Charles Kennedy
A Tragic Flaw

Greg Hurst spent fifteen years as a political journalist at Westminster, first with *Southern Newspapers* and then, from 2000 to 2007, with *The Times*. He reported on British politics throughout Charles Kennedy's period as leader of the Liberal Democrats and saw Kennedy frequently during his leadership and accompanied him throughout the General Election campaigns of 2001 and 2005.

He was subsequently assistant news editor at *The Times* and, since 2009, has been the newspaper's Education Editor. He writes and broadcasts regularly on public policy and current affairs.

He is married with three children and lives in Maidenhead, Berkshire.

'I will lift up mine eyes unto the hills, from whence cometh my help.'

Psalm 121, *King James Bible*

Charles Kennedy:

A Tragic Flaw

Greg Hurst

Methuen

First published in Great Britain 2006 by
Politico's an imprint of
Methuen & Co Ltd
35 Hospital Fields Road
York
YO10 4DZ

This revised paperback edition first published by Methuen, 2015.

2

A CIP catalogue record for this book is available from the British Library.

ISBN 978 0 413 56430 6

Typeset by SX Composing DTP, Rayleigh, Essex.
Printed and bound in Great Britain by CPI Group (UK) Ltd, Croydon, CR0 4YY

Contents

To my wife Christine
and our children Richard, Lucy and Jessica

Foreword by Rt Hon Lord Steel of Aikwood

I can think of no other occasion when the death of a former back-bench MP caused the House of Commons to hold a special tribute session. That happened for Charles Kennedy, and I sat watching in the peers' gallery opposite Sarah and Donald as heartfelt tributes were paid not just by the Prime Minister and other grandees but Members of all parties who recalled him with both respect and affection. I was also struck by how in the days following his sudden death complete strangers would speak to me in the street or on public transport to say how sad they were at his passing. All that showed how greatly he touched people, even those who had never met him.

Those who were privileged to count him as a friend were devastated. I had supper with him – typically in the ordinary Commons cafeteria – just before the general election when we talked not just about that but about the family croft where I had visited him and his parents and to which he had now fallen heir. To be among the few dozen at his burial in the highland hillside Kennedy tiny burial ground – not even a cemetery – was an experience I shall always remember.

This updated biography pays due tribute to the most successful Liberal/Liberal Democrat leader of the post-war era, his hugely successful TV persona, but most important to the man himself – staunch Catholic faith which he never paraded publicly and his struggle with the awful disease of alcoholism.

In 1979 or 1980 I was a judge at an inter-university debating competition in Bristol, and we had to choose the best individual speaker of the evening. It was a red-haired member of the Glasgow team.

Afterwards I happened to sit next to him at dinner and he said he was a member of the university Labour Club. I said: "Charles, having listened to your speech I think you should reconsider your party orientation" which was my clumsy way of asking him to join the Liberal Party. He didn't, but joined the SDP when it was formed in 1981. In the '83 election I was doing a whistle-stop tour of Scotland by jet which included a brief stop to support my old friend and colleague Russell Johnston in Inverness. As we huddled in the back of a rain-soaked pick-up bellowing encouragement through a loudspeaker Russell asked: "Have you met the SDP candidate for Ross & Cromarty? That is him under the umbrella at the back."

"No", I replied, at which Charles shook my hand and said "Oh yes you have".

We often laughed about that, and the rest is history – well recounted here.

David Steel
August 2015

Preface

This is a story about politics: about talent, conviction, ambition, rivalry, frustration. It spans the drama and excitement of political crises and election campaigns to the everyday pressures and constraints of representing and leading a voluntary movement. It is in essence also a human story with a resonance reaching well beyond politics. It chronicles prodigy and achievement, but also human frailty, mistakes, unfulfilled potential, divided loyalty and personal misfortune. Politics happened to be the stage upon which it was played out, but it could have been any number of others. The human traits at work in this narrative are universal and easily recognisable in many walks of life. In the period covered by this book the Liberal Democrats faced particular challenges, many of them the growing pains of a small party adjusting to the realities and disciplines of greater strength at Westminster. I hope, however, that this narrative is of interest to readers of all political persuasion or of none. Similar dynamics are found in all major political parties, although owing to the size and limited means of the Liberal Democrats these were writ much larger than they might otherwise have been. Therein, I think, lies much of the interest.

This is not an authorised biography. The book was conceived and commissioned well before Charles Kennedy's resignation as leader of the Liberal Democrats but changed significantly as a result, with its structure altered and timing brought forward. I intended from the outset to write from an independent perspective. Charles Kennedy always struck me as a likeable and fundamentally decent man, not a conventional politician but an obviously human one in his strengths and weaknesses, and therefore an interesting subject for a biography. He also happened to be leader during a pivotal period for the Liberal Democrats, as they grew from a minority party to become a more serious political force. As a political journalist with *The*

Times, I saw Charles Kennedy frequently while he was leader and I reported at the time on many of the events covered in the book. I watched him at Westminster, accompanied him on visits and throughout the 2001 and 2005 general election campaigns, saw him at party events and interviewed him many times. He did not wish to be interviewed for this book but did allow his closest political friends and former staff to speak to me with his knowledge and approval. As with most of the people I interviewed for this book, they were happy to speak about certain areas or events but not about others. Charles Kennedy was also helpful in clarifying some biographical and factual details at the end of my research, for which I am grateful.

Naturally in the course of my research I spoke to a large number of other people known to me and suggested by others, many of them sympathetic to Charles Kennedy but many, too, who were less so. I listened to and weighed up their varied opinions and strived throughout to produce a balanced account. Some I spoke to were happy to be identified; others agreed to be interviewed only on condition of anonymity. Although those in the latter category were often very helpful in informing my understanding of events, I have avoided wherever possible quoting unidentified sources.

I am particularly grateful to Dick Newby and Anna Werrin, both of whom gave me several lengthy interviews and acted as intermediaries with Charles Kennedy. Chris Rennard was unfailingly helpful on campaigning and party history and meticulous in his attention to accuracy. Richard Grayson, as a historian, was particularly generous in loaning me papers and other documents of interest. He read several passages and made useful suggestions. Paddy Ashdown, David Steel and David Owen were each generous in seeing me and giving me the singular viewpoints of former party leaders; Paddy Ashdown was especially helpful. Duncan Brack, who initially planned to be Charles Kennedy's biographer, was good enough to share some of his thoughts with me and, with the consent of both, I made use of a taped interview he conducted with Charles covering his childhood, student days and early years in the Commons.

I am also grateful to Catherine MacLeod for her introductions in Fort William; to John Morrison for explaining to me the intricacies of Glasgow's student tradition of parliamentary debating; to Robin Downie for painting a vivid picture for me of life in Glasgow University Union; and to Jonny Hardman, who trawled the union's extensive – and haphazard – debating records on my behalf.

Alan Gordon-Walker, who was then at Methuen, allowed me considerable freedom as an author but helped me with the structure of the book. Jonathan Wadman, my original editor, was quietly professional and effective. My mother Elizabeth Hurst, a former teacher of English literature, read the manuscript and provided a helpfully detached point of view. Any errors that remain are, of course, my own.

My greatest professional thanks are due to Peter Riddell, my former colleague at *The Times*, who encouraged my plans for this book, introduced me to Methuen and was a constant source of ideas, support and wise counsel. I sought his advice over many things, large and small, and he read most of the chapters in draft form, making many suggestions that improved the book; I owe him a great deal. Philip Webster, *The Times*' former political editor, was similarly generous with his shrewd judgment and unstinting support.

When Charles Kennedy died in June 2015 I revised the book to take in the period after he stepped down as leader of the Liberal Democrats and I am grateful to Methuen for publishing this new edition. I saw no reason to change the earlier narrative, other than for minor additions or corrections, but added two chapters on Kennedy's subsequent life and career, and some further analysis and discussion on his legacy in light of the Liberal Democrats' experience in the coalition government and the calamitous defeat for the party in the 2015 general election.

In researching the new material I received generous help from many people who knew Charles Kennedy. I wish to thank Conn O'Neill, in particular, for his detailed accounts of campaigning with Kennedy in Ross, Skye & Lochaber, which were supplemented by others including Duncan Mackay, Jamie and Flora Stone, Candy Piercy and Lindsay McCallum; Father Roddy Johnston and Father Roddy McAuley for their insights into Charles Kennedy's faith; Donald Cameron of Lochiel for a history of the Kennedys' cemetary at Clunes; Niall Rowantree and Chris Sibbald for colourful descriptions of his rectorial elections at the University of Glasgow; friends and former staff including Jim Wallace and Jackie Rowley; and Catherine MacLeod and Alastair Campbell. Others must remain anonymous.

I am blessed with a close, supportive and resilient family. When researching and writing new chapters it was a delight to discuss these with our teenage children, Richard and Lucy, who were encouraging and understanding. Our younger daughter Jessica was patient and accepting of my absence. My brother Dominic read an early draft and made helpful and perceptive suggestions. My parents and mother-in-law gave constant support. Most of all, however, it was my wife Christine who stepped in to give me time to write. I am in their debt.

Greg Hurst
July 2015

1

The orange revolution

One ordinary, dull day in mid-November, the sky fell in on Charles Kennedy. As with any upset in the troposphere, its impact was gradual rather than immediate. But the build-up of pressure it caused was so severe that, when it exploded, it knocked him off his feet and destroyed his six-year tenure as leader of the Liberal Democrats. Modern British politics has seldom witnessed a more dramatic series of events than those set in motion on that overcast autumn afternoon. And yet, on the day in question, almost nobody realised anything had happened.

Charles Kennedy was driven a short distance across the capital from the House of Commons to the London School of Economics, off the Strand, to address a lunchtime meeting hosted by the university's Liberal Democrat Society. He arrived fifteen minutes late, and was directed into a small lift and taken up six floors to the Shaw Library, a large handsome room with a striking glass dome in its ceiling, chandeliers on either side, and lit by big windows with aspects onto jumbled London rooftops. There, surrounded by bookcases and stern portraits of Sidney and Beatrice Webb, two of the LSE's socialist founders, and several of its subsequent directors, around a hundred students were seated on metal and plastic chairs. Some slouched on red armchairs towards the back. Kennedy's speech should have been a routine occasion. He was giving a series of such lectures on political themes; this one was on involving young people in politics and advocated votes at sixteen. Sitting beside him at the top table was Tim Farron, an industrious new Lib Dem MP and the party's youth spokesman, who had written the speech and introduced his leader. Kennedy cracked a few jokes, noticing a student in the front row wearing a Che Guevara T-shirt, to whom he quipped: 'I can see you're not a Liberal Democrat.' But his speech[1] itself was delivered slowly.

Tim Farron may have winced inwardly when Kennedy several times departed from his carefully crafted script but did not notice anything untoward and concentrated on chairing the meeting. After his oration, Kennedy chatted briefly with his undergraduate hosts, who considered his message a little dull but were otherwise appreciative, before he was ushered away, with his aides explaining he was expected at another engagement.

One member of the audience, however, departed far from happy. Julia Goldsworthy, a young, bright, conscientious Lib Dem MP also elected seven months earlier, returned to Westminster and confided to a handful of more experienced colleagues that she thought her leader had been drunk. What should she do? The correct procedure, fellow MPs told her, was to inform the party's chief whip, Andrew Stunell. Perhaps they thought a novice MP would flinch from doing so, but she did.

'I didn't think it was very well delivered. I didn't want to know anything more, apart from to know that it had been noted. I saw the chief whip. I felt it was necessary,' Julia Goldsworthy explained. 'I have seen Charles making fantastic performances. That was not one of them. I felt it correct to feed that back.'

What she did not know was that Charles Kennedy was an alcoholic. Only his most senior MPs, who worked with him closely and saw him most often, shared this secret. All had been assured repeatedly that he had submitted himself to professional treatment and forsworn alcohol. There had been a series of spectacular crises linked to his drinking which had punctuated his leadership, and elaborate efforts to cover up its manifestations. Stumbling his way through a speech at the LSE was minor in comparison, although it became significant nonetheless. Already a new Lib Dem MP had glimpsed a problem which, despite rumours and innuendo within Westminster, was known for certain to only a few. More importantly, despite promises of action spanning several years, it was evidence that his alcoholism was unresolved.

Earlier that morning, as they gathered for their weekly meeting, several of the party's senior spokesmen had seen so for themselves. The Lib Dem self-styled shadow cabinet assembled as usual at 10.30 a.m. in a Commons committee room, to discuss a paper by David Laws, the welfare spokesman. It proposed a higher state pension age of sixty-seven and reform of public sector pensions, in return for a more generous state pension for all and reduced means testing. Steve Webb, a former professor of social policy who was previously the party's pensions spokesman, criticised the plans as unaffordable. As the argument developed Charles Kennedy, who was chairing the meeting, remained uncommunicative and distant. Some present did not notice. Others did, and realised he was drunk.

'In this discussion he was self-evidently not in control, visibly recovering from the night before. His speech was slurred,' said one member of the shadow cabinet. 'It was difficult in those circumstances to have a serious discussion on a very important and weighty political issue. I felt all through the meeting we had a useful discussion but Charles was not really engaged in it.'

At least one of those present told the leader's office afterwards his performance was completely unacceptable and he must understand the seriousness of such behaviour; his leadership was at stake. That evening, three or four hours after his LSE speech, Kennedy was due to chair a meeting of the Lib Dem federal policy committee but pulled out and went home early, missing a series of Commons votes, including one on a controversial Conservative motion to nullify government plans to liberalise licensing laws. MPs were told he was 'feeling unwell'. The following day Kennedy was back at the Commons, and stayed around that evening to take part in six divisions, although Lib Dem MPs who spoke to him in the chamber noted he smelt strongly of alcohol. Early the next morning, Thursday 17 November, he set off for a train trip to Newcastle to hoist the Lib Dem flag in the city ahead of metropolitan borough elections in the spring.

What, precisely, happened on that Great North Eastern Railway service once it left King's Cross was to become the stuff of legend amongst Liberal Democrats. Kennedy and his junior press assistant, Courtney Cooke, alighted from their first-class carriage at Peterborough, the first stop, and caught another train back to London. Word was sent to Newcastle that the visit had been cancelled; a reception committee was awaiting Kennedy at the station to take him to a lunch with business and civic leaders and, later, to open a tram service. As news of the aborted excursion reached Westminster, journalists began bombarding Lib Dem MPs with telephone calls to ask what had happened. It was one of the unexpected, unnerving episodes with which some Lib Dems had become wearily familiar. Most knew nothing about what had happened, but were forced to defend their leader and parry reporters' inevitable, speculative inquiries about alcohol. Jackie Rowley, press secretary to Charles Kennedy, swiftly toured the parliamentary press gallery telling journalists he had turned back for 'personal family reasons'. She hinted heavily that his infant son Donald was ill, but told journalists

Kennedy had insisted she should not disclose details, telling her: 'Sarah and I will not have our private life discussed.' A handful of short news items were published[2] but Jackie Rowley appeared to have been successful in quashing a potentially embarrassing story. The media's restless focus moved on.

To several of the emerging generation of able, ambitious Lib Dems, however, this was a watershed. For two or three years, some had known of Kennedy's alcoholism but had been reassured by senior party figures that 'appropriate action' was being taken. Indeed, from the spring of 2004 until the general election a year later, the Lib Dem leader's performances had improved, with fewer drinking episodes. But during the campaign itself their tolerance ended when Charles Kennedy launched the party's manifesto. He arrived late, red eyed, having barely slept, and stammered over details of its flagship plan for a local income tax as a disorientated man might stumble through fog. Certain MPs became convinced the abject embarrassment of the manifesto launch was due not to lack of sleep following the birth of his child, as Charles Kennedy himself claimed, but another lapse in his struggle with alcoholism. To them, ruining the publication of their manifesto in a general election was beyond the pale. This was the big moment for an opposition party trying to make the weather in a fiercely fought election. Should they tolerate a leader unable to perform? A by-election in the Lib Dem seat of Cheadle in the weeks after polling day had saved Kennedy although, for several of his sharpest MPs, he had been given his last chance. Among those most concerned were some unlikely people. They included Ed Davey, a former party researcher and management consultant; David Laws, previously an investment banker and the Lib Dems' head of policy; Norman Lamb, whose background was as a solicitor and local councillor; and Sarah Teather, a former charity worker who entered the Commons in the Brent East by-election to become its youngest MP. By instinct these were loyalists, not rebels.

The week following the abandoned Newcastle trip, as Lib Dem MPs reassembled at Westminster after the weekend, they began to discuss its implications with one another. Alternative accounts of what took place on the ill-fated journey began to circulate among Lib Dems, suggesting Charles Kennedy was taken off the train in another drink-related episode, and that the explanation from the leader's office was untrue, which caused distaste. MPs started to share drink-related anecdotes about Kennedy. The story of his performance at the LSE, witnessed by Julia Goldsworthy, was passed among senior MPs along with other episodes such as his conduct at that morning's shadow cabinet meeting and recent performances at Prime Minister's questions. Over cups of coffee in Portcullis House, drinks in the Commons smoking room, at supper in the Members' Dining Room or in impromptu discussions and telephone conversations, many of the party's frontbench spokesmen began sharing their despair at their leader. Rapidly the discussions spread among shadow cabinet members, chiefly Vince Cable, Michael Moore, Norman Baker, Don Foster, Sandra Gidley, Andrew George and John Thurso. They asked themselves if their leader was likely to change and, with the evidence suggesting otherwise, whether they could face another four years like the previous parliament. The phrase many began to use was: 'the current situation is not sustainable'.

Their immediate anxieties tapped into a wider frustration which had applied since the general election that Kennedy had failed to map out a strategic direction for the coming parliament and let the party drift. The annual conference two months earlier had been a political shambles, with platform defeats over European Union spending and privatising the Royal Mail, plus a sense that Kennedy's policy review had failed to rein in an increasingly personalised debate between social and economic liberals. Nor had the party been given the opportunity fully to debate the lopsided results of its election campaign. This yielded a dozen gains and massive swings from Labour, exceeding expectations. But there was a net loss of two seats to the Conservatives. The Lib Dems' so-called decapitation strategy of trying to unseat prominent Tories backfired and the Conservatives deployed a new armoury using marketing data to identify target voters, telephone canvassing and direct mail leaflets. Some Lib Dems felt a massive opportunity was missed in the election. Others in marginal seats wanted evidence that the party had learned lessons from the Tories' campaigning tactics. It amounted to a general dissatisfaction at the way the party was led, alongside specific concerns among the handful fully aware of Kennedy's alcoholism and his string of broken commitments to deal with it.

With discontent in the party's upper ranks apparently widespread, MPs began to troop in to see Menzies Campbell, who was both their elder statesman and their deputy leader, to pour out their concerns. This was not a new phenomenon. The threshold of Menzies Campbell's spacious, modern office in Portcullis House, with framed certificates of his prowess as an Olympic sprinter on the walls, had at various stages over the past three years become a familiar port of call for Lib Dems wishing to unburden their despair at Charles Kennedy's drinking. To a degree, all those aware of his condition had become complicit in continual efforts to cover up its symptoms and shield him and the party from their consequences. This time things were different. Some of those at the forefront of the disquiet – Ed Davey, David Laws, Norman Lamb and Sarah Teather – represented the new generation of Lib Dem talent. They made it clear to Menzies Campbell they were no longer prepared to endure it. Norman Lamb was ready to resign from the front bench in despair. The mood amongst his colleagues was almost as bleak.

Menzies Campbell confided in his long-time political ally Archy Kirkwood, saying he feared some spokesmen might resign. The two men discussed Menzies Campbell's responsibility to the party as deputy leader. Archy Kirkwood, who had left the Commons at the election but had been made a peer, introduced a different perspective. As a former chief whip, he well knew that several others in the Lib Dem shadow cabinet had been wrestling with similar concerns for years. His calculation was that four more malcontents might have tipped the balance against Kennedy. The text book, he counselled, said when such dissatisfaction was shared by 50 per cent of the shadow cabinet plus one more, the leader would have to submit to a motion of no confidence and would lose. Moreover, if there ever was a time to do so, it was in the first year of a parliament. Archy Kirkwood's advice for these so-called Young Turks was that, if they were serious and convinced they could meet the '50 per cent plus one' test, they had a course of action available to them.

His suggestion injected a sense of purpose into the calculations of Lib Dem parliamentarians and their hushed conversations over a period of three weeks. They did not meet together privately as a group but conferred individually, sounding one another out in chance meetings in the corridors and division lobbies of the House of Commons, and then shared impressions with others. A few MPs outside the shadow cabinet were brought into the discussions, notably Alistair Carmichael, Matthew Taylor and Nick Harvey, as the view began to harden that Charles Kennedy had indeed lost the support of a critical number of his senior MPs. A draft letter was worked on to convey this to the leader, with the intention that it would be signed by a large proportion of the shadow cabinet – led by Menzies Campbell and, if he agreed, Simon Hughes – and given to Charles Kennedy before the Christmas recess of Parliament, allowing him time to consider his position over the holiday period and prepare a dignified exit strategy. All were agreed it should be done in absolute secrecy, with Kennedy able to bow out with dignity, in a manner of his choosing and citing his own reasons, although the more determined among them pressed the case that he must use his traditional New Year message to announce his resignation. Simon Hughes, the party's president and another potentially pivotal figure, was approached by Archy Kirkwood but prevaricated, saying he wished to consult friends before responding. The plan stalled.

The dilemma was that none of Kennedy's critics was willing to offer leadership. The key office holders had conflicts of interest. Menzies Campbell, the deputy leader, had long regretted not standing against Charles Kennedy when Paddy Ashdown stepped down in 1999. Simon Hughes, the party president, was certain to stand if Charles Kennedy quit. Vince Cable, the next most senior frontbench figure, had harboured leadership ambitions of his own and was reluctant to move against Kennedy. The chief whip, Andrew Stunell, had been told many times previously of concerns at Kennedy's drinking and senior MPs lacked confidence in his willingness to act. The terrible responsibility of confronting the leader was left to more junior members of the shadow cabinet.

There was, of course, another dimension to consider. Were members of the shadow cabinet to succeed and create a vacancy for leader, what next? Mark Oaten had been positioning himself for a future leadership election. Ed Davey had considered standing himself. There was a danger of a divergent election with five or more candidates. There was a real fear amongst them that Simon Hughes, after twenty-two years of campaigning with grassroots party activists, might win in such circumstances. Those leading the mutiny regarded Hughes as a left-wing populist. Several said they must rally behind one candidate: 64-year-old Menzies Campbell, perhaps on a caretaker basis. Young cardinals often prefer old popes. Yet through this period Campbell's position remained somewhat opaque. Back in the summer he appeared to have accepted he would no longer become leader and had considered leaving the front bench.[3] He was undergoing health checks following treatment for cancer three years earlier. As the autumn crisis developed, he was uncomfortable with the potential conflict of interest arising from his twin roles as deputy leader and possible candidate: MPs such as Andrew George, for instance, were urging a different course of action, saying Charles Kennedy must take a sabbatical for intensive treatment for his alcoholism, with Menzies Campbell as interim leader, after which Kennedy should return. Campbell indicated to such people that he saw it as his duty to prepare for any eventuality. Gradually, however, as more senior MPs urged it upon him, it became clearer that Menzies Campbell was likely to stand for the leadership should Charles Kennedy resign. This was rarely made explicit but became the agreed assumption. The dynamic began to change.

Even before a plan – still less a plot – had fully formed, things went disastrously wrong. Ed Davey took a telephone call, followed by a visit to his Commons office, from Philip Goldenberg, a short, bearded, rotund corporate lawyer. Goldenberg, deputy chairman of the Lib Dems in England, held a place in Liberal Democrat history, having proposed to Paddy Ashdown the idea of a joint Cabinet committee with Labour. Philip Goldenberg shared the sense of dissatisfaction with the general election result and was encouraging moves to replace Charles Kennedy. As the pair discussed current events, Ed Davey brushed aside entreaties to stand himself in the event of a leadership election. The issue, he said, was how to convey the loss of confidence among senior spokesmen to Charles Kennedy. Mark Oaten was the member of the shadow cabinet closest to Kennedy, Ed Davey said. His role would be crucial, but Oaten's position was complicated by the fact that he was a potential candidate for the leadership himself. Oaten had to decide where he stood. Philip Goldenberg knew Mark Oaten well and offered to help. He telephoned Oaten immediately and was invited up to Oaten's spacious garret office on the sixth floor of the Norman Shaw South building. There, Mark Oaten was adamant he would not be part of any move against Charles Kennedy and he would certainly not rally behind Menzies Campbell. He called it a 'stitch-up' from which the biggest beneficiary would be his younger rival Nick Clegg, one of the new intake of Lib Dem MPs. Oaten said he remained loyal to Charles Kennedy, to whom he had been parliamentary private secretary. But, if there had been a loss of confidence, the right course of action was for a group of senior MPs to go and see the leader. Knowing how the leader's office worked, he suggested the person to start with was Anna Werrin, Kennedy's long-time assistant. But Mark Oaten was insistent that, should it come to that, he would not relinquish his ambitions and would stand himself.

Philip Goldenberg had a crystal clear message to report back. But at this critical juncture, technophobia got the better of him. On departing, he fished from a pocket his battered red mobile phone and attempted to ring back Ed Davey, pressing the 'dialled numbers' button on the handset to repeat his last call. The moment a familiar voice answered, he blurted out his findings.

'Hello Ed, I have seen Mark,' he began. 'Mark said to me if there is going to be a delegation, it had better go and see Anna in the first instance.'

Suddenly his error became apparent. The voice at the other end of the line interrupted: 'No, no, no, this is Mark, not Ed.'

Amid embarrassment, the conversation was rapidly terminated. The last dialled number in his telephone was not Ed Davey's but that of Mark Oaten, who despite his own leadership preparations kept close contacts with Charles Kennedy and his tight-knit inner circle. What might have seemed to him a private initiative by a Lib Dem activist suddenly looked like a conspiracy. Ed Davey and his colleagues assumed, correctly, that their discussions would be reported straight back to the leader's office. From then onwards, the essential precondition of their moves to seek Charles Kennedy's resignation – that of absolute secrecy – was lost. Things began to fall apart.

Believing their discussions should move beyond snatched conversations in corners, furtive discussions over cappuccino, and grammatically wanting text messages, several other members of the shadow cabinet at last proposed a meeting. It was to be away from Westminster and lengthy enough to agree on the text of the letter of no confidence, allow all those shadow cabinet members present to sign it, and then proceed to a discussion of what should happen next. Nick Harvey, an MP who had been close to Paddy Ashdown and was exiled on the back benches under Kennedy, agreed to host the gathering in his large, modern town house in Kennington, a few minutes' walk from the Commons. He fixed a date for supper for ten people on Tuesday 13 December, and began making arrangements for Charles Kennedy's future to be carved up on his light oak dining room table, even engaging a caterer for the occasion. So clandestine was it meant to be that a cover story was concocted: should anyone ask, the dinner would be to commemorate the hundredth anniversary of Henry Campbell-Bannerman's landslide general election victory in 1906, the high water mark of the Edwardian Liberal Party when it won 400 seats.

From then, events began to spiral out of control. On Friday 9 December, the *Guardian* published a story reporting pressure on Charles Kennedy to quit; it said some members of his shadow cabinet favoured a different strategy to Kennedy's of working with David Cameron, the new Conservative leader whose election was confirmed that week, in the event of a hung Parliament.[4] Advocates of such an approach wanted to begin informal talks with the Tories in the New Year, it reported. Many Lib Dems suspected the chief source to be Mark Oaten; indeed, Oaten disclosed subsequently that he had had lunch two days earlier with one of the story's authors, Julian Glover, in the Members' Dining Room, where a caterpillar crawled across

Oaten's plate.[5] The article added to the febrile atmosphere among senior Lib Dems and heightened suspicions that Mark Oaten was professing public loyalty to Charles Kennedy while privately undermining his position. Rumours circulated that Oaten had a leadership campaign team ready, was preparing a regional tour, had asked staff to obtain directories of local Lib Dem officers and candidates, and had approached potential donors.

That afternoon Nick Harvey, who was taking a constituency surgery in North Devon, was telephoned by a reporter from the *Daily Mail* who put it to him that he planned to host a dinner at his house the following Wednesday at which Charles Kennedy's future would be discussed. Nick Harvey was able to answer, truthfully, that he would not – but only because a single detail was incorrect. His supper party was planned for Tuesday, not Wednesday. Shaken, he called colleagues to cancel the dinner. Charles Kennedy's allies had again got wind of their plans and launched an aggressive pre-emptive strike.

That night came further drama. Andrew Neil, the broadcaster, disclosed on his television show that he had been told 'on good authority' that Charles Kennedy planned to announce his resignation in March at the party's spring conference at Harrogate.[6] This triggered a rash of media stories over the weekend speculating on Kennedy's future, led by the *Mail*, which named Nick Harvey as one of the plotters but made no mention of its potential scoop of the conspirators' supper planned at his house.[7] Kennedy's office was furious with Andrew Neil's assertion, which they knew to be wrong, and lodged an official complaint, thus seeking to divert the story into one of a row with the BBC rather than a leadership crisis. The counter-attack from the leader's circle continued as Anna Werrin sent a terse e-mail to Norman Lamb accusing him of acting as chief whip to the rebels due to meet at Nick Harvey's house and giving notice, presciently, that Kennedy would stand as a candidate even if the shadow cabinet succeeded in forcing a leadership contest.

Kennedy's critics appeared to have been routed. Their plans had been leaked. Leadership speculation and anonymous attacks on Kennedy were peppering the tabloid press. Shadow cabinet members had not even had a chance to meet privately and discuss in detail a credible course of action, while their hope that he would be persuaded to bow out gracefully appeared utterly misplaced. Two MPs, Nick Harvey and Norman Lamb, had been implicated by the leader's office and risked being disciplined or denounced to the newspapers. Things were getting ragged, and a little nasty.

Then, however, the leadership made a grave miscalculation. As Lib Dem MPs returned to Westminster on Monday, news began to circulate that certain newspapers were being briefed by Charles Kennedy's office that he would issue a rebuke to his shadow cabinet when it met the following morning and tell members not to brief against him.[8] The notion that they, not he, were the problem incensed several and stiffened their resolve. In snatched conversations throughout the day, MPs discussed how to respond. Archy Kirkwood made discreet approaches to MPs, including Sandra Gidley and John Thurso, about a plan to avoid a direct confrontation with Charles Kennedy at the meeting. Instead he proposed that the chief whip, Andrew Stunell, should take soundings from shadow cabinet members afterwards to see if they retained confidence in Kennedy's leadership. After the 10 p.m. Commons vote David Laws, Sarah Teather, Ed Davey and Michael Moore returned with Norman Lamb to his flat in Marsham Court where, over glasses of wine, all agreed to back up such a request. With a curious sense of orderliness, they decided they would intervene alphabetically.

Members of the shadow cabinet arrived the next morning at their usual meeting room on the committee corridor of the Commons to find a notice saying the venue had been changed. They were directed through Westminster Hall, up a flight of stone steps and along a short passageway to the Jubilee Room, with its dark oak-panelled walls, powder blue Pugin wallpaper with flower patterns, and oil paintings. The tables had been pushed together to form a long rectangle around which the meeting took place. Charles Kennedy, seated at one end with Menzies Campbell on one side and Andrew Stunell on the other, duly threw down the gauntlet. In a controlled, assertive tone he opened the meeting by telling them he would stay as leader. If anyone managed to force a leadership election, he would stand as a candidate. And, if anyone had a problem with that, they should come and see him by 2 p.m. and offer their resignation. He spoke powerfully, for three or four minutes. On concluding, he clearly intended to move on to the first agenda item, the government's White Paper on school reforms.

As he paused, a solitary hand was raised, indicating a wish to speak. It was Sandra Gidley, taking up the proffered gauntlet. She told Charles Kennedy calmly that this was not quite good enough; she was constantly having to answer questions about him, and had done so at a constituency dinner over the weekend. 'I think you need to know exactly how much support you have in your shadow cabinet,' she told him. 'It is all becoming very difficult. Other people have concerns about your leadership.'

She proposed members of the shadow cabinet talk to the chief whip, saying they might have a more frank discussion and find it easier to express their concerns to a third party. Even before she finished, she began to be heckled by Mark Oaten and Lembit Öpik. Again appearing to have foreknowledge of the rebels' plan, Mark Oaten, who was called next, tried to ridicule her proposal, saying colleagues with concerns should air them to Charles Kennedy in person. Lembit Öpik, who followed, charged the atmosphere by suggesting that to do otherwise was cowardly.

Then came a slight pause before Menzies Campbell intervened, proposing that the discussion went 'below the line' – meaning the half-dozen or so party or leader's staff should leave, to allow a candid discussion among parliamentarians. Charles Kennedy rejected this, saying the senior staff would have to deal with the outcome and should hear what was being said. But Menzies Campbell, looking a little stiff, did say the proposal to involve the chief whip 'had some merit'. John Thurso came in to support the plan, saying there was clearly a problem, the party was quietly tearing itself apart in public. He introduced the resonant phrase 'this is a boil that has got to be lanced.' In the subsequent discussion, which was tense but calm with no raised voices, all but one of those who spoke agreed the question had to be resolved. These included Simon Hughes, although most of his contribution was an attack on anonymous press briefings. Ed Davey looked his leader in the eye and told Charles Kennedy that he had lied on his behalf, but was not sure he would do so again. Charles Kennedy winked at Sarah Teather before bringing her into the discussion, perhaps expecting support. But she too said she had concerns, despite the affection she had for him, and wanted the chief whip involved. Phil Willis, a friend of Kennedy's, was the only other MP present to offer support before the discussion concluded. It lasted about thirty minutes.

Awkwardly, Charles Kennedy then took the meeting through its formal business for a further hour with updates on the education White Paper, the Racial and Religious Hatred Bill and a Lib Dem spending review to identify £15 billion of cuts in Whitehall budgets, introduced by Chris Huhne. Once it finally broke up, the outcome was slightly uncertain. Charles Kennedy had trumped the plan to make his chief whip the conduit for those who had lost confidence and invited them to come and see him instead. Patently, however, his opening gambit that those inclined to do so should tender their resignations – 'back me or sack you' – looked academic in light of the mauling he had received. Several members of the shadow cabinet chose to see both the chief whip and the leader, using the first to rehearse what they would say to the second, but again a clear plan of action had been disrupted.

Charles Kennedy returned to his office and spent the afternoon and following day holding one-to-one meetings in his Commons office with senior MPs, although he telephoned some others rapidly and put them on the spot, asking where they stood. David Laws, the recipient of one such call, told Kennedy his position was unsustainable. In face-to-face meetings Norman Baker, close to tears, told him the same, as did Norman Lamb and, tearfully, Sarah Teather, all citing his alcoholism. Menzies Campbell, too, told Charles Kennedy he must quit for the sake of his family. As MPs beyond the shadow cabinet began to be invited in, Alistair Carmichael told him it was time to stand down. During all these meetings, which were booked in fifteen-minute slots, MPs found Kennedy serenely calm and friendly. Meanwhile Sandra Gidley, sticking to her original proposal, saw only the chief whip and told him Charles Kennedy should go.

Again, however, the dynamic changed. *The Times* published on its front page an account of the shadow cabinet revolt,[9] finally forcing the unfolding drama into the open. Under the ensuing glare of media attention, and not entirely clear of the conclusion of their shadow cabinet discussion, MPs flitted in and out of one another's offices, congregated mainly on the third floor of the modern Portcullis House building, as a result of which several opted to give Kennedy one last chance. Ed Davey told his leader the position was unsustainable but gave him a choice: fundamental change or you go. Don Foster, emotionally, told Kennedy he not could afford another lapse in his battle with alcoholism but offered support. Michael Moore, who had been uneasy that no firm plan was in place should Kennedy quit, told him his office was dysfunctional and his leadership lacked grip, but urged him to believe in himself and play to his strengths. Vince Cable, always an uncertain rebel, asked Kennedy if he did indeed have a serious problem with alcohol and about his abandoned train journey to Newcastle the previous month. As he did throughout, Kennedy gave assurances that he did not have a drink problem and said that the Newcastle episode had nothing to do with alcohol. Andrew George told Kennedy he was an outstanding leader but remained unconvinced he had conquered alcoholism, or, as he awkwardly put it, 'the problem you know I often raise with you'. John Thurso, another of those telephoned early on by Kennedy, similarly believed that his leader must deal with his drink problem, but refused to discuss such personal matters other than face to face and was never offered a meeting.

Much of the media attention was by now focusing on that evening's weekly parliamentary party meeting in the Commons, at which Charles Kennedy would face his MPs for the first time since the crisis had become public knowledge. The leader's office saw a chance to regain the initiative. The rebels' strategy throughout had been to contain their grievances tightly within the shadow cabinet, with only a handful of exceptions, and convey their loss of confidence to the leader privately. The remaining forty or so Lib Dem MPs were therefore bewildered by the crisis that enveloped them without warning and many were intensely angry to read in newspapers about events of which they knew little or nothing. After threading their way through a phalanx of reporters in the corridor to Committee Room 11, backbench MPs were ripe for a diversionary tactic of blaming the press. Charles Kennedy spoke strongly for about eight minutes, pledging to improve his performance but saying he would stay on, and was greeted by a supportive banging of desks. Mark Hunter, victor of the Cheadle by-election, then gave a ringing endorsement of his leadership, followed by other aggressive attacks on the 'Tory press' and tributes to Kennedy, led by Bob Russell, who challenged Kennedy's critics to stand up and declare themselves. There were further loyalist speeches by Phil Willis, Mike Hancock, Bob Russell, Mark Oaten, Lembit Öpik and Greg Mulholland. It became clear that the parliamentary party's chairman, Paul Holmes, had lined up a series of Kennedy allies to set the meeting's tone. No other members of the shadow cabinet spoke, having delivered their views privately to Charles Kennedy and not wishing to betray the secret of his alcoholism, which further skewed the balance of the debate and created an eerie atmosphere. Bravely, Julia Goldsworthy struck cautiously against the tide, saying: 'There is an issue that has to be resolved.' Lynne Featherstone, another new MP, was more direct, telling Charles Kennedy: 'It would be disingenuous of me not to mention that I have concerns about your personal habits.'

After an hour Tim Razzall, Charles Kennedy's strategist and chief adviser, emerged from the meeting to tell waiting journalists that all but one of the dozen MPs to have spoken so far had backed the leader, suggesting he had seen off his critics and won an endorsement to carry on. Inside, as the meeting continued, more coded criticism followed from Alistair Carmichael, Nick Harvey and Danny Alexander. Incredibly, given his private conversations earlier with his most senior spokesman, when Charles Kennedy left the room he too declared himself 'gratified by the overwhelming level of support that was expressed for me and my continuing leadership'. The

Kennedy camp claimed he had seen off an aborted coup.

Several of his critics gathered afterwards, gloomy and confused, for a glass of malt whisky in the ground-floor office of Alistair Carmichael in the Norman Shaw North building, where Scottish Lib Dem MPs were meeting ahead of their staff Christmas party. With people drifting in and out, including Menzies Campbell and Archy Kirkwood, they discussed with one another what to do next.

'I said, "That's it, for better or worse, that was a great performance by Charles. Forget it,"' John Thurso said. '"You have had your shot and it missed." That was the general view for an hour.'

The Scots MPs piled into taxis to take their staff for supper at Savoir Fare, a French restaurant in New Oxford Street, where they sat as a group of around twenty in the basement. During the meal Michael Moore, uncertain if he could get a signal in the room, pulled out his WAP phone and scrolled through the news stories on BBC Online. There he found an article portraying Menzies Campbell as the instigator of a plot against Charles Kennedy, based on inferences drawn from Campbell's refusal to speak to reporters as he left his meeting with the leader earlier that day. Michael Moore passed his mobile handset to Menzies Campbell, who read the piece with mounting fury. So incensed was Campbell that he left the restaurant and, from the street outside, telephoned Charles Kennedy's press secretary to protest.

Michael Moore said:

> Ming was raging, as we all were. This seemed to be a destabilising attempt by somebody close to Charles. He basically at that point went out of the restaurant, he rang Jackie Rowley to make it clear he wasn't doing so and to say how dark a view he would take of any attempt to undermine him.

John Thurso later shared a taxi home with Campbell where they discussed the conversation. Thurso said:

> Ming was incandescent with rage. He said: 'I cannot believe Charles would do this. He cannot know about this.' He rang Jackie Rowley and said: 'I am being portrayed as if it is all my fault, this is a victory for Charles. If I am being put up as a scapegoat then I will tell everything I know, because I will not have my integrity called into question.' Ming was incredibly upset. He felt he had covered for and protected Charles on a vast number of occasions and never spilled the beans.

The following afternoon, amid more media stories accusing him of disloyalty,[10] Menzies Campbell issued a terse statement saying he had no intention of standing against Charles Kennedy, who would have his full support for as long as he remained leader.[11] In fact, relations between them had all but broken down. From this moment it was clear Menzies Campbell would be a candidate to replace Kennedy if he resigned, although no campaign was ever put in place. More MPs pledged support to Campbell, among them Chris Huhne, another talented new MP, although this later became a source of controversy when he stood as a candidate for the leadership himself.

Rivals were also circling. On the day the shadow cabinet revolted, an e-mail from Mark Oaten was circulated to Lib Dem members, setting out Oaten's achievements as home affairs spokesman, in what looked like blatant self promotion.[12] The following weekend, with Charles Kennedy vowing to continue, Oaten gave a newspaper interview effectively setting out his stall as a candidate.[13]

Meanwhile Kennedy's critics were regrouping. The evening after the parliamentary party meeting at which Kennedy's supporters rallied, Ed Davey, Norman Lamb, David Laws and Sarah Teather planned a melancholy supper together in Shepherd's restaurant in a mood of collective gloom at the damage wreaked on the party and the inconclusive outcome. But new critics of Kennedy began to emerge, urging them not to let matters lie as it became apparent there were other MPs outside the shadow cabinet who had not spoken but shared the concerns. Chris Huhne, who had played little part in events thus far, urged them to try again, saying that once started the mutiny must be pressed to its conclusion. Susan Kramer and several others were of a similar view. The circle of unhappiness among mainstream Lib Dems was widening, not narrowing. Chris Huhne was particularly forceful. That evening Huhne, Vince Cable and several MPs had been invited to meet Paul Marshall, a millionaire hedge fund entrepreneur and Lib Dem supporter, who occasionally hosted symposiums on subjects such as taxation or the Canadian Liberal party. These had grown out of *The Orange Book*,[14] a challenging collection of largely economically liberal policy essays edited by Paul Marshall and David Laws, to which most of those invited that evening were contributors. David Laws and Ed Davey planned to send their apologies but Chris Huhne exhorted them to keep their appointment with Paul Marshall and to use the occasion for a serious discussion about how to press the leadership crisis to a conclusion. After a short taxi ride, David Laws,

Ed Davey, Norman Lamb, Sarah Teather and Chris Huhne reconvened in Paul Marshall's spacious thirteenth-floor office in an art deco building near Charing Cross, with panoramic views of the River Thames; instead of highbrow policy they discussed brutal politics.

Vince Cable, a slightly donnish economist, had until this point been ambivalent about the insurrection, having refused to support the first, abandoned letter of no confidence in Kennedy or to accept an invitation to Nick Harvey's similarly aborted supper. Cable had, however, begun to doubt Charles Kennedy's private assurance that he did not have a drink problem and realised that his younger colleagues had passed a point of no return. Those gathered in Paul Marshall's office were determined to act. They had no wish to involve Menzies Campbell or Simon Hughes, due to their positions as deputy leader and party president and as potential candidates. They entreated Vince Cable, the next most senior member, to take charge and discussed plans for a second letter of no confidence, which they proposed to sign and deliver collectively to Charles Kennedy; this time, only members of the shadow cabinet who could be sworn to secrecy would be included. A brusquely short draft had already been prepared. Cable at first resisted but Chris Huhne led attempts to prevail on him to change his mind, arguing that the party would otherwise look a laughing stock that no donor would wish to support. After a long discussion Cable agreed.

He set two conditions. First, he said he would himself compose the letter asking Charles Kennedy to consider his position over the Christmas recess, which he felt should be respectful in tone and allow Kennedy time to go in a manner he chose. Second, Cable said he would keep the only copy, so that it could not be misused, and would deliver it himself. Although not what they initially envisaged, the others readily agreed. It was a critical moment. The *Orange Book* group had decided to see through the ramshackle insurgency to a decisive conclusion.

Over subsequent days, eleven senior MPs signed Vince Cable's carefully crafted and respectful letter asking the leader to 'reconsider his position', most doing so in his office in Portcullis House: Cable himself, Norman Baker, Ed Davey, Sandra Gidley, Andrew George, Chris Huhne (although not technically in the shadow cabinet), Norman Lamb, David Laws, Michael Moore, Sarah Teather and John Thurso, who did so via an exchange of faxes from his ancestral castle in Caithness, thereby inadvertently creating a second copy. Nick Clegg, who after some debate had declined to join his *Orange Book* allies at Paul Marshall's gathering, refused an invitation to sign, thinking the plan politically unwise and without a clear idea of what would happen next. The signatories did not quite constitute a majority, given that the shadow cabinet had twenty-three members, but once the three potential candidates were removed from the equation (Menzies Campbell, Simon Hughes and Mark Oaten), and two office holders from the Lords (Tom McNally and David Shutt), eleven was an ominous number. There were three or four others Vince Cable had not spoken to. So nervous were some that Vince Cable would have second thoughts that Ed Davey prepared a reserve letter, similarly worded, to go ahead without him, should he falter. But, with Parliament about to rise for the Christmas recess, Vince Cable arranged to see Charles Kennedy, requesting that his chief of staff, Dick Newby, be present as a witness, and told him of his letter. In a move that was later misrepresented, Cable, who had the document in his pocket, explained to Charles Kennedy he would not hand it over now but thought that Kennedy should know the strength of feeling amongst his colleagues. His position as leader was no longer sustainable, Cable explained, and he should use the Christmas period to prepare an exit strategy and depart in a civilised manner. They parted amicably and Vince Cable, thinking Kennedy had little option but to do as he urged, locked the letter away and left shortly afterwards for a family wedding in India and to visit a village in Sri Lanka being built for people made homeless by the tsunami a year earlier.

Hitherto, Charles Kennedy's drinking had been hinted at in press reports of the crisis but not more than that. This changed with the intervention of Paul Marsden, a former Labour MP, who, bizarrely, defected to the Lib Dems in 2001 but then returned to support Labour again for the general election four years later, though he did not stand again as an MP. Paul Marsden, who had by now quit the Commons, wrote a newspaper article[15] that discussed directly Kennedy's drinking, laced with anecdotes from his encounters with the Lib Dem leader.

Jackie Rowley told journalists that Charles Kennedy 'strenuously denies' having a drink problem but no writ for libel was issued. The effect was to force the subject of his drinking into the public domain. Charles Kennedy, in a pre-arranged television interview, was asked if he'd had medical support to deal with his drinking, to which he replied, again untruthfully: 'No, no, no, that is not the case, it is a matter on all fronts – if there's something my doctor really wants me to do over this holiday period, as a matter of fact, it is give up smoking.'[16]

Three days later Andrew George went to see Charles Kennedy a second time, explained he had signed Vince Cable's letter but told his leader he could survive if he made a public statement admitting to a drink problem. Two other members of the shadow cabinet made a similar proposal, one via Dick Newby, who took soundings on the idea from MPs, and the other in a private letter to Charles Kennedy. Andrew George told Kennedy that if he agreed to do so, he would ask Vince Cable to withdraw the letter seeking his resignation. Over the Christmas recess Andrew George followed this up with several telephone calls to Charles Kennedy appealing to him to make a public admission of alcoholism, but urging him not to call a leadership ballot himself. Each time Kennedy told him he was reflecting on the idea.

As Lib Dem MPs dispersed to their constituencies or on holiday, several were struck by the absence of any initiative from the leader to shore up his position. Instead of telephone calls to MPs, peers, council leaders and regional party officers to urge unity, there was silence. Charles Kennedy fulfilled his engagements, unwisely telling reporters there was plenty of young talent in the party should any of the shadow cabinet want to quit. He issued a New Year message, which the mutineers had intended would be a resignation statement but instead accused the Government of presiding over worsening inequality.[16] Sporadic discussion of Charles Kennedy's position continued in the media but essentially there was a lull in hostilities as, true to their agreement, the eleven signatories observed their oath of silence about the letter locked, undelivered, in Vince Cable's safe in Twickenham.

Hopes of a ceasefire began to fray as, in the absence of direction from the top, Lib Dems began airing contrary solutions in the media. Simon Hughes called it unacceptable that complaints about Kennedy should continue, saying the 'water was tested before Christmas and the majority view was that Charles should stay on'.[18] He pleaded with Kennedy's critics not to do anything further until after the May local elections. This latter theme was taken by Tom McNally, who urged MPs to postpone any leadership challenge for the sake of Lib Dem council candidates, but called for 'a radical, rapid and sustained change in the style and content' of Kennedy's leadership.[19] This was trenchant stuff. The idea of postponing the agony, however, horrified others. Susan Kramer, the party's former candidate for London mayor and now an MP, interrupted a family holiday in Turkey to give an interview by mobile telephone calling for a leadership election within weeks, with Charles Kennedy as one of the candidates, to 'clear the air'.[20] Susan Kramer, concerned for her party's elections in her London borough of Richmond, said the leadership question could not be 'allowed to bleed'.

Norman Baker endorsed her call that evening but proposed an alternative, a vote of confidence among the party's sixty-two MPs,[21] an idea taken up by others. Throughout the day the chief whip, watching in despair from his constituency in Stockport, circulated ever more exasperated pager messages to his MPs. One told them to refer media requests to the party's chief press officer. A second implored: 'Pls [sic] share your views with me before airing them in the media.' His last read: 'Putting it another way. Use your common sense and shut up.'

Such was the fracturing backdrop when, the following morning, Charles Kennedy's office took a telephone call from an executive at ITN, who dropped a bombshell. Its evening news bulletin at 6.30 p.m. would report that Kennedy had submitted to treatment for alcoholism. Worse, the story's reporter was Daisy McAndrew (née Sampson), who had been Kennedy's press secretary for his first two years as leader and knew of his drinking. Finally, his 'bunker' was forced to accept this was the endgame. Three years earlier, Charles Kennedy had been on the brink of making a public admission of his drink problem but backed out on the morning of a planned press conference. Now his team revived the plan, in a last, desperate attempt to spike the ITN story. They resolved to make the announcement first, on his own terms, in the hope that MPs who had urged such a course of action upon him would be honour bound to offer support. But Kennedy decided to go further by himself initiating a leadership ballot, appealing over the heads of his mutinous MPs for the backing of rank-and-file members. In private he had called this 'the nuclear option'. Arrangements were hastily made for a press conference at 5.45 p.m., billed as a 'personal statement' by Charles Kennedy. He pressed the nuclear button.

Lib Dem MPs, still largely out of the loop, were informed in a short pager message of the impending press conference as news of the event flashed around Westminster. Amid feverish speculation first that Charles Kennedy would announce his resignation, then that he would admit to treatment for alcoholism, the story took yet another twist. Sky News and the BBC revealed the existence of a letter of no confidence in Charles Kennedy, signed by eleven members of his shadow cabinet, whose existence was leaked to them by one of the tight circle of signatories. Much emphasis was laid in subsequent news reports on the fact that the letter had not been delivered, deepening the confusion and portraying those behind it as vacillating or lacking courage.

Charles Kennedy, looking strained yet self-possessed, delivered his statement[22] in a characteristically direct manner to a throng of reporters and a bank of flashing cameras crammed into the boardroom at the party's headquarters in Cowley Street. He had, he said, been coming to terms over the past eighteen months with a drink problem. It had been a struggle and he had learnt the hard way of the need to face up to this medical problem. Charles Kennedy said:

> I've sought professional help and I believe today that this issue is essentially resolved. I have chosen not to acknowledge it publicly in this way before because, if at all possible, I wanted to overcome it privately. In a sense, this admission today comes as something of a personal relief. I should have been willing to talk about it more openly. I wish I had.

This issue lay beneath much of the current leadership speculation among his MPs, he admitted, but said he considered himself capable and in good health and remained politically determined as leader. Then came the disastrous addendum. It was only fair now, he said, to give party members their say over the continuing leadership. Kennedy announced he was requesting that the party immediately put in place steps to hold a leadership election, saying it was open to any colleague who believed they could better represent the party's long-term interests to stand against him. This was nonsense, as he well knew. Menzies Campbell, Simon Hughes and Mark Oaten had all said previously they would not stand against him. By evening all had issued statements confirming they would not do so.

With Charles Kennedy's statement dominating media headlines, Lib Dem MPs, who were scattered across their constituencies, focused not on the confirmation of his drink problem but on the looming leadership ballot. Many were aghast. The following day became one of gruesome political theatre as Lib Dems took to the media airwaves to demand his resignation in ever more graphic terms. Nick Harvey set the ball rolling, dismissing Kennedy's ballot as an absurd charade triggered only after extracting commitments from others not to stand. Chris Davies, then leader of the Lib Dem MEPs, called him a 'dead man walking'.[23] Jenny Tonge, a peer, suggested that to have an alcoholic leader was untenable, saying: 'Quite honestly, if you are looking for someone to play the part of Tarzan, you wouldn't employ a one-legged actor.' Matthew Taylor, his eyes moist, pleaded with Kennedy on Sky News to quit, for his family's sake. At this moment Vince Cable returned from Sri Lanka to find himself bombarded with calls from journalists about his letter, some asking if it would indeed be delivered. Thinking on his feet, Vince Cable said yes and arranged to travel to the Commons to hand it over in person. Once there he again had a curiously civilised conversation with Charles Kennedy, telling him on arriving 'this is the dreaded letter,' at which both men laughed. Still, however, Kennedy seemed not to grasp the severity of his plight, later giving newspaper interviews to declare his intention to soldier on.[24]

Away from the drama being played out on rolling news channels, events of still greater significance were gathering pace. Ed Davey and Sarah Teather decided in an exchange of telephone calls early in the day to resign from the front bench. Initially their idea was to encourage all the eleven signatories of Vince Cable's letter to stand down too. But, recalling Charles Kennedy's fateful reference to younger talent waiting in the wings, they agreed to demonstrate that the loss of confidence in him ran far wider by extending the invitation to junior MPs. Both began an exhaustive series of calls to parliamentary colleagues, initially proposing that they quit together at 5 p.m. that day. Their aim was to break the wave of damaging media coverage and to force Charles Kennedy's resignation before the Sunday newspapers dished out the inevitable details of his drinking episodes. Soon they were being helped by Norman Baker, Julia Goldsworthy and Nick Clegg, whose patience with Charles Kennedy finally snapped and who rang both Dick Newby and Anna Werrin to say he was withdrawing support. By lunchtime twenty MPs were ready to resign, when the plan changed again.

Anxious to act honourably, Andrew George, in a freelance initiative from Cornwall, announced he had written to Charles Kennedy giving notice that he would resign on Monday if he remained leader. He did so in a radio interview[25] during which, in a moment of farce, his constituency organiser, Antony 'Chunky' Penhaul, reversed the MP's car into a wall outside his office in Penzance while Andrew George talked to London by mobile phone. His intervention threatened more chaotic choreography at the conclusion of an already messy, drawn-out affair. When Norman Lamb, too, declared himself ready to resign unless Kennedy quit, Ed Davey and Sarah Teather synchronised the mass resignation threat to be issued that day, if necessary, but to take effect after the weekend. Ed Davey telephoned the chief whip, hoping if Kennedy resigned immediately their initiative need never be made public. Davey was unable at first to make contact and left a message for Andrew Stunell. When Stunell called back, Ed Davey told him that twenty MPs were ready to quit. Charles Kennedy himself then telephoned Ed

Davey. In a tense, difficult conversation, Kennedy intimated that he was considering his position and asked for a reprieve over the weekend. Ed Davey said he would call back. He consulted colleagues including Sarah Teather and David Laws, and they concluded Kennedy had not given a definitive commitment to resign. With news of their plan threatening to leak out, they went ahead slightly later than envisaged, e-mailing a statement[26] to the Press Association just before 6.30 p.m., by which time their number had risen to twenty-five, among them the brightest of the new intake of Lib Dem MPs. They were seven short of a majority of the parliamentary party but, with three of the signatories to Vince Cable's letter not even among them, and a BBC survey later claiming a tally of thirty-three rebels, it was clear the game was up.[27]

Charles Kennedy, doorstepped by television crews as he arrived back at his Georgian terraced town house in south London, put on a brave face. He called for a period of reflection; cited, as he had done for several days, messages of support that had poured in from party members; and said he planned a quiet family weekend. Simon Hughes attempted early on Saturday to broker an eleventh-hour compromise, under which Kennedy would stand down temporarily until May, but it was too late. Again notices were issued for a press conference at Cowley Street, scheduled for 3 p.m. Reading his resignation statement,[28] Kennedy showed all the qualities that made him one of the best known and liked politicians of his generation. He was composed, fluent, unsentimental, and even humorous. He announced he would stand down immediately, conceding he had lost the support of a critical number of his MPs although not of party members, and finished with some advice for his successor, effectively a summary of his guiding philosophy as leader. Liberal Democrats, he said, should resolve internal differences such as those between social and economic liberals on their terms, not those dictated by others who did not share their goals. The party should hold fast to liberal principles and at all costs remain politically independent, avoiding relations with other parties that would blur the Liberal Democrats' identity to voters. With that, and a final, rueful smile, he left the stage, beaten but unbowed.

2

Happy Highland days

Charles Kennedy is an enigma. As leader of his party he was almost universally liked by his MPs in Parliament, but brutally deposed by them. He never had another job other than that of full-time politician at Westminster, yet felt himself an outsider in the House of Commons. He was known as vivacious, sociable, witty and was so in demand as a regular media performer he earned the sobriquet 'Chat Show Charlie', but in fact was a painfully shy and stubbornly private man with very few close friends. He was blessed with a brilliant talent as a communicator, shrewd political judgement and an intuitive ability to read the public mind and yet, as leader of the Liberal Democrats, his public performances were frequently diffident, pedestrian and forgettable. He could rise to the most testing challenge, then lose his way when the pressure of external events subsided. To understand fully these interplaying melodies of temperament and circumstance one must trace back to his childhood, his political awakenings as a student and the exceptional events that propelled him into Parliament at the threshold of his adulthood.

Charles Peter Kennedy was born on 25 November 1959 into a very ordinary family in a unique part of Britain. His father Ian Kennedy was a draughtsman for the North of Scotland Hydro Board and would draw plans for hydroelectric power turbines. His mother Mary was the daughter of a Clydeside dockworker. They had two older children, Ian and Isabel. Charles, the youngest by six years, was named after his uncle, Charles MacEachen, his mother's brother, who served in the Second World War as a merchant navy steward and was killed in 1943, aged twenty-one. His sister Isabel later moved to Canada, where she worked as a missionary and later as a teacher, while his brother Ian went to work as a lorry driver for the local authority highways department. It was by all accounts a happy family environment.

Charles developed a passion for astronomy, fascinated by the Apollo astronauts landing on the moon, and saved up to buy a small telescope. As a teenager he developed a devotion to the pop musician David Bowie. Far from being overlooked as the youngest, he was often indulged by his parents, particularly by his mother, and enjoyed a strong, close relationship with them, although he grew used to the company of people older than himself.

What would otherwise have been an ordinary, working-class childhood was made unique by its setting. The family lived on the outskirts of Fort William, the principal town of Lochaber in the West Highlands, ringed by mountains and set against a vast salt-water loch, Loch Linnhe, where the Kennedys had deep roots as crofters, plying a tradition of small subsistence farming that spanned generations. The small, flat plain behind their home, directly beneath Ben Nevis, had been tilled by Kennedys since 1801. Their seven-acre croft was given to Charles Kennedy's ancestors in an act of benevolence by the Cameron of Lochiel, the local laird. He encountered them as they made their way to emigrate to Canada, walking with all their worldly goods to catch a boat from Corpach, a small port on Loch Linnhe, having been evicted in the beginning of the Highland clearances.[1] Generations of Kennedys are buried in the family graveyard on a hillside in Lochaber, including Charles Kennedy's great- great-grandfather. There are Highland roots, too, on his mother's side. His maternal grandfather was from Arisaig, a small settlement in a bay on the west coast near Mallaig, and his maternal grandmother was from Glasgow, where they settled to find work. Both were native Gaelic speakers and returned to the Highlands once they retired.

In his early boyhood the family croft was still tilled by Charles's grandfather, Donald Kennedy, who, following Highland tradition, combined crofting with work as a ploughman at Achintee in Glen Nevis. Donald Kennedy was a well-known figure in Lochaber. He fought with the Lovat Scouts during the First World War and was gravely wounded in his left arm at the battle of Ypres; one of his younger brothers died prematurely after surviving a gas attack in the trenches. Donald Kennedy, also a Gaelic speaker, was a small but powerfully built man and, like his two surviving brothers, a renowned athlete. He captained Fort William at shinty, the Highlands derivative of hockey, in 1912 and despite his injured arm continued to compete as an athlete on his return from the war. Donald Kennedy competed in the Highland Games in short sprints and in the long jump, the high jump, the light and heavy hammer, the shot put and the caber. His mode of transport was a battered old Ferguson tractor and he was enraged by post-war legislation requiring a licence to drive it on the roads around Fort William. According to family lore, Donald Kennedy once literally let loose a bull in a china shop. Following another crofting custom, he travelled down to Carlisle to buy a bull to service the herds of several neighbours as well as his own. On his return by cattle train, the bull charged off from Fort William station and found its way into a gift shop, from which he managed to extricate it without a single breakage.

When Ian and Mary Kennedy married in 1950 the croft was sub-divided, another Highland tradition, and next door they built the two-storey home where Charles and his older brother and sister were brought up. As a boy Charles Kennedy was just old enough to remember his grandfather, who lived next door in a modest single-storey croft, ploughing their acreage with a brown shire horse, Nellie, and being taught to help milk his tiny herd of cattle, muck out the horse and shear sheep under the gaze of a working farm collie. He later described the family's amusement on occasions when his grandfather would come next door to use their telephone. Being unfamiliar with the device, he would bellow into the receiver as if it worked on the same principle as an ear trumpet.[2] Long after his death, Charles Kennedy renovated his grandfather's simple crofter's bungalow to turn into his own home when visiting the constituency, next door to his parents, and restored his grandfather's plough and potato planter as garden ornaments in tribute to his memory.

When growing up, neither of his parents spoke Gaelic, knowledge of which was then considered a disadvantage. In another break with the past, Ian Kennedy sold his father's cattle herd and taught himself the draughtsman's skills by which he made his living. Instead of athletics, his gift was music. An accomplished fiddle player of semi-professional standard, he won many musical competitions, toured three times playing his fiddle in the United States and was much in demand as an entertainer. He and Mary Kennedy, who accompanied him on the keyboard, would play often at local fêtes, ceilidhs and concerts, making the couple well-known figures in and around Fort William. The family lived modestly but comfortably, eating much home-grown and home-reared produce, with a network of relatives close by. Charles Kennedy would observe later that in such an environment social class mattered much less than what a person contributed, and the Kennedys were respected as active members of a small, strong community to which they had long-standing ties. Ian and Mary Kennedy were Roman

Catholics and Charles served as an altar boy at St Mary's Catholic Church in Fort William. His parents instilled in their children their own sense of duty, good manners, respect for others and community, and Charles retained in his adulthood a deep, if not always evident, Catholic conscience. Charles Kennedy said later: 'We were brought up to respect people in authority and to consider their word as good as law. I was extremely fortunate and perhaps unusual in never having been let down by my parents, teachers or other elders.'[3]

In such surroundings Charles Kennedy enjoyed an exceptionally secure, happy and, perhaps, sheltered childhood, made idyllic in his early years by helping with the husbandry chores on his grandfather's croft. Its location was also exceptionally beautiful. Wildlife abounded; the river Lochy flowed, shallow but wide, fast and cold, just across the road. All around was the physical presence of the Highlands. Beyond Fort William there were sloping moors grazed by sheep and cattle. The high, remote hills studded with granite outcrops, birch, oak and pine forests, tumbling streams and still, cold lochs present a landscape breathtaking in its beauty. It changes utterly with the seasons: white with snow, bleak and foreboding in winter; bright green in late spring and summer with moorland grass and bracken shoots inter-spersed with lines of purple heather; and pale yellow and brown by autumn. Brought up in a unique, enclosed environment, Charles Kennedy marvelled at seeing double-decker buses and elevators when the family ventured into Glasgow to spend summer holidays visiting his mother's relatives. The geography of the Highlands, sparsely settled with small communities sharing a keen sense of identity and cooperation, made a lasting impression on his character and political instincts. Indeed, it is striking how several of the close political friendships he formed later, of which there were relatively few, were with politicians representing Highlands and Islands constituencies: Russell Johnston, Bob Maclennan, Jim Wallace and John Farquhar Munro. Even Calum MacDonald, a Labour MP with whom he opened a tentative Lib–Lab dialogue after the general election of 1992, represented the Western Isles.

Charles Kennedy grew up with neither his grandfather's athleticism nor his parents' aptitude for music. Once at school he found himself invariably the last to be picked for games teams. The only sports to interest him were swimming and golf, for which his enthusiasm was at one stage sufficiently strong for his father to build an eighteen-hole putting green in the back garden. He was a shy boy but obviously bright. He attended St Columbus

Roman Catholic Junior School, a newly built school within walking distance from his home, whose construction was still being completed when he was due to start. His mother kept him at home, rather than send him temporarily to another school, and he picked up what he could from watching children's television until the school opened a couple of months later. His family's choice of school, later renamed Lochyside Primary School, proved an important one. Charles Kennedy later said he owed his political career to the fact that the school was sufficiently small for a teacher to pick up on a mild defect in his speech that meant he had difficulty pronouncing 'th' and 's' sounds. He recalled:

> I went on to receive one-to-one speech therapy and, although it was for only a short time, I still have vivid memories of these sessions, saying 'this thing' and 'that thing' until I was blue in the face and playing a lot of snakes and ladders. The treatment corrected the defect and, to this day, I am grateful to the teacher who spotted it.[4]

Able to speak without lisping, it was at secondary school that Charles Kennedy found his forte. He attended Lochaber High School, within sight of the family croft, a large mixed comprehensive school built in 1960 serving a wide area of the west coast and the Highlands, where students were taught Gaelic and played shinty. Its catchment area was so large that the school had a hostel where several dozen students, who lived long distances from Fort William, boarded during the week. Charles Kennedy was good at essays, struggled at science, tried his hand at acting and generally kept up with his studies without exerting himself, establishing a pattern that many people would note throughout his career. 'He always did just enough work to get by,' his father told one interviewer.[5]

The stage was an environment where he thrived. Boyhood parts in plays, including taking the part of the lion in *The Wizard of Oz*, culminated in his taking a leading role in a school operetta in his final year. He played Pooh-Bah in *The Mikado*, devoting such attention to the role that he rewrote some of his lyrics to include humorous references to contemporary politics. His performance, in elaborate costume and make-up, stole the show. School friends recalled how he delighted the audience by exiting the stage to one side, dashed around backstage to appear from the other wing, and ad-libbed comically in one performance during which a stool he used as a prop gave way. He put his head between his knees and stared at the broken stool as the audience roared with laughter. Charles Kennedy was a performer. Indeed, his mother thought he could have made a career on the stage, had politics not beckoned.

Fortunately for the young Charles Kennedy his school offered another avenue for performing. Soon after Kennedy arrived at school the head of English, Bob Dick, set up an extra-curricular debating society. Debating was at the time a keenly contested activity, stimulated by a Scottish schools debating tournament sponsored by the Scottish *Daily Express*. Charles Kennedy joined the debating society in his first year at senior school and by his third year, under the tutelage and encouragement of Bob Dick, was selected for Lochaber High School's debating team, where he excelled. It was, furthermore, a door to a new world. It enabled him to win the acclaim of his peers and others, to take days away from school to travel to new places, meeting journalists, politicians and other interesting figures; it was to become his short cut to success. Kennedy explained: 'I liked argumentation and I like speech making. It was just something that I instinctively took to, the experience of standing in front of a whole lot of people and putting forward an argument and trying to persuade them round to your way of thinking.' Contemporaries from his school days recalled his style of public speaking as extremely flamboyant, including bursting into song, which would invariably capture the attention of his audience.

Fiona Kenny, his debating partner in the school team, said: 'Debating gave Charles confidence. I never saw Charles nervous before a debate. We loved that experience. We would take a day off school, we would set off in Bob Dick's car, listening to *Bridge over Troubled Water*. They were happy days.'

Three times Kennedy reached the finals of the Scottish schools debating competition, held in the debating chamber of Glasgow University Union. Not only did this bring prestige to the school and its representatives; it gave the young Charles, then in his mid-teens, his first experience of staying away from home in a Glasgow hotel, one he found overawing. Mingling with pupils from other schools opened his eyes for the first time to class differences as he came across teenagers from fee-paying schools in Edinburgh, Glasgow and Dundee. He noticed they appeared totally at home in a hotel and had a clear sense of the profession they planned to follow in later life. Charles Kennedy's background was humble although by no means poor, and he remained proud of his family and his Highland antecedents. But this sense of the ordinary boy pitched into an unfamiliar and slightly daunting arena returned to him as he made his maiden speech in the House of Commons[6] and was evident at times even after he became leader of the Liberal

Democrats. Fiona Kenny said: 'We learned never to be afraid, not to be intimidated by public school people. Charles and I used to have a trick, which was to actually appear nervous when you mixed with people beforehand and then go into the debate and deliver your first point and absolutely destroy them.'

Charles Kennedy quickly learned the arts of guile and ruthlessness in competitions, such as a skilful use of debating rules that permitted a request from an opponent for a point of information. Fiona Kenny said:

> He was really strategic even at that age. Another trick was, if someone offered you a point of information, you would say: 'I will take that in a minute,' and wait sixty seconds, by which time they would have forgotten what they were going to say. He was merciless in destroying his opponents.

To his chagrin, the year after he left Lochaber High School the tournament was won outright by Fiona Kenny and her new debating partner, but their efforts helped to establish Lochaber High School with a reputation during the 1970s as one of the foremost debating schools in Scotland. The real credit lay with Bob Dick, a kindly man who commanded the immediate respect of his pupils and with whom Charles Kennedy remained in close touch during his passage through university and into politics. Kennedy also befriended Charles Graham, a political journalist on the Scottish *Daily Express*, who judged the competition. This type of mentor relationship between the young, promising pupil and encouraging, older teacher was one he replicated in politics with Roy Jenkins, Russell Johnston and Mark Bonham Carter.

Coming into contact with pupils from across Scotland had a further effect on Charles Kennedy. As well as meeting confident children from independent schools, he encountered poor teenagers of his own age from tough inner-city schools in Glasgow whose aspirations in life did not stretch beyond getting a job, of any sort, or a house of their own. It was his first glimpse of social inequality and was a powerful contributor to a gradual political awakening in his middle teens. His grandfather Donald had been a Highland Liberal, a political lineage that traces back to Gladstone's defence of crofters after the Highland clearances. His father Ian occasionally flirted with the Scottish National Party, but in the main his parents voted for Russell Johnston, their local Liberal MP, although his mother was a passionate socialist and identified with Labour. The earliest political memory for the young Charles was of

Harold Wilson's re-election as Prime Minister in 1966, when photographs of Wilson as a twelve-year-old schoolboy on the steps of Downing Street were widely published. But his interest was not initially fired by politics at Westminster, which was pretty far removed from the life of a boy in the West Highlands, but by events the United States. Even at the age of eight he registered the assassinations of Bobby Kennedy and Martin Luther King in 1968 and recalled later being moved by both. Five years on he was rushing home from school to catch up on news reports of the Watergate congressional hearings, which he followed with a passionate interest. Politics in Britain started to register with him when Edward Heath began preparations to take Britain into Europe's Common Market, and particularly during the referendum campaign to confirm Britain's entry in 1975. The cross-party alliances that came together in both camps fascinated him. He was drawn to the arguments of Edward Heath, Roy Jenkins and Jeremy Thorpe in the 'yes' camp but impressed too by the campaigning against from Tony Benn, Peter Shore and Barbara Castle. Aged fifteen, in a rare break with his family lineage, Charles Kennedy joined Fort William Labour Party, convinced that Harold Wilson – who began life an ordinary boy from Huddersfield – would do more to address the social inequalities that troubled him than would Jeremy Thorpe. His interest in the Labour Party was strong and deep. At the age of seventeen he wrote a prize-winning essay on why the death of Tony Crosland had deprived Labour of its greatest potential future leader. Already Kennedy was thinking himself of a career in politics. 'Charles knew from day one what he wanted to be. He wanted to be a member of Parliament,' said Fiona Kenny.

For understandable reasons, Kennedy subsequently played down his commitment to the Labour Party but he remained a member for six years, spanning the remaining two years of his school life and four years as an undergraduate. As indicated by his regard for Tony Crosland, he was attracted to those on the moderate right of the Labour Party and not at all by the growing militancy of the left. Charles Kennedy wrote later that he found many Labour activists engaged in fighting a dogmatic class war that was to him both surprising and thoroughly unpalatable; Highland radicalism has a gentler, although perhaps more profound character. Nonetheless, the young Charles Kennedy was a Labour man.

As a bright, talented pupil he made his family proud by going on to university. As a prominent and gifted schools debater, although not yet a champion, there was one university for him to choose above any other. The University of Glasgow had a tradition of debating more formal and developed than any other in Scotland. The Glasgow University Union organised the Scottish schools debating competition and hosted the finals in its debating chamber, where pairs of pupils were judged on their debating skills by the university's students. Charles Kennedy won a place at Glasgow to read English, leaving school after his fifth year and going up in the autumn of 1977, two months before his eighteenth birthday, for a four-year honours degree course. This was the norm in Scotland, but after three years he switched to study politics and philosophy. He was able to do so after being awarded a repeat year grant, available to certain students who changed faculty, giving him an additional year at Glasgow, where he spent a total of five years as an undergraduate: sufficient time for a student lifestyle to become not a phase but a habit.

His student life revolved overwhelmingly around Glasgow University Union, a formidable stone building of three storeys built in 1930, with Scottish baronial features, that was home to an autonomous student body established in 1885. The union offered its 5,000 student members a reading room and library for study, meeting rooms, a bar, catering facilities, a large snooker hall and other entertainment. But, above all, it had a substantial debating chamber, complete with an extensive strangers' gallery and aye and no division lobbies, which was at the heart of an active and highly organised tradition of student debate. Glasgow offered a style of student debating unlike any other British university, stemming from a decision taken in 1892, when the union's first rules for debates were drafted, to base these as closely as possible on the standing orders of the House of Commons.[7].

Students would join one of six clubs, most based broadly on political parties but in essence debating teams: Conservative, Liberal, Independent Socialist, Scottish Nationalist, Social Credit and Distributis. The university Labour club did not have a debating team, thinking such activity bourgeois and middle class, and dismissed it as semantics. Each year members would choose a leader for their club. In Glasgow parliamentary debates, of which there were six in each academic year, clubs would take turns to be 'in government' with the leader taking the role of Prime Minister and presenting a short Bill of perhaps four clauses, and the other clubs would offer various forms of opposition or support. The parliamentary debate would begin at 1 p.m. and continue, with a dinner break from 5.30 to 7.30 p.m., until 1 a.m. through a series of rounds: an opening afternoon round, unpointed open period for maiden speakers, mid-afternoon, closing afternoon, opening evening, mid-evening rounds, and question time – a moment for satirical sketches on the stage known as the 'Stunts'. In the closing evening round club leaders made ten-minute speeches, the leader of the opposition spoke for twelve minutes and the Prime Minister addressed the chamber for as long as he chose. Debaters dressed formally in suits, while clerks robed in red gowns sat at a clerks' table. They operated an intricate system of marking to score speakers' contributions, which counted towards an inter-club debates trophy, and published a debates report with comments or 'crits' on main speeches. As in the House of Commons, there was a Speaker presiding over the debate, an order paper, although this listed those due to speak in a manner more like the House of Lords, and in debates students never referred to one another by name but instead used the third person and constituency names were conferred on each member. Another departure from Commons debating etiquette was that speakers might be jeered noisily from the gallery, or even pelted with chips, making it a testing and character-building environment.

It was an atmosphere in which Charles Kennedy thrived. He joined the Social Credit club, as the one closest to the Labour Party's position, and was styled the Honourable Member for Lochaber, after his school rather than the area of the Highlands where he grew up. By another quirk of Glasgow tradition he otherwise used the formal moniker Charles P. Kennedy, and was listed as such on all union records. Debating was not simply a student pastime. For undergraduates such as the young Charles Kennedy, it was a way of life. Parliamentary debates were the focus of great anticipation and each was followed by a legendary post-debate party through the night. Between these were a host of others of a different nature: Dialectic Society events, inter-varsity debates, lunchtime debates, Beer Bar debates. From 9 a.m. debaters would gather at one of the round tables in the union's Smoke Room and start an impromptu group discussion that would continue throughout the day. The debaters' table might equally turn its thoughts to philosophical disposition as to banter or personal abuse; it was a culture of quick-witted discourse and point-scoring.

As an experienced schools debater Charles Kennedy rapidly established his reputation for public speaking at Glasgow. After little more than a year the clerks, dutifully recording their debates reports, or 'crits', had spotted an emerging talent. One observed: 'You are rapidly becoming the Mr Nice Guy of Social Credit debating, a sort of dialectic plumber who enters the debate to unblock a club line . . . This was an excellent speech – well thought out and convincingly delivered by a speaker who is continually growing in power and authority.'[8]

By his third year he became both his club leader and the union's convenor of debates, organising debating events and joining the union's board of management. He and Fiona Kenny, who joined him at Glasgow having stayed at school until her sixth year, presciently renamed their debating club the Social Democrats, intended as a centre-left grouping for Labour students rather than as a forerunner to the party he later joined. In January 1980 came the moment to which every Glasgow debater aspired. With the new Social Democratic club having its turn 'in government' for the year's fourth parliamentary debate, Charles P. Kennedy took the role of Prime Minister, denouncing Margaret Thatcher as he spoke to the resolution: 'That this house has no confidence in Her Majesty's Government in Westminster'. The Glasgow custom was for the order paper to list club speakers according to a humorous or topical theme: the British Empire or Catholic Church, for example, or citing literary quotations for each speaker. Kennedy eschewed such frivolity. His order paper listed his speakers as if they were members of his Cabinet.[9] Significantly, among a subsidiary tally of privy counsellors cited beneath them was the name of Donald Dewar, a former Glasgow union debater and then backbench Labour MP for Glasgow Garscadden. Kennedy's instincts still lay with Labour.

As debates convenor he became further absorbed into the world of student debating. He became secretary of the Scottish Students Debating Committee, organising inter-varsity competitions, and then its acting chairman after the incumbent withdrew, although minutes of the meeting record that Kennedy's elevation was agreed 'after some discussion'.[10] Kennedy himself represented Glasgow in such debates and travelled widely. In addition to speaking at other Scottish universities, particularly the ancient universities, he eventually joined debating tours overseas, including to the United States.

Having delivered his prime ministerial speech, Charles Kennedy was thereafter known as the Rt Hon. Member for Lochaber. It also entitled him to put his feet on the table in the debating chamber, another Glasgow quirk. Having reached the status of senior debater he was much in demand for parliamentary and other debates in his remaining years, rarely preparing speeches in advance beyond a few jotted notes but developing a distinctive style of oratory. Fiona Kenny said:

> There was a period when Charles's style changed and he just got a confidence where it was not so much about what he said, it was about the way he said it. He started holding

his hands apart and bringing his fingers to meet again. He just started to look parliamentary. He had a group of fellow students who coached him and supported him, thinking at that point about him being president of the union.

He excelled in the mid-evening and, particularly, government pre-question time rounds. For these Glasgow parliamentary debating protocol required a discursive and philosophical speech on the nature of the Bill before the house. Kennedy would deliver this in the soft, conversational tone he deployed later in the Commons and, particularly, at party conferences. John Morrison, another member of his debating club, recalled: 'He was very good at that. In fact if you wonder where Charles got the conversational conference speech style, you can go directly back to government pre-question time and mid-evening rounds of the Glasgow University Union.'

Just as Glasgow debating in the early 1960s produced a generation of star debaters, led by John Smith, Donald Dewar and Menzies Campbell, the era of the late 1970s and early 1980s saw another peak in its debating history. Several of that generation went on to senior roles in the media, although Charles Kennedy's contemporaries included Liam Fox, who contested the leadership of the Conservative Party in 2005. Liam Fox recalled:

> He was a renowned and quite feared debater. He could always speak well without notes and you always had the impression that he could virtually speak on any topic without very much preparation. He was aggressive and very skilful as a debater and won a lot of trophies for the university. It was at a time when Glasgow was particularly pre-eminent in debating and we held most of the country's debating trophies. There were a lot of very good debaters, most of whom you can recognise in the House of Commons because they tend to have much the same style.

Among those who saw him debate at the time was David Steel, the Liberal Party leader, who was asked to be a judge at an inter-university debating competition at Bristol in 1980. He and Eric Heffer, the second judge, selected the debaters from Glasgow University as the winning team and as the best individual speaker chose Charles Kennedy. On the basis of his speech, David Steel suggested to Kennedy afterwards that he consider leaving Labour for the Liberal Party. David Steel recalled: 'At the dinner afterwards he happened to be sitting next to me, and I said to him: "Having listened to your speech, I think you should rethink your political orientation," by which I meant join the Liberal Party.'

Such was Charles Kennedy's rhetorical reputation in Glasgow University that at one annual general meeting of the Dialectic Society, which shared a union tradition of passing satirical resolutions, it approved a motion based on an adaptation of the black power slogan that read: 'Say it long, say it loud, I'm Charles P. Kennedy and I'm proud.'

On one occasion, Kennedy was accused while speaking from the front bench of breaching the chamber's standing orders that forbade the drinking of alcohol other than whisky. This was based upon the House of Commons practice that permits Chancellors of the Exchequer to fortify themselves when presenting their budgets. 'The Right Honourable Member for Lochaber is drinking alcohol,' one student interrupted with a point of order. 'It's water, Mr Speaker, Sir,' Charles Kennedy replied, with a twinkle in his eye. 'There's a lemon in it, it must be gin and tonic,' another objected in a further point of order. 'Ah, it's plain water,' came Kennedy's riposte, 'with a goldfish in it.'

His oratory did, however, let him down on occasions. After one speech in the chamber, having perhaps spent too long in the Beer Bar beforehand, the clerks dispensed with their usual critique running to three or four paragraphs in the debates report, and instead recorded a three-line poem:

> CPK, what can we say?
> You walked in,
> You drank some gin.[11]

In his penultimate year at Glasgow he and Fiona Kenny – the first mixed debating team to represent Glasgow University Union – reached the final of the *Observer* Mace for student debating. Fiercely proud of its traditions, Glasgow University Union had won the Mace on eight previous occasions, more than any other university, but not since 1974. The following year Charles Kennedy won the trophy for Glasgow with a new partner; Kennedy was the proposer and Clark McGinn, a fellow philosophy student, the seconder. Ironically, their task was to argue the case against proportional representation. The return of the Mace to Glasgow University Union was the cause of much celebration. That year Kennedy also helped to make history by speaking in a marathon debate organised by the Dialectic Society that set a record for the world's longest.

Central though debating was to Charles Kennedy and his fellow debaters, it was one of many facets of student life at Glasgow University Union. Games such as snooker were an important part of union life for many students, entertainment was organised and the union retained many of the attributes of a private gentlemen's club. There was even a barber's shop in the basement, where short-back-and-sides haircuts and wet shaves with an open razor were available. While immediately comfortable with student debating, this shy boy with a West Highland reserve and Catholic upbringing was at first less at ease with the decadence of undergraduate life. His best friend, Murdo Macdonald, later recalled how he and their small circle of close friends had to 'socialise' their scarecrow-like companion, with his orange hair and big ears, and encourage him to gravitate from nursing a half-pint of lager towards drinking gin and tonics at the pace of other students.[12] As he cut a dash in the chamber with his dexterity in debate, however, Charles Kennedy became a prominent union figure, growing extremely self-confident with a wide circle of acquaintances, although his intimate friends remained few and he preferred discussing politics to small talk, and never talked of his personal life. On joining the board as debates convenor, Charles Kennedy was expected to wear a jacket and tie to its meetings, held around a substantial oval table in the wood-panelled boardroom with its cavernous fireplace. Any student who attended inappropriately dressed faced a vote of censure, while a union member who was discourteous to one of the board risked a fine in guineas.

Women were not permitted to become members of the union; they were entitled to debate but not to represent Glasgow University Union in competitive debates: this was the 'men's union'. There was a heavy drinking culture, particularly amongst the sporting societies, exemplified by a yard of ale produced in the Beer Bar for drinking competitions. Black-tie dinners might end with drunken undergraduates clambering on top of one another to form precarious human pyramids. During some lunchtimes, porno-graphic films would be shown in the sedate Reading Room. These were named 'The Freds' after a producer of 1940s Tom and Jerry cartoons; bizarrely, a short animation would be shown as a pretext, after which the screen would switch to pornography while the Tom and Jerry cartoon soundtrack continued. A vein of misogyny ran through some of the union's corporate life that came to a head in the year Charles Kennedy joined the board over whether to admit women as members, a subject referred to as 'mixing'. The Queen Margaret Union, the women's union, decided to open its doors to male students in 1979 and the university put the men's union under pressure to reciprocate or face financial penalties. The board, having taken counsel's opinion, called a special general meeting in February 1980, and proposed an amendment to the union's constitution to admit women as members. This was carried by a substantial majority, although 139 students voted against, in a demonstration of the undercurrent of resentment at the prospect of allowing women equal status within the union.[13]

This was the backdrop of rancour and division against which, a few months later, Charles Kennedy was elected president of the union, succeeding his friend John T. Macdonald, and with his closest friend Murdo Macdonald as honorary secretary. It was an uneasy atmosphere since, having been party to the board's proposal to 'mix' the union, Kennedy was one of those seen by the misogynist minority as having betrayed its 95-year history as a men's union. To new women members, meanwhile, he was one of the establishment in a body that opened its doors to them only reluctantly. On the first evening of the new term, entry to the union's Beer Bar was closed to freshers as a 'night of shame' was staged to mark its passing as an all-male redoubt. The *Glasgow Herald* published a photograph of a group of students, several of them long haired, scruffily dressed and clutching the pint jug beer glasses of the era, with Charles Kennedy on the edge of the group immaculately dressed in a suit and tie. His year as president saw further controversy as the union's catering and bar staff went on strike early in 1981, after it emerged that the union's employees were paid less than counterparts at the university academic staff club. As union staff mounted a NUPE union picket at the front entrance, Charles Kennedy and members of his board were at times called upon to unload barrels of beer and other supplies delivered to the rear of the building.[14]

It was not all rows and back-biting. Stories abound about the under-graduate antics at Glasgow of the youthful Charles Kennedy. He earned the ire of the academic authorities by masterminding an ironical campaign for the election of Reginald Bosanquet, a former television newsreader with a reputation as a *bon viveur*, as rector of Glasgow University in 1980. His efforts – under the banner 'Reggie for rector' – were surprisingly successful, and Charles Kennedy bequeathed to his student successors for the following three years a somewhat detached Reggie Bosanquet as their representative on the university's court. He earned the nickname 'Taxi Kennedy', although accounts differ as to its origins. Some contemporaries attribute this to a penchant for summoning cabs for the shortest journeys within the university campus paid for with taxi 'chits' charged to the union's account; others to tales of him taking taxis back to Glasgow after missing the last train from

Dundee, Aberdeen or other cities. There were even accounts of taxi races to Glasgow airport and or other destinations across the city at the union's expense. The invitation that year for Daft Friday, the annual twelve-hour union ball that began with a sherry party, followed by the Bridie dinner, and proceeded through the night to end with breakfast, was issued in the style of a newspaper report on the attempted assassination of 'President Kennedy'. The President's taxi, it reported with student humour, had come under fire from a sniper in Bosanquet Boulevard. 'Three shots pierced the silence . . . as the President's taxicade came under fire,' the spoof report said. 'The President lay slumped on the floor. Fortunate, this, or else he might have been hit . . .'

As a larger-than-life student character, who exhibited a laidback attitude to a role as president that carried serious responsibilities, he attracted criticism too. At one meeting during his term as president, another board member raised allegations of financial mismanagement against Charles Kennedy and secured agreement to set up a committee of inquiry to investigate these and report back. This process was swiftly stopped as two of senior trustees who had been absent called an extraordinary board meeting and protested that such a procedure was out of order. Instead the union's auditors were invited to consider the allegations and found nothing irregular.

For most of his time at university Charles Kennedy's involvement in politics was confined to debate, his theoretical political studies and union politics, much of it based on personalities rather than on ideology. Political student activism had a separate focus, on the Students' Representative Council, where in the same era Wendy Alexander and Sarah Boyack, who both later served as Labour ministers in the Scottish Executive, cut their teeth. Charles Kennedy was a union man, not a student politician. A visit with fellow union members to the Strangers' Gallery of the House of Commons fired his own ambition for a career at Westminster but its direction was determined by the decision of Roy Jenkins, Shirley Williams, David Owen and Bill Rodgers, the so-called Gang of Four, to break away from the Labour Party. In January 1981 he and three fellow students from the Labour club, Stephen Boyle, Stephen Kerr and John Morrison, went to a meeting at a Glasgow hotel of the Council for Social Democracy, established in the Limehouse declaration of principles by the Gang of Four. John Morrison decided immediately to join the fledgling party that was launched two months later as the SDP but Charles Kennedy, ever cautious, held back. John Morrison recalled: 'I was smitten at that point, I said I am leaving [Labour], I am joining the SDP. I made that decision, I crossed that Rubicon, but Charles at that point said: "I will wait a while. I like what they are saying but I am staying in the Labour Party."'

It was not until November, with the Liberal–SDP Alliance riding high in the opinion polls and just before the Crosby by-election that brought Shirley Williams back into the Commons, that Charles Kennedy resigned his membership of the Labour party to join the SDP. Among those who persuaded him to do so was Iain MacCormick, the former Scottish Nationalist MP for Argyll and a former Glasgow debater and fellow Highlander, who stood for the university's rectorship while Kennedy was union president. They stayed in touch and, after MacCormick joined the SDP, he invited Charles Kennedy for drinks at his mother's house in Glasgow and urged him to follow suit. Iain MacCormick recalled: 'I said: "Look, Charles, why don't you bloody well join the SDP?" We had a long conversation and I was very glad in the end to know that he decided to join the SDP, really glad, because I knew that this guy had so much potential.'

Finally, in January 1982, Kennedy had a taste of real-world politics when the city's constituency of Glasgow Hillhead fell vacant on the death of its Conservative MP, Sir Thomas Galbraith, precipitating a two-and-a-half-month by-election campaign that gave Roy Jenkins his opportunity to return to Parliament. With other SDP students, Charles Kennedy worked hard as a footsoldier in the campaign, canvassing and delivering leaflets. After a spoiler candidate changed his name by deed poll to Roy Jenkins, he and other SDP students were sent on the day of the ballot in late March to parade outside polling stations wearing a heavy sandwich board with the message 'Number 5: the Rt Hon. Roy Harris Jenkins'.

Debating and student union politics took up so much of Charles Kennedy's life that his obvious ability was not always apparent in his academic studies. At times he neglected these, especially during his year as union president. His English tutor, Philip Drew, worried that Kennedy's work was being overlooked, called him in relatively early on and asked the young man what he wished to do with his life. Journalism, perhaps teaching, or possibly politics, Charles Kennedy told him. The first two needed a degree, Professor Drew pointed out, but concluded: 'If all else fails you can always go into politics.'[15] When he applied himself, Charles Kennedy was clearly bright. Raymond Plant, later Master of St Catherine's College, Oxford and a Labour peer, taught him moral philosophy as a visiting professor at Glasgow and thought him 'an exceptionally able pupil'.[16]

'His aim had been to read for a joint degree in English and philosophy, but the politics course caught his interest and he switched,' said Robin Downie, his philosophy tutor for his final two years. 'Academically he was a good student. Often the Glasgow Union office bearers do not do well. But he continued with his studies while being president and debating round the world. He was awarded a good 2:1, which included some first-class papers. On my advice he wrote a philosophy dissertation instead of one of his written exams. His theme was political and private morality, and that was given a good first-class mark.'

Even so, Charles Kennedy would often be late with his essays, although he would always telephone with an explanation and offer a new delivery date. Even during his final exams, Professor Downie had to stop him from participating in lunchtime union debates and plead with him to concentrate on his examinations.

On graduating from university, Kennedy spent the summer trying his hand at the only career path that really appealed to him beyond politics. He took a summer job at Radio Highland, a dual-language local BBC radio station in Inverness that broadcast in both English and Gaelic. Kennedy, who worked on the English language output, was taken on as a temporary reporter but in a small community radio station had ample opportunities for broadcasting. One of his early items broadcast was entitled 'Hitler's Boat', an account of the voyage of a German vessel up the Caledonian canal. Fellow journalists thought him a natural communicator with the potential for a career as a journalist, although Kennedy was still very clear that he wished to be a member of Parliament. Gregarious and brimming with self-confidence, he was known in the radio station as 'Charles-Charles' due to his habit of introducing himself to anyone and everyone, saying: 'I'm Charles; Charles Kennedy.' He was paid for his work, although it was not a permanent, salaried position, and it turned out to be the only job he would experience outside Parliament. Long afterwards, his curriculum vitae would meticulously include this brief holiday job as 'journalist and broadcaster'. Iain MacDonald, his senior producer, said: 'He was offered the option of sticking with that particular route because he was good at it. He thought long and hard about it and came back to me and said: "I have decided to go to the States, I may never get the chance again."'

Charles Kennedy decided to cut short his brief foray into the outside world when, after five years as a student, he opted for more. He met an academic, Audrey Olmstead, on one of his undergraduate debating tours who suggested to him that he go to study in Bloomington, Indiana. The university had a department of speech communication headed by an expert in speech rhetoric, Jeffrey Auer. Kennedy applied for and was awarded a Fulbright scholarship to study for a master's degree at the University of Indiana, where he held the title of associate instructor and coached debating teams while studying political rhetoric. It was a post tailor made for Kennedy and he loved it. He appreciated great orators whatever their political colours or the violence of their views, admiring, for instance, Enoch Powell as well as Michael Foot and Roy Jenkins. He also grew fascinated by Robert F. Kennedy and for years afterwards would cite as an inspiration Bobby Kennedy's quotation from Aeschylus: 'Some men see things as they are and ask themselves, why? I dream of things that never have been and ask, why not?' Such academic detachment when studying the political arts, akin to the debating skills that allowed him to win a prize arguing the case against proportional representation, can be both a strength and a weakness in politics itself. The ability to appreciate, and even anticipate, the case made by an opponent can aid strategic thinking; but, particularly in a leader, it must be matched by conviction and passion to rally one's own side. Charles Kennedy would often hark back to his year in America as one of the happiest of his life, as well as a powerful influence on his worldview; he was impressed by the 'can-do' approach he noticed in Americans, but also found differences in view that made him feel more consciously European than previously. Not even six years of study sated his appetite for student life and, having been invited to stay on for a further two years, he had embarked on a PhD on the political rhetoric of Roy Jenkins when British politics suddenly summoned him back.

Keen to pursue his ambition to enter politics, Kennedy applied in his final year at Glasgow University to be added to the SDP's list of approved parliamentary candidates. He attended an interview in Edinburgh where he was seen by the party's candidates panel of Bob Maclennan and Dick Mabon. Many young men of twenty-two might have been intimidated by the prospect but not this accomplished and experienced debater. Bob Maclennan recalled:

> We had a long list of people to see and he was somewhere in the middle of the list, but he was so fascinating that we took a lot of time to talk to him. We thought he was amazingly mature. He was dressed very smartly for the interview in a grey suit, very formally, and although he had a very youthful face he seemed to have a

very sophisticated understanding of politics; quite astonishing in someone of his years.

Even so, the interviewers were taken aback by his answer to their final question. 'I said to him: "You want to be on the list but I presume that's not for the next election, which is probably going to be next year?"' said Maclennan. 'And he said, "Oh no, I want to stand at the next election."'

Bob Maclennan, MP for Caithness & Sutherland, who had quit Labour for the SDP, decided Kennedy would be perfectly suitable to stand in the forthcoming general election. The SDP was a small organisation and Maclennan was subsequently in charge of negotiations with the Liberals over which seats the two Alliance parties would contest in Scotland. He fought particularly hard to claim for the SDP the constituency in Ross-shire, next to his own north Highlands constituency, on a hunch that there was a local sense of opposition to the sitting Conservative MP but not yet an obvious alternative for the electorate to turn to. The Liberals wanted to claim the Ross-shire seat for themselves, pointing out it had been represented by a Liberal MP, Alasdair Mackenzie, from 1964 to 1970. But the Liberals had come a poor fourth place in 1979, having lost their deposit in 1974. They also had a stronger organisation in Argyll & Bute, which their candidate in the previous election, Ray Michie, was keen to contest again and boundary changes apparently made it a better prospect. Two other seats in the Highlands and Islands, Inverness and Orkney & Shetland, were held by Liberals, while neither party was strong on the Western Isles, which was in nationalist hands. Bob Maclennan secured an agreement that the Alliance candidate in Ross-shire should be from the SDP, not a Liberal, and set about arranging for Charles Kennedy, who was by then in Bloomington, Indiana, to contest it. 'I got in touch with people there and introduced him to the local party,' Bob Maclennan said. 'And because we had, in those days, a sort of area party arrangement it was very easy for me to get him looked at seriously.'

Charles Kennedy duly applied for the nomination, although the final boundaries of the constituency were still unclear. There were two proposals before the boundary commissioners, one of which included Lochaber and his home town of Fort William. So low were the local expectations for victory that it was very late in the electoral cycle that he was invited for interview. In the interim period the new constituency's boundaries were settled as it became Ross, Cromarty & Skye, covering a vast area of the north Highlands and no longer Fort William, which transferred to Inverness, Nairn & Lochaber. Charles Kennedy thought he had no chance of being selected. But, sitting in the university library in Bloomington, Indiana, on a sheet of paper he listed in one column all the negative factors likely to count against him: that he was too young, lacked experience, was a student in the Midwest of America. In the opposite column he converted each into a positive response, suggesting, for example, that in such a large, redrawn constituency it would be an advantage to have a young, energetic candidate eager to traverse it with vigour.[17] He flew back from Indiana, with a return ticket in his pocket, to climb another rung up the ladder of SDP politics.

When the young man from Indiana arrived for the selection meeting at a hotel in Tain, there was a further negative factor he had overlooked from his library list. While in the Midwest he grew a ginger beard that, to the mixed audience of assembled SDP members and Liberals, who formed the majority, counted against him every bit as much as his youth. He was one of six candidates but captivated the meeting with his opening speech. Calum MacRea, a long-standing Liberal and GP from Uig on the north of Skye, recalled: 'Immediately he spoke you could see that he was a young man with a great future, He had a very personable attitude. He had a great way with people. I was very impressed with him. He shone out so much compared with the others.'

When the contestants withdrew to allow members to make their choice Dr MacRae, representing the Skye Liberals, rose to declare at the outset: 'Well, as far as I am concerned there is only one individual and that's young Mr Kennedy.'

Young Mr Kennedy was indeed selected. Before he departed for Indiana to get his affairs in order he was taken aside and told, with a gesture towards his ginger beard, to 'get rid of that nonsense'. He returned to his studies in Bloomington, expecting an autumn election. Six weeks later, having completed his spring semester, he flew back to Fort William and, within two days, Margaret Thatcher called a general election for June. There was no time to nurse the new constituency over the summer, as Kennedy had assumed he would do. The campaign started immediately.

When he reported to the local SDP headquarters in Dingwall ready to fight the election, Charles Kennedy was clean shaven. Accompanied by Ian Kennedy, his father, as driver and Mary, his mother, as companion, he began a traditional campaign, touring small village halls, auction marts (livestock markets), schools and similar venues, several in a day, to speak about local agriculture, the fishing industry, and transport links. Given the distances between meetings in a constituency 200 miles across, his team soon found audiences being kept waiting as their candidate negotiated his heavy schedule. John Farquhar Munro, then chairman of the local SDP branch, explained:

> We decided the best thing to do was to get old Kennedy with a violin, he would go on ahead to the next venue, play them a few tunes on his violin there, until Kennedy got along, and when Kennedy arrived he would take off to the next one. I don't think they were particularly interested in hearing Charles Kennedy because they were so enthralled with Ian Kennedy playing his violin.

The SDP, never very strong in Scotland, was outnumbered by local Liberals who added their own flavour to his campaign, tapping into the Highland Liberal tradition. His agent, Sandra MacDonald, and her husband David were Liberals, and his election address was published in red and yellow, the traditional colours of Scottish Liberals, rather than the blue and red of the SDP. The seat was held by a Conservative, Hamish Gray, who had represented Ross & Cromarty since 1970 and was a middle-ranking member of the government as minister of state for energy. It was widely assumed that he would hold the seat although the boundary changes meant it now included Skye, which had a strong Liberal vote and was previously represented by Russell Johnston, the Liberal MP for Inverness, who grew up on the island. The closure of an aluminium smelter at Invergordon, near Cromarty, a symbol of the area's industrial fabric, also provoked a backlash against the Conservative government. As Charles Kennedy addressed dozens of meetings from Dingwall to Kyle of Lochalsh, across to Broadford, Dunvegan and Portree on Skye, by ferry to the tiny island of Raasay and a host of other far-flung Highland communities, voters began to warm to the eloquent young man from Fort William escorted by his fiddle-playing father, and audiences began to swell. Calum MacRae recalled: 'He had a sort of charm about him which you seldom see. He could take over a crowd. In a sparse population he soon got to be known.'

John Farquhar Munro said:

> From his accent and his diction and his presentation it was very obvious he was West Coast and Highland to the backbone. And then when they realised who he was, son of Ian Kennedy the violin player, grandson of Donald Kennedy the great athlete

crofter, that immediately gave him a credibility and he became acceptable as one of themselves.

Fortunately for Kennedy, his Catholicism was never brought up at his selection meeting in an area where pockets of sectarianism could still be found. Some local members were furious on discovering his religious roots, but this came too late to matter. Over its final weekend a buzz of excitement caught the campaign as the SDP headquarters in Dingwall had a flurry of visitors and telephone callers asking to join the party. Charles Kennedy, never one to overstate his case, had been careful until that point to talk of getting a good result rather than of winning. Now his campaign team told him he must use the few days remaining to talk of victory and of restoring to the constituency its Liberal heritage, albeit under the new colours of the SDP. John Farquhar Munro said: 'We said to Charles: "Look, there is no use us going out there campaigning and to these meetings for the last three or four days suggesting we are going to do very well. Tell them we are going to win the seat."'

When the polls closed on 9 June, ballot boxes had to be transported from the outlying islands and more distant polling stations before the count could begin the following morning at Dingwall town hall, making it the last constituency to declare in the 1983 general election. Initially bundles of ballot papers began to stack up for the Conservatives, making it appear that they were ahead. At one point Hamish Gray approached his youthful opponent and told him: 'Mr Kennedy, time for you to get your school bag back on your back and get out of here; you have lost the election.' But, as the count continued, the faces of Tory scrutineers began to lengthen as the SDP's piles of ballot papers grew. When the result was declared at lunchtime it was a sensation: Charles Kennedy gained Ross, Cromarty & Skye with a majority of 1,704, unseating one of Margaret Thatcher's ministers and in complete defiance of a national swing to the Conservatives. He was elated, but shell shocked; Hamish Gray was devastated. The victor barely had a chance to celebrate before Grampian Television telephoned asking to interview Charles Kennedy in its studios in Aberdeen. Within half an hour he was ushered into a taxi for the long drive to the north-east coast for a television interview. During the journey the student-turned-politician faced the reporter accompanying him and asked: 'Do MPs get paid?'

Many people have since pointed to Charles Kennedy's election to the House of Commons at his first attempt, aged twenty-three, as an example of the good luck that appeared to bless his early rise in politics. In fact, it may have been the worst thing that could happen to an ambitious young man endowed with such natural talent. He had never tested his political convictions in the world beyond the microcosms of university campuses. He had never been paid a salary nor had to buckle down to the discipline of a job. He was a bachelor, and henceforth as a public figure his relationships would be subject to the public gaze. Most important was the question of whether, deep down, he believed he had truly earned his place in Parliament on his own merits. Charles Kennedy subsequently apologised to several other older and more experienced candidates who failed to get elected in 1983, including Menzies Campbell, who narrowly failed to win North East Fife at his second attempt, implying there was something undeserving about his own victory. Amid the euphoria of his triumph in Ross, Cromarty & Skye may have been sown the first seeds of self-doubt.

3

Star of the SDP

Staff and supporters gathered at the SDP's headquarters at Cowley Street in London endured a wretched election night in June 1983. The new party won 25.4 per cent of the popular vote and came close to pushing Labour, with 27.6 per cent of the vote, into third place. But the SDP's support was spread too thinly to be effective, still less to achieve its aim of breaking the mould of two-party politics in Britain. On the eve of the general election, the SDP had twenty-nine MPs, the great majority of them defectors from Labour. Of these, just five were re-elected: Roy Jenkins, David Owen, Bob Maclennan, John Cartwright and Ian Wrigglesworth. The vanquished included Shirley Williams and Bill Rodgers, two of the original Gang of Four, and many of its most prominent founding parliamentarians. It was a rout.

Late the following morning the nucleus of party workers returned to Cowley Street to welcome Roy Jenkins, their leader, for one of those ghastly formalities: a morale-boosting visit to their headquarters. No one felt like celebrating. The previous night their dreams had been shattered. Suddenly, their mood was distracted by the most unexpected consolation. From the final count of the election, in a far away seat in the Scottish Highlands, came news at lunchtime of a stunning SDP victory, the only gain ever made by the party at a general election. There, the 23-year-old Charles Kennedy had come from fourth place to unseat a minister of state. In almost farcical scenes, party staff began scouring maps to find out where, exactly, Ross, Cromarty & Skye was, while Alec McGivan, the SDP's national organiser, went in search of a biography of this young man of whom they all knew nothing.

Immediately Kennedy was given a taste, albeit from afar, of how turbulent a period the aftermath of a general election can be. Roy Jenkins, the man who more than any other had attracted Kennedy to the SDP, was forced out as leader by David Owen, who threatened to stand against him unless he resigned. Michael Foot threw in the towel as leader of the Labour Party. Soon afterwards a dispirited David Steel announced he would take a three-month sabbatical, having been talked out of resigning as Liberal leader by friends. Archy Kirkwood, a new Liberal MP and his former political assistant, persuaded a local postman to open the post box in Ettrick Bridge in the Borders where Steel had deposited a letter of resignation and retrieve it. The political landscape was changing.

When the young Charles Kennedy made his way to London to swear the oath of allegiance in the Commons it was under the leadership of David Owen. He was introduced to his leader at his first meeting of the SDP's six-strong parliamentary committee – a far cry from the group of sixty-two MPs Kennedy himself later led. The young MP was dispatched on a familiarisation visit to Cowley Street, where the party's national secretary, Dick Newby, was deputed to instruct the unexpected MP on the political realities that lay ahead. Dick Newby said:

> The only thing I can remember advising him was that, because they were such a small group, he would be absolutely inundated with everybody wanting him to do everything. And he just needed to not do everything, or try and do everything, but decide what he was interested in and just focus on a few things and do those well.

Kennedy gave his maiden speech on 15 July,[1] five weeks after his election, during a Friday debate on the younger generation. Traditionally, Commons maiden speakers pay tribute to their predecessor and avoid controversy, in return for which they are heard in respectful silence, without interventions or other interruptions. With the boldness of youth, Kennedy tested the boundaries of both conventions. He lavished praise on Alasdair Mackenzie, his Liberal forebear in Ross & Cromarty. But when he came to Hamish Gray he referred to a row generated by Margaret Thatcher's decision to grant his predecessor a peerage and bring him back into the government as a minister of state in the Scottish Office. Kennedy said mischievously:

> I am optimistic and encouraged by what happened to Lord Gray, and I hope it sets a trend by the government. I hope that three million people, many of whom lost their jobs largely as a result of government policies, will shortly be placed, as a result of Prime Ministerial decision, in much better jobs.

Much of his speech was about youth unemployment, especially in the Highlands, and Kennedy attacked as shameful and disturbing the gap opening between young people who had a job and those who did not. He made a plea for proportional representation, saying the current voting system disenfranchised many people who thought their votes would not matter, and arguing that electoral reform would usher in a more tolerant, caring and compassionate government. He also called for home rule for Scotland, saying devolved government would make Highlanders, and all Scots, feel more involved in their political institutions. It was a fluent piece of oratory, clear in its message and nicely judged to weave into the tenor of the debate. Several subsequent speakers were unusually laudatory in their congratulations. Sir Nicholas Bonsor, a Tory MP who spoke next, called it an outstanding contribution; Hector Monro, who followed later, said Kennedy had delivered his speech exceptionally well; while Bob Dunn, the junior education and science minister who responded for the government, marvelled that Kennedy showed no apparent nerves and spoke without notes.

Office space within the parliamentary estate was considerably restricted in the early 1980s and many MPs would share a room. Kennedy found himself allocated a suite of two rooms to occupy with Roy Jenkins in St Stephen's House, across the road from Big Ben. One office was tiny, the other much larger. Jenkins took the smaller room, which barely had space for his desk, chair, and his beloved books and paintings. Kennedy shared the larger office with his own and Jenkins' two assistants. It was a perfect metaphor for the two men's changed circumstances. Roy Jenkins, having held two of the great offices of state, dreamt of being Prime Minister and gambled his future on launching a new political party, was squeezed alone into an office little larger than a cubby hole. Charles Kennedy, the 23-year-old accidental MP, worked in the room beyond with their parliamentary staff. Initially Kennedy addressed him as 'Mr Jenkins' until he felt sufficiently confident to call him Roy. But Roy Jenkins was by no means condescending to his young colleague. He took care, and considerable time, to explain to Kennedy how the House of Commons worked, entertained him for lunch at his country house at East Hendred, Oxfordshire, and made introductions for him in London society, such as to the Bonham Carter dynasty. Roy Jenkins, politically courageous, wise, well read, liberal, became a powerful mentor figure to Charles Kennedy and remained so throughout his life.

With only six MPs to put the SDP case in Parliament, it was all hands to the pump. Owen appointed the young Charles Kennedy his spokesman on health, which as a former doctor and health minister he could help with, and social security, plus Scotland and Northern Ireland for good measure. Kennedy's task was not so much to develop new ideas as to assimilate the canon of existing SDP thinking on two very important policy portfolios and to work with the outside experts who were a feature of the party's policy-making. His relationship with David Owen became coloured by later events but at the time was a good one on both sides. They had much to do with each other, particularly on health policy as the SDP embraced the then radical concept of the internal market. David Owen recalled:

> It was a nice post for a young person to be in but I could watch it a little and help him. I would like to think I tried pretty hard to help him through what was a hell of a transition. He had suddenly come back from America, burst into this whole thing, and I think he handled it all extremely well.

Kennedy probably never worked as hard on his policy portfolios again. It was as social security spokesman that he made his first speech to the SDP conference at Salford that autumn, speaking on poverty and welfare reform and earning a standing ovation. He was also forced to think on his feet as he faced the steep learning curve in adapting from student to parliamentarian. As Scottish spokesman, for instance, he found himself due to take part in the annual Commons debate on the rate support grant order for Scotland. Jim Wallace, a Liberal MP who entered the Commons at the same time, said: 'I remember Charles coming to me and saying: "Can you give me a bit of help with this debate? What are rates? How do they work? I've never paid them."'

Throughout his political career, Kennedy showed a remarkable ability to absorb factual information by skim-reading a briefing paper, committing the salient details to his short-term memory and, crucially, grasping instinctively the political significance of the issue at stake.

Much later in his first parliament, when the two Alliance parties appointed joint spokesmen in preparation for the next general election, Kennedy became Alliance spokesman on social security. Archy Kirkwood, who had held the same role for the Liberals, met Kennedy outside the Commons chamber as he was about to speak on a set of benefit regulations being laid by the government after the 10 p.m. vote.[2] Kirkwood briefed him on his own party's position and watched Kennedy speed-read the regulations and explanatory notes for the first time before entering the chamber. Archy Kirkwood recalled:

I took the trouble to go and sit behind him, knowing that what he knew about this subject could go on the back of a postage stamp. He made a six-minute speech which was word perfect. Anybody who listened to that from outside would have thought, that's a very useful contribution to the debate.

Initially, Kennedy employed as his Commons assistant a young graduate who had worked for Shirley Williams. On leaving a few months later his assistant introduced Kennedy to a friend, Anna Werrin, whom she recommended as her replacement. Charles Kennedy, always preferring informality, took Anna Werrin for a drink and agreed to hire her as his parliamentary assistant, sealing a pivotal political partnership that would span more than twenty years. It was, in some ways, a curious choice. Anna Werrin, who was young and well spoken, did not have a background within the SDP. She was a member of the Labour Party, having joined at university, and remained so when she came to work for Kennedy. David Owen, for whom she would also perform policy work, later discovered her affiliation to Labour and raised this with Kennedy, who refused to see it as a problem. Anna Werrin let her links with Labour lapse but only joined the Liberal Democrats much later.

Despite having travelled widely with Glasgow University Union debating teams, Kennedy remained a relatively unsophisticated young man. When he came to London to claim his seat it was only his third visit to the capital. Initially he stayed with a friend in Hammersmith, arriving with no real idea how far it was from Heathrow airport. He was fortunate in that he had colleagues prepared to guide him through the transition to Westminster politics. Bob Maclennan, having spotted Kennedy's talent from the outset and helped him secure the nomination for his Highlands seat, became a close friend. He recalled:

I remember it as a pretty comfortable period, that he adapted very quickly, that he was a hand in a glove here. I remember him being very well liked, across the House. He had an ingratiating impact on people, not only in his party. He was never harsh in his manner of address, was wry rather than confrontational to those with whom he didn't agree, and often if he did agree with somebody he said so.

Russell Johnston, the Liberal MP for Kennedy's home town, was another with whom Kennedy formed a strong friendship. Important as all these men were to Charles Kennedy's political education, however, they were all considerably older than he was. His closest friendships were with two Liberal

MPs: Jim Wallace, who succeeded Jo Grimond as MP for Orkney & Shetland, and Malcolm Bruce, who won Gordon in Aberdeenshire from the Conservatives, one of five Liberal gains. Jim Wallace, the youngest Liberal MP at twenty-eight, was the closer in age but still five years older than Kennedy, and married. Malcolm Bruce was fifteen years his senior. The trio, all Scots, shared a flat together while they found their feet in London. Once he had done so, Kennedy bought himself a small, one-bedroom mansion flat in Ashley Gardens, behind Victoria Street and within walking distance of the Commons. Ashley Gardens became his London political base for two decades, although later he bought a bigger flat across the corridor in the same block which came up for sale, and kept the first as an investment. Occasionally he would host parties there but it remained very much a bachelor flat: visitors would notice that his small kitchen was well stocked with little-used cooking equipment and utensils, while on a notice board were pinned well-thumbed leaflets from local take-away pizza restaurants.

As Britain's youngest MP, Charles Kennedy had a certain celebrity cachet from the outset. He played up to this a little, priding himself on his regular attendance at the Brit awards for pop musicians: in fact, his musical tastes were eclectic and in that era he was very taken with a Frank Sinatra album, *Sinatra at the Sands*, which was hardly contemporary. His fluency as a communicator, his sense of humour and punchy turn of phrase made him in demand from the media as a broadcaster and newspaper columnist. He began to accept invitations to appear on or present radio and television programmes on topics beyond politics, earning him the nickname 'Chat Show Charlie'. Towards the end of his first parliament he was broadcasting regularly on BBC Radio 4's *Today* programme, the nation's foremost political discussion show, with the Tory MP Julian Critchley and Labour MP Austin Mitchell, in what became known as the 'Critch, Mitch and Titch' act. He even installed an ISDN line in his London flat to facilitate broadcasts from his home.

Kennedy was well liked by Liberals and, indeed, had friends in other parties too. Placatory by nature and finding himself the subject of flattering media attention, Kennedy sailed serenely by the divisions and strains within the Alliance as the election slowly approached. His one significant foray into the front line of Alliance feuding came after a joint defence commission set up by David Owen and David Steel to resolve their parties differences over replacing Cruise and Polaris nuclear missiles. This was almost wrecked by David Steel, whose comments to a pair of journalists over lunch in May 1986 were interpreted as saying the commission would reject a replacement for Polaris; in fact its report fudged the issue. David Owen, a former defence minister and MP for Plymouth Devonport, where the nuclear submarine fleet was based, reacted with a forceful speech declaring Britain should remain a nuclear weapons state. Rather than overcoming the differences between the Alliance parties, the commission exposed them. David Owen's trenchant intervention caused irritation among SDP colleagues who were well disposed towards the Liberals. At the party's autumn conference at Harrogate, Owen chose Charles Kennedy for the delicate task of opening a debate on defence. It was, in Owen's view,

> the one time I gave him a tough call. You saw some of the qualities that became more obvious: the certain wit and a little laid back. He defused the crisis very well. It was interesting. It was the point when I realised he was his own man and he had character. He did it his way, which he was perfectly entitled to do.

Such efforts were short lived. A few days later the anarchic Liberal assembly, meeting in Eastbourne, swayed by an emotional speech from Simon Hughes and supported by Michael Meadowcroft and Archy Kirkwood, defied its leadership and voted by a narrow margin for an amendment saying that the defence capability of the European pillar of NATO must be non-nuclear. The assembly then went further, instructing the party's policy committee to use the motion as the basis of Liberal policy in negotiations with the SDP about Alliance defence policy. It was a disaster, forcing David Steel to disown the decision and gravely damaging the credibility of the Alliance.

Like any first-term MP, much of Kennedy's focus was to ensure his re-election. Initially he would travel back to the Highlands almost every weekend, taking the Thursday night sleeper train via Edinburgh to Fort William, where he would return to his parents' house, or via Glasgow to Inverness, where he would stay with his agent, Sandra MacDonald, and her husband David in Dingwall at the heart of his constituency. Later Kennedy took a flat in Strathpeffer, a Victorian spa town twenty minutes' drive from Dingwall, and used this as a constituency base. On the advice of Bob Maclennan, he introduced telephone surgeries for weekends when he remained in London or for constituents living in remote areas, whereby once a month he would advertise a freephone telephone number for constituents to ring between certain times. The operator would stack calls as they came in, and as Charles Kennedy finished one call, another would be put through. It was a pioneering service at the time, although it could tempt a less conscientious member of Parliament to dispatch constituency work from a telephone in London rather than travelling back in person. Over summer recesses Kennedy twice teamed up with Bob Maclennan, Russell Johnston and Jim Wallace for Highlands and Islands tours by the region's MPs, in another example of his closeness to Liberal colleagues in neighbouring seats.

By the time of the 1987 general election, Charles Kennedy's position in his seat was strong. He had spoken regularly in the Commons on constituency issues, such as forestry, agriculture, fishing and the oil industry. He was better known in the seat and had achieved a profile of sorts through his media appearances. Nonetheless, he took no chances. The full Kennedy campaign was redeployed as he spoke at seventy public meetings during the four weeks of the general election, with his father Ian playing the fiddle and mother Mary providing companionship and support. This time Anna Werrin came up to Dingwall to help in the organisation of his campaign headquarters. Their efforts paid off as he increased his majority spectacularly to 11,319, achieving 49.4 per cent of the vote as Conservative support in the seat plummeted.

Fighting a constituency-based campaign in the west Highlands again removed Kennedy from the destructive tensions at the top of the Alliance campaign. David Owen focused on attacking Labour as unfit to govern, in particular over its defence policy, and talked of achieving influence by holding the balance of power. His preference was explicitly for an arrangement with the Conservatives if no party won a Commons majority. David Steel, by contrast, launched his fiercest assaults on Margaret Thatcher and spoke of offering a non-socialist alternative to Conservative rule. This inherent instability in the Alliance, with two leaders so obviously at odds with one another, contributed to another miserable election for the SDP, whose representation in the Commons fell to five. Roy Jenkins and Ian Wrigglesworth were defeated. Of the two SDP by-election gains during the parliament, Rosie Barnes held on by a narrow margin in Greenwich while Mike Hancock lost by 200 votes in Portsmouth South. Shirley Williams, in Cambridge, and Bill Rodgers, in Milton Keynes, failed in their attempts to return to the Commons. Instead of a parliamentary breakthrough, it was another humiliation. Although 3.1 million people voted for the SDP, just short of 10 per cent of those who participated, and despite an intensive target seats exercise supported by its wealthy trustee David Sainsbury, it again failed to make headway against the two dominant political parties. Its very future as a separate party was now in doubt. The case for a merger with the Liberal Party, which managed to hold its ground with seventeen MPs, was bound to return with a vengeance.

David Owen launched a pre-emptive strike against supporters of a merger. Outside his hotel in Plymouth, where he held his seat of Plymouth Devonport with a slightly bigger majority, he held an informal press conference on the day after the election. Asked about a merger, he replied: 'The partnership is of two parties and two strands of British politics – social democracy and liberalism. I will stay SDP leader for as long as the SDP exists and they want me to stay as their leader.'[3]

David Steel reacted over the weekend by inviting television cameras into his house in Ettrick Bridge, in the Borders, to film him writing a memorandum ostensibly to the officers of the Liberal Party setting out his own thoughts on the future of the Alliance. Steel summarised three options: for the Liberals and SDP to operate separately; for them to grow together; or what he called a 'democratic fusion' of the two parties – a merger. He was explicit that this latter option was the one he favoured and went so far as to propose a name: the Liberal Democratic Alliance. David Steel was widely accused of trying to bounce the two parties into a merger; certainly events moved very quickly. Roy Jenkins and Shirley Williams, from the SDP, called for a merger, as did the Liberal MPs Paddy Ashdown and Alan Beith. On the Monday after the election, the SDP's national committee met for the first time. Shirley Williams, who as party president was the committee's chairman, proposed a recommendation for the party conference in Portsmouth of a ballot of all members seeking approval to open negotiation on a merger or, as she put it, 'union with the Liberal Party'. Since there were fewer than ten SDP MPs, Charles Kennedy and his handful of colleagues were automatically members of the national committee, on which supporters of David Owen's vision of a separate party had a majority. The Owenites blocked Shirley Williams's plan, arguing that four days after an election was an inappropriate time to consider such a far-reaching move, but calculating also that the campaign for a merger must not be allowed time to mobilise. Instead, the committee agreed to reconsider the relationship of the SDP with the Liberal Party at a special meeting in a fortnight's time; hostilities had been postponed.

Two days later, after the Commons reconvened to elect the Speaker, the SDP's parliamentary committee of MPs and peers held its first meeting of the new parliament and unanimously re-elected David Owen as leader. Owen then issued each of them with copies of a secret memorandum, individually numbered in case of a leak, with his own proposal for the future of the Alliance. His plan, in the form of a draft resolution to the party's national committee, was a startling document advocating not David Steel's least preferred option of the SDP and Liberals reverting to become separate parties but splitting the SDP itself in two. Owen described his proposal as an amicable divorce, with SDP members who wished to merge with the Liberals able to transfer their membership to the new party but those who did not remaining in the SDP as a separate party. A consultative ballot would be held immediately – before the conference – giving each member the choice. The assets currently held by the party would be split between pro and anti-merger members according to how they voted. Those who did not cast a vote would stay members of the SDP. His memorandum went as far as to set out the proposed questions for the ballot he envisaged, asking simply whether members wished their registration to remain with the SDP as a separate party or be transferred to an SDP group to negotiate with the Liberals with the aim of forming a merged party. It stated: 'The resources of the SDP, its financial and physical assets, will be split fairly on a proportional basis between those who decide to transfer their membership and those who remain members of the SDP. The national committee will appoint an independent arbitrator to preside over such an allocation.' His resolution continued: 'It is vital that there is no personal acrimony between the Social Democrats and our Liberal partners and that we retain the spirit of partnership that has been a feature of the Alliance in the past and will be important for the future.'[4]

David Owen's move was based on a calculation that a split within the SDP was inevitable: only he could know the lengths to which he was prepared to go to resist being dragged into a merged party, or what he saw as a take-over by the Liberals. The four other MPs, including Kennedy, and the two peers present rejected his plan outright and urged a compromise in line with David Steel's less favoured option that the two Alliance parties grow closer together. This should include, Rosie Barnes suggested, a single leader by the next general election. David Owen withdrew his memorandum, collecting up each numbered copy, and its contents remained secret until the publication of his memoirs four years later. Instead Bob Maclennan was tasked with drafting an alternative resolution to the national committee offering a so-called federal option, under which the SDP and Liberals would grow together, as an alternative to a full merger. The meeting approved a further suggestion from Bob Maclennan to end the system of the Alliance fielding joint parliamentary spokesmen in Parliament, which surprised and upset some Liberal MPs.

Bob Maclennan published his resolution a week later at a press conference with John Cartwright, Rosie Barnes and Charles Kennedy. It ran to three pages, and proposed the questions for a ballot of SDP members. They were to be offered two choices: a closer constitutional framework for the Alliance but preserving the identity of the SDP as a separate party; or a total merger of the SDP with the Liberal Party which involved the abolition of the SDP. The four MPs were thought to be doing so with David Owen's backing, although in fact the plan was their alternative to his wish to divide the SDP in what he called an amicable divorce. Furthermore the foursome was assumed to be recommending unanimously to the SDP's 58,000 members the first option, of moving together.

In the intervening days, however, the debate within both parties over whether to merge polarised sharply and deteriorated to a level of intense personal antipathy between the protagonists. David Steel poured cold water on the option of growing together, despite having himself put it forward days earlier, saying the relationship between the SDP and Liberals could not stand still; it must move towards a union or backwards towards a separation. John Cartwright attacked those pressing for a merger as combining 'the sensitivity of Genghis Khan with the strategic genius of Ethelred the Unready'. Roy Jenkins accused the five SDP MPs of doing more to damage the Alliance than Margaret Thatcher or Neil Kinnock, which must have hurt Charles Kennedy, his protégé, greatly.

Kennedy, placatory by nature and still a relative newcomer to national politics, had successfully kept out of the simmering merger debate throughout the previous parliament. He had close friends who were Liberal MPs and certainly did not share David Owen's instinctive mistrust of Liberals. The crucial dimension for him was his constituency party. Since his selection in 1983, the Liberals and SDP members in Ross, Cromarty & Skye had effectively operated as a merged local party, with Liberal members considerably in the ascendant. Bluntly, without Liberal support he could not expect to hold his seat. Kennedy's agent, Sandra MacDonald, and her husband David, both Liberals, told his young MP that anything other than a merger was not up for discussion. If Charles Kennedy defied his local party he faced the possibility of moves to deselect him or to stand a Liberal candidate against him.

David Owen had kept a public silence since his anti-merger remarks in his impromptu Plymouth press conference the day after the election and, just before the crucial national committee meeting, he travelled to Oslo for talks at an international commission on disarmament and security. While in the Norwegian capital he decided he must respond to escalating attacks on his position by supporters of a merger. He composed a public letter to his party's members outlining the case for a continuing SDP, regardless of the outcome of the members' ballot. The SDP, he wrote, had by virtue of being a separate party injected toughness into Alliance policy positions on a host of issues: the Falklands war, the miners' strike, the right to buy for council house tenants, the market economy, anti-terrorism legislation, integrating tax and social security benefits and maintaining a nuclear deterrent. Some senior figures in the party, he said, sincerely wished to merge the two parties, and indeed had wanted to from the beginning, and if they won the ballot they could open negotiations to do so. But he believed it essential to maintain the SDP as a separate party 'for the medium term at least'. Owen wrote:

> I for my part will remain a member of the SDP for as long as it exists but I have no intention of being persuaded to become a member of a merged party. Though I am naturally flattered by expressions of support for me to lead such party, it is not for me.

His letter contained another sentence saying that, as a democrat, he would accept the judgement of his party's members. In fact, neither of the options drafted by Bob Maclennan was to his taste. If a majority of members backed a merger he had made it clear he would break with them; if they chose a closer federation, he had imposed a clear limit on how far this could take the two parties.

Charles Kennedy had until this point been treading a delicate path between the wish of his local, Liberal-dominated Alliance supporters for a merger and the determination of his fellow MPs to preserve the party they joined, the SDP. Suddenly he reached a fork in the road. His two closest counsellors in the party had gone in different directions. Roy Jenkins was assertively in favour of a merger and Bob Maclennan, who represented workers at the Dounreay nuclear reactor site at Caithness and was wary of the Liberal activists' hostility to nuclear power, was opposed. All Kennedy's instincts were for accommodation and conciliation, but in such polarised circumstances there was no prospect of either. So nervous was he before the critical meeting of the SDP's national committee that he was accompanied to the venue by Anna Werrin, who waited outside for him in her car while inside he took the most difficult decision of his life.

As members of the national committee gathered in the boardroom at Cowley Street on Monday 29 June, the opening discussions on the merger concentrated on arrangements for the ballot. The wording of Bob Maclennan's draft resolution had prompted protests from supporters of a merger, led by Shirley Williams, and at the meeting he agreed to remove references to preserving the SDP as a separate party or the abolition of the SDP. The questions would simply be:

> Option 1. Do you want the national committee to negotiate a closer constitutional framework for the Alliance, which preserves the identity of the SDP?
>
> Option 2. Do you want the national committee to seek a total merger of the SDP with the Liberal Party into one party?

Once the timing and other arrangements for the ballot were decided, and calls to conduct the ballot jointly with the Liberals rejected, the committee discussed which option it would recommend to party members. In the course of the discussion Kennedy asked David Owen to clarify his own position. Owen reiterated that he would not join a merged party, going beyond even his letter to SDP members that talked of continuing the SDP for the medium term. Owen was categorical: he would never join a merged party. He said: 'He knew, of course, my real position, which was that I actually believed we should separate. So I gave him a reply which probably hinted more that, yes, I thought we would be bound to separate.'

Charles Kennedy's response caught the meeting by surprise, albeit delivered in rather rambling fashion, and changed the balance of the debate. 'In that case, I shall vote for Option 2,' Kennedy declared.[5]

Kennedy's position in the SDP was still junior. His views probably carried less weight not merely than those of his fellow MPs but also than many of the well-known figures at the top of the party: people like Polly Toynbee, David Marquand, Dick Taverne and Sue Slipman. But although opponents of a merger won the subsequent vote by eighteen to thirteen to endorse Option 1, Kennedy's decision became pivotal. It severed the unity of the party's five MPs, who were in the unique position of having been returned to Parliament three weeks earlier as representatives of the SDP. In the poisonous atmosphere of infighting amongst people who had hitherto been close allies, Kennedy was branded 'Judas'.

David Owen recorded in his autobiography his deep disappointment and surprise, saying :

> Charles' decision would do great damage to our chances of winning the membership ballot for a federal solution, for now the parliamentary party was divided. I was tempted, even at that late moment in the meeting, to break my silence and table my amicable settlement resolution, which I had brought to the meeting as a precaution.[6]

This episode was later portrayed as Charles Kennedy standing up to David Owen. In fact, it was more complicated. The four other SDP MPs, including Kennedy, had already stood up to David Owen at the meeting of their parliamentary committee, when they rejected his plans to split their party in an amicable divorce. Having been thus defeated, Owen had played little part in drawing up their alternative of a proposed ballot on two compromise options, although the first option was clearly the only palatable one for him and other opponents of a merger. Kennedy was actually breaking ranks with his fellow MPs, and particularly with Bob Maclennan, his friend, constituency neighbour and author of the compromise motion. Bob Maclennan admitted:

> I was taken aback by what happened. I did feel uncomfortable because we had talked it through and Charles hadn't gone through his entire reasoning with me. I had tried to get him to tell me before the meeting, but I knew that he wasn't quite sure, and I think he was waiting to see how David Owen would behave.

The following weeks were a terrible trial to Charles Kennedy. He alone among the five SDP MPs began campaigning for a merger but continued to attend strained meetings of the parliamentary group. Among SDP supporters the gloves came off as they fought one another over the party they loved. Kennedy, whose advance in politics thus far owed much to bonhomie and charm, was plunged to the forefront of a vicious internecine war as friendships and alliances were shattered, insults flew, and the Alliance – and the SDP specifically – became a laughing stock. It was a miserable time, more traumatic than anything in his life before or since, and left him terribly hurt.

Kennedy joined the 'Yes to Unity' campaign run from the home of William and Celia Goodhart in Notting Hill, although with political heavyweights such as Roy Jenkins, Shirley Williams and Bill Rodgers championing the case for merger, and cheered on from the sidelines by David

Steel, Kennedy was not a major figure within it. As the only MP backing a merger he remained important nonetheless. He was used, for example, to take a press conference with young SDP parliamentary candidates who were in favour of a merger. During the campaign Kennedy issued an appeal that the message of the SDP and the Alliance 'should not be lost in a welter of self-indulgence and self-destructive recrimination'.[7] It was a forlorn hope. The ballot was conducted in the same venomous spirit that poisoned meetings of the SDP's national committee. The pro-merger camp was accused of breaking an agreement that there should be no canvassing by sending leaflets to 30,000 members, drawing complaints of the misuse of confidential area membership lists. The anti-merger campaign, run from Rosie Barnes's party headquarters in Greenwich under the banner 'Vote for the SDP', took full-page advertisements in the *Guardian* and *Independent* on the day most members received their ballot papers, saying the SDP's distinctive policies and appeal would be lost forever in a merger. Both moves prompted complaints to the Electoral Reform Society, which upheld a further objection over an attempt by Owenites to include on the ballot the national committee's recommendation to vote for Option 1, the anti-merger federal alternative. David Steel gatecrashed the proceedings by using a Liberal party political broadcast to press the case for a merger, saying: 'Six years is long enough for an engagement. It's time for wedding bells.'

During the campaign other influential members took up Owen's position that they would not join a merged party, including the SDP's trustees, David Sainsbury and Leslie Murphy. In a joint article for *The Times*, they argued:

> Political parties are not companies. They depend totally on the enthusiasm of their members, and their destinies cannot be settled, therefore, by simple majority votes. If people do not like the way a party is going they will simply leave it. A merger should, therefore, take place only if there is an overwhelming majority in favour.[8]

When the result of the ballot was declared, on 6 August, the pro-merger Option 2 was carried by 25,897 (57.4 per cent) against 19,228 (42.6 per cent), on a high turnout of 77.7 per cent. While a clear victory, it was not the overwhelming majority seen by Owen's supporters as necessary to make a merger work. David Owen had already written his resignation statement and quit immediately as leader of the SDP. Members had voted for the party's leaders to open merger negotiations with the Liberal Party but suddenly found their captain jumping ship. Not only was there an urgent task at hand in guiding the SDP into the talks ahead; moves began to revive David Owen's proposal for amicable settlement, which had not been put to the membership, for a continuing SDP that would continue to use the party's title. On the day he resigned, Owen agreed to a request from Rosie Barnes to address a fringe meeting at the forthcoming party conference in Portsmouth to launch the Campaign for Social Democracy, an obvious echo of the vehicle for the original creation of the SDP. This was ominous. Such was the bad blood between the two sides that a continuing SDP under Owen might not cooperate in another alliance with the merged party, but act in competition against it.

Charles Kennedy stepped into the breach, tabling a motion for a debate at the Portsmouth conference whose intention was to absorb the SDP's title into the merged party and so stop David Owen's supporters from establishing a continuing SDP. The Kennedy motion sought to set out terms for the merger negotiations, saying these must aim for 'a new party incorporating the SDP and the Liberal Party'. In characteristically emollient fashion, his motion said the negotiating team appointed by the SDP's national committee should represent the opinions of those both for and against the merger, in addition to establishing the new party on the principle of 'one member, one vote' – the clarion cry against trade union block votes and electoral colleges in the Labour Party that underpinned the formation of the SDP. Although there was speculation that Bob Maclennan, the joint architect of the SDP's constitution, was about to change sides and join the merger negotiations, Kennedy was still the sole MP to have backed the merger. A flurry of newspaper stories appeared tipping Charles Kennedy to stand for the vacant post of leader of the SDP, to take the party into the talks and, perhaps, become deputy leader of the merged party.

Even at that early stage, Kennedy did not lack ambition. In the period before the merger he and his friend Jim Wallace, then an equally ambitious Liberal MP, joked with one another in the Commons one evening that they might one day find themselves competitors to lead the same party. Jim Wallace said:

> He and I had a conversation in which we could envisage circumstances in which we took it as read it would be a merged party and that he and I could end up as rivals for the party leadership. And the agreement we had was, whichever of us was better placed, the other would back him.

But, still aged only twenty-seven, Kennedy knew in the malicious hot summer of 1987 that time was on his side; it would be foolish to do anything other than wait. Roy Jenkins, Shirley Williams and Bill Rodgers led attempts to persuade him to take up the interim position of SDP leader, enthusiastically supported by Alec McGivan, the SDP's national organiser.[9] Kennedy deftly took himself off to Turkey on a last-minute holiday with his former constituency chairman John Farquhar Munro. From a hotel in Kusadasi, on the Aegean coast, Kennedy ran up a telephone bill of £200 in international calls: Roy Jenkins was in Italy, Shirley Williams in Wyoming, Bob Maclennan in New Hampshire and other SDP MPs were in locations as far flung as the Caribbean. Some of Kennedy's more senior colleagues again pressed him in long-distance telephone calls to lead the party into the merger talks; again he demurred. John Farquhar Munro recalled:

> I was saying to him: 'Too young, Charles. Supposing you had the thing for ten years: at forty you've done it all. Leave it alone.' Half the time the telephone wasn't working, you didn't need to try and phone before two o'clock in the afternoon. You'd go and ask at the desk, say: 'What's wrong with the phone?' They'd say: 'Technical.'

There was a procedural hurdle, too. The SDP's much-admired constitution stipulated that candidates for leader needed to be nominated by 15 per cent of SDP MPs, in effect one other member of Parliament. Kennedy could not stand as leader against the wishes of his four fellow MPs and it was becoming clear that Bob Maclennan was now ready to lead the negotiations. Although the author of the defeated option for a closer federation of the Alliance parties, Maclennan decided he should accept the verdict of the members' ballot rather than follow David Owen towards schism. He also had a clear view of how the SDP should conduct itself in the talks, hoping, if he bargained hard enough, the merged party might retain the 'hard centre' elements of the SDP rather than being taken over by Liberals, some of whose instincts on policy he mistrusted. He even hoped David Owen might reconsider his position and remain within such a party.[10] Several senior Social Democrats had grave doubts about Maclennan's qualities as a leader; hence their willingness to back Charles Kennedy, but Kennedy put aside their differences over the summer and agreed to nominate his Highland neighbour as leader. From Turkey he telephoned a statement to that effect for the British press.

Oddly, all five SDP MPs were briefly linked with the vacancy for leader in one form or another. Bob Maclennan initially tried to persuade Owen to withdraw his resignation. Rosie Barnes, a fierce anti-mergerite who had arrived in the Commons only in January, dropped broad hints that she would challenge Charles Kennedy if he stood.[11] Owen was content for the post to be left vacant but offered to support John Cartwright should he stand. But when the tiny yet fractured parliamentary party assembled at the Commons after the holiday period in August, the sole candidate was Robert Maclennan, nominated by Charles Kennedy. During the meeting, which lasted two hours, Maclennan's anti-merger colleagues tried to persuade him not to do it, but he was elected unopposed, mercifully sparing the party's bewildered membership another ballot. Kennedy joked that it was appropriate for a party in mid-life crisis to be led by someone with such manifest experience of mid-life.

At the party conference that followed, Charles Kennedy enhanced his growing reputation as a politician to watch as he opened the passionate six-hour debate on the SDP's future by moving with great verve his amendment trying to lay claim for the merged party to the SDP's title. He attacked David Owen's notion of an amicable separation as 'illogical nonsense' and was cheered as he declared: 'I've witnessed reruns of old battles and old scores in old parties and I want no part of it. They were old battles to which I was not a witness, old scores to which I was not a party, and old parties in which I am not interested.'

This speech, skilfully distancing himself from the wrangles with the Labour Party of the SDP's founders, was a brilliant performance that rallied the party in probably the most difficult period in its short history. With his intuitive skill at capturing the mood of an audience, he gave them the powerful unifying message many craved. His speech drew a standing ovation and marked the moment when Charles Kennedy began seriously to be talked of as a future party leader. Amidst the wreckage of the party's civil war over the past twelve weeks, SDP members who were prepared to submit themselves to a merged party could take comfort that they had a new star in their midst. His amendment was carried overwhelmingly and, although it had no legal status and could not prevent David Owen from continuing with his rump SDP, it was seen at the time as a significant setback for Owen.[12] A counter-motion, essentially outlining David Owen's terms for an amicable divorce, was defeated by 228 votes to 151.

But there were two further ominous developments at the Portsmouth conference, one obvious, the other less so. At their fringe meeting, Owenites launched their Campaign for Social Democracy and by the end of the year were claiming a membership of 15,000, the minimum Owen thought necessary to form the base of a new political party. Whatever the view of the majority in the conference hall, David Owen had a mission of his own to continue. Meanwhile, in the opening conference hall debate, another amendment was narrowly carried, by 166 votes to 148, calling for a discussion of SDP and Liberal policies before the merger negotiations were completed. This amendment was introduced at the particular behest of Bob Maclennan, who used his conference speech as leader to appeal to members still sceptical about a merger not to pre-judge the outcome of the negotiations ahead. He laid great emphasis on the importance to the SDP's distinctiveness of clarity on policy and said he was not ready to cast aside the achievements of six hard years; he would enter the merger talks with the advantage of knowing where SDP members stood on the dominant policy questions facing the country. It would not do to dust down the Alliance election manifesto, which he called the product of an honourable committee compromise that obscured its priorities and blurred its focus. Maclennan declared: 'As your leader I do not intend to lead any member of this party towards a leap into a limbo. Instead, I intend to seek a determined stride forward for social democracy.'

Quite how seriously Bob Maclennan intended to take his quest for clarity on policy for the merged party was not immediately apparent. The Liberal assembly met twelve days later in Harrogate and overwhelmingly voted for a merger after a debate in which Russell Johnston, Kennedy's friend and other constituency neighbour, spoke passionately in favour. Charles Kennedy himself was invited to the assembly as one of several SDP guests and was given a standing ovation, before a speech in which he acknowledged the sacrifice of Liberal Party history at stake in a merger. David Steel, always a big-picture rather than details man, spoke from the assembly floor, urging: 'Serious deliberations are necessary and valuable in setting up our new direction, but, I beg you, let them be brief. Let the deliberators be locked in a room for a month if necessary but let them get on with it.'[13]

Some chance. His own assembly insisted on electing a large Liberal negotiating team of seventeen, meaning, once the SDP had fielded an equivalent number, the talks involved thirty-four people, plus officials of both parties. They were interminable. Over the following five months, discussions were held at Cowley Street, at the Liberal Party headquarters off Whitehall, at the Reform Club and in the House of Commons. They sat late into the night. The SDP contingent, which included Charles Kennedy, had the advantage of being headed by its party leader, who set about the task in a style that was robust, if slightly out of character for the donnish barrister. David Steel left the task of leading the Liberal team to Tim Clement-Jones, who had to contend with a group deliberately chosen to represent the spectrum of opinion in his party. SDP negotiators pressed the case for a constitution similar to their own with a properly constituted biannual party conference as the sovereign policy-making body, a federal policy and executive committee and the principle of balloting all members on matters that touched on the party's fundamental values and interests. The Liberals tried to preserve their recent emphasis on community politics and a voice for party councillors and other activists who were used to wielding power through quarterly meetings of the unrepresentative Liberal council. This body at one point tried to overrule the Liberal negotiators by calling for the parts of their outline agreement to be redrafted.[14] During these endless meetings, often preceded or interrupted by discussions within each party's negotiating teams, Charles Kennedy struck an unlikely alliance with one of the most hard-line Liberals, Rachael Pitchford, leader of the Young Liberals, as the only two smokers among the negotiators.

Having stunned the press and the electorate with the ferocity of their infighting over the decision to merge, the pro-union SDP elements and Liberals now invited mockery by their bickering over the details of what appeared a simple concept. John Grant, a former MP, resigned from the SDP delegation in exasperation at the Liberals' behaviour. The talks ground on, whittling the areas of disagreement down to the new party's name and a reference to NATO in the preamble of its constitution, but they broke their deadline to conclude by Christmas; both parties had scheduled special conferences to approve the outcome before spring campaigning began for the local elections. But Bob Maclennan's wish for a policy prospectus was deliberately pursued separately from the unwieldy negotiation process. David Steel took the view that, since the idea had come from the SDP, he awaited an SDP initiative.[15] Bob Maclennan set about drafting a policy document with two young assistants, Hugo Dixon and Andrew Gilmour, true to the spirit of Maclennan's conference speech in Portsmouth, that of promising a determined stride forward for social democracy. Their prospectus, *Voices and Choices for All*, proposed abolishing universal child benefit, extending VAT to food, children's clothes, newspapers, household fuel and financial services, and phasing out mortgage interest tax relief, all to raise money for tackling poverty, plus continued development of civil nuclear power and retaining the new Trident nuclear deterrent. Some were eye-wateringly radical, not to say controversial, policies.

Three days before Christmas, a preliminary discussion on the policy prospectus was held with David Steel, Alan Beith, chairman of the Liberal policy committee, and Bob Maclennan and his assistants at Steel's house at Ettrick Bridge but they did not go into details. The two leaders then departed for Christmas holidays, Maclennan to the United States and Steel, a little later, to Kenya. Their absence further squeezed an already tight timetable for its agreement ahead of a final meeting of the negotiating teams on 12 January. Steel delegated oversight of the document to Alan Beith, who raised some objections with its principal authors. Once Steel returned from Africa, with the deadline looming, he was distracted by firefighting over the new party's name and reference to NATO, in addition to the policy prospectus.

With a press conference to unveil the policy document arranged for noon on 13 January, the final marathon negotiating session began only the afternoon beforehand at Cowley Street to finalise the new party's constitution. They were still talking by the evening when Charles Kennedy, Tony Greaves from the Liberals and two colleagues adjourned to a pizza restaurant to go over the preamble to the constitution.[16] Their end product, which included the reference to NATO, was enough to prompt the resignation of Michael Meadowcroft, a former Liberal MP, who went on to establish the rump Liberal Party. It was around midnight, and after an ultimatum from an animated Bob Maclennan, who told the Liberals they had five minutes to accept or the merger was off, that the SDP's preferred name was accepted: the Social and Liberal Democrats, dropping the established title of the Alliance. Three more Liberals, Tony Greaves, Rachael Pitchford and Peter Knowlson, duly walked out in protest at the name.

Only then did Robert Maclennan and David Steel get to work on what was by now called the leaders' policy document. The Liberal policy committee, meeting separately that evening, raised a series of grave objections and demanded major changes.[17] Steel and Des Wilson, a former Liberal party president, went back to Cowley Street and argued for the postponement of the press conference but Bob Maclennan refused. Instead the two leaders, both exhausted, stayed until 5 a.m. to work on redrafting the document. They were too late. The contents were leaked to the press overnight and David Steel returned to the Commons, after two hours' sleep and a bath, to be told by Jim Wallace, his chief whip, that the Liberal MPs would not accept it. Steel asked Bob Maclennan to come to his Commons office and, ninety minutes before the scheduled press conference, told him quietly he was no longer prepared to go ahead with its launch; Maclennan could go alone and announce to the journalists that the whole merger was off or, as, Steel had suggested, they could postpone the press conference. Steel made clear that he would resign as the leader of his own party if the merger failed in such circumstances.[18] Maclennan proposed instead a postponement of the press conference until 5 p.m. and, in the meantime, offered to address the Liberal MPs. As the two leaders talked, senior Liberal figures and some from the SDP, including Charles Kennedy, who was summoned in a telephone call by Tom McNally,[19] milled in the anteroom outside in an air of chaotic anxiety. Once their meeting concluded, a large number of journalists had already gathered for the press conference in the Jubilee Room of the Commons. Indeed, a number were thumbing through the policy prospectus. The Liberals had impounded their copies in David Steel's office but others were blithely handed out by SDP officials. One of Robert Maclennan's staff, Simon Coates, was allotted the task of announcing the delay, explaining that 'the two leaders had not had the chance to consider the final draft of the policy declaration with their parliamentary colleagues'.

Bob Maclennan and Charles Kennedy met the Liberal MPs in a Commons committee room in one of the most traumatic meetings any had witnessed. Maclennan attempted to address them but was unable to and began to weep. Simon Hughes and Malcolm Bruce, sitting together, correctly anticipated he would make a rush for the door and effectively rugby-tackled Maclennan to prevent him leaving. Charles Kennedy, seeing his older friend and colleague in distress, led him over to one side by a window to calm him down and, with their backs to the Liberal MPs, the pair talked quietly for about twenty minutes before the meeting continued.[20] It was an important moment in Kennedy's political and personal maturity, as he found himself supporting the man who guided him though his first steps in national politics.

Rescuing the merger from its chaotic predicament proved surprisingly straightforward. At the reconvened press conference, the leader's policy document was withdrawn. David Steel consigned this to its unfortunate place in history, borrowing a phrase from a satirical Monty Python sketch and likening it to a dead parrot. A team of six – Tom McNally, David Marquand and Edmund Dell from the SDP and Des Wilson, Jim Wallace and Alan Leaman from the Liberals – had by the weekend produced a short summary of existing Alliance policies that was agreed without difficulty by the negotiators and policy committees of both parties. But the process had been deeply damaging to the credibility of the merged party and to most of those involved. It conveyed exactly the sense of frenetic anarchism associated with the Liberal Party of old that the merger with the more sensible SDP intended to banish. Bob Maclennan made one further error of judgement. After formally agreeing with the Liberal Party to the merger, and approving the diluted policy summary, Maclennan took Charles Kennedy for a final attempt to persuade David Owen to drop his opposition and join the new party. Maclennan left Cowley Street telling television crews: 'My young colleague Charles Kennedy and I are first going to Limehouse to see David Owen.'

This declaration, which Owen happened to see on the television news, surprised and infuriated him. He had agreed to see Maclennan with the expectation of hearing he was no longer prepared to endorse a merger and would recommend that members voted against in the forthcoming ballot. This was on the basis of telephone calls made by Maclennan to an intermediary, John Grant. David Owen, who was at home celebrating his daughter's birthday, was first tempted to turn off the lights and not answer their knock. Instead he invited the pair into his house for five minutes, telling them icily they should have known his answer, that he thought their behaviour disgraceful, and showing them out in humiliating fashion. Owen spent the remainder of the evening on the telephone to journalists, denouncing the visit by Maclennan and Kennedy as a cheap publicity stunt.[21]

Joining this ill-advised visit to David Owen was the only misjudgement by Charles Kennedy during the entire miserable episode but it deserves to be seen in a charitable light. He owed much to Bob Maclennan, as a friend and colleague, and it was reasonable for the two SDP MPs to stick together as they went into the merged party with the larger Liberals. After the disaster of the leader's policy prospectus, Owen and his two remaining SDP MPs established a Social Democratic Parliamentary Party and maliciously withdrew the whip from Maclennan and Kennedy.[22] This event aside, Kennedy showed sound judgement, resilience and maturity beyond his years as history was made around him. This period of great strain had a profound formative impact upon him and earned him admirers among Liberals as well as within the SDP. As both parties held special conferences to endorse the merger, Malcolm Bruce told almost 2,500 Liberals who squeezed into the Norbreck

Castle hotel in Blackpool: 'How can you send me out of this conference to look Shirley Williams and Charles Kennedy in the eye and say we don't have a future together?' Kennedy himself, speaking at the equivalent SDP conference in Sheffield, admitted the vain hope of impressing David Owen had been the root cause of the policy document's tone, saying: 'Perhaps we negotiated too much with a view to appeasing absent friends.'

David Steel even suggested to Kennedy that he stand for the leadership of the new party, not with the intention of winning but to lay down a marker for the future; again, wisely, he resisted such overtures. Charles Kennedy was prepared to support David Steel, but Steel's authority was undermined by the debacle of the leaders' policy document and the Liberal Party leader decided against putting his name forward. Kennedy, like many in the SDP, instead voted for Paddy Ashdown, the former captain in the Royal Marines, who entered Parliament in the same year as Kennedy as a Liberal MP, and to whom it fell to pick the merged party up off the floor.

4

Exile under Ashdown

The first two years in the life of the Social and Liberal Democrats were wretched ones. The merged party – the SLD – had vast debts, which spiralled beyond £500,000. Members argued over, and twice changed, its name. The party's opinion ratings were seldom above 10 per cent and for a period dipped below 5 per cent. Many of Charles Kennedy's new parliamentary colleagues squabbled and sulked. David Owen and his guerrilla army of SDP refuseniks lurked on the sidelines, waiting to pounce on strategic errors. Paddy Ashdown summed up the bleak situation at a meeting with party officers and staff over his first summer as leader. He told them: 'We were an organisational shambles, financially bankrupt, electorally irrelevant and inherently split between the two old parent parties, the Liberals and the SDP.'[1]

The very day Paddy Ashdown was declared leader two Inland Revenue officials turned up at Cowley Street, the headquarters of the merged party, and tried to remove its computers in lieu of unpaid staff national insurance contributions. During his leadership campaign, Ashdown suggested that the party use the short title 'the Democrats', and at his first autumn conference in Blackpool persuaded members to adopt the new name, although on a split vote of 650 to 500. This was popular with those who came to the new party from the SDP. Shirley Williams spoke emotionally in the debate, saying the merger must be a marriage, not a take-over by the Liberals. But Ashdown later rued it as his worst mistake. Alan Beith, his rival in the summer leadership election of 1988, had proposed the name 'Liberal Democrats', articulating resistance from the old Liberal Party to dropping the word 'Liberal' from the short title. Despite the conference vote, which Paddy Ashdown characteristically used his authority as the new leader to push through, most fellow MPs resented the name 'Democrats' and it became the subject of escalating tensions within the new parliamentary party of nineteen MPs. Charles Kennedy and Bob Maclennan, as the only two to arrive via the SDP, gave vigorous backing to Ashdown but were outnumbered. Alan Beith twice threatened to resign the party whip over the issue. Around half of the MPs effectively detached themselves from Ashdown's leadership and threatened to call themselves Liberal Democrats anyway. Towards the end of his first year as leader Paddy Ashdown, with his own authority at stake plus the constitutional sovereignty of the new party's conference, told his MPs he would quit if they did so.[2]

Recognising defeat, Paddy Ashdown accepted that his own preferred title of 'Democrats' had to go but insisted the change be endorsed by the party at large, not MPs unilaterally. He balloted the membership after the autumn conference in 1989 and with the members' approval, the SLD changed its name to the Liberal Democrats – as the Liberals had wanted all along. This ended the controversy over the name within the party but for at least a year afterwards some confused journalists were still referring to the new party as 'the Democrats'.[3] At the same annual conference in Brighton the dominant Liberals scored another victory over the old SDP by removing from the party constitution the reference to NATO, ostensibly on the basis that a permanent legal entity should not include the name of a temporary organisation. Charles Kennedy, having sat through exhaustive negotiations to keep the NATO reference as a symbol of robustness on defence policy, spoke against the motion in the conference debate. But Tom McNally, another friend from the SDP, was asked by Ashdown to argue in favour and the vote was carried.[4] Liberal instincts were clearly in the ascendancy as terms of the merger were deftly unpicked.

Unsurprisingly, the electorate was not much tempted by a ragged party shorn of any elected politicians of national stature and whose very name was uncertain, even to itself. Its only well-known MP in this period was David Steel, who was given a six-month dispensation from frontbench duties to write his memoirs before returning as foreign affairs spokesman and was then abroad a good deal with Liberal International. In a run of parliamentary by-elections the Social and Liberal Democrats' vote plummeted, complicated by David Owen's continuing SDP standing in opposition to them. To the bemusement of voters, the SLD and SDP fought each other tooth and nail until the merged party gradually established the upper hand. At one point, in July 1989, Bob Maclennan and Charles Kennedy briefly entertained hopes of a restoration of relations with the three SDP MPs, and persuaded Paddy Ashdown to meet with their former colleagues. Ashdown, however, took a hard line when he did so. He offered them his party's whip, saying they could sit as Social Democrats while his other MPs styled themselves Liberal Democrats under the umbrella name Democrats, which at that point Ashdown was battling to save. But he insisted on Owen's resignation as leader and the abolition of the SDP, and the meeting came to nought.[5] Owen's continuing SDP soldiered on until the following year when, in a by-election in Bootle, Merseyside, its candidate achieved just 155 votes and came in seventh place, behind candidates from the breakaway Liberal Party and the Monster Raving Loony Party. Nine years after its launch, the last remnant of the SDP was wound up, having faded to a grotesque shadow of its former self.

Amidst this fight for the very survival of the merged party, Charles Kennedy found professional solace in one of the most satisfying tasks of his career. He was appointed to a select committee to consider the televising of proceedings in the House of Commons, a proposition that met fierce opposition from traditionalists. The committee, chaired by John Wakeham, the Leader of the Commons, took evidence from broadcasting organisations, parliamentary officials and the political parties, and went into great technical detail on camera positions and sight lines in order to satisfy opponents to accept a year's experiment. Kennedy, who had considered a career as a broadcast journalist, took a great interest in the inquiry and much later would point to its success as one of his most fulfilling experiences at Westminster.

Just as the electoral threat from the continuing SDP receded, however, another loomed in the path of the merged party. In elections to the European Parliament in June 1989, with half its MPs mutinous and the name issue unresolved, the SLD was humiliated by a surge of support for the Green Party. The Greens came third with 1.8 million votes, 15.2 per cent, pushing the Social and Liberal Democrats into fourth place with 812,547 votes, just 6.6 per cent. It marked the nadir in the new party's fortunes. During the inquest that followed Charles Kennedy was challenged in a television debate by Mo Mowlam, a Labour frontbencher, to cross the floor of the House of Commons and rejoin Labour. 'If ever there was a time to do so, that would have been it, but the thought never crossed my mind,' Kennedy wrote later.[6]

As with many fringe movements confronted with sudden success, the Green Party rapidly buckled. But the conclusion Kennedy drew, along with many others, was that their party became complacent in assuming that its commitment to environmental policy was understood by voters and this should have been more explicit in campaigning. It was a lesson he never forgot. Once he became Lib Dem leader, Charles Kennedy made a point during election campaigns of talking continually of a 'green thread' running through his policies. A much wider dynamic was at play in the European elections of 1989, however, that revolved simply around the lack of credibility achieved by the Social and Liberal Democrats thus far.

This was illustrated after the resignation of Nigel Lawson as Chancellor in the autumn of 1989, when Charles Kennedy used one of his infrequent contributions at Prime Minister's Questions to gloat at the Conservatives' discomfort. Did Margaret Thatcher feel a leadership challenge would clear the air, he asked her? Coldly, Margaret Thatcher dismissed his question, replying that a party which could not even decide its own name was hardly in a position to advise anyone.[7] Kennedy got his revenge three months later, at the height of the political controversy over the poll tax, the flat rate charge per adult that replaced the rates system for funding local authorities. Margaret Thatcher primly insisted on calling this the community charge, with a stubbornness that encapsulated her refusal to listen to the steadily rising criticism that her policy was socially iniquitous and politically catastrophic. In a rare lapse of self-control at Prime Minister's Questions, she inadvertently used the vernacular term adopted by her critics and referred to the 'poll tax'. Charles Kennedy, instantly spotting her slip, drew loud laughter from the opposition benches when he rose to offer her warmest congratulations on having, at last, got the title of her policy correct.[8]

Such moments of light relief aside, the whole episode of the merger and its shambolic aftermath must have been a galling experience. Charles Kennedy, intent while still at school on becoming a member of Parliament, joined Labour when it was a party of government. He left, after months of caution, when the SDP was leading both the Conservatives and Labour in the opinion polls and held promise of being a dominant political force, certainly a contender for government. Now the political heavyweights who lent the SDP such gravitas were dispersed: Roy Jenkins to the Lords, Shirley Williams married and living in the United States, David Owen now Kennedy's opponent. Kennedy found himself in a weak minority party battling for its very survival whose activists and MPs had a peculiar proclivity for quarrelling over issues regarded by the electorate as bizarre. Neil Kinnock, meanwhile, was leading Labour away from the grip of the hard left and back towards electoral respectability. It is unclear whether Charles Kennedy was actually cut out to be a minority party politician at all, as opposed to a career politician within a major party; it certainly was not the original path he chose when, despite his family's Highland Liberal sympathies, he opted instead for Labour. He was never much interested in the detail of policy, nor driven by obvious passion. It takes a peculiar mixture of tenacity, conviction and unworldliness to take seriously a political cause regarded by the man in the street as largely irrelevant or simply odd. Charles Kennedy possessed none of these qualities. The inauspicious beginnings of the Social and Liberal Democrats heralded a series of tests of his commitment over the next decade that he did not always navigate with ease.

He was initially keen to be involved under Paddy Ashdown's leadership. The week after Ashdown's election Charles Kennedy went to see him to say he hoped for 'something important' as a frontbench role.[9] Ashdown subsequently appointed him spokesman on trade and industry within an economic policy team led by Alan Beith. A year later he was moved to become health spokesman, this time within a health, education and welfare team headed by Archy Kirkwood. With the Conservative government about to embark on controversial health reforms, his move was presented to journalists as a promotion although, tellingly, there were suggestions that Ashdown felt Kennedy had yet to fulfil his potential as a policy spokesman.[10] This became a recurring theme as Charles Kennedy developed a reputation for inactivity in his policy portfolios. He was never associated with developing new policy ideas of his own. He was a man for the broad sweep of an argument, and instinctively grasped the political dimensions and strategic context, but was not one for the details. Similarly, he enjoyed the tertiary stage of politics when concepts were argued over with opponents and communicated to the electorate, not the hard graft of developing, testing and adapting individual policy proposals.

The frontbench role he enjoyed most was that given to him by Paddy Ashdown after the 1992 general election, when he became Europe spokesman. Throughout his career the European Union was the subject in which Charles Kennedy consistently showed the keenest interest. In 1992 it was also the focus of a mounting political crisis of the kind that fascinated him as the Maastricht treaty negotiated by European leaders, agreeing in principle to a single European currency, required ratification by each EU state. John Major, who succeeded Margaret Thatcher as Prime Minister, introduced a Bill to ratify the treaty in Parliament that became the target of a sustained and bitter parliamentary rebellion by hostile Conservative MPs. Several times it seemed the government would be brought down over the Maastricht treaty in a series of knife-edge votes in the House of Commons late at night across a period spanning a year.

One episode in particular proved difficult for Charles Kennedy. The Liberal Democrats supported the Bill to ratify Maastricht, despite a clause in the treaty negotiated by John Major giving Britain the choice to opt out of joining the single currency. Labour opposed the Bill on the pretext that Major won a similar opt-out from its labour protection measures, the so-called social chapter. The controversy began when John Major halted his Maastricht Bill after the treaty was put to a referendum in Denmark, where it was rejected by the narrowest of margins. Major agreed to the Labour Party's request for a paving debate before resuming with its committee stage. This paving motion in November 1992 was effectively turned into a vote of confidence in the Conservative government, whose economic credibility lay in ruins after the devaluation of the pound two months earlier on Black Wednesday. As it became clear that the votes of Liberal Democrat MPs were likely to keep the Conservatives in power, Charles Kennedy led a call for his party to change tack. He did so first in his weekly column in the *Scotsman*, describing the paving motion as a contrivance and implying his party might therefore not support it. This was pounced upon by George Robertson, Labour's spokesman on Europe, and Alex Salmond, leader of the Scottish National Party, as evidence of a potential split. Kennedy did indeed urge his party to change tack at a special meeting of the parliamentary party the day before the debate. Otherwise, he told colleagues at the meeting, the Lib Dems would prop up the Tories in office. Several of the party's elder statesmen immediately weighed in against him. Russell Johnston asked how such a stance would be seen on the streets of Paris, Rome and Berlin. Roy Jenkins and David Steel also supported Ashdown, who led all but one of his MPs – the Eurosceptic Nick Harvey – into the aye lobby the following night, where they were welcomed by the Conservatives but subjected to savage abuse from Labour MPs. John Major survived the main vote with a majority of just three, thanks to the Liberal Democrats. Paddy Ashdown wrote rather disparagingly in his diaries of Kennedy's role before the Maastricht paving debate, accusing him of 'getting wobbly' and suggesting he lost his nerve.[11] But several colleagues believed Charles Kennedy was more in touch with public opinion, and certainly with the majority view among Lib Dem members, in questioning whether John Major's handling of the legislation meant the issue at stake had gone beyond the merits of the Maastricht treaty to one of his effectiveness as Prime Minister. After a prolonged economic recession and a disastrous few months for John Major since the election, very many voters had already lost confidence in the government. It took courage for Charles Kennedy to raise this and to challenge Ashdown's approach. Ironically, Kennedy and his friend Jim Wallace, who shared his doubts, were left to defend their party's position alongside Ashdown on television after the votes. Jim Wallace recalled: 'Charles and I were the two that were left to front the cameras. I remember the two of us saying ruefully: "Where are all these others who were out there and have disappeared like snow off a dyke?"'

The Commons debates on Maastricht were another powerful formative experience for Kennedy. It was a period of raw parliamentary politics as the substantial group of Conservative MPs opposed to the treaty tried to ambush, outwit and defeat their own government. With John Smith, the new Labour leader, determined to exploit John Major's difficulties, the Liberal Democrats were drawn into the government's tactics and were of vital importance to the parliamentary arithmetic. Kennedy, who always had a visceral dislike of Conservatives, found himself involved in extensive contacts with Tory ministers and whips for discussions on the Bill's forthcoming stages and votes, most of which were taken on the floor of the Commons rather than in committee. It brought him close to the process of government for the first time and all concerned had to immerse themselves in the complexities of parliamentary procedure and voting majorities. The Liberal Democrats' consistency in supporting the Maastricht Bill throughout won the party a degree of publicity and credibility, and Kennedy later paid tribute to Ashdown's achievement in leading his united party through the process.[12]

Nevertheless his relationship with Paddy Ashdown, as illustrated by the Maastricht paving debate episode, was difficult. The two men were quite different in background and temperament. Ashdown, a privately educated English Liberal, was forty-seven when he was elected leader, with experience as a soldier, diplomat and, briefly, in business and as a youth worker. He kept his military manner, with a penchant for early morning meetings at 8 or 8.30 a.m., formal position papers on strategy and a style of command in which he unquestionably led from the front. Charles Kennedy, the young Highlander from the SDP who never had a job outside politics, operated on instinct rather than military-style planning. He was frequently, indeed routinely, late for most appointments and baulked at Ashdown's tendency to make snap judgements and decide his preferred outcome in advance of meetings and then push it through with dispatch. Ashdown conceded:

> In many ways I suppose we represented the alpha and epsilon of the Liberal/SDP Alliance both geographically – we came from different parts of Great Britain, opposite ends in a way – but also in terms of personality. You could scarcely get two people who were more different than Charles Kennedy and Paddy Ashdown: both in their background, their upbringing and in their personalities.

There was, however, a deeper dynamic to the poor relationship between the pair. Paddy Ashdown struggled with some of the political arts required of a leader. He worked himself hard to improve his public speaking and delivery in the House of Commons, taking lessons from one of his MPs, Liz Lynne, a former actress. He saw in Charles Kennedy's natural gifts as a speaker, debater and media performer the very talents he strove with so much effort to master. Ashdown conceded:

> I always hugely admired his extraordinary skills. I remember once saying to Roy Jenkins while listening to Charles speak, I can't remember where, maybe at a conference, 'I would love to be able to speak like that.' Charles's sharpness of wit in particular was an astonishing thing, which I have none of.

But Ashdown became exasperated by Kennedy's unwillingness to use his talents to greater effect by refusing to submit himself to self-discipline and sheer hard work. He said:

> Charles is an immensely gifted man, immensely gifted. He has all the politician's gifts, and I don't mean that in any sense pejoratively. He is a good speaker, he gets on with people, he gets the best from them, but application is not his greatest skill. This is not lack of ability, this is just lack of application. You have to remember where I come from. I get up at 5, 5.30 in the morning, do a hundred press-ups, not literally but metaphorically, and start ringing people at 6.30 having contained myself up until then not to disturb them too early, whereas Charles is completely different on that. So, yes, I think it would be fair to say I deliberately gave him two pretty heavyweight portfolios – trade and industry was pretty heavyweight then, it is less heavyweight now – health in particular, and I think it is fair to say that while he did not portray any lack of ability, he certainly portrayed a certain laid-back attitude to the job which annoyed me enormously. The truth is that Charles can do something with one hand tied behind his

back better than many politicians, probably including myself, can do with both hands and all our energy behind it. So, yes, it was irksome.

In an early one-to-one meeting Ashdown, with typical directness, rhetorically asked Charles Kennedy how they would ensure he would not just be a chat show politician. His young colleague took quiet but deep offence. Once Charles Kennedy became leader, friends of Ashdown persuaded him to remove from the draft manuscripts for his diaries a significant number of unflattering references to his successor to avoid a row that might damage the party. Relations between them were never warm but cooled progressively as those close to Ashdown thought Kennedy was not pulling his weight, while Charles Kennedy was impatient to be more involved or used by the party.

This was one of the motivations for Kennedy when he stood to be president of the Liberal Democrats in 1990, replacing the former SDP MP Ian Wrigglesworth. The presidency offered a role in overseeing the running of the party, a platform for speaking at conferences, a political profile as a party spokesman across policy areas and an opportunity to build a base of support among members to further his future leadership ambitions. He stood against Tim Clement-Jones, who ran Paddy Ashdown's leadership election campaign, but benefited from sensitivity within the party to the claim of a Liberal take-over. Kennedy was elected by a wide margin of 24,648 votes (82.2 per cent) to Tim Clement-Jones's 4,818 (16 per cent), with a third candidate getting negligible support. Kennedy's election as president, initially for two years, was again hailed in several newspapers as a further step along the road to becoming the party's future leader.

Although the ballot for the presidency took place in July, Charles Kennedy had to wait until September to step formally into the role at the annual conference in Blackpool but an opportunity immediately presented itself to enhance the standing of the battered party. A fortnight after the ballot Ian Gow, the Conservative MP for Eastbourne, who had been Margaret Thatcher's parliamentary private secretary, was murdered by the IRA with a bomb placed beneath his car outside his home in Sussex. His murder provoked widespread revulsion and a public debate about whether it would be right for opposition parties to contest the by-election caused by his death. After agonising over this decision, Paddy Ashdown concluded the Liberal Democrats should not, on the ground that the IRA must not be allowed to decide whether or not a constituency was represented by a Conservative MP.[13]. In typically autocratic fashion, Ashdown consulted the party's general secretary, Graham Elson, and the chairman of the Liberal Democrats in England, Peter Lee, but not the incoming president or other officials or MPs. The federal executive committee discussed plans for the Eastbourne by-election in ignorance of their leader's intentions. Paddy Ashdown was on the brink of issuing a statement announcing that the Lib Dems would not contest the by-election when Chris Rennard, the party's newly appointed director of campaigns, learned of it with twenty minutes' notice. Rennard, a large man who cut his teeth in the roughhouse street politics of Liverpool in the era of Trevor Jones 'The Vote' and was an experienced Liberal party official, thought the Lib Dems had a fighting chance of winning Eastbourne, despite its apparently safe Tory majority of 16,923. He enlisted the help of Archy Kirkwood, who was tasked by Ashdown to rebuild the party's organisation, to stop any statement being issued, sending him a note beginning 'Paddy has gone mad'. In a similar tone, and at some personal risk, Rennard then faxed a letter to Paddy Ashdown himself saying he was appalled at the prospect of such a statement being made without any consultation with the party's director of campaigns. He wrote:

> Your job is not to do what the Labour and Tory parties want but to stand to up to them . . . It will not be seen to be bold and courageous to recommend not fighting – it will make you a laughing stock in Walworth Road [Labour's party headquarters], Downing Street and eventually in the quality press that you threw away this chance.[14]

Although angered by the fax, Paddy Ashdown was persuaded to hold fire and, subsequently, to field a candidate. Chris Rennard got to work preparing the ground for a by-election strategy he was to follow under three successive Lib Dem leaders by portraying the party that began in a third place, in this case Labour, as out of the race and the Lib Dems as the sole challengers to the incumbent Conservatives. After a hiatus of two months the Tories opted for a by-election the week after their autumn party conference, four days before Ian Gow's memorial service in London. This meant moving the writ on the final day of the Lib Dem conference at Blackpool, coinciding with Paddy Ashdown's leader's speech. It fell to Charles Kennedy, as the new president, to introduce the leader. Knowing this would be televised live, Chris Rennard gave Kennedy a script urging Lib Dems to flock to Eastbourne where the party needed all their canvassing skills and enthusiasm. Fearful that Charles Kennedy might make a verbal slip and inadvertently send thousands of party volunteers the wrong way along the south coast to Bournemouth, he wrote the destination of Eastbourne in inch-high letters.

With the campaign formally underway, Charles Kennedy followed his own call and threw himself into the by-election Paddy Ashdown had not wanted to contest. He was the star turn at morning press conferences, then still a staple part of by-election ritual, and boosted the morale of volunteer Lib Dem helpers by working alongside them and socialising with the campaign team. Chris Rennard said: 'The night before he was doing a press conference he would go out canvassing, go out with the campaign team. Afterwards he would go round headquarters, and we would say: "Who fancies going out for dinner with Charles?"'

One evening he joined a group of around eighteen Lib Dems for supper in an Italian restaurant in Eastbourne and afterwards declared he would pay for their wine, a bill of around £90. Kennedy waved away their protests, telling them: 'It's only one chat show appearance.'

Before another morning campaign press conference Charles Kennedy was put forward by the Lib Dems for a local radio station interview that illustrated his skill as a politician. He knew next to nothing about the area and his sole preparation was a two-minute briefing from Chris Rennard about car parking charges introduced by a local hospital. 'Charles spoke for five minutes, using every single fact from the briefing, making it seem he was on top of a local issue about Eastbourne hospital and the world's greatest expert on something he didn't know anything about.'

Labour's faltering efforts in Eastbourne played directly into the Lib Dems' hands. Two days before Ian Gow's murder, the local Labour party selected as its candidate Peter Day, a left-wing councillor who refused to pay the poll tax. Labour's national executive committee by-election panel deemed him unsuitable and, late in the campaign, imposed a replacement, Charlotte Atkins. The Conservatives were widely expected to hold the seat but caused distaste by their heavy emphasis on appealing to voters not to do the IRA's bidding, branded 'emotional blackmail' by the local newspaper. One Tory newsletter stated baldly that any result other than a massive vote for the Conservative candidate 'will be a moral victory for terrorism'.[15] The Lib Dems selected as their candidate David Bellotti, a councillor in Lewes who had fought the seat in 1979, who campaigned resolutely on local issues, particularly on crime. They flooded the constituency with volunteers – 800 arrived to deliver leaflets over the final weekend. Not even a cut in interest rates by 1 per cent in the campaign's penultimate week, accompanying sterling's ill-fated entry into the European exchange rate mechanism, stemmed the massive swing towards the Lib Dems as they gained the seat with a majority of 4,550. The result stunned both the Conservatives and Labour and was a turning point in the fortunes of the Liberal Democrats, proving they could challenge the Tories in areas such as south-east England where Labour was weak. Furthermore it demonstrated that, despite their difficult beginnings, the Lib Dems had held fast to the basic art of winning elections. The Eastbourne by-election brought back hope to the party and was a forerunner to a string of similar by-election gains from the Conservatives at Ribble Valley, Kincardine & Deeside and, in the 1992–97 parliament, Newbury, Christchurch, Eastleigh and Littleborough & Saddleworth.

Charles Kennedy enjoyed his role as president enormously, particularly his first two years. As a young man without family ties he was free to spend weekends visiting far-flung local constituency parties and student groups, using his talent for after-dinner speeches and getting himself better known among members. At the end of his term he stood for a further two years, beating Martin Thomas by a tighter but still comfortable margin of 25,956 votes to 10,813. He would take great care in preparing his president's address at annual party conferences, and in his four years these became events in their own right, whose hallmarks were humour, punchy political attacks on opponents and motivational appeals to the party faithful, wrapped in whimsical flights of fancy, often peppered with literary allusions.

He began his first speech as president by declaring: 'As long as humankind retain their civilisation; as long as birds sing in unclouded skies; so long will endure the power of the compassionate spirit.' At Bournemouth in 1991 he attacked the economic record of John Major and Norman Lamont, his Chancellor, saying: 'Major and Lamont are to caution and prudence what Burke and Hare are to eternal rest.'

Kennedy's four years as president gave him a prominent front-of-house role in the party but barely brought him closer to Paddy Ashdown's inner circle. To run the party's 1992 general election campaign Ashdown brought in Des Wilson, a former Liberal Party president and skilled campaigner. His terms were that he would report directly to the leader; he had complete control over the resources and organisation of the Lib Dems' campaign without being accountable to the party's federal executive committee, chaired by Charles Kennedy as president. Des Wilson, who had a low opinion of most of the party's MPs, further insisted on fronting the campaign himself and remained sensitive throughout to others beyond Ashdown sharing the media spotlight with him. While Charles Kennedy was, in fact, one of the few MPs whose abilities Des Wilson rated, Kennedy had a much more peripheral role in the election campaign strategy than he might have liked, and certainly than a party president could have expected.

Like most Lib Dems, and indeed most political commentators, Charles Kennedy approached the general election of 1992 expecting a hung Parliament in which the Conservatives would lose their majority but Labour would have too few seats to govern alone. Characteristically, Paddy Ashdown worked out his negotiating position in advance and decided to seek four Cabinet posts as the price of a coalition deal: for himself, David Steel, Alan Beith and Menzies Campbell.[16] More junior roles as Ministers would be sought for Charles Kennedy, Malcolm Bruce, Jim Wallace, Simon Hughes and Matthew Taylor. Paddy Ashdown insisted that the party fight a campaign within its means, to avoid leaving destabilising large post-election debts, but senior Lib Dems still saw scope for gains at the expense of a deeply unpopular Conservative Party and privately hoped to emerge with a total of thirty seats. The Lib Dems began the election strongly, with Des Wilson's campaign drawing praise. But in the final week they lost ground sharply as Neil Kinnock allowed the campaign to become bogged down on the question of a proportional voting system for the House of Commons as the condition for a Lab–Lib coalition. Thanks to the prospect of Labour and the Liberal Democrats entering talks on voting reform, the Conservatives were able hit both parties with a single blow by campaigning on the dangers of constitutional change. The Lib Dems' fortunes also became tied to those of Neil Kinnock, whose triumphal manner at a Labour election rally in Sheffield crystallised doubts in the minds of floating voters about his suitability as a Prime Minster. John Major confounded all expectations and, in the teeth of a savage economic recession, was returned with a Tory majority of twenty-one. The Lib Dems failed to hold any of their three by-election gains and ended with twenty MPs, a net advance of just one. The outcome was a crushing blow to Charles Kennedy and many others, who had anticipated being part of a coalition government. He was plunged into a post-election gloom as, like many in the Labour Party and the Lib Dems, he despaired at how the Conservatives could ever be defeated.

One possibility that Charles Kennedy was keen to explore was that of closer cooperation with Labour. The conclusion drawn by many Lib Dems from the election result was that Labour could not win on its own, and would need a progressive alliance with the Lib Dems, possibly involving electoral reform, to do so. Much later in Paddy Ashdown's leadership, Kennedy was portrayed as hostile to collaboration between the two parties but his position was always a pragmatic one. His own political instincts remained much closer to Labour's position on central issues such as higher state spending on public services and addressing poverty; in the Conservatives they shared a common enemy. When he agreed with an opponent he tended to say so. A month after the election Paddy Ashdown made a speech at the guildhall in Chard, Somerset, calling for dialogue with Labour to construct a 'non-socialist alternative to the Conservatives'. Charles Kennedy, who was closer to a number of Labour figures, was used by them to explore the Liberal Democrats' thinking. Robin Cook, then running John Smith's leadership campaign, dined with Kennedy at a Chinese restaurant in Pimlico to discuss Lib–Lab relations, although for his two years as Labour leader John Smith remained cool towards the Liberal Democrats.

An illustration of Charles Kennedy's closeness to some Labour politicians came on the night of the Newbury by-election in May 1993, as the Liberal Democrats overturned a five-figure Tory majority to win by an incredible margin of 22,055; Labour, with 1,151 votes or 1.99 per cent, lost its deposit. Kennedy spent the evening in broadcasting studios commenting on the result and was approached by Peter Mandelson, who ran Labour's by-election campaign and quietly asked him not to be too hard on Labour in order not to jeopardise future relations between the two parties. A week later Charles Kennedy attended a private dinner with a dozen Labour and Lib Dem MPs and peers, to discuss informal cooperation in parliamentary seats at future elections. One of the Labour MPs present was Calum MacDonald, who represented the Western Isles, indicating Kennedy's willingness to discuss cooperation with an MP from a different party in his own Highlands and Islands region.

The clearest indication of Charles Kennedy's embrace of Lib–Lab co-operation came with the launch in September 1993 of the *Reformer*, a quarterly journal that strove to sharpen thinking on strategy and policy among Liberal Democrats. Kennedy was the chairman of its editorial advisory board, which comprised senior figures who came to the party from the SDP plus mainstream Liberals. It was seen in the party as a factional move, clearly offering an alternative focal point to *Liberator*, the publication of the unreconstructed Liberal left run by a self-styled collective. In its first issue the *Reformer* declared its mission to help elect 'another radical reforming government of the centre-left' and contributors included the Labour MP Frank Field, arguing that a Lib Dem working group on policy to tackle unemployment should be broadened to encompass Labour and trade union representatives. The journal's inaugural editorial, in a first edition devoted to unemployment, chastened Liberal Democrats for instinctively calling for increased public spending and higher taxes as solutions to economic problems. Less presciently, it also questioned the Lib Dems' commitment to an independent central bank, calling this 'hardly a corner-stone for the rebuilding of our economy for the twenty-first century'. Gordon Brown achieved precisely that with the same policy four years later.

The *Reformer* continued to explore the boundaries of cross-party dialogue in future editions, in addition to urging Liberal Democrats to be more realistic and coherent in policy development. John Monks, general secretary of the Trades Union Congress, wrote about Europe; Gordon Borrie, chairman of the Commission on Social Justice, set up by John Smith, wrote on welfare reform. Its fourth issue, in the summer of 1994, offered an insight into how its largely social democratic board viewed the election of Tony Blair as leader of the Labour Party. The original purpose of the SDP in replacing Labour as the principal opposition to the Conservatives could no longer apply, its editorial concluded: 'Most obviously, it buries the vision of replacing Labour. As a party riddled with extremism, nonsensical policies and riven with internal division, Labour still did pretty well in the 1980s. As a – at least more – united social democratic party, they are here to stay.'

Liberal Democrats should react by veering neither to the left or right but stand their ground, stay true to their beliefs and values, welcome Labour's shift towards them and confine their criticism to areas where they disagreed, the *Reformer* advised:

> If Tony Blair's project to modernise the Labour Party succeeds, and it is in our interest that it does succeed . . . let us seek to differentiate ourselves in the areas where the policies we believe in are, simply, better. We should avoid differentiation for its own sake. Articulating philosophical differences will do us nothing but harm.

Charles Kennedy was not a frequent contributor to the *Reformer* in its early days but attended editorial meetings and was closely associated with a publication consistently urging preparations for a coalition with Labour. Several figures involved with the *Reformer* joined or rejoined Labour as Tony Blair began to refashion it as a social democratic party, notably Andrew

Adonis and Roger Liddle, but also the former joint editor Sally Prentice and sales manager Mark Glover. Its columns conveyed a mounting sense of excitement after Paddy Ashdown formally abandoned the Lib Dems' previous stance of 'equidistance' between the main parties and ruled out any post-election deal with the Tories. The journal's issue in the winter of 1995 called on the Lib Dems and Labour to lay 'the foundations of a two term reforming Government of the centre-left'. The accompanying editorial was explicit:

> The Liberal Democrats are now committed to the ideal of a centre-left reforming Government. If achieved through a hung Parliament, then inevitably Labour will be the senior partner in it. The pretence, still held by too many, that a hung Parliament can operate like a hung council must be abandoned. In those circumstances for the Liberal Democrats to pick and choose when to support the Government would lead to instability, an early election and the certain loss of hard-won gains.

To suggest, as some did later in Ashdown's leadership, that Charles Kennedy was opposed to cooperation with Labour was utterly mistaken. He was, however, becoming increasingly detached from his party. In a reshuffle in July 1994, Kennedy was passed over for the post of foreign affairs spokesman in favour of Menzies Campbell, who turned down Ashdown's entreaties to become Treasury spokesman. According to colleagues, Menzies Campbell protested he did not know the difference between a rate of interest and a rate of exchange and told Ashdown that 'economics is not my bag'. Charles Kennedy stayed in his post as Europe spokesman, with a notional increase in status to team leader, but was effectively denied one of the big roles in a still small parliamentary party. When Ashdown later set up a small team, the Jo Group, named after his press secretary Jo Phillips, to monitor the Lib Dems' relations with Labour, he surprised friends by the vehemence of his insistence that it should not include Charles Kennedy, a former party president who knew many Labour figures. After the 1997 election Ashdown offered Kennedy a barely enhanced role as deputy foreign affairs spokesman, under Menzies Campbell, but without a place on the leader's committee; Kennedy turned this down. Bob Maclennan, now president, intervened and suggested to both men that Kennedy become spokesman on agriculture and rural affairs. This matched Charles Kennedy's constituency interests and offered him the opportunity to travel around the country. Agriculture policy had been the subject of fierce controversy owing to the Conservative government's handling of the mass infection of cattle with BSE. Kennedy did demonstrate a flash of brilliance in this post when Jack Cunningham, as agriculture minister, overreacted to cautious scientific advice of a remote health risk and banned the sale of beef on the bone. Kennedy got ahead of the Conservatives and used an obscure Commons procedural device, known as praying against the regulations for the ban, to force a late night debate. He opened this with a commanding, witty and highly political speech before leading both Tory and Lib Dem MPs through the division lobbies to vote against the ban.[17] Nevertheless this remained a peripheral post and a further sign of the young pretender's detachment from Ashdown's leadership.

From the mid-1990s Kennedy's political career had begun to drift. He carried the burden of having been tipped from an early age as a future leader but had few concrete achievements to point to in fulfilment of such promise. On handing over the role of president he had no prominent position in the party. He was excluded from discussions on strategy and outside the group of ambitious MPs close to Ashdown. He filled the void with even more media work, writing newspaper columns and supplementing his lucrative extra-curricular activities with after-dinner speeches arranged through agencies. In an error of judgement, he even continued such paid after-dinner speaking in his first months as leader. He became best known for participating in television shows that strayed from politics into light entertainment: *Celebrity Countdown*, *Through the Keyhole*, *Clive Anderson All Talk*, *Call My Bluff*, *A Kick in the Ballots* and *Wogan* were among the many, and he appeared several times on *Have I Got News For You?*. Such broadcasting provided a foil for his quick wit and helped him develop a reputation with the public as a more approachable politician but at the expense of a corresponding loss of respect in other quarters, including among fellow Lib Dem MPs. Kennedy had never been one to spend his evenings at the oval table in the middle of the Members' Dining Room used by Liberal Democrat parliamentarians. As his media work blossomed his absence from the dining table, like that of Simon Hughes, whose politics was always rooted in grassroots activism away from Westminster, came to be resented by older MPs and was a frequent topic of discussion among them. Matthew Taylor, a fellow MP, recalled:

> There was an amazing lack of understanding that it was beneficial to the party. When Charles was doing the chat shows he knew he could only do that if he was prepared to be slightly flippant about the party and not everyone got that. There was a tendency to see it as disloyal to the blokeish parliamentary club. But for the membership it is not seen in that light at all. It is seen as hugely beneficial to the party.

There was another reason from Kennedy's detachment from some of his colleagues in the Commons. After devoting more than ten years of his early adulthood almost exclusively to politics, he used his third parliament from 1992 to 1997 to spread his wings and reclaim some of his personal life. Some of his media appearances were simply fun, a contrast to the treadmill that the House of Commons could become once his initial, almost boundless enthusiasm began to fade for the political world at Westminster that he gatecrashed so young. He cultivated new interests, particularly in music; he loved going to the opera or West End musicals, of which *High Society* was an especial favourite. When entertaining visitors at his flat he would always play music from a kaleidoscope of tastes. These ranged from his teenage fixation with David Bowie, whose album *Station to Station* remained an all-time favourite, to Scottish folk, Frank Sinatra and classical music, introduced to him by his mother. Occasionally he would throw parties at his flat in London, although he always kept a separate social circle in northern Scotland in the schizophrenic life that single MPs with seats far from Westminster are destined to lead. Although by now his life was predominantly based in London, on many Thursday evenings he would catch a sleeper train to the Highlands, either to Inverness or home to Fort William. There in the mid-1990s, he renovated his grandfather's croft next door to his parents' home. This modest 1930s bungalow, with its tiny rear garden looking out on his crofter's plot, became a haven for Kennedy where he would write, think and take delight in simple pleasures such as a fascination with watching the birds feeding at his bird table.

There was a sense in this period in which Charles Kennedy, out of favour with his party leader and still a bachelor, cast around for a sense of purpose. He cultivated friendships with political reporters in bars at the House of Commons. Later, some prominent journalists from outside the parliamentary lobby system wrote of going on spontaneous heavy drinking sessions with Kennedy. His image as a somewhat louche politician was reinforced when he bet against his own party's optimistic predictions in the European elections in 1994 and wagered £50 that the Lib Dems would win only two seats, at odds of 50-1. When his tip proved correct he collected his £2,500 winnings in person and found his bet front-page news in the tabloid press.[18] In the years that followed Kennedy put on more than a stone in weight, a consequence of his unhealthy diet and unsuccessful efforts to give up smoking. He once appeared in the Commons on crutches, complaining he had banged his right knee of the edge of his bath, and was left walking with a stick by another injury he blamed on dropping a coffee mug on his right foot. He was a man sorely in need of direction and, indeed, of a wife.

The House of Commons in the 1980s and 1990s routinely sat late into the night from Monday to Thursday and imposed a punishing lifestyle on MPs. It was difficult enough for a member of Parliament who was married; for a young man not in a permanent relationship, and surrounded by colleagues a generation older, it could be rather a lonely life. With a gregarious nature and a position as a talented young MP that gave him a certain celebrity, Charles Kennedy had plenty of opportunities to socialise and often enjoyed spur-of-the-moment gatherings or invitations. But beneath the bonhomie he remained a surprisingly shy man who did not easily form close relationships. Girlfriends found that there were already two women with a powerful influence over his life: his mother, to whom he remained very close, and Anna Werrin, his Commons assistant, who organised every aspect of his political role. Friends said he would take out girlfriends, especially early on as he found his feet in London, but neglect to ring them back and arrange subsequent dates. He did develop and sustain serious relationships. One of the first was with Sophie Davis, Jim Wallace's secretary in the Commons, whom Kennedy dated in his late twenties. The longest relationship of his bachelor days was with Georgina Capel, a literary agent, who introduced him to literary circles in his early thirties and with whom he was close. He later dated Hannah Gardiner, a press officer for the Liberal Democrats. He was still single at thirty-eight when, in the year after the 1997 general election, he began to see Sarah Gurling. She was a former Lib Dem councillor who worked at Cowley Street during the campaign and was the younger sister of James Gurling, a friend who helped to produce the *Reformer*. He and Sarah Gurling had briefly gone out together previously but now began a long and tentative courtship that ended in their marriage only after he became leader.

During the 1997 election Charles Kennedy again had no involvement in strategy or planning; he was used widely for media interviews and broadcasts but to communicate messages decided largely by others. For the first time he was also seriously alarmed that he might not hold his own seat. As Tony Blair relentlessly pushed Labour on a path of modernisation to recapture the aspirations of the middle classes, Kennedy faced as his Labour opponent Donnie Monro, the singer with Runrig, Scotland's most popular rock band. Although defending an apparently comfortable majority of 6,505 in a four-way contest, Kennedy had several reasons to be anxious. Labour was polling exceptionally strongly, even in areas where it had traditionally been weak. In the Highlands and Islands, Labour was trying to tap into the radical crofting tradition in an initiative led by the Labour MP Brain Wilson. Kennedy's seat had been extensively altered by boundary changes to become Ross, Skye & Inverness West, shedding areas he had represented in East Ross and taking in Labour wards in Inverness, injecting an element of uncertainty. Donnie Monro, a Gaelic speaker born on Skye, was a well-known figure who threatened to challenge Charles Kennedy's appeal to Highland instincts. Kennedy had never been one to concern himself with the organisation of his local party. It had a small membership and was not well prepared for the election; again Anna Werrin was dispatched to Dingwall to organise his constituency campaign, although in the event Kennedy's apprehension proved overdone. He saw off Labour's challenge with his majority dropping to 4,019 but was given a fright.

Elsewhere the election results were an overwhelming endorsement of Paddy Ashdown's strategy of trying to surf alongside Labour on the tide of popular feeling against the Conservatives. Thanks to a heavy concentration on target seats and massive tactical voting by Labour supporters, the Lib Dems more than doubled their number of MPs to forty-six, despite a drop in their overall share of the vote to 16.8 per cent. Yet the scale of Labour's landslide victory and the rout of Conservatives dashed Ashdown's still secret intention to take his party into a coalition with Labour. Since the autumn of 1994 Paddy Ashdown had been meeting Tony Blair in private to discuss conditions for a Labour–Liberal Democrat coalition, even in the event of a Labour majority. They even discussed the longer-term possibility of a merger between their parties. They differed on the conditions for an eventual merger, with Blair keen to heal the rift between Labour and Liberals since the early twentieth century but Ashdown, whose vision was a pluralist one of separate parties working together, saying a merger could only come about organically after a period of cooperation, perhaps of ten years.[19] In the event, Tony Blair won a majority in the House of Commons of 179, the largest for a century, and baulked at the opportunity to invite Ashdown and the Lib Dems to come into government with him at the very beginning. Instead they settled for a Cabinet committee for leading figures from both parties, officially called the Joint Consultative Committee with the Liberal Democrats, to discuss the implementation of a joint programme of constitutional reform agreed in opposition between Robin Cook and Bob Maclennan. Ashdown styled his approach as one of constructive opposition, ready to support and work with the new government where they agreed and confine criticisms to areas of genuine difference.

Blair and Ashdown continued to discuss the prospect of the Lib Dems joining a coalition administration over the following eighteen months in clandestine meetings in Downing Street. It was only once the Labour Party rejected proportional representation for the Commons – for the Lib Dems the keystone of the Cook–Maclennan constitutional reforms – that their long and ardent courtship was finally broken off.

Only a handful of Lib Dem MPs and advisers knew of Ashdown's extensive talks with Tony Blair, known as 'the Project'. Charles Kennedy was not one of those involved or consulted, although he was privately kept informed of developments by Bob Maclennan. In the months after the election, many Liberal Democrats remained in a state of excitement at their electoral breakthrough in the Commons. Labour set about legislating for a Scottish Parliament, a National Assembly for Wales, a mayor and assembly for London, and incorporating the European Convention on Human Rights into UK law, and it agreed a proportional voting system for European elections: all Lib Dem policies. While declaring himself 'unpersuaded' of the case for change, Tony Blair went through the motions of asking Roy Jenkins to chair a commission to consider an alternative to Westminster's first-past-the-post voting system. But there was concern from the outset at the Joint Consultative Committee and the creation of a formal link between the Lib Dems and the Labour government.

Charles Kennedy shared such concern. For him, the outcome of the general election had tilted the pragmatic arguments away from a coalition with Labour. Had Labour failed to achieve a majority, or perhaps even emerged with a precarious overall majority as John Major did in 1992, the Lib Dems might have expected to wield real influence as junior coalition partners. With Tony Blair in such dominant control over the Commons, the Lib Dems risked tying their electoral fortunes to another party without the strength to influence its programme. Kennedy played a waiting game to see whether his leader's strategy bore fruit, particularly via Roy Jenkins's Commission on Voting Reform. Subtly, however, he began to position himself as the advocate of a different approach. At an away-day for MPs at Wadham College, Oxford in July 1997 he was cheered by colleagues when he proposed that the Lib Dems chart a different course by trying to replace the Conservatives as the main opposition party, thus going into direct competition with Labour.[20] He later returned to this theme in the middle years of his period as Lib Dem leader. In Eastbourne, at the party's annual conference, Kennedy gave warnings in interviews that the Lib Dems were in danger of pulling their punches against Labour, said the JCC must be ring-fenced to constitutional affairs and spoke of 'blood on the carpet' if Ashdown tried to take the party into a coalition.[21] For all this, however, Kennedy was not involved in efforts by a substantial number of MPs to stop Ashdown's strategy.

While at Eastbourne he and Jane Bonham Carter, a long-time friend and companion, bumped into Menzies and Elspeth Campbell at the conference hotel and agreed to have supper together in the dining room. Over their meal Kennedy and Campbell, a supporter of Ashdown's 'project', discussed the succession once Ashdown stood down, whenever that might be. Menzies Campbell offered Charles Kennedy a pact. His proposed that if Ashdown quit in the first half of the parliament, Kennedy should agreed to support the 56-year-old Campbell to become leader and wait for his chance to come again; if Ashdown went in its second half, Campbell would agreed to back Charles Kennedy. Menzies Campbell thought they had come to such an understanding but Kennedy, who when asked to do the bidding of another often reacted with caution mixed with stubbornness, was non-committal. 'I remember being surprised that such a sensible suggestion was not openly agreed to by Charles,' Jane Bonham Carter recalled. 'He was sphinx-like.' The discussion, echoing one between Kennedy and his friend Jim Wallace a decade earlier, was never revived when Paddy Ashdown stepped down in the middle of the parliament and the two men prepared separate leadership campaigns, with neither approaching the other to return to it.

By the turn of the year, Ashdown's position was dangerously exposed. His party was suspicious, restive and fearful of its independence while he held covert and ever more urgent discussions about forming a coalition government. He struggled to get agreement from his MPs for a strategy paper that left all options open on the party's relationship with Labour ahead of a debate at the Lib Dem spring conference in Southport. Charles Kennedy and Simon Hughes, both emerging as leading doubters of his approach, headed those against. Kennedy, by now actively engaged in the party once again, told friends before the Southport conference that he was thinking of supporting or even tabling himself a motion ruling out a coalition in that parliament. The *Reformer*, having to this point remained consistently supportive of Lib–Lab cooperation, adopted an abruptly different tone in its issue of spring 1998. Its editorial stated that 'despite New Labour's huge majority, the

prospect of a centre-left coalition has become the issue of greatest concern ...
Southport must be the point at which this stops.'

In the event, Kennedy held back from tabling an amendment echoing
such a view. Had such a motion been carried if would have fatally
undermined Paddy Ashdown. The outcome in Southport was almost as bad
for him. Delegates forced on Ashdown an amendment saying any 'significant
change in strategy' – code for a coalition – would need the support of three-
quarters of the party's MPs or members of the federal executive committee,
or a two-thirds majority at a special conference, and then go to a ballot of
members, a so-called triple lock. Ashdown, in a black temper, consulted
advisers over whether to use his leader's speech at Southport to announce his
resignation. He held off for a further ten months to allow the Jenkins
commission to report and see the Bill enacting a new voting system for the
European elections through Parliament, but at Southport he had effectively
reached the end of the road. He and Tony Blair tried one more roll of the
dice, announcing via a joint statement in November a review of the JCC to
extend its remit beyond constitutional affairs. Ashdown told his MPs of the
move by letter just before an incendiary meeting of the parliamentary party
lasting three and a half hours. Backbenchers protested, rightly, that they were
being bounced into a course of action and had little choice to accept without
undermining their leader. Paddy Ashdown got his way. By then, however,
the direction of travel within the Liberal Democrats had changed and his
victory proved pyrrhic.

In was in the period just after the Southport conference that Charles
Kennedy made his most audacious move against Ashdown. Six weeks later,
with campaigning for the local elections in full swing, Kennedy gave an
interview to the BBC attacking his leader's approach of constructive
opposition as 'a contradiction in terms if ever I heard one' and comparing it
to 'riding two horses'. He went further, setting down a clear marker for the
future:

> I think if, by the halfway mark in this parliament, we fail to deliver Blair or we fail to
> deliver PR, then obviously serious internal head-scratching would have to be done.
> That would be a rethink. It needn't, I think, affect Paddy Ashdown's personal position
> but it's difficult for any leader to have to so fundamentally recast his strategy.

Kennedy's remarks coincided with the Welsh Liberal Democrats' conference in Swansea, and dominated the opening day's headlines. At the

opening press conference, Paddy Ashdown was asked to respond and did so with resolute force. Affecting a joke, he told journalists: 'Charles is an ambitious fellow. He has started too early and is riding the wrong horse.'[22]

It was a very serious public falling out, with the potential to damage both men. Ashdown wrote a stiff note to Charles Kennedy, calling his interview 'VERY unhelpful', dismissing his explanation that the remarks were taken out of context and proposing they meet soon. Paddy Ashdown recorded a vivid account in his diaries of the showdown that ensued between them late the following Wednesday afternoon, giving a rare glimpse of Kennedy showing real passion. Flushed and grimacing, Charles Kennedy went to Ashdown's office in the Commons to say he could not believe his leader had attacked him so openly. Kennedy protested he had not intended to do the same, and twice told Ashdown: 'I do not want your job.' Paddy Ashdown upbraided him for disturbing the party's political messages before the local elections and said he was bound to react strongly to such criticism. He did concede, however, that he had not been as frank with Kennedy in the past as he should have been. Ashdown told Charles Kennedy he was one of only three people talented enough to succeed him as leader – referring to Nick Harvey and Don Foster[23] – and therefore had no wish to damage him. They parted on friendly terms, with Charles Kennedy offering a handshake on leaving. Ashdown wrote: 'It was a sharp confrontation which lasted about ten minutes. He was perfectly polite, but red in the face with anger. He has, however, a very direct way of looking at you, which I admire. He held my eyes throughout and was perfectly coherent.'[24]

From the middle of 1998, Charles Kennedy's friends in the party began to press him to think seriously about standing for the leadership when the moment came. He became more active in the *Reformer,* both in editorial discussions and writing for the journal, and was encouraged by James Gurling to write a book combining policy discussion with autobiography to position himself for the future, although it did not at that stage progress beyond brain-storming and planning discussions. His nascent leadership campaign first gathered on 4 January 1999 as James Gurling, Richard Grayson, Clive Parry, Neil Stockley and Justine McGuinness, all friends from the *Reformer* team, met to discuss rumours that Paddy Ashdown might quit and make loose plans on the assumption of a summer leadership election. Ashdown successfully concealed his intentions and surprised his party by announcing his resignation on 20 January, telling only selected colleagues and staff before breaking the news to senior spokesmen and then the parliamentary party meeting late that afternoon. Unsurprisingly, Charles Kennedy was not one of those told earlier by Ashdown. He learned the news from David Laws, the party's policy director, who worked from the Commons office of Malcolm Bruce next door to Kennedy's in 7 Millbank, across the road from the Palace of Westminster. Initially Kennedy thought it simply a rumour but shortly afterwards his telephone rang: it was Tim Razzall, the party treasurer, confirming the news and opening overtures to the heir apparent. Thanks to his media profile, experience as party president and careful distancing of himself from Ashdown's strategy of cooperation with Labour, Kennedy was immediately seen as the frontrunner. Shrewdly, he kept a low public profile, although his small team swung immediately into action. That evening, after the parliamentary party meeting at which Ashdown read his letter of resignation to his startled MPs, Kennedy met James Gurling, Richard Grayson, Clive Parry and Neil Stockley in the central lobby of the Commons and took them to the television interview room in the Lords, where they were later joined by Sarah Gurling as they discussed his campaign. This group was striking both for its youth and the absence of any other MPs. When they reassembled at Charles Kennedy's flat on Sunday evening they were joined by Dick Newby and, to the surprise of some, Tim Razzall, the party's treasurer, who was sufficiently close to Ashdown to join him on annual family skiing holidays. Both men, who became his closest advisers, were peers; fellow MPs were slower to offer support. The first to do so was Matthew Taylor, who approached Kennedy in the Central Lobby of the Commons to ask if he would stand. Significantly, his second question was: 'Do you want to do the job?' Some in the Kennedy camp wanted a woman to head his campaign, ideally Shirley Williams. But after some discussion Matthew Taylor, who was English, a Liberal and had a political base in the Lib Dem stronghold of the West Country, was asked be its chairman, with Bob Maclennan as treasurer.

The timing of Paddy Ashdown's departure was awkward. The process of choosing his successor was to begin only after the local, Scottish and Welsh elections in May and European elections in June; candidates were discouraged from campaigning before these and therefore initially did so surreptitiously. It also meant a long, draining leadership election. Ashdown, who recognised that Kennedy was the clear favourite, admitted to colleagues a drawn-out campaign would 'expose . . . candidates' deficiencies'[25] and so held particular perils for the frontrunner. This was not simply skulduggery; not unreasonably, Ashdown wanted his party to have a genuine choice. Yet

Kennedy benefited from Paddy Ashdown's failure to bring on sufficiently obvious alternatives. Ashdown had deliberately made Nick Harvey, whose political judgement he admired, his chairman of campaigns and communications in order to get him better known among party members, but the field rapidly became overcrowded. Curiously, Nick Harvey found himself in competition with two other Ashdown confidants with similar views on continuing his legacy of cooperation with Labour. Days before his resignation Ashdown took Menzies Campbell to supper at the Reform Club and, falsely, assured him he would quit in June or later, without realising his friend would wish to stand. Campbell was caught unawares by the announcement and considered putting his name forward but decided against after failing to persuade Don Foster, another Ashdown ally, to drop out and support him. Paul Tyler, Ashdown's chief whip, even considered throwing his hat into the ring. The larger their number, the more difficult it would be for lesser-known candidates to become noticed during the campaign. Nick Harvey pulled out, saying first he would back Menzies Campbell, who subsequently did the same.

The Kennedy campaign team met monthly during the purdah period when leadership candidates were supposed to be concentrating on the local elections, often using the boardroom of Tim Razzall's corporate finance company, Argonaut, or the Congress Club in Westminster, a basement dining club a stone's throw from the Commons. Its key figures were Razzall, Jane Bonham Carter, who was by then Razzall's partner, Dick Newby, Matthew Taylor, James Gurling as agent, and Anna Werrin as organiser and progress chaser, although they were joined by other figures from the party such as Graham Elson and Candy Piercy who arranged canvassing operations. Minutes of their monthly meetings convey a collective sense of brisk efficiency and political acumen, as they made preparations for the vote, a postal ballot of the party's 82,827 eligible members. They discussed the nomination procedure, obtaining membership lists from candidates standing in the European elections, finding volunteers for telephone canvassing and whether to use direct mail. But the minutes betray a sense of creeping complacency, too. A note of their meeting to plan Kennedy's campaign launch, for instance, reported: 'CK campaign is behind in its active supporters database and needs a big key contacts list to ensure a large majority.'[26]

Charles Kennedy surprised some of his critics with his public composure in this opening period, with the media eager for stories on leadership candidates and the party under orders to concentrate on election campaigning. He refused media interviews and his own campaign preparations were kept secret, while the clumsy attempts of rivals to dine journalists and raise their profiles gradually tumbled out. It was only in June, after the European elections, when the new voting system helped the Liberal Democrats to achieve another breakthrough with ten MEPs, that the leadership contest could break into the open. The Kennedy campaign set up shop above a Shell petrol forecourt at Westminster as a base for telephone canvassing and contact with party members. The preparations for his book were boiled down into a 10,000-word manifesto, combining his life story, philosophical roots in liberal thought and outlook on policy, with a heavy emphasis on social justice. This was intended to address doubts about his interest in policy and convey what, actually, he stood for. A planning brief for the document produced for his campaign team identified as its purpose, highlighted in bold type, to establish his credibility and ownership of Liberal Democrat core values, to develop and communicate a vision for the party, and to show passion for politics and for the leadership. As with other campaign literature its cover was illustrated by a striking black-and-white portrait photograph of Charles Kennedy over the title 'a vision for new times', adapting the campaign's slogan 'a new leader for new times'. The design of such literature, provided by William Sieghart, projected a sobriety and professionalism that set it apart from those of rival candidates and underscored his status as frontrunner.

For all their moody photographs, neat covers and spiral binding, however, his campaign publications still left unanswered the fundamental question of the moment: what would he do as leader; and, in particular, what would he do about the Lib Dems' relations with Tony Blair and Labour? For all his distancing of himself from Paddy Ashdown's strategy, Kennedy's proposition to the members was remarkably cautious. He told them he would continue the arrangement for senior Lib Dems to meet ministers in the Joint Consultative Committee within its current remit of constitutional reform and foreign affairs, but go no further and hold Tony Blair to his commitment to a referendum on a new voting system for general elections. As the favourite to become leader, it was naturally wise to keep his options open. It was certainly in his nature to do so. He had also been under some pressure, particularly from Roy Jenkins, to tone down his criticism of Ashdown's closeness to Blair. The result was that Kennedy's position was seen as ambiguous, strong on tone but slight in detail.

The position of Simon Hughes was not fundamentally different on future relations with Labour. He pledged to stay in the JCC, extend its discussions to civil liberty issues such as the right to trial by jury, but 'democratise' the Lib Dem representation on the committee, implying ordinary party members could be elected to a seat at its table. But the safety-first style of Charles Kennedy's campaign and drawn-out nature of the election gave Simon Hughes the opportunity to build momentum as the candidates traipsed around twenty hustings meetings and tried to interest the media in the contest. Only two MPs, Steve Webb and Tom Brake, nominated Simon Hughes but he surprised his critics by producing a well-organised grassroots campaign network and enthused party activists by fighting an energetic election. In a dig at Kennedy, his campaign literature stated mischievously: 'He has never been a member of any other party.' Simon Hughes's position as the conscience of the Liberal left and the radical tradition, his unpredictable populism and his reputation for disorganisation left many MPs anxious to prevent him become leader. In a pattern repeated throughout Kennedy's subsequent leadership, senior Lib Dems began to rally to Charles Kennedy in order to stop Simon Hughes from taking charge of the party. Don Foster withdrew to endorse Kennedy after exchanging letters with him to elicit a cautious undertaking that, in certain defined circumstances, he might consult the party on extending the remit of the JCC. Menzies Campbell, Nick Harvey, Paul Tyler and Archy Kirkwood, all of whom wanted Lib–Lab cooperation to continue, did likewise, taking his support to more than half the party's MPs. Soon the party establishment was pretty much behind Charles Kennedy's campaign, although his apparent strength of support owed much to the failure of Ashdown's circle of senior MPs to agree on a single candidate from their number, the wish to thwart Simon Hughes and Kennedy's success in attracting the 'career vote' of those who expected him to win.

The most intriguing candidate to stay in the race was Malcolm Bruce, then the party's Treasury spokesman. Kennedy had been his close friend when they entered Parliament together and his best man when Bruce remarried the previous year. In Tony Blair's first two years in office, as the Conservatives struggled with the unfamiliar role of opposition, Malcolm Bruce led a series of highly successful attacks on the government's economic record, talking of a 'black hole' in the public finances and then of a 'war chest' of surplus revenues. He and Charles Kennedy cooperated to a degree during the contest. Malcolm Bruce totted up the aggregate costs of Simon Hughes's spending pledges, for instance, reckoned they reached £38 billion, and shared the figures with Kennedy. But Malcolm Bruce was unable to differentiate himself in a field of five, the others being Jackie Ballard and David Rendel, both of whom later committed the cardinal sin for Liberal Democrats of losing their seats at general elections.

By the final three weeks it was clear that Simon Hughes had picked up a strong following among grassroots members, skilfully tapping into their mistrust of Lib–Lab cooperation by accusing Kennedy of shifting his position. Hughes's vigour as a campaigner stood in contrast to criticism of Charles Kennedy's less frenetic style, and was exacerbated by sniping at Kennedy's image as a chat show politician and barbs that his views on policy and political philosophy were opaque. The notion of a close contest injected excitement to its closing days. Once the results were declared, on 9 August 1999, the Kennedy campaign was no longer thinking in terms of the 'large majority' envisaged in early planning meetings, which implied achieving well beyond 50 per cent in the first round. The candidates, Lib Dem MPs, peers and officials assembled in the crowded basement of the Royal Commonwealth Club off Whitehall for the declaration. On first-preference votes, Kennedy polled 22,724, Simon Hughes 16,233, Malcolm Bruce 4,643, Jackie Ballard 3,978 and David Rendel 3,428. It took four counts as David Rendel, then Jackie Ballard and finally Malcolm Bruce were eliminated and their next preference votes redistributed before Kennedy passed the 50 per cent threshold, with 28,425 votes to Simon Hughes's 21,833, to be elected leader. It was a less convincing mandate than he had hoped for and the campaign had raised as many questions as it had provided answers about Charles Kennedy's intentions as leader. He still had much to prove. Taking the podium to make his victory speech Kennedy gave one, final flash of the quick-witted, self-deprecating humour that would rapidly become suppressed by the responsibilities of leadership. Surveying the ranks of senior Lib Dems and journalists, he began with: 'From here on it's downhill all the way.'

5

Reluctant leader

On becoming the Liberal Democrats' leader, Charles Kennedy's position was weaker than it appeared. He inherited from Paddy Ashdown a party strengthened beyond recognition: financially secure, if not wealthy, with forty-six MPs, ten MEPs, seventeen MSPs in Edinburgh who were junior partners in a coalition government in Scotland, six AMs in Cardiff, and some 4,800 councillors. The election of so many Lib Dem parliamentarians within two years ushered in opportunities for the party to employ far more professional staff than at any time previously. Yet Simon Hughes had captured the activists' vote in the election. Kennedy's support came from a significant number of MPs who still harboured reservations about his character and political strategy and largely from 'armchair' members, among whom he was the best-known candidate owing to his media profile. Defeated leadership rivals led by Jackie Ballard gave noisy warnings, despite her own modest vote, that Kennedy had been given only a limited mandate. Moreover, morale among staff in the party's headquarters was very low after a disagreement over who should lead planning for the general election campaign. Charles Kennedy had been urged to intervene but would not and it resulted in the departure of the chief executive, Elizabeth Pamplin. It was far from a firm political base. Beneath the smiles and victory celebrations Charles Kennedy was a leader remarkably lacking in self-confidence.

He had an inauspicious start. Eager to emphasise his campaign commitments to social justice, Kennedy arranged on his first day as leader to visit a housing estate in Brixton, south London, where he called on a Jamaican pensioner to hear her anxieties about local crime rates. Inexplicably, before doing so he and Sarah Gurling invited the press to the Atrium restaurant in Westminster, where, to the embarrassment of other diners, they were photographed enjoying a 'light summer lunch'. It was their first media event together and was meant as her public introduction as his companion. Instead it gave newspapers the opportunity to contrast the surroundings of the fashionable central London restaurant where Kennedy had lunch with the crime-ridden inner-city community he then visited, and reinforced negative impressions of Kennedy as an insubstantial, media-orientated figure.[1] At another early engagement, however, Charles Kennedy quietly demonstrated the collegiate side to his nature he had promised. A press conference was called in the National Theatre to introduce Susan Kramer, the winner of a ballot of members in the capital to be Lib Dem candidate for Mayor of London. Party officials told Susan Kramer beforehand to let the new leader take the limelight. On arrival, Kennedy did the opposite. Susan Kramer recalled:

> As we walked up the stairs and saw the cameras, Charles just turned to me and said: 'They have not turned out for me, they have turned out for you. I am going to introduce you and you can take the press conference.' I just have never seen anybody in a leadership role in politics who could be so generous. Charles has less ego than anybody I have ever met in politics. It was his first press conference, he could have insisted on trying to dominate it, but he realised what was best for the party. It made a huge difference to me, at the beginning point of the mayoral campaign, to be treated with that kind of respect by the leader of the party.

Kennedy, worn out by a seven-month leadership campaign, had one more shot in his armoury before heading off on an overdue holiday in the Bahamas. To demonstrate a readiness to challenge taboos, and his instinct for shifting moods in public opinion, he called for another look at the case for decriminalising the use of cannabis as part of a Royal Commission to reconsider drugs laws.[2] Ministers had a month earlier rejected the case for decriminalising the use of cannabis for medicinal purposes, despite growing pressure across the political spectrum to do so. The idea of a Royal Commission had been adopted, to the dismay of Paddy Ashdown, by the Lib Dem conference in 1994 amid much controversy. By dusting down the policy and putting it centre stage Kennedy showed a willingness to take risks, and signalled a more liberal approach to social policy than Labour and generated considerable public debate.

Early August was not an easy time to take over as leader. The House of Commons was in recess. The office of the leader of the Liberal Democrats was being redecorated, and its small staff had decamped temporarily to a basement room elsewhere in the Commons. For several weeks, Charles Kennedy continued to work from his office in 7 Millbank as he and his team focused on preparations for his first party conference. Its agenda had been set before the leadership election and so Kennedy's speech was the chief preoccupation. He decided it should range widely, under a loose theme of reconnecting politics with the voters, and he delighted colleagues by circulating to them in advance drafts of sections that dealt with their policy portfolios; spokesmen were given the opportunity to suggest changes, which were marked with their initials and returned, in another popular manifestation of his consensual style after the route-march of the Ashdown years. The conference, in the genteel surroundings of Harrogate, was largely successful and marred only when Simon Hughes, unhelpfully if not inaccurately, declared that Charles Kennedy had 'never been a great policy promoter' nor 'an ardent position taker' and said the direction he planned to take the party in was unclear.[3] With the air of one flexing his muscles Hughes, who had been Ashdown's health spokesman, announced he wished to become both home affairs spokesman and deputy leader, a post elected by the party's MPs and held by Alan Beith.

Throughout his leadership Charles Kennedy found party conferences nerve-wracking, knowing that the attention given them by the media heightened pressure on him and his party not to make mistakes. Before his inaugural conference speech as leader he was visibly anxious. The outline was drafted by Richard Grayson, his incoming speechwriter, based on discussions with Kennedy about the general approach he wished to take. Chunks were added or rewritten by Kennedy, and amendments suggested by others in his team or by policy spokesmen. As a result the text changed many times. Much later Kennedy's advisers concluded that this pattern, which set a template for future speech-writing, was a profound error and robbed him of the distinctive style of oratory at which he excelled. 'One of the things we first got wrong was slightly taking his own voice away in speeches when he became leader,' Anna Werrin said.

When it came, his speech was most striking for its low-key, conversational tone – the reverse of a typical, tub-thumping politician's speech. Without modern sound amplification such a style would have fallen flat but Kennedy carried it off, proving himself a politician of the television age. He talked of the divide between rich and poor, opposed tax cuts at the expense of better-funded public services and revived the idea of a local income tax. He told members he would maintain current cooperation with Labour on constitutional reform, would not rule out further cooperation, and summed up his approach thus: 'The Liberal Democrats are nobody's poodles; but we are not Rottweilers either.'

The speech was reasonably well received, with its genial, emollient style appreciated more by Lib Dem delegates than by the watching media. It was, however, far removed from his inspirational oratory to the SDP conference at the height of the merger controversy nine years earlier. Once back from Harrogate, Charles Kennedy began to assemble a new front bench team. It was a clumsy, drawn-out process. For their post-election holiday a month earlier he and Sarah Gurling stayed in the Bahamas at the villa of Tim Razzall with his partner Jane Bonham Carter, an old friend of Kennedy's. While there Charles Kennedy asked Razzall to run his general election campaign, replacing Nick Harvey as chairman of the party's campaigns and communications committee. In similar fashion, the others of his core leadership campaign team transferred en bloc to new roles: Dick Newby, a Yorkshireman with a direct manner who had run the SDP, became his chief of staff, Richard Grayson his director of policy, and Anna Werrin effectively his head of office, although some MPs were slow to appreciate the extent of her influence. Matthew Taylor was rewarded by being appointed Treasury spokesman and Bob Maclennan became spokesman for constitutional affairs.

A first batch of appointments, including that of Simon Hughes to the post he lobbied for as home affairs spokesman, was announced the day after the conference. The final list was not published until three weeks later, creating needless uncertainty. It was an awkward task, since several colleagues had stood against Kennedy or considered doing so and a group of senior MPs remained close to Paddy Ashdown and the strategy of seeking a coalition with Labour. Yet, as in subsequent reshuffles through his leadership, a dislike of confrontation made Kennedy stall the process and conduct it by telephone rather than swiftly in face-to-face meetings. He created two new posts. His friend Malcolm Bruce was moved to become chairman of the parliamentary party, with a brief to act as a link with other Lib Dem parliamentarians and as a cross-portfolio party spokesman. In another innovation Kennedy created a post of leader's parliamentary private secretary, given to Mark Oaten, who had run Don Foster's abandoned leadership campaign.

Mark Oaten was involved in planning several subsequent front bench reshuffles. They were always similarly elongated, messy affairs and always created ill feeling. The process would begin with Anna Werrin and Dick

Newby, and later Mark Oaten, presenting lists of names to Kennedy, who would take advice from Tim Razzall. Then the chief whip would be brought in to discuss the logistics and point out omissions. Typically, an MP removed from the front bench would be found a place on a select committee in consolation. Mark Oaten said:

> He found it extremely difficult. The stumbling block was that Charles would promise to make the difficult phone calls which would unlock the whole thing and he just wouldn't do them. He would hate making the phone calls and he would classically leave all of this until very late on a Sunday evening, and that would be when he would make the phone calls.

Another innovation introduced by Charles Kennedy was to style his front bench as a 'shadow cabinet'. This drew protests from the Conservatives that such a title held no constitutional basis, and was mocked in sections of the media, but eventually the name stuck. It also provoked a spirited debate among Lib Dem MPs about the relationship between the shadow cabinet and the weekly meeting of the parliamentary party. Some questioned whether it was right for the shadow cabinet to meet and take decisions before these were considered by the parliamentary party meeting, or if a spokesman who lost an argument in the shadow cabinet on a Tuesday morning should be able to reopen the discussion at the meeting of all MPs on Wednesday evening. Kennedy, in his consensual style, patiently let colleagues argue these points at length over several weeks before the change was accepted. In another break from Paddy Ashdown, in the Commons he chose to speak from the front bench below the gangway. This was where Kennedy had cut his teeth in the SDP, whose MPs in the 1980s jostled for seats on this bench with left-wing Labour MPs such as Dennis Skinner while the Liberals sat more sedately in the row behind. After the 1997 election the Liberal Democrats commandeered this front bench as well, this time after scuffles with Conservative MPs, although Ashdown always spoke from an end seat on the second bench. Kennedy felt more comfortable speaking from the floor of the House but, with no bench in front of him and no despatch box to lean upon, was visually exposed. The House of Commons can be an intimidating place for any speaker; for a Liberal Democrat, with 417 Labour MPs ranged on the benches opposite, 164 Conservatives behind and around, and only 45 colleagues offering support, it was a particularly hostile environment. Despite his prowess as an undergraduate debater and conference orator,

Kennedy struggled to make an impact each week at Prime Minister's Questions, the forum in which opposition leaders are inevitably judged. Liam Fox, the Conservative politician who was his contemporary at university, observed:

> People have often asked why Charles was not a great performer in the House of Commons. I think there is a disadvantage for the Liberal [Democrat] leader in that they are not actually at the dispatch box. At the dispatch box in the House of Commons it is much more like you were trained in Glasgow. You are actually pretty close, eyeball to eyeball, against your opponent. From where the Liberal [Democrats] sit in the House of Commons they are actually quite a long way from the centre of the action, as it were. Both the distance and the fact of the openness of it are, I think, disadvantages.

Kennedy would tell friends how the ordeal would often prey on his mind from the Sunday evening or Monday of each week. As Liberal Democrat leader he had the disadvantage of being called after the Leader of the Opposition and therefore every Wednesday took into the Commons chamber alternative or reworked sets of questions, typed on A5 paper, in case William Hague, the Conservative leader, stole his thunder and raised the topic he planned to. Kennedy was entitled to two questions each week but did not have the option of splitting them, raising one subject first and another in a later question. His friends tried to persuade him to revert to speaking from the second row as Paddy Ashdown had done but he disliked speaking from a raised position and always refused.

One further complication dogged Charles Kennedy's performances in the Commons. The front bench below the gangway from where he chose to speak was also the place where Edward Heath sat in his honorific position as Father of the House, the MP with the longest continuing service. Kennedy, never partisan by instinct, actually admired Edward Heath for his single-mindedness as Prime Minister in taking Britain into the European Community and the two got on reasonably well. But when Kennedy's advisers replayed video footage of his hesitant performances at Prime Minister's Questions they became aware that the somnolent posture of Edward Heath beside him made the visual impression still worse. Each week thereafter Mark Oaten made a point of squeezing onto the bench next to Edward Heath and giving the former Prime Minister a vigorous nudge just before Charles Kennedy rose to speak.

The electorate picked up on Kennedy's discomfort with parts of his role. Several months after he became leader, the Liberal Democrats commissioned some private research from their polling company, Martin Hamblin, which conducted a series of focus groups of between seven and a dozen voters in four marginal or target seats – Richmond, Cardiff, Taunton and Aberdeen – between late November and early December. Participants were asked their view of Kennedy and shown photographs of him and a party political broadcast in which he featuring. Most had a very favourable impression of Charles Kennedy, particularly women, but were unsure what he stood for. There was, the research found, 'a good deal of nostalgia for Paddy Ashdown when comparing the two'. It concluded: 'It was felt Charles Kennedy could look vulnerable, young and not relaxed and that sometimes he seemed "white knuckled" or unsure of what to do with his hands. The broad consensus was that he looked better when pictures were not set up or posed.'[4]

In Liberal Democrat circles things felt rather different. Kennedy's relaxed, open style was widely appreciated. His readiness to consult was welcomed. He encouraged policy spokesmen to develop their own ideas, and would regularly tell parliamentary party meetings: 'Let a thousand flowers bloom.' 'He was a breath of fresh air,' recalled Norman Baker, MP for Lewes.

In theory Kennedy maintained an open-door policy in which any colleague was free to come and see him at any time; in practice few did so and he never broke out beyond the tight inner circle around him. His colleagues found the self-assurance Kennedy had displayed as an aspiring politician no longer there once be became leader. They noticed a weight appeared to have landed upon his shoulders. He looked unsure of himself, at times he looked unhappy. He grew much thinner, shedding a stone and a half in his first months in the role. Those who harboured doubts about his character complained he appeared reluctant to lead and his strategic direction was unclear. Away from the Commons he found it more difficult to relax. His diary would be crammed with official engagements months in advance and in social situations the higher public profile that came with being party leader heightened his feeling of self-consciousness. Even his friends admitted he had changed.

'It can be a lonely job and it is a tremendous responsibility,' said Jim Wallace, who by this point was deputy First Minister in the Scottish Parliament and spent little time in the Commons. 'Did a weight descend on him? That's right, it did. That's leadership, and it probably did blunt his effervescent character.'

Still more significant was the knowledge that Kennedy did not have the automatic support or unconditional loyalty of a significant group of his MPs, including senior figures who previously had enjoyed close access to the leader. Mark Oaten observed:

> You really had a new team and a new order coming through that were very nervous and sensitive about the previous team that had been there. That led him to stick very much to the people that had been involved with his leadership campaign. It was quite hard for other people to be involved in that inner circle. I thought that that inner circle would break down as time went on; it never did.

An illustration of tensions between Kennedy and his Ashdownite MPs arose early on over one of his appointments in the leader's office. Richard Grayson, a thirty-year-old academic and director of the Lib Dem think tank Centre for Reform, was originally given three roles in the leader's office. In addition to being director of the party's policy unit and responsible for the leader's policy work, Kennedy intended that Richard Grayson should be in charge of the team of up to a dozen senior parliamentary researchers working for MPs in the Commons. Their budget had been substantially enhanced thanks to the government's decision, three months before Kennedy became leader, to increase the state funds to support the parliamentary work of opposition parties. In line with a recommendation from the Committee of Standards in Public Life, this so-called Short money went up threefold, in the Liberal Democrats' case from around £370,000 to more than £1 million a year. In an example of the limited power of a Liberal Democrat leader, the party's MPs decided that ownership of the research team should lie with the parliamentary party as a whole and not be run by a figure so close to Charles Kennedy. It was therefore agreed that a planned new post of head of research would report not to Richard Grayson in the leader's office but to Paul Tyler, who as chief whip was accounting officer for the budget. The power struggle was given added edge as, once the post was advertised, among the applicants was Julian Astle, who had been appointed to the leader's office under Paddy Ashdown and had worked for Nick Harvey and Archy Kirkwood. It appeared that the control of the researchers might be stripped from Charles Kennedy's appointee and given instead to someone with close links to the Ashdownites. Although Paul Tyler conducted the interviews, held in a small committee room off Westminster Hall in the Commons, Kennedy personally sat in on them and ensured the job went to someone else. Mary Polak, one of the senior researchers, was duly appointed.

Such suspicion was again illustrated during his first Christmas recess of Parliament, when Charles Kennedy told his MPs the party must make an impact over the holiday period and issued instructions that MPs were not all to go away at once. Menzies Campbell, as foreign affairs spokesman, had for several years led a delegation of Lib Dem MPs on a familiarisation visit to the United Nations in New York in early January. Despite Kennedy's edict he did so again, taking with him Don Foster, Nick Harvey, Paul Tyler and Michael Moore. While they were there, some criticism of Charles Kennedy appeared in the British press, accusing him of failing to make a sufficient impression in his first months as leader. While in New York, Don Foster was interviewed on BBC Radio 4's *Today* programme and asked about the attacks on his leader. Trying to be helpful, Foster appealed for Charles Kennedy to have at least six months before anyone made a judgement; back in Britain this was interpreted as a warning that Kennedy had been placed on probation and given a deadline by which to prove himself. The Kennedy camp viewed the quintet, four of whom had contemplated standing for the leadership, with the utmost suspicion and henceforth they were referred to in the leader's office as the 'Manhattan Five'.

Fortune intervened to give Charles Kennedy a chance to display his judgement as a political crisis developed in Wales. Thanks to the programme of devolution, on which Liberal Democrats cooperated with Labour, the Lib Dems were junior partners in a coalition government in Scotland. In Wales, the picture was more complicated. Labour's original candidate to lead the Welsh assembly, Ron Davies, quit after being robbed by a stranger he met at a haunt for gay men on Clapham Common. In the election to choose his successor, Tony Blair intervened heavily to support Alun Michael and block the candidacy of his rival Rhodri Morgan, a popular if maverick figure in Wales. Alun Michael won the nomination but at the price of much bad blood within the Welsh Labour Party and became caricatured, unfairly, as 'Blair's poodle', the man parachuted in to run Wales for the Prime Minister. The first elections to the National Assembly for Wales in May 1999 saw Labour win twenty-eight seats, three short of an overall majority. Instead of following the Scots' example of a Lab–Lib coalition, Alun Michael, whose Labour AMs were tribal in outlook, tried an experimental approach of decision-making in consultation with the assembly parties. It proved short lived as the Conservative group leader, Rod Richards, led a reversion to a traditional form of confrontational politics. Alun Michael was soon left running a minority Labour government.

This was first manifest in a censure vote five months later against his agriculture secretary, Christine Gwyther. Her appointment had upset Welsh farmers, as she was a vegetarian, although there was an undercurrent of misogyny too, and her handling of the BSE crisis drew criticism. By February 2000, opposition parties in Cardiff were preparing for a vote of no confidence in the leadership of Alun Michael himself. Ostensibly, the cause was a demand for additional money from the Treasury to match European Union aid for west Wales and the south Wales valleys. The sub-text was a wish to remove Alun Michael and, in so doing, poke Tony Blair in the eye. The six Lib Dem assembly members were happy to join Plaid Cymru and the Conservatives in toppling him and, such was his unpopularity, they even received private encouragement from Labour AMs to do so. Alun Michael had attempted a series of discussions with opposition parties about how to restore stability to the assembly, and rescue its reputation with Welsh voters. In the weeks before the vote, he offered the Lib Dems a coalition with two seats in his executive cabinet or a looser collaboration of advance consultation on major policy decisions such as the budget. He was rebuffed.

The antics of the small Lib Dem group on the assembly in joining the oppositionist tone of this new era for Welsh politics was the cause of some exasperation, not only in Labour circles but also amongst certain Lib Dem parliamentarians. The Liberal Democrats, after all, had helped to bring the assembly into being and had an interest in making it work. Tony Blair, who had invested political capital in the leadership of Alun Michael, began making overtures to the Liberal Democrats at Westminster to help save his First Secretary. Blair telephoned Charles Kennedy in the first week of February asking him to press his assembly members to open talks with their Labour counterparts or at least not insist on a conclusive no-confidence vote. After going away to think about it and consult with colleagues Kennedy rang back late on 3 February. Unable to reach the Prime Minister, he simply left a message with the duty clerk at Downing Street with his response: the Lib Dems' position remained that the Treasury must provide the additional funds for Welsh aid now. Charles Kennedy was in no mood to be helpful.

Tony Blair then attempted to play his trump card. Paddy Ashdown, who had observed a loyal silence since quitting as leader, was invited to Downing Street on 7 February, two days before the no-confidence vote in Cardiff. Blair told him privately that Gordon Brown would find the £1.2 billion of additional funds to match EU aid for Wales over six years. The snag was he could not announce this until July when he published his comprehensive spending review of all government budgets. Blair proposed the Lib Dems agree to a short-term coalition with Alun Michael until July and, when the additional Welsh aid was announced, the partnership could be extended for the remainder of the assembly's four-year term. He asked for Ashdown's help.

Paddy Ashdown had wanted a Lib–Lab coalition in Cardiff from the outset, like that in Edinburgh, and after the Welsh assembly elections the previous May had pressed Blair to intervene to achieve one. If Alun Michael were overthrown now his likely successor would be Rhodri Morgan, who both Blair and Ashdown judged – incorrectly – would be even less keen on cooperation with the Lib Dems. Paddy Ashdown thought it probably too late to rescue Alun Michael but agreed to try. Later that day he invited Mike German, leader of the Lib Dem AMs, who was visiting London, to his Commons office, where Ashdown urged him to reconsider and think through the risks if Alun Michael was defeated. He put further pressure on Mike German by putting Alex Carlile, a Lib Dem peer, in touch with Paul Murphy, the Welsh secretary, to discuss the outline of a potential deal. Paddy Ashdown also lobbied Kennedy himself. After several attempts by Ashdown to ring him the previous afternoon, Charles Kennedy returned his call on the morning of 8 February and the two had an inconclusive discussion. Paddy Ashdown gave warning that the party was passing up on the chance to deliver on its policies in Wales. Kennedy, determined not to interfere, simply stalled. Ashdown tried two more avenues. Over lunch at Brooks's club, he secured Roy Jenkins's agreement to use his influence with Charles Kennedy to rescue the cause of coalition government based on a proportional voting system in Wales. Having asked Kennedy's permission to do so, he then met Richard Livsey, MP for Brecon & Radnorshire and leader of the Welsh Liberal Democrats, and told him forcefully he was spurning an opportunity to bring long-term benefit to Wales.

Kennedy, however, had a different agenda. As a Scottish MP he was better tuned to the politics of devolution. His instinct was to leave the matter to be settled in Cardiff and let events take their natural course. It was a very different approach to leadership. He and his advisers saw a further chance to demonstrate that the terms of trade between Labour and the Lib Dems, and in particular between Blair and Kennedy, had changed. When Tony Blair telephoned him a third time, Charles Kennedy again refused to help, telling him simply: 'It's devolved.' When Blair continued to press him, Kennedy repeated: 'You don't understand. It's not my decision; it's their decision. It's devolved.'

At a parliamentary party meeting that evening Ashdown and Lembit Öpik, one of two Welsh Lib Dem MPs, were lone voices in arguing for a coalition. Instead, MPs backed Richard Livsey in opposing a deal. At the end of the discussion, Charles Kennedy declared this a matter that should be settled in Wales without his interference or that of other MPs; to do anything else might have provoked Richard Livsey's resignation. It was not, he said, the job of the Liberal Democrats to act as 'parliamentary pooper scoops'. If the former remark was a discreet dig at Ashdown's lobbying, the latter was an unusually blunt put-down. Meanwhile, at the assembly building in Cardiff Bay, Alun Michael was sharing a last supper of fish and chips with Rhodri Morgan in his fifth-floor office while awaiting a response from the Lib Dem AMs to a final overture. News of their rejection was final conveyed to him by Michael Hines, Mike German's special adviser, who was sent up to say the Lib Dems were not interested and, indeed, had left the building for a curry.

During the day Paddy Ashdown reported back to Downing Street on his discussions in telephone calls to Jonathan Powell, Blair's chief of staff, and Pat McFadden, his political secretary. In an eleventh-hour attempt to stave off defeat in Cardiff the following day, Gordon Brown took the risk of being seen to pre-empt his spending announcements due in July by briefing Welsh newspapers that he 'would not let the people of Wales down'. It was not enough for Labour's opponents and, given the denigration of Alun Michael in Wales, events there had gathered a momentum of their own. On 9 February, knowing he faced defeat, Alun Michael resigned as First Secretary before the vote of no confidence had even taken place. It was a major embarrassment to Tony Blair, who was still enjoying an extended political honeymoon, exacerbated by the timing of the announcement. Alun Michael told Blair at lunchtime of his intention to resign but not when he would so do. At Prime Minister's Questions at 3 p.m., Blair was challenged by a Conservative MP to back his First Secretary, and told the Commons that Alun Michael was 'doing an excellent job'. When another Tory MP received a pager message with news that Alun Michael had resigned, William Hague skilfully made a show of breaking the news to the Prime Minister. As Blair counter-attacked, six times during the exchanges he conspicuously denounced the Welsh nationalists and Conservatives in the assembly, but not the Liberal Democrats.[5]

It made for good parliamentary theatre and was damaging to Blair. However, the opposition party leader who emerged from the episode with the greatest credit was not William Hague but Charles Kennedy, who showed himself able to resist formidable pressure and hold fast to the liberal instinct that devolution means letting others take responsibility for decisions. It was a very different approach to leadership; Kennedy sat back and let things happen rather than trying to give a lead. Yet it had its effect. Against Blair's expectations, Rhodri Morgan opened drawn-out coalition talks with the opposition parties in Cardiff. These did not begin in earnest until after July, when the extra Welsh aid from the Treasury was confirmed. Kennedy asked to be kept informed but left them to it. Only after his AMs asked for help did he dispatch David Laws, who had helped to draft the partnership agreement for the Lib–Lab coalition in Scotland and the subsequent deal on tuition fees, to draft a similar document for Wales. Once the talks concluded in October, Labour had agreed to 114 of the Lib Dems' manifesto commitments for Wales, some of them minor but including smaller school class sizes, free school milk, a bigger student hardship fund, a larger health budget and a freeze in prescription charges. The outcome was a Lib–Lab coalition that governed in Wales until the assembly elections of spring 2003. The day before the formal agreement, the six Lib Dem AMs gathered in Mike German's office for a final conference call with Kennedy. Mike German said: 'We said to Charles we had all agreed, some with great trepidation, but were ready to go ahead with it. He wished us luck and said: "It sounds like you have a good deal. If that's what you want to do, I will back you all the way."'

The Alun Michael saga gave Kennedy the chance to show his judgement; now an opportunity arose to demonstrate his electoral appeal. In late February the Conservative MP for Romsey, Michael Colvin, died with his wife Nichola in a fire at their Queen Anne-style Edwardian mansion. It was a terrible tragedy but politics moves inexorably on; his death meant a by-election. On first sight Romsey, covering the picturesque Test valley in Hampshire, looked a reasonably safe seat. Michael Colvin held it with a majority of 8,585, or 16.5 per cent, over the Liberal Democrats in the 1997 general election, the nadir of Tory electoral fortunes. But the Lib Dems' analysis provided an insight into both their campaigning tactics and electoral strategy. The voting figures broke down as 46 per cent Tory, 29 per cent Lib Dem and 18.5 per cent Labour. Chris Rennard, by now a peer but still campaigns director, judged the Conservative vote could be shaved slightly but almost all the Labour vote could be 'squeezed' by encouraging tactical voting: he calculated he could win. The first weekend after the fire, Rennard travelled to Romsey to discuss preparations for the by-election with the executive of the local party.

His optimism was not universally shared. Mike Hancock, a Hampshire MP and friend of Kennedy's from the SDP days, told colleagues that hopes of a Lib Dem victory were unrealistic. There were further doubts as to whether an attempt to harvest protest votes against the Conservatives could still work now the party was in opposition. Once the campaign was under-way, *The Times* published a leading article saying the seat was 'a most improbable target for Mr Kennedy' and predicting the Conservatives' share of the vote should increase substantially.[6] To his credit, Charles Kennedy took the view that it was not his role to second-guess his party's campaigning experts. He placed his trust in Rennard's judgement and made six campaign visits to Romsey, although he remained nervous about its prospects until Chris Rennard decamped to Hampshire to direct the campaign in person. Both men were taking a considerable risk. The Conservatives moved the writ for the by-election to be held on 4 May, the day of local council elections, which required the attention of the party's director of campaigns and the leader. Both knew, however, that by-elections were becoming less frequent and presented the Lib Dems with a rare opportunity to fight their opponents on an equal footing, due to campaign spending limits. The Lib Dems threw the kitchen sink at Romsey.

The Liberal Democrats used their by-election campaign in Romsey to road-test themes for the general election expected the following year. Gordon Brown's decision to freeze public spending for his first two years as Chancellor meant the Lib Dems' message from the 1997 election, of raising taxes to pay for better public services, still resonated. They campaigned in Romsey on the condition of local hospitals and schools, with a big emphasis on the plight of pensioners, blaming Conservative underfunding of health and education rather than Labour's record, and proposing modest tax rises to fund investment in public services. They chose as their candidate Sandra Gidley, a local pharmacist and former mayor of Romsey, and combined their messages with local factors such as the closure of sub-post office branches and building on greenfield sites. Unsurprisingly, given the traumatic manner of their MP's death, the local Conservative party was not well prepared for a by-election. After a delay, and some internal disagreement, they rejected as their candidate Liz Perry, the association's 29-year-old chairwoman, who was seen as the favourite. Instead they chose Tim Palmer, an Eton-educated gentleman farmer and Tory councillor just across the county border in Dorset, who was more in Michael Colvin's image. When Conservative election literature described him as a 'local' candidate born in Hampshire, Chris Rennard sent a researcher to London to check his birth certificate at Somerset House and birth announcement in *The Times*, and discovered he had been born in London. Lib Dem literature mercilessly used this fact to discredit the Tory campaign, saying their 'local' candidate was born in London, lived in Wiltshire, was a councillor in Dorset yet was standing for election in Hampshire. Such crass oversights aside, the Conservatives mounted an energetic defence of the seat led by John Hayes, a vice-chairman of the party, and supported by large numbers of Tory MPs, their staff and young volunteers.

Beyond the trench warfare in Romsey's suburbs and villages, a more significant battle was taking place as Charles Kennedy went head to head with William Hague for the first time. The young Conservative leader, having abandoned his initial strategy of modernising the Tory party and trying to break from its recent past, had reverted to high-profile populism to shore up his core right-wing vote. In his speech to the Conservatives' spring conference in March he attacked the government's policies on asylum, Europe and political correctness and said if Labour won a second term Britain would feel like a 'foreign land', where Britons felt strangers in their own country. He courted controversy by offering sympathy to a Norfolk farmer, Tony Martin, convicted of murder for shooting dead a teenage burglar fleeing his property. He launched a so-called Save the Pound roadshow to campaign against Britain's entry into the euro, taking it to Romsey in mid-April. Most controversially, Hague unveiled an uncompromising policy of detaining all applicants for asylum on arrival and claimed that Britain faced a flood of asylum seekers, which threatened to provoke a return to demonstrations by the far-Right National Front.[7] Such populism was the antithesis of liberalism and contrary to all Charles Kennedy's political convictions. Operating on instinct, in the final week of the campaign Kennedy gave a series of interviews and speeches attacking Hague's language and accusing him of pandering to the worst type of minority prejudice. At Prime Minister's Questions on the day before polling he returned to the attack on William Hague, telling the Commons: 'When one is talking about issues such as asylum and immigration, particularly with elections approaching, to use saloon-bar language is nothing more than gutter politics.'[8]

It was one of his most effective Commons performances as leader. By doing so, Kennedy turned the by-election into a duel between the two opposition party leaders and so generated considerable interest in the contest. Charles Kennedy was always inclined to be realistic about his party's prospects, disliking the tendency of politicians to overstate their case. Four days before the poll, Chris Rennard was furious to see a story in *The Times* reporting a belief by 'senior Liberal Democrat sources' that Romsey was a tough nut to crack and the Lib Dems were unlikely to win the by-election.[9] Assuming, correctly, that the Conservatives would use such an admission in campaign literature, Rennard began making enquiries as to the source of the story. He was taken aback to discover it emanated from Charles Kennedy himself, in conversation with the paper's reporter, James Landale. Over the final weekend the Conservatives were confident from their canvass returns that their vote had held up sufficiently to retain the seat, albeit with a reduced majority, betraying a fundamental misunderstanding of the dynamic of a by-election upset. To achieve the type of swing required to capture a seat the Lib Dems depend on late momentum, often generated by media coverage and reinforced by intensive leafleting. By the final weekend they need not be ahead, only close enough to be in contention. Even when the postal votes were counted the Lib Dems remained behind; Sandra Gidley saw the results on the desk of her agent, Gerald Vernon-Jackson, and assumed she had lost. At the count, however, Rennard was sufficiently confident of victory to break with usual practice and encourage Sandra Gidley to attend early enough to provide pictures for the television news as she arrived to applause from Lib Dem supporters. She won the seat with a majority of 3,311, taking 50.5 per cent of the vote to the Conservatives' 42 per cent, and squeezing Labour's share to just 3.7 per cent, causing it to lose its deposit. Charles Kennedy, awaiting the result at home, was swiftly put through to Sandra Gidley, his forty-seventh MP, on a mobile phone so that she could be filmed accepting her leader's congratulations. The following morning he travelled down to Romsey to walk through the town centre, thank the voters and revel in his triumph.

It was a stunning result, overshadowing respectable Conservative gains of almost 600 seats elsewhere in the local elections and badly weakening William Hague's credibility. The conclusion drawn by many was that Hague's core vote strategy of right-wing populism might work in low turnout contests such as town hall elections but had repelled moderate voters in Romsey, which saw a higher turnout of 55 per cent. It thus raised questions about William Hague's chances of winning the general election with such an approach. For the Liberal Democrats, the result suddenly raised the prospect that they might realistically seek to win further seats from the Conservatives in the election, rather than battle to hold their gains from last time. For the first time, too, it demonstrated that in their quietly spoken, self-deprecating leader they had a unique electoral asset. Voters clearly liked this unassuming man, who possessed a knack of talking in a way people understood and identified with, yet showed political courage and conviction too. For Charles Kennedy, after his uncertain start, the victory was an important boost to his self-confidence and an encouragement to trust his own political instincts.

Like his electoral appeal, Kennedy's style of working was unconventional. He disliked formal meetings, although in his new role he was forced to endure many, and he was at his most comfortable in relaxed surroundings tossing ideas around with his closest advisers. He liked them to argue around him; he would absorb their points and choose between them. Initially his leadership campaign team carried on meeting, at least monthly, with his staff and formal advisers joined by James Gurling and Clive Parry. This was variously called the Diary Group or Office Group. A more formal body, the Leader's Advisory Group, comprising the chairmen of party committees and heads of departments at Cowley Street, was also set up and met fortnightly, but had little power or influence. Several months into his leadership the structure changed, with the creation of the Small Office Group of those advisers with whom he worked the closest. Its core members were Dick Newby, Tim Razzall, Anna Werrin, Mark Oaten, Matthew Taylor, Richard Grayson and Daisy Sampson, his press secretary. They would also met fortnightly to discuss plans for forthcoming events, immediate strategy and topical events, although the membership was fluid and policy spokesmen might sometimes attend. A wider circle, the Large Office Group, would meet every three months or so, often at a venue away from the Commons, for a broader discussion on strategy followed by supper. Such gatherings might include Jane Bonham Carter; Malcolm Bruce; Clive Parry; the president, Navnit Dholakia; the party's chief executive, Hugh Rickard, later Chris Rennard; Julian Ingram, a polling analyst; and, later, Robert Bean, who ran a branding and marketing company. After a year or two, the Small Office Group met less frequently as its function was increasingly replaced by informal, often spontaneous meetings of those closest to Kennedy, although tellingly very few MPs were ever involved. Towards the end of the day, when the mood took him, he would come to the doorway of his inner office, beckon to his staff and anyone he felt comfortable with who happened to be in the anteroom, and say: 'Come in, come and have a gossip.' As Mark Oaten said:

> We would classically have a gossip, chat, a bottle of wine shared amongst all of us, and we just talked through. He would sit back in his chair, kick his shoes off, sit there with a cigarette, and that was the point when you really saw Charles working, much more engaged. That's how it worked. It didn't work with formal meetings at all. The big decisions of the day were nearly always taken in that kind of environment.

Having taken the helm halfway through a parliament, the overwhelming focus of Charles Kennedy and the Liberal Democrats was on preparation for the next general election. At the end of May all of his MPs, candidates and agents in target seats gathered for the weekend at the Jarvis International Hotel in Bristol for an extended election-planning exercise. Kennedy, who arrived a day early for strategy discussions with his office team, gave a speech of welcome on the first evening, and candidates were then subjected to a mock session of the television programme *Question Time*, with Tim Razzall in the role of its host, David Dimbleby. Candidates took turns on the platform, two at a time, defending the party's policies and practising rebuttals while MPs acted the roles of Labour or Conservative panellists attacking the Lib Dems' positions. Training for television and radio interviews was provided for candidates over the weekend, during which there were presentations on market research, the Romsey by-election campaign and key election messages. These were calibrated overwhelmingly to attack the Conservatives, from whom any election gains were expected to come. A more covert aim of the event was to encourage prospective parliamentary candidates to meet Charles Kennedy informally, at coffee breaks and mealtimes, and see him at close quarters in an environment that displayed his strengths as leader to best effect. In one session he gave a presentation on the platform in the form of an interview, the format he found most comfortable.

A much wider initiative to raise Charles Kennedy's profile was his book, first mooted in the year before he became leader and revived after his election as a vehicle for introducing curious electors to him more fully. Of course, as leader he did not have time to write such a tome himself. Some of its outline had been incorporated into his manifesto for the leadership contest. Over the following nine months Richard Grayson and Matthew Baylis, a researcher in the leader's office, produced drafts which Charles Kennedy annotated in longhand on every page, often adding biographical details and political anecdotes, in addition to personal reflections. With typical prescience, Kennedy was in the vanguard of latching on to a sense of disaffection with conventional politics among a growing number of disillusioned voters. He made this a theme of the book, entitled, with an unfortunately hubristic play on words, *The Future of Politics*. While his analysis of an emerging disconnection between governors and governed was timely, and his biographical passages revealing, it remained a curious work. Kennedy set out, he explained in the preface, to answer these questions: 'What makes this Kennedy fellow tick? What makes him angry, what makes him sad? What fires his passion? By the way, does he possess passion? Why is he a Liberal Democrat . . . ?'[10]

Whether he answered them is open to doubt. The book was arranged around a theme of freedom, as he sought to marry his social democratic instincts with a classically Liberal focus on the individual. Therefore, his chapter on social justice had the title 'Freedom from poverty', that on the environment was 'Freedom to breathe' and a section on devolution was 'Freedom to govern'. Yet beyond this structure was a startling lack of original thinking on policy or a strand of political thought that was identifiably his own. He talked of 'social justice audits' for all policies emanating from Whitehall, embraced community bartering schemes or local exchange and trading systems, and experiments with direct democracy allowing citizens rather than politicians to take executive decisions. It would, of course, have been odd for a political leader to publish a radical and detailed set of policies not destined for his party's manifesto a year before a likely general election. Nevertheless, Kennedy's book firmly entrenched his image as a man for mood and strategy rather than policy.

The book, published in advance of the September conference and serialised in *The Times*, did achieve its short-term aim in generating publicity for Kennedy. The conference was, however, not a good one for him. It was his bad luck that, in his opening years as leader, almost every conference appeared jinxed by a major political crisis that dominated the news agenda. His first spring conference had coincided with a move to close mass car production at the Rover plant in Birmingham; the following year's coincided with the outbreak of the foot-and-mouth epidemic. The autumn conference at Bournemouth in 2000 was completely overshadowed by a fuel crisis as soaring crude oil prices provoked blockades of oil refineries by road hauliers and farmers. Fears of petrol shortages triggered extraordinary and irrational panic buying of fuel by motorists, generating very long queues outside petrol stations. Many of them ran dry. Ministers, caught unawares by these direct action protests, were forced to take emergency measures to coordinate tanker supplies. The public reaction was at first confused, with severe alarm at the disruption of petrol supplies but fairly wide sympathy with the fuel protestors, many of them small businessmen who claimed to represent millions of motorists. This view held, despite television pictures of overweight truckers, suddenly self-appointed arbiters of access to public services, debating whether to allow tankers through their blockades to supply hospitals. Much of the public debate centred on demands to cut the rates of fuel duty set by the Treasury, instead of the underlying cause of short-term fluctuations in crude oil markets. In the frenetic political atmosphere, the Conservatives briefly overtook Labour in opinion polls for the first time since 1992.[11]

One of the reasons for recent rises in fuel duty was a conscious government policy, introduced by the Conservatives and continued by Labour, to raise tax on petrol by a rate higher than inflation, the so-called fuel duty escalator. This was an environmental policy, which Liberal Democrats had supported. On the opening morning of his party conference, the Lib Dems announced that Charles Kennedy would make an 'emergency statement' on the fuel crisis. It would have taken a brave leader to make the environmental case for higher fuel tax in such a climate. Already a clamour had been raised for lower duty. Instead he did neither, calling for a freeze in real terms on fuel duty over five years by earmarking extra VAT receipts generated from future rises in fuel prices to be returned to the government's transport budget. This policy was agreed by the parliamentary party before the summer recess, after the disproportionate number of Lib Dem MPs representing rural areas lobbied hard to protect the interests of rural motorists. At least Kennedy resisted populist pressure for a cut in fuel duty, but the Lib Dems had compromised on their environmental credentials. It was not their finest hour. Nor was Charles Kennedy's main speech on the final day of the conference much better. A lively debate had taken place among his advisers over the optimum length of a conference address, with Dick Newby favouring a much shorter, focused delivery. His view prevailed over that of Richard Grayson, the principal speechwriter, and in Bournemouth the leader's speech ran to barely thirty minutes. Among delegates in the hall it went down well, as Charles Kennedy delivered it with a passion some doubted he possessed. It was less well received by the media, partly arising from a sense that its brevity failed to meet expectations of such an occasion. Peter Riddell, writing in *The Times*, called it 'one one of the most vacuous leader's speeches I have ever heard at a party conference'.[12]

Just over a year into his leadership, Charles Kennedy still cut an uncertain figure. The following month Menzies Campbell's wife Elspeth, who always had a soft spot for Kennedy, invited him to stay overnight with them in Edinburgh before attending the funeral of Donald Dewar, the Labour politician who led the Scottish Parliament and was regarded as the father of the Scottish nation. In the following morning Elspeth Campbell prepared a formal breakfast on her best china for their house guests, who included David and Judy Steel. When Kennedy emerged to join them he waved away Elspeth Campbell's hospitality. 'What would you like for breakfast?' she asked him. 'Do you have any Diet Coke?' Kennedy replied meekly. Fortunately, Elspeth Campbell was able to retrieve a can intended for a grandchild.

The company, who were joined by Archy Kirkwood, the former Lib Dems' chief whip, proceeded to the service in a formal funeral car arranged by the Campbells, which drove them in sombre style along the M8 motorway for the funeral in Glasgow. Afterwards, the assembled ranks of Scotland's great and good repaired to the finery of Glasgow Art Gallery where, in Presbyterian fashion, guests were offered tea, coffee or soft drinks but no alcohol. Kennedy slipped away and found a pub where he could have a drink.

Liberal Democrat members were broadly happy with Charles Kennedy's more open, consultative style of leadership but the media, collectively, was pretty unimpressed. Leadership from the front makes waves and offers a clear story to report. Kennedy's collegiate approach was more like that of a naval convoy, destined to travel at the speed of its slowest ship, and more incremental than exciting. Furthermore, he had a disarming tendency to admit to his frailties and mistakes. Just past the halfway point into his first year he was challenged in one interview over whether he had made an impact, and replied: 'Oh no, definitely not. New leaders never make sufficient impact in their first six months.'[13]

Commentators took some time to adjust to this novel candour from a politician, although some were slow to appreciate that many voters liked it. He was criticised for inactivity, lacking passion and a failure to give a lead, all of which had elements of truth, but he was assumed, too, to lack ambition. As Dick Newby said:

> One of the advantages of Charles, and disadvantages, was that he was ruthlessly realistic about the party's position. And this is why he never overclaimed, because he didn't

believe it. So he didn't want to overplay in terms of where we could get to. Some people thought that reflected his personal lack of ambition, which wasn't the case at all. It was just that he thought his credibility required him to be realistic.

Such criticisms resurfaced at his next conference in Torquay the following spring, where he was met by further accusations that he was failing to take advantage of a slump in support for the Conservatives under William Hague.[14] This time Charles Kennedy resolved not to ignore his critics but to respond. He decided at short notice to drop a large section from the draft of his leader's speech dealing with policy and instead reworked into the text a defence of his approach to the role of leader. When he entered the stage, after an embarrassing interlude when he was announced before he had been fetched from backstage, Kennedy took off his suit jacket and walked the stage in his shirtsleeves as he mounted a defence of his style of leadership. He was able to do so thanks to a new, larger autocue system placed on balconies behind his audience that he could read from wherever he stood on the stage. 'It's said I'm laid back. Well, that's true, but that's because I'm tolerant and because I'm a liberal,' Charles Kennedy told his audience. 'And I'm proud of that, but I'm also ambitious for our party and I'm ambitious for our country.'

It was not brilliant oratory. It was certainly far removed from the rhetorical flair described by his contemporaries at Glasgow University, and even from his platform performances as an emerging talent in the SDP and early years of the Liberal Democrats. But it was what he felt comfortable with, and made a virtue of the attributes singled out by his critics. The reluctant leader was beginning to find his voice.

6

In Blair's tent

Overwhelmingly the biggest strategic question facing Kennedy before the election was his party's relationship with Labour. The legacy of Paddy Ashdown's courtship with Tony Blair was that most commentators viewed the Liberal Democrats entirely through the prism of what leverage they could wield over the Prime Minister, and what they might get in return. Many newspapers reported Charles Kennedy's first conference speech, for instance, as an overture to Labour. The *Financial Times* headline, 'Deeper links with Labour signalled', was typical.[1] There was a widely held assumption that, should he fail to work with Tony Blair, he simply risked irrelevance. This was a source of continuing exasperation to Charles Kennedy. Blair's commanding majority in the Commons meant a coalition was not a realistic proposition and not likely after the election either. Kennedy's goal from the outset was to identify and explain a distinctive role for the Liberal Democrats that was independent of Labour. In one television interview, he put it thus: 'I do not think you can run a political organisation on the basis of always thinking of yourselves as some kind of adjunct to another political organisation.'[2]

More often, he would simply say it did not make sense for a Coca-Cola salesman to spend his time talking about Pepsi. Whatever his view, two items of unfinished business were left on the table from the Blair–Ashdown 'project'. The Joint Consultative Committee of senior ministers and Lib Dems remained in existence. The government was also still committed, in theory, to a referendum on Roy Jenkins's recommendations on voting reform for Westminster. Informally, and more importantly, there was in effect an open invitation from Downing Street to explore other areas of potential cooperation between the parties.

Tony Blair, still very keen on Lib–Lab collaboration, appeared to share the same assumption about the Lib Dems' prospects as the commentators. When Paddy Ashdown told the Prime Minister privately in early December that he intended to quit, six weeks before he told his own MPs, Blair replied: 'So, will I get Charles Kennedy?'[3] In another perhaps more telling remark, Tony Blair was said to have asked Ashdown once: 'Charles Kennedy – all that talent. Why is he so idle?'[4]

On a personal basis, Tony Blair and Charles Kennedy had known each other for many years and got on reasonably well. They entered the Commons at the same time and, in their first parliament, the office used by Kennedy in St Stephen's House was along the same corridor as that shared by Blair and Gordon Brown. Blair and Kennedy occasionally appeared on television together, particularly in a series of broadcasts during the 1992 election campaign and its aftermath. When Tony Blair, then a member of the shadow Cabinet, wanted to find out more about Paddy Ashdown's thinking on collaboration between their two parties he used Charles Kennedy as an intermediary, since Kennedy was better known to Labour reformers than his leader. They had a furtive meeting over a meal at the Hampstead home of Derry Irvine, the shadow Lord Chancellor, to discuss scope for cross-party cooperation.[5] Also in attendance was Peter Mandelson, then a newly elected Labour MP, whom Kennedy knew through Roger Liddle, a friend from the SDP. There were even half-hearted attempts to encourage Kennedy to rejoin the Labour Party. The dinner at Derry Irvine's home bore eerie overtones of later meetings between Tony Blair and Paddy Ashdown once Blair became leader of the Labour Party and the two men hatched out their 'project' for formal cooperation between their parties. Blair also attended a supper in the Reform Club with the A1 group, a discreet dining club of twenty or so senior figures from the SDP of which Kennedy was a member, when the hosts and guest tested their respective visions of social democracy.

On Kennedy's election as leader, Tony Blair broke off his summer holiday to telephone with his congratulations and they agreed to meet soon. In the ensuing years they met many times, more often than the political world appreciated: alone, informally for dinner, with teams of advisers, across the Cabinet table in the JCC, spontaneously at state or parliamentary occasions. Relations between the two were friendly although not close, and Kennedy was always conscious of the firm limits placed on Lib–Lab cooperation by his own party. At their first formal meeting, at Blair's invitation, Charles Kennedy took along with him Tim Razzall, Dick Newby and Anna Werrin.

As he did on every such occasion, Kennedy insisted they enter by a side route via 70 Whitehall, as Ashdown had for his clandestine assignations, and then along corridors in the Cabinet Office, rather than through the front door of 10 Downing Street. 'We never went through the front door of Downing Street, because he thought it was pompous,' Dick Newby said, 'and he was very keen not to look as though he was desperate to be in Downing Street.'

On arrival, the Lib Dems were shown into the Cabinet Room to await the Prime Minister and, while they did so, Kennedy told his advisers: 'I am going to make absolutely certain that these discussions start on my terms.' When Blair appeared, Charles Kennedy asked: 'I hope you don't mind me smoking, Tony?' 'Not at all, not at all,' replied Blair, although it meant they all had to relocate, and they held their meeting outside in the Rose Garden where Kennedy could light a cigarette. As with subsequent meetings, which tended to be in Tony Blair's study, known as the 'den', they had a general discussion about the political landscape, possible areas of cooperation and talked about an agenda of work for the Joint Consultative Committee. Generally Tony Blair would be accompanied by three or four advisers from a cast of Jonathan Powell, his chief of staff, who sat silent but observing; Charlie Falconer, his Cabinet Office Minister and political fixer; Sally Morgan, his head of government relations; Pat McFadden, his political secretary; Andrew Adonis, from his policy unit; and Anji Hunter, his office gatekeeper.

During one visit to Blair's study, Charles Kennedy noticed a bizarre ornament on top of a television set. It was a Billy Bass singing fish plaque, a curious adornment given that the Prime Minister had the government art collection at his disposal. At intervals, the battery-operated fish would turn its head out towards the room and, loudly, sing 'Don't worry, be happy'. Kennedy asked what on earth such a gadget was doing in the Prime Minister's study. Blair replied that it had been brought back for him by John Prescott after a holiday in Florida. Next time Kennedy bumped into John Prescott, he mentioned having seen the singing fish. John Prescott responded: 'How else do you think I know what buggers are seeing the Prime Minister? They always say to me, "That's a very good present you gave him."'

Sometimes Kennedy would go to see Tony Blair alone, but advisers of both leaders eventually put a stop to such one-to-one meetings. Tim Razzall said:

> It was always a mistake, and we had various discussions over the years, initially with Anji Hunter and latterly Sally Morgan, to the effect that it wasn't a good idea for them

to meet alone, which both sides agreed. Nobody ever knew what they had agreed, because their recollections were not necessarily the same. This was a particular concern with people in Downing Street.

The JCC's programme had already worked through the areas of constitutional reform on which the two parties could reach political agreement. Left in its in-tray were those that were more politically problematic or on which they disagreed. The most obvious was the Jenkins report on proportional representation for the Commons; Kennedy was naturally interested in PR for local elections in England, although this was not part of the Cook–Maclennan agreement and Tony Blair was not enthusiastic. As with directly elected regional assemblies, it fell under John Prescott's departmental responsibilities. Prescott was tribally hostile to the Lib Dems and against cross-party cooperation, and would have nothing to do with the talks. Delayed freedom of information legislation did subsequently find its way into law, though in a diluted form unpalatable to Liberal Democrats. Reform of the House of Lords, the second major area of unfinished business from the Cook–Maclennan agreement, foundered as Blair disregarded Lib Dem pressure for an elected second chamber. Realistically there was little scope for progress within the JCC on constitutional reform, its original purpose.

The second area within the JCC's remit was foreign affairs, particularly Europe. Since Roy Jenkins had inculcated in Charles Kennedy a passionate conviction in the European Union, this was potentially the more fruitful area of partnership with Tony Blair. At his first party conference as leader, Kennedy made a point of speaking at a fringe meeting organised by Britain in Europe, a new cross-party pressure group formed as the vehicle for a yes campaign in a referendum to take Britain into the euro. The following month Charles Kennedy shared a platform to launch Britain in Europe at the Imax cinema in Waterloo, south London with Tony Blair, Robin Cook, the Foreign Secretary, and the Conservative politicians Michael Heseltine and Kenneth Clarke. All were taking risks in doing so, but Charles Kennedy probably the least of any of them. The Liberal Democrats had consistently been the party most supportive of the EU and Kennedy was trying to execute a conscious growth strategy for his party of appealing to centrist Conservative supporters who shared his views on Europe. Crudely, the Lib Dems and Kennedy himself gained disproportionate publicity from such cross-party initiatives, but for him Europe was an article of faith, irrespective of popular opinion. In subsequent discussions with Blair at Downing Street, Europe was the issue on which he consistently tried to take the initiative. Repeatedly, he urged the Prime Minister to begin making the case for Britain's membership of the single European currency and start campaigning for it, regardless of his plans for a referendum on the issue, to avoid losing the argument by default. Tony Blair's refusal to do so was a source of exasperation to Kennedy, given that their parties were both in favour of British entry to the euro, albeit under different conditions. Charles Kennedy continued dutifully to attend events for Britain in Europe, despite suspicions in its early days of an umbilical link to Downing Street regardless of its all-party status.

The JCC found worthy, if perhaps more peripheral, work to do. Its first meeting of the Kennedy era, around the long oval table in the Cabinet Room on 13 December 1999, had a heavyweight cast list. On one side sat Tony Blair and five Cabinet ministers: Robin Cook, Jack Straw, Mo Mowlam, Margaret Jay and Charlie Falconer. On the other sat Charles Kennedy, Menzies Campbell, Simon Hughes, Bob Maclennan, Bill Rodgers and Dick Newby. They discussed House of Lords reform, freedom of information legislation and Europe. Afterwards, the JCC published a joint statement by the parties setting out a common position on institutional reforms for an enlarged EU ahead of the forthcoming Inter-Governmental Conference. The statement was circulated to Lib Dem MPs the day before publication in February 2000 with a covering note headed 'strictly private and confidential'. Despite such sober formalities, it amounted to little more than a position statement ahead of complex pan-European negotiations in which compromise was inevitable. Following its second, and final, meeting in July 2000, the JCC issued an agreed position on desired reforms to the United Nations' peacekeeping and humanitarian capabilities ahead of a UN millennium summit in New York. The Lib Dems were pleased, believing they had persuaded the government to accept large parts of Lib Dem policy on UN reform. The JCC paper was issued in September of that year with a 4 a.m. embargo, as though it conveyed international significance. It was in the same mould: earnest, idealistic, erudite, yet destined to be of tangential importance in the stark realities of international diplomacy.

Tony Blair remained deeply committed to Lib–Lab cooperation. Having perhaps overestimated Charles Kennedy's readiness to work with him, Blair gave Lib Dems the impression that he began to woo harder as Kennedy's caution became more apparent. Curiously, like Kennedy, Tony Blair was profoundly influenced by Roy Jenkins and shared Jenkins's analysis that the split between the Liberal Party and the Labour movement that spawned the Labour Party in the early twentieth century was an anomaly from which the Conservatives had benefited disproportionately. Nine months into Kennedy's leadership, Blair gave an interview to the author Robert Harris for an American magazine explicitly committing himself to a merger of the two parties. Blair said:

> I've never given up on that goal and I still believe it can be achieved. The truth of the matter is that we are basically driven by the same value systems. There may be differences on policy, but that's more to do with being different parties – almost the accident of being in different parties – rather than some great division of ideas.[6]

For Tony Blair, such cross-party dialogue was also part of a wider strategy. Fundamental to the electoral appeal of his New Labour coalition was a process of working with centrist politicians and others in a non-partisan fashion to push the Conservative Party further to the margins. It became known as Blair's 'big tent' style of politics. There was, however, a fundamental difference in Blair's motivation to that of the Lib Dems. The aim of Kennedy and his party was to work with Labour as separate parties with the ultimate goal of a coalition based on electoral reform. Events showed that Blair's approach was to try and draw the Lib Dems, and others, into a pavilion over which the red flag of Labour fluttered: Blair's instinct was hegemony, not pluralism.[7] Tony Blair's commitment to Britain in Europe was genuine, if ultimately unconsummated, but again sharing a platform with Michael Heseltine and Kenneth Clarke had the same wider political purpose. There was a similar undercurrent when he appointed Chris Patten as one of Britain's two European Commissioners, overruling William Hague's original nomination. Businessmen, pop stars, sportsmen and a host of others might at various times find themselves ushered into Blair's 'big tent', invited to undertake or endorse apparently apolitical initiatives in the national interest yet inadvertently running the risk of being misrepresented as cheerleaders for the government.

In their meetings, Blair continually pressed Charles Kennedy to broaden the remit of the JCC to include policy areas where their parties had similar positions, such as pensions, education and the health service. As Paddy Ashdown had been after his party's conference in spring 1998, Kennedy was constrained by conference resolutions. Even had he wanted to, he would have been unable to agree to more than a protracted and potentially divisive series of internal party consultations on such a proposition. He had no real interest in maintaining, and certainly not in extending, a controversial mechanism inherited from his predecessor that had little scope to influence government policy yet risked contaminating the Lib Dems' independence. As Tim Razzall said: 'Charles was thought of as being against all this. Actually, he didn't see the point of it because it wasn't achieving anything. He didn't have any principled objection to it. But if you couldn't get PR through, what was the point?'

The only occasions when Kennedy displayed belligerence were when opponents of Lib–Lab cooperation within the Labour Party, such as John Prescott, Gordon Brown and Jack Straw, appeared to be manoeuvring to block progress on Labour's manifesto commitment to a referendum on Commons voting reform. Roy Jenkins had recommended 'AV-plus', combining the alternative vote for single-member constituencies and a list system for multi-member regions. This had effectively been abandoned. Realistically Kennedy knew, as the general election approached, that Labour would not fulfil its commitment to hold a referendum before then. Tony Blair was now offering a referendum in the next parliament on the alternative vote, although it was doubtful whether Blair would have convinced the Labour Party to accept this. Lib Dem members would certainly have looked with suspicion on the alternative vote, which is not a proportional system at all even though the party stood to gain from such a change. Charles Kennedy's goal was to prevent Labour's next manifesto from blocking the possibility of Commons voting reform altogether. He indulged in some sabre-rattling at his conference at Torquay in spring 2001, and there was much activity involving go-betweens. Kennedy and Richard Grayson visited Robin Cook at his Commons office; they urged the Foreign Secretary, whose instincts were pluralist, to put pressure on Blair and emphasise how important another commitment to PR would be to Lib Dem members. Finally, Charles Kennedy met Tony Blair in late March and – extraordinarily – negotiated the wording of a passage for Labour's election manifesto. Kennedy, Dick Newby and Tim Razzall went to the Prime Minister's large, oak-panelled office behind the Speaker's chair in the Commons, where the deal was struck. Tony Blair would not commit himself to a referendum in the next parliament. But he did agree to instigate a review, after the next set of devolved elections in Scotland and Wales in 2003, of the new voting systems in operation and to carry out a reassessment the Jenkins report. It was a compromise, but at least it kept the cause of voting reform alive. The agreed section for Labour's manifesto read: 'We will review the experience of the new voting systems and the Jenkins report to assess whether changes might be made to the electoral system for the House of Commons. A referendum remains the right way to agree any change for Westminster.' This was one of the few, indeed perhaps the only, tangible political achievement of Kennedy's dialogue with Blair and proved an empty pledge.

No review of electoral systems had reported by the end of the following parliament. In response to the Liberal Democrats' lobbying, they were allocated significantly more peerages, triggering protests from the Conservatives. This enhanced their influence as holders of the balance of power in the Lords, but Charles Kennedy disliked using this extra and enhanced patronage as he customarily agonised over whom to send to the Lords. Mark Oaten recalled: 'Again that was always a painful thing for Charles. It was like having to do a shadow cabinet reshuffle, deciding who was going to get the peerages.'

The negotiations with Tony Blair's office over numbers of peers were always drawn out. Ahead of the 2001 general election, for instance, Kennedy was invited to submit names for a dissolution honours list, by convention for retiring MPs. Paddy Ashdown was effectively on the proposed list already, as a former party leader. Charles Kennedy was invited to submit two more names, and had in mind proposing Bob Maclennan and Ray Michie, his constituency neighbours in the Highlands. Before doing so, however, his office haggled, trying to bid up the numbers by citing the Cook–Maclennan agreement and arguing about parity in relation to the Conservatives. First Downing Street agreed to expand the number of Lib Dem nominations to four, enabling Richard Livsey to take ermine. Finally, aided by the delay in the general election due to the foot-and-mouth epidemic, which allowed the negotiations to continue, Downing Street allotted the Lib Dems one extra space on the list and Ronnie Fearn, the only other retiring Lib Dem MP, was put forward for the fifth peerage.

The relationship between the Liberal Democrats and Labour presented Kennedy's team with challenges when it came to developing policy for his first election manifesto. Richard Grayson observed:

> We were very clear when Charles became leader that one of the major problems that we had was a lack of differentiation from the Labour Party because we were talking about some of the same things. They were doing our constitutional affairs agenda and we were doing their social affairs policy.

Kennedy inherited from Paddy Ashdown a radical policy paper, *Moving Ahead*, following a re-examination of policy conducted in short order in the spring and summer of 1998. One of its more controversial proposals, to transfer schools to neighbourhood schools trusts away from local authorities, and so threatening their position as monopoly providers in the state sector, was unceremoniously defeated at the autumn conference of that year. Among Charles Kennedy's friends, the review, executed by David Laws although chaired by Mark Oaten, was regarded as having a 'libertarian, sub-Thatcherite agenda' at odds with the party's centre-left instincts. *Moving Ahead*, disparagingly referred to among them as 'Shuffling Sideways', was quietly dropped and, under Kennedy's leadership policy, development went back to the drawing board.

Charles Kennedy's own outlook remained essentially that of a social democrat. The reasons that attracted him to the Labour Party in 1975, of a wish to address inequality and a concern about the poverty and those at the margins of society, still resonated as strongly. He believed in a market economy but, perhaps through growing up in an interdependent Highland community, he had powerful collectivist instincts. Charles Kennedy's attitude to public services, for instance, was coloured heavily by egalitarianism and a belief in the ethos of public servants which led him to hold back from radical reforms that implied controversial changes to working practices. Although he was greatly influenced by Roy Jenkins, his liberalism was more temperamental. Laid back, informal, disliking confrontation, he was uncomfortable with authoritarianism and genuinely liberal by instinct. His respect for others and willingness to take people at face value was also natural, and characteristic of Highland communities. Kennedy constantly ruminated on strategy and positioning, but was never a font of policy ideas, which he left to others.

In theory he now had the opportunity to craft a policy platform in his own image; in practice, with little more than two years from an election, there was insufficient time to introduce, develop and explain wholesale changes. With less coverage in the media, Lib Dems tended to communicate key policies earlier in the electoral cycle to ensure they were understood by voters. Early on Richard Grayson, in discussion with James Gurling and Clive Parry from Kennedy's leadership campaign team, decided upon constructing the election manifesto on the idea of freedom, as with Kennedy's book. In deference to social democratic sensibilities the draft manifesto, drawn up by

Richard Grayson and Matthew Taylor, was later entitled *Freedom in a Liberal Society* to avoid connotations of rampant individualism or licentiousness. But its emphasis was consciously a social liberal one, with a redistributive social justice agenda married with decentralised government as the precursor to individual liberty, instead of equality as an end in itself. As Richard Grayson commented:

> There was a strong sense that he had to talk about values. Because of the need for differentiation and because of the centre of gravity in the party it was very consciously saying that social liberalism, as set out by people like Hobhouse[8] a hundred years ago, was the way forward. We needed to come up with a political language that enabled us on the one hand to talk about liberal values but also allowed us to talk about social justice.

Like his predecessor, Charles Kennedy decided to chair the party's federal policy committee although his role tended to be confined to that of trouble-shooter. Where he did have an input into the manifesto it tended to be eclectic. He was very keen, for instance, on the idea of a tick box on tax returns that would enable taxpayers to express a preference on how a small proportion of their tax should be spent, such as increasing the health or education budget. His enthusiasm for social justice audits found its way into the manifesto, as did a proposal for replacing the Barnett formula for allocating money to Scotland and Wales. When the final manifesto, *Freedom, Justice, Honesty*, was published in the spring of 2001, it was accompanied by a briefing paper pointing out that, of its 250 specific policy pledges, 180 were new or had been redeveloped under Kennedy's leadership. Yet for all such context, the Lib Dem's broad policy position remained remarkably similar to that in the 1997 election. The central proposition was for a modest increase in taxation to improve the funding of public services, attacking the Conservatives' legacy of underfunding the health and education services but accusing Labour of failing to do enough to address it. This was symbolised by an extra penny on income tax to finance higher spending on education. The larger tax rise, however, was the proposal for a new top rate of income tax at 50p on incomes over £100,000 a year. The chief beneficiaries of Lib Dem largesse were to be pensioners, with a more generous state pension and free long-term care, school pupils and university students, who were offered smaller classes and a return to free tuition, and the National Health Service, with an emphasis on budget increases rather than reform.

Freedom and social justice, two of the manifesto's themes, combined values and policy. The third, honesty, essentially was built around Charles Kennedy himself. As a new leader fighting his first general election, the Lib Dems wished to use every opportunity to get Kennedy better known. After his success in the Romsey by-election, Kennedy's style of politics was presented by the party as an asset in its own right: open, down to earth and, above all, straightforward. Polling evidence suggested to Tim Razzall and Chris Rennard, the election's strategist and tactician, that voters saw Kennedy as an honest, trustworthy figure. This was after a period when the Conservatives' image had still not recovered from a series of personal scandals that beset its ministers in the mid-1990s, while Tony Blair and his government had acquired a reputation for 'spin'. Large photographs of Charles Kennedy adorned posters and campaign literature in both of the elections he fought as leader.

Although the Liberal Democrats were keen to use their manifesto to distinguish themselves from Labour, the dialogue with Tony Blair was part of an electoral strategy, too. Labour's landslide victory in 1997, when the Lib Dems made their electoral breakthrough by more than doubling their number of MPs, was the result of massive tactical voting by supporters of both parties. It was in their mutual interest to continue a grand alliance against the Conservatives, a strategy referred to by Tim Razzall in political discussions as 'two against one'. Charles Kennedy would mistakenly call it 'two plus one', but the point held. As the general election approached, the focus of Kennedy's discussions with Blair shifted from policy to politics, including a meeting in the 'den' in Downing Street specifically to discuss the general election. Occasionally, such cooperation was portrayed erroneously by the Conservatives or in the media as deals over target seats. In fact, both sides established from the outset that they could not stop local activity by their supporters. Labour and Lib Dem campaigners would continue to fight each other vigorously in 'ground war' battles where electoral arithmetic pitched them against one another, or as local issues dictated. The simple fact was that such seats were the minority. Tim Razzall explained: 'It was massively in our interest, and indeed it was massively in Labour's interest, to make sure that our respective guns were firing primarily at the Tories and not at each other, because there was very little electoral damage either party could do to each other.'

Tony Blair and Charles Kennedy agreed to coordinate their national campaigns to maximise the electoral damage both could wreak on the

Conservatives. Blair nominated Charlie Falconer to execute the agreement, Kennedy proposed Tim Razzall. The pair met weekly with Razzall, always alone, visiting the grand room in the Cabinet Office occupied by Falconer. On occasions Falconer would be joined by Pat McFadden from Downing Street or Douglas Alexander, Labour's campaign coordinator, who was close to Gordon Brown. At these meetings the two sides discussed the broad outlines of their campaigns and what policy themes they would introduce on which days, with Razzall several times changing his planning grid in order not to get in Labour's way. Such coordination continued throughout the election campaign as Charlie Falconer, from Labour's headquarters in Millbank Tower, and Razzall, in Cowley Street, would talk every evening by telephone. Tim Razzall explained:

> There will have been examples where we adjusted our grid to make sure that we were going on the same topic, but that's really *de minimus*. The real impact was the fact that Labour did not turn their guns on us. The major objective for us was to ensure that they did not, because that would have cost us seats. Instead of us being able to squeeze the Labour vote in the constituencies where we had to squeeze it, the Labour vote would have gone up.

Throughout the election, Kennedy soft-pedalled in his attacks on Labour, saying Tony Blair's first term had been 'a disappointment' but a return of the Conservatives would be 'a disaster'. Even so, the campaign itself got off to an awkward start. With the epidemic of foot-and-mouth disease causing serious disruption and political controversy in agricultural communities, Tony Blair delayed the general election and the county council elections due on 3 May by five weeks. Given their relative penury, this had serious repercussions for the Lib Dems: an aircraft and battlebuses for Kennedy were chartered, venues for press conferences and rallies were booked, staff had been hired for the campaign. They had already made reserve plans for an earlier election on 5 April, increasing their outlay. Blair consulted the Lib Dems before deciding to delay the election, and Charles Kennedy was initially against before, reluctantly, he accepted the epidemic would inhibit campaigning in rural areas. When Tony Blair finally telephoned Kennedy at home in Fort William on 'leader terms' to give notice of his decision, Kennedy pointed out he had read the news on the front page of the *Sun* newspaper that morning.

One reason for the doubts about Kennedy's leadership harboured by some of his MPs was the inexperience of those around him. Not only would this be Charles Kennedy's first election as leader; Tim Razzall had not run such a campaign either. Richard Grayson was relatively young. Anna Werrin had no roots in the party and became a member only shortly before Kennedy's leadership campaign. The financial firepower at their disposal was also limited. The £2 million election budget was less than three quarters that of the Lib Dems' campaign in 1997, in part because of a steep fall in membership and a new law restricting political donations and requiring their disclosure. The campaign was severely constrained by lack of resources, even after several successful emergency appeals to donors. In an internal campaign report afterwards, Chris Rennard told colleagues: 'Without the help of a very small number of significant donors (including the Joseph Rowntree Reform Trust) who negotiated with me directly, then our campaign would have probably been a disaster in terms of seats won.'

Boldly, Charles Kennedy set himself the twin goals of winning more seats and improving the Liberal Democrats' share of the vote, which had fallen progressively since the high-water mark of the Alliance campaign in 1983. Essentially, however, the aim was to consolidate the gains made in 1997, many of which were won with perilously thin majorities. Although there were additional target constituencies, predominantly held by the Conservatives, it was a defensive rather than an offensive campaign. Resources and campaign activity were heavily concentrated in the relatively small number of held and target seats. Election planning was built around a structure of highlighting one Lib Dem policy as the main issue of each day, requiring discipline from Charles Kennedy to stick to chosen messages in interviews and press conferences. Indeed, the entire campaign was a considerable test for the still inexperienced leader. His day would begin at 6.45 a.m. with a strategy meeting at Cowley Street, a briefing at Local Government House at 7.30 a.m. for panellists and a morning press conference at 8 a.m., with media interviews afterwards. Eschewing experiments with modern campaigning, the Lib Dems stuck to a traditional leader's battlebus tour, a concept introduced by David Steel in the 1979 election, although Kennedy first tended to fly by chartered aircraft to a regional airport from where he would make his onward journey by battlebus. He would make two such visits daily, to hospitals, schools, police stations, or any venue matching the day's policy theme. The aim was to feature on regional television news programmes in two different areas that night. After evenings spent giving media interviews or addressing rallies, the itinerary included a 10.30 p.m. briefing at Cowley Street with Tim Razzall, Chris Rennard and Dick Newby, although this rarely happened; Kennedy preferred to unwind in an apartment booked for him for the duration, where Tim Razzall and Anna Werrin had similar arrangements.

The early morning press conferences, so timed to avoid clashing with similar events staged by Labour and the Conservatives, proved remarkably successful. By starting first, the Lib Dems often had their policy issue of the day broadcast verbatim on early television news bulletins. Jaded journalists covering the election tended to use the event as a warm-up before tackling William Hague and Tony Blair later on. Towards the end of the election, Kennedy's quick wit and bantering style generated a good-natured atmosphere with correspondents that helped his media coverage, given the Lib Dems' decision to make a virtue of their leader's straightforward manner and to use his image so extensively in campaign material. Following the example of David Owen in the 1987 election, Kennedy answered the inevitable question of whether he expected to win the election by responding, disarmingly, that he probably would not – hence his more realistic goals of more seats and more votes. The Lib Dems' vacuous campaign slogan, 'Real Chance for a Real Change', tried to capture such frankness with its double emphasis on a real or genuine appeal. Deliberately, while he was out on the road, journalists were given direct access to Charles Kennedy, striking a contrast with the way Tony Blair and William Hague were often kept at arm's length from reporters.

The most peculiar aspect of the campaign was the political space ceded to Charles Kennedy by his opponents. Labour, as Tim Razzall had hoped, largely left the Lib Dems alone. The odd taunts, such as Gordon Brown theatrically reading out an improbably long list of Lib Dem spending pledges, were exceptions, not the rule. More curiously, the Conservatives also largely ignored the Liberal Democrats and concentrated their fire on Labour. Charles Kennedy had to do very little rebutting of attacks from rival parties and simply ploughed his own furrow. He emphasised throughout that he wished to conduct a positive campaign, and he put the Lib Dems' case in a reasonable tone and skilfully engaging manner that was quietly effective. He made the case for tax rises to fund public services by saying 'you can't get something for nothing'. He would refer to figures supplied by the party, putting a cost to every manifesto commitment, and say 'what you see is what you get'.

Kennedy was fortunate that, unlike in the elections of 1983, 1987 and 1992, there was no expectation of a hung Parliament and therefore no serious or concerted examination of the Lib Dems' negotiating position in the event of coalition talks. Indeed, he repeatedly pointed to the Lib Dems' role in coalitions running both Scotland and Wales as a means of bolstering the party's credibility, with little or no fear this would lead to distracting questions about coalitions at Westminster. The biggest drama was not political at all. One morning, just after Kennedy's aircraft took off from London City Airport for a school visit in north Norfolk, it was hit by a fearsome gust of wind. The 46-seat plane, an ATR 42, dropped suddenly and sharply, sending trays of breakfast snacks and coffee crashing upwards and then down before the aircraft stabilised. It could have been far, far worse. Three weeks from polling day Charles Kennedy began to style the Lib Dems the 'effective opposition'. This ended the Ashdown approach of constructive opposition and prepared the ground for the new parliament by challenging the Conservatives for the role of holding a re-elected Labour government to account. At first Charles Kennedy, in an interview with *The Times*,[9] used the phrase 'moral opposition'; this was hastily adapted to avoid sounding sanctimonious, and the term 'effective opposition' stuck.

Never a physically robust man, Kennedy found his gruelling schedule extremely tiring as the campaign went on. The pressure of such close contact with journalists throughout the day, which Chris Rennard and others encouraged, was particularly demanding on a shy, private man. He would frequently catnap on his battlebus, although his smaller backup bus did not have private quarters at the rear where he could sleep or unwind. He was also nervous about the result in his own seat, which he was able to visit only at weekends. Chris Rennard sent Candy Piercy, one of his experienced campaign officers, to Ross, Skye & Inverness West, to organise Kennedy's constituency campaign and put his mind at rest. Several times Sarah Gurling spent days on the road with Kennedy to provide support and company. At intervals Murdo Macdonald, his best friend from university, joined him on his battlebus to keep him company, tell jokes and help him relax. The importance of such support to Kennedy was affirmed in his own submission to the party's internal election report. This was a practical and logistical analysis to aid preparations for future campaigns, not a political or strategic commentary, and so by its nature his contribution dealt with humdrum details. Nonetheless, his candid reflections on how he coped with the greatest political test of his life had a plaintive quality to them, giving a rare glimpse of the inner man:

> Given the intense focus on the leader individually as the campaign progresses, it is vital

that the tour accommodates the personality and whims of the person in that role; equally, that the personnel in the most immediate and politically sensitive contact with the leader are those with whom he or she is most comfortable.[10]

Several times in this report he referred to his mounting fatigue and to the need for future itineraries to allow for more private rest time in comfortable surroundings, and for an hour or two at the end of each day to enable him to watch the television news and get an overview of the election campaign:

> As the campaign wears on, it becomes increasingly important for the travel time to be dead time in between stops; additional off the record briefings can be extremely tiring and that's where the gaffes can most easily occur. Generally, we all pushed ourselves to the physical limits and perhaps beyond on the tour.

He concluded: 'My final – wholly – self-serving thought is that the leader will always turn in a better performance if allowed to reside at home.'

Given Charles Kennedy's exhaustion, it was a tribute to his determination that he navigated the final stages of the campaign still sticking to his messages of the day and without significant errors. The Lib Dems' poll ratings remained static during the election's opening exchanges, as William Hague stole a march on Labour with a rapid and well-executed launch of his manifesto. But the Tory campaign, focusing on the core issues of saving the pound, immigration and tax cuts, imploded once Hague's headline figure for £8 billion of tax cuts was extrapolated to £20 billion by his junior Treasury spokesman, Oliver Letwin. Meanwhile Tony Blair, after an uncertain start during which a woman angry at her partner's hospital care harangued him, retained his commanding lead in the polls and began to campaign on a pledge to reform public services. As polling day neared a handful of Conservative-inclined commentators launched attacks on the Liberal Democrats as their position strengthened but it was too late for them to have an impact. Charles Kennedy increased his share of the vote to 18.8 per cent. He gained seven seats from the Conservatives, lost two back, and took one from Labour, raising his tally of MPs to fifty-two. Chesterfield, the sole gain from Labour, was targeted by Chris Rennard with the aim of securing at least one Lib Dem MP in every region. This aim was to encourage a 'cluster' effect whereby one Lib Dem victory would make it easier to gain a foothold in nearby constituencies. In another milestone, the party held all seven seats where Lib Dem MPs retired or stood down. Rapidly the notion entered Lib

Dem folklore that the two MPs who lost their seats had ignored Rennard's textbook approach to constituency campaigning: Jackie Ballard, who lost in Taunton, by disregarding advice to circulate regular leaflets highlighting her local work in the constituency, and Peter Brand, who was defeated in the Isle of Wight, for gratuitously introducing controversial issues in his campaign literature. On the back page of Peter Brand's final election newsletter was a column setting out his liberal views on capital punishment, abortion, euthanasia and fox-hunting. A typical Lib Dem leaflet would have appealed for tactical voting by Labour supporters. Horrified, Chris Rennard suggested on seeing the newsletter that Peter Brand pulp the whole 40,000 print run, and offered to pay for a replacement from central funds, but he was rebuffed. The effect was to strengthen considerably Chris Rennard's grip on the Liberal Democrats' campaigning culture. Elsewhere the most notable feature of the results was how little changed. Tony Blair won a second landslide victory with a barely reduced Commons majority of 167; the Conservatives made just one net gain, prompting William Hague's immediate resignation.

The outcome of the election was greeted among senior Liberal Democrats with a profound sense of relief. For one thing, pundits' expectations that the party would lose ground following its gains in 1997 were proved wrong. The party continued to advance. For another, it illustrated that the Lib Dems could continue to be successful under Charles Kennedy, their reluctant leader. Indeed, the polls again demonstrated the electoral appeal of this unusually self-deprecating politician. Kennedy himself drew self-confidence from what was, in Liberal Democrat terms, a successful election. He subsequently began to exert his wishes at weekly meetings of his shadow cabinet and parliamentary party. There were fourteen new MPs, some who had gained seats and others who had replaced retiring Lib Dem MPs; this tilted the balance in the parliamentary party in Kennedy's favour. Although his self-doubt had not left him, he had proved his abilities as leader both to his party and to himself.

A new parliament gave Charles Kennedy and his small leadership team the chance to make fundamental changes in policy and strategy. In the months before the election, he had sketched out plans for a review of policy covering public services, particularly health and education, to reconsider whether the Lib Dems' position of calling for higher government spending would be viable after another four years. This would put into the melting pot the totemic Lib Dem policy of proposing an extra penny on income tax to raise money for education, a centrepiece of party manifestos since 1992. To drop it would allow Charles Kennedy to make a decisive break with the past, especially as the National Health Service was becoming the more important focus of political debate. This argument was captured by Julian Ingram, the party's market research adviser, who in his own submission to the Lib Dems' internal post-election report, noted: '1p for education has worked well but now looks tired compared to the money Labour has and will invest in education.'

In the final stages of the election campaign, as Labour's victory appeared certain, Tony Blair had laid emphasis on reform of public services, including greater use of the private sector in service delivery, and triggered protests from trade unions and the left. This ideological divide was mirrored within the Liberal Democrats with a very small number, led by Mark Oaten, pressing for the party to adopt a more economically liberal approach to the private sector and choice in public services. This was resisted by the great majority of Lib Dem activists, among whom social liberalism had held sway for a generation and whose views were represented most vigorously at Westminster by Steve Webb and Evan Harris, a former junior doctor whom Kennedy promoted after the election to the key post of health spokesman. Sensing these tensions, and the likely policy direction of the re-elected Labour government, Kennedy opted for a big policy review chaired by Chris Huhne to channel and control such internal policy debate. Chris Huhne, an ambitious Lib Dem MEP, had been a parliamentary candidate for the SDP in the 1983 and 1987 elections. He then concentrated on a career in journalism and the City, telling friends in the party he would return to politics only when the Lib Dems were sufficiently established to have safe seats. The PR list system for European elections offered him just that and he was elected to the European Parliament in 1999. During his policy review he embarked on an extensive series of consultations with party members around the country, getting himself sufficiently well known in the process to establish a base for his campaign for the leadership of the party in 2006.

Still more important to Charles Kennedy in mapping out his plan for the new parliament was the future of the Joint Consultative Committee, the formal link of cooperation between Liberal Democrats and Labour ministers. On this issue, Kennedy again proved the value of his more subtle style of leadership. When he had become leader, this committee had been the chief focus of debate within the party: the subject of resignation threats, conference resolutions, indeed, the principal point of differentiation between the candidates in the leadership election. Less than two years on, it had ceased to become a matter of real contention. To get to this point Charles Kennedy did very little. He allowed it to meet and to explore future areas of work within the severe restrictions laid down by the party. He rarely talked about it to the media and he concentrated his attentions elsewhere. He let the JCC wither on the vine.

His new strategy of effective opposition, unveiled during the election campaign, clearly required independence from the government. In the weeks afterwards, Kennedy set about a series of careful consultations within the party about the future of the JCC. In mid-July, the fifty-two Lib Dem MPs were invited to a five-hour meeting in Methodist Central Hall, across Parliament Square, where the JCC was one of the chief items for discussion. There were calls from some, such as Phil Willis, to pull out and signal the end of collaboration with Labour. A number of those who had been involved in Paddy Ashdown's strategy of constructive opposition were more questioning. In typical Kennedy style, everyone was allowed to express a view, after which he concluded the discussion, thanked them for their thoughts and left no one the wiser as to where he himself stood. Privately, however, he had long ago resolved to end his party's involvement with the JCC unless Tony Blair made a sudden concession large enough to justify it carrying on. The question was how to do so in a manner that would not jeopardise a benign relationship with Labour that had worked manifestly in the Liberal Democrats' interest during the election. Dick Newby said:

> Charles always regarded it, I think, as a pointless exercise, but we had to find a way of demonstrating to ourselves whether it was a pointless exercise or not and so, as it were, give it a chance. But equally we had to find a way of withdrawing from it without being petulant.

With his post-election party conference approaching in the autumn, Charles Kennedy told Blair he wished to withdraw from the JCC and wanted its position resolved by then. Even at that late stage Tony Blair was loath to give up on his commitment to Lib–Lab cooperation and, after a series of negotiations, at Downing Street's request it was agreed that the JCC be suspended, not wound up. This was finally announced, after a delay, in a mutually respectful joint statement by Blair and Kennedy, saying:

> We both believe that the committee has done useful work and it remains available to resume its work if further constitutional items become ready for discussion. We both remain committed to constructive parliamentary dialogue and will continue to

undertake joint work on specific issues where appropriate.[11]

There was an attempt by the Conservatives to portray this as an equivocal position by the Liberal Democrats, but the statement was largely recognised for what it was: the end of formal links with the government. Dick Newby said: 'We agreed with this compromise because that is what they wanted and the form of words made it absolutely clear it in reality that there was nothing doing.'

In the event, the planned announcement coincided with the terrorist attacks of 11 September in America and no longer seemed to matter. The following week, in his conference speech, there was a slightly awkward moment when Kennedy drew a ragged cheer from some delegates as he referred to the suspension of the JCC and then proceeded to praise its work. The activists knew it would never be revived. Charles Kennedy had cleared the decks of the final vestige of his predecessor's strategy, and did so with a subtlety and skill that was underappreciated. While Tony Blair's popularity remained high, Kennedy ensured that the Lib Dems continued to benefit from tactical voting by Labour supporters. Yet already there were signs that the electoral appeal of Blair and his government was faltering. Kennedy ensured that the Lib Dems were positioned to reap the benefits rather than suffer damage by association. With a mandate of his own from the electorate, a bigger parliamentary party and an independent political base, he had laid the groundwork to pursue a strategy of his own. Having reached this point, it was never quite clear what Charles Kennedy's alternative vision was. In part, this was because international events rapidly intervened. There was a downside, too, in his style of leadership of wishing to keep strategic options open and trying not to commit himself when conditions might change due to events beyond his control. The result was a lack of clarity that drifted like a cloud over the remainder of his leadership, sometimes thinning to allow a clearer vista of what lay beyond, yet at other moments massing thick and dense to obscure any view.

It had been an important, and successful, year for Charles Kennedy. Over the Christmas recess, at his croft in Fort William, he sealed his journey towards becoming a happier, more self-assured politician by asking Sarah Gurling to be his wife. Three weeks later, announcing their engagement to the press, he revealed coyly that he went on bended knee to do so. 'I'm a traditionalist,' he explained.[12] They married in July 2002 at the Chapel of St Mary Undercroft, in the crypt beneath the House of Commons, with a congregation of 150, which to the couple's delight included Tony and Cherie Blair. Kennedy, wearing a lounge suit with a thistle in his buttonhole entwined with an English rose, chose Tim Razzall as his best man. It was a traditional order of service, with hymns including 'Praise, my soul, the King of Heaven' and 'I vow to thee, my country', but made ecumenical by the presence of a Catholic priest, Father Michael Seed, who assisted in blessing the marriage. Dick Newby's wife Ailsa, an Anglican vicar, gave the address and James Gurling read the first lesson, from the Sermon on the Mount in Matthew, chapter 5, verses 1–10: 'Blessed are the meek; for they shall inherit the earth.' The second reading, by Charles Kennedy's sister Isabel, was of Shakespeare's sonnet 'Shall I compare thee to a summer's day?'. A lone piper played the 'Skye Boat Song' and, as guests left the chapel, Ian Kennedy played his fiddle in Westminster Hall as they made their way to the wedding breakfast in the Members' Dining Room, where they ate chilled asparagus with champagne vinaigrette, traditional roast leg of lamb and chilled pear soufflé.

By this stage, criticism of Kennedy's leadership had quietened to such a degree that his office overlooked the formality of his re-election for the new parliament. The party's constitution required a ballot for the post of leader to be called by the first anniversary of a general election, a procedure spared only if the leader was a member of the government. His staff found out about this rule too late to complete the nomination procedure in time and Kennedy was re-elected unopposed in the summer of 2002 just after the one-year deadline. Tony Blair and Charles Kennedy remained committed to working together where it suited them, and continued to do so. By his nature, Kennedy preferred to pursue such contacts with meetings, telephone calls or liaison by staff when the need arose, rather than through a formal structure such as the JCC. He would see or talk to Blair at the request of either side and their relationship remained friendly, although Blair grew increasingly irritated by the Liberal Democrats' policies. Several times he and Kennedy had sharp exchanges in the Commons as Tony Blair attacked the Lib Dems' spending commitments as unrealistic, and expressed mounting impatience with their opposition to student tuition fees and their refusal to embrace reform of working practices in the public services.[13]

A tentative dialogue was explored by political emissaries of both to see what scope remained for working together with the aim of isolating the Conservatives, now led firmly from the party's right wing by Iain Duncan Smith. Discreet dinners were held in a private room at the Marriott Hotel in

County Hall, across the River Thames from Westminster. Blair was represented by Sally Morgan, Charles Clarke, the chairman of the Labour Party, and his general secretary, David Triesman; from the Lib Dem side were Tim Razzall, Dick Newby and Anna Werrin. Much of their discussions was on policy. With the Conservatives having ended the convention of the official opposition offering bipartisan support on Northern Ireland policy, for instance, they talked about how the Liberal Democrats could work in cooperation with the government. Charles Clarke and David Triesman also met Tim Razzall and Chris Rennard for hearty breakfasts at the Cinnamon Club, a fashionable Indian restaurant at Westminster. They discussed issues such as changes to election law and state funding of political parties, although the tenor of these meetings was different as Charles Clarke wanted to seek cross-party agreement on such issues, including if possible with the Conservatives. Such contacts fizzled out once Charles Clarke left the post of Labour Party chairman the following year. By then, however, a new issue was emerging that would pitch Tony Blair and Charles Kennedy onto opposing sides as British foreign policy edged towards its most controversial episode since the Suez crisis in 1956, and the United States prepared to invade Iraq.

7

Against the war

On the afternoon of 11 September 2001, Charles Kennedy was sitting in his Commons office with the television flickering from a wall mounting as events began to unfold in America that would dominate British politics for years to come. Kennedy happened to have with him Paul Keetch, his defence spokesman and one of the Lib Dem MPs he was closest to. Together they watched as the twin towers of the World Trade Centre in New York, having been struck by hijacked passenger aeroplanes, burned and then collapsed. From the outset it was clear very many people would have died in a terrorist attack unprecedented in its savagery. This was underlined as a third hijacked aircraft was flown into the Pentagon and a fourth crashed in a field in Pennsylvania.

Having spent a happy year in Indiana as a postgraduate student, and having cut his political teeth defending NATO in the SDP, Charles Kennedy had a broadly Atlanticist outlook. Although rapidly there were calls in the United States for a military response against the perpetrators, Kennedy's instincts were to offer support to the Americans. Paul Keetch, who took a certain macho pride in representing Hereford, the garrison town of the SAS, was robust in the advice he offered Charles Kennedy. In one statement the following day, Paul Keetch said: 'All terrorists, of whatever origin, share in the guilt of those who perpetrated these terrible acts.'[1] With Menzies Campbell, the foreign affairs spokesman, away in Australia and unable to contribute to developing the party's response, the initial position of the Liberal Democrats was surprisingly firm. Three days later, as Britain was still numb with shock from the graphic media coverage of the terrorist attacks and the scale of death and injury, Tony Blair asked for Parliament to be recalled. The evening beforehand, as Lib Dem MPs reassembled at the

Commons for their first parliamentary party meeting since the attacks, the first signs of unease at the party's initial stance began to emerge. Alistair Carmichael, who had been elected less than three months earlier as MP for Orkney & Shetland, voiced concern that declaring war on terrorism was too simplistic a response. He was followed by several others who expressed similar doubts.

When the Commons met at 9.30 the next morning, it was a sombre, but remarkably prescient occasion. The Prime Minister declared in a statement, as he had from the outset, that he would stand by the American government and people in their time of need; the terrorists responsible had made themselves the enemies of the entire civilised world. He concluded his statement with a little-noticed but profoundly important observation, reflecting a fear he had long held:

> We know that they would, if they could, go further and use chemical, biological or even nuclear weapons of mass destruction. We know, also, that there are groups of people, occasionally states, who will trade the technology and capability of such weapons. It is time that this trade was exposed, disrupted and stamped out. We have been warned by the events of 11 September, and we should act on the warning.[2]

The recalled sitting marked the first Commons performance of Iain Duncan Smith as leader of the Conservative Party; his election had been due to be announced on 11 September itself, but was delayed by a day in a mark of respect. As a former guards officer, whose father had been an RAF war hero, Iain Duncan Smith felt his duty lay in putting Britain's national interest ahead of party politics. He offered Tony Blair unequivocal backing in supporting Britain's closest ally:

> Over the coming days and weeks, there may be some who counsel caution over the full measure of support that the Prime Minister has already declared. By contrast, I assure him that he will have our total backing throughout in maintaining his position of unflinching support for the United States in its search for the perpetrators and its subsequent actions.

Very unusually, the official opposition had promised the government full backing throughout, provided it held fast to its position. It would be difficult to overstate how profoundly the terrorist attacks of 11 September affected British public opinion; Iain Duncan Smith caught the national mood on the day itself. Unwisely, he had committed himself to a similar position in future, too. Charles Kennedy's response was not markedly different but, tentatively, he asked more questions, including about the role of the United Nations, and gave no commitment over his future response. Kennedy asked:

> It seems almost inevitable that there will be some sort of military response at some point, although at the moment we do not know where, when, or against whom. Will the Prime Minister confirm that he does not rule out a further recall of Parliament, especially if, as I imagine they will be, British service people are to be involved in such action? An American writer once observed that the terrorist attempts to wash an impure world clean with the blood of innocent victims. The impurity here is the dreadful deed of the terrorist. On that, this House stands shoulder to shoulder in full support of our American cousins.[3]

Menzies Campbell, the Lib Dems' distinguished foreign affairs spokesman, who had just returned from Australia, struck a slightly different tone in the debate that followed. He observed that terrorism would be more easily put down when its causes were understood. He, too, offered support for America and noted that NATO had, for the first time, invoked Article 5 of its founding treaty permitting self-defence after an armed attack. Crucially, he added: 'But this is a sovereign House of Parliament and . . . cannot give a blank cheque for military action. NATO operates by consensus.'[4]

Ten days later the Liberal Democrats were due to hold their annual conference in Bournemouth. Such was the continuing public mood of shock, anger and incomprehension that questions were raised as to whether it was appropriate for the conference to go ahead at all. Kennedy himself was very nervous about doing so. Of course, it did meet but, as with so many of Kennedy's early conferences, it was darkened by the shadow of external events. The terrorist attacks of 11 September were by now attributed to Osama bin Laden and his al-Qaeda terrorist network, which operated training camps in Afghanistan under the protection of its Islamic fundamentalist Taliban regime. The United Nations Security Council had already given authority for 'all necessary steps' in response and America was seeking allies for a military attack to overthrow the Taliban in Afghanistan. Charles Kennedy had been briefed extensively by Tony Blair on his reasons for supporting President Bush and on the opening Sunday of the conference held a lengthy meeting of his MPs in a gloomy atrium at the Highcliffe Hotel in Bournemouth. Kennedy and Menzies Campbell endorsed action against the Taliban while a small but vocal group, including Jenny Tonge, Steve Webb, Alistair Carmichael, Richard Younger-Ross and Richard Allen, voiced doubts about the wisdom of such a military response. Kennedy, conscious that the Liberal Democrats bore a heavy responsibility as the first political party to debate the emerging war on terrorism, was determined to keep his MPs broadly committed to the same course of action and prevent any from making intemperate public comments. Dick Newby observed:

> The party could have split three ways with the pro, anti and abstainers: there was history of this in the Liberals. Charles was absolutely determined to get everybody on board. People were concerned that we did establish a bit of distinctiveness from the Americans. It was much more difficult to get unanimity on Afghanistan than it was on Iraq. There was just a wider variety of view.

Kennedy did this by qualifying his initial stance, offering support to America but conditionally, and reserving the right to criticise if the need arose. In an emergency statement to his conference the following morning, Kennedy made a careful criticism of the martial language used by President Bush, saying: 'War is not the word, nor crusade.' He tempered his previous declaration of standing shoulder to shoulder with America, and picked up Menzies Campbell's phrase of 'no blank cheques'. He told the conference: 'That's where the candid friend comes in: standing shoulder to shoulder, but always there for the occasional cautionary tap on the shoulder . . . There are no blank cheques to be issued.' The conference approved a motion endorsing a military response, provided it was precise, proportionate and consistent with international law. Those with doubts were allowed their say in the debate and most held to the more cautious line agreed; Jenny Tonge, who held an important post as international development spokesman, came closest to breaking ranks by declaring: 'We must bomb this area, but we must bomb it with food and aid. It's cheaper than military action and may win over a lot more hearts and minds.'

The conference was relatively successful. The Liberal Democrats were largely insignificant to a massive diplomatic and military effort generated from Washington, which Tony Blair was doing his best to influence through private channels to President Bush while maintaining total support in public.[5] Yet at least in the context of British discussions of these events, Iain Duncan Smith's position of total backing had given Charles Kennedy an

An MP at 23: a victorious Charles Kennedy is chaired from the 1983 election count in Dingwall by George Burness (*left*) and John Farquhar Munro. (*Press and Journal*, Aberdeen)

A besuited Kennedy *(front row, extreme left)* with fellow Glasgow University students before women were admitted to the union. (*Glasgow Herald*)

'Chat Show Charlie': appearing on an edition of *Celebrity Countdown* with Edwina Currie *(second left)* and the hosts, Richard Whiteley and Carol Vorderman. (Channel 4 Television)

Urging SDP members to merge with the Liberals at a conference in Sheffield in 1988. (Times Newspapers Ltd)

An overweight Kennedy speaking at a Liberal Democrat conference in 1994.
(Times Newspapers Ltd)

With Tim Razzall, his chief adviser, whose influence came to be resented.
(Times Newspapers Ltd)

With Tony Blair. 'I like Charles,' Blair told one Labour Party conference.
(Times Newspapers Ltd)

Without a despatch box, Kennedy found addressing the Commons difficult.
(PA/Empics)

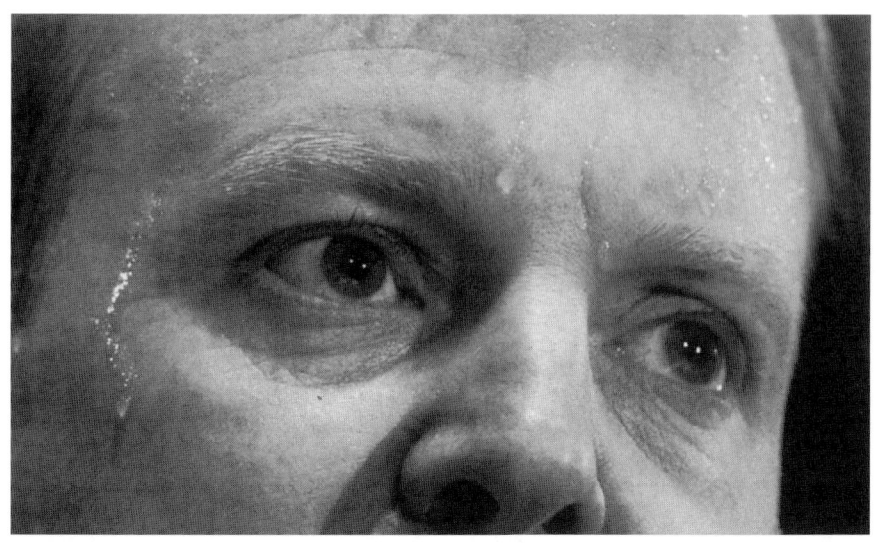

Perspiring and clearly unwell, addressing the Liberal Democrat spring conference at Southport in 2004. (Phil Noble/PA/Empics)

Giving his statement at Cowley Street in January 2006 in which he admitted to a drink problem. (Times Newspapers Ltd)

Enjoying Highland traditions at the Glen Finnan Highland Gathering.
(Credit: Conn O'Neill.)

Kennedy with David Owen, Russell Johnston and others in the late 1980s when merger talks were rife. (Credit: Highland Press.)

Kennedy the Highland Man at Mallaig Harbour. (Credit: Conn O'Neill.)

opportunity to strike a distinctive role. Unlike Paddy Ashdown, or indeed David Owen, Kennedy was not naturally comfortable offering a commentary on military diplomacy or strategy. He needed advice. He could, of course, have turned to Ashdown himself. Owing to his lesser-known background in intelligence Paddy Ashdown, who was now in the Lords, had contacts among dissident Afghans and mujahedeen fighters, whom he put in touch with MI6 as potential allies against the Taliban. He even invited two of them to the Highcliffe Hotel in Bournemouth during the party conference, where he introduced them to Menzies Campbell over coffee. Perhaps understandably, Kennedy preferred to avoid a perception of being in his predecessor's shadow and did not seek Ashdown's counsel. Indeed, he issued instructions to the party's press office that Paddy Ashdown should not discuss the likely military intervention in Afghanistan on national media outlets and should be confined to the local media. Ashdown spoke strongly in favour of the Afghan campaign in subsequent parliamentary party meetings attended by both peers and MPs, and made two speeches in the Lords expounding his view, but did so from the back benches.

Instead Charles Kennedy turned for military advice to a figure who was to become central to his policy stance over the next eighteen months. Tim Garden was a retired air marshal who, on leaving the RAF, became director of the Royal Institute of International Affairs at Chatham House, the foreign affairs think tank. There he got to know John Roper, the Lib Dems' chief whip in the Lords, who asked him to help with the party's work on foreign and defence policy for the Joint Consultative Committee. Having done so, Tim Garden was invited to join a working group updating Liberal Democrat defence policy; he became a member of the party and worked closely with Paul Keetch, the defence spokesman. As Charles Kennedy put together a small war cabinet to offer him policy advice on the Afghan campaign, Tim Garden was asked to be a member. The group, comprising Menzies Campbell, Paul Keetch, Shirley Williams, William Wallace, John Roper and Kennedy's own staff and researchers, met weekly in his Commons office. Having decided at the outset to offer cautious support, while reserving the right to question and criticise if necessary, the judgements were not particularly controversial. The bombing, which began on 7 October, had United Nations authority, Tony Blair took care to keep Kennedy informed of events, the British contribution to the fighting capacity in Afghanistan was relatively small and the Taliban regime collapsed in the second week of November. The Liberal Democrats placed emphasis on the need for humanitarian relief and post-conflict reconstruction of Afghanistan, but were able to support the military action without significant dissension. Charles Kennedy rose to the challenge. More importantly he had found a style of working he was comfortable with, using a small circle of advisers meeting regularly to offer expert advice that formed the basis for developing his position throughout the Iraq conflict.

The foreign affairs response to 11 September formed only one of the political repercussions. Another was a move by the government to put in place sweeping new counter-terrorism legislation aimed at curbing the deadly threat posed by violent Islamic extremism. As he had in building the case for military action, Tony Blair tried to proceed on a basis of cross-party cooperation – he had little choice, given that the new anti-terrorism powers were to be rushed through Parliament within two months and he had no majority in the Lords. Again, this presented the Liberal Democrats with an opportunity to contribute to a national debate, this time in the field of civil liberties, an area where the party had an obvious locus. The government's proposals were extremely controversial, especially a power to detain indefinitely and without trial foreign terrorist suspects who could not be deported as they faced torture in their country of origin. They would, however, remain free to leave the country. In order to appease mainstream British Muslims, a separate offence of incitement to religious hatred was tacked onto the Bill, sitting uncomfortably with emergency legislation to deal with terrorism. The Conservatives, represented by Oliver Letwin, now their home affairs spokesman, opted to work closely with the Liberal Democrats in scrutinising the Bill in both the Commons and the Lords, often tabling joint amendments with Simon Hughes, who led for the Lib Dems. They extracted substantial concessions from the government, time-limiting the most contentious new power of detention without trial – which three years on was struck down by the law lords – and forcing ministers to withdraw their attempt to outlaw incitement to religious hatred after repeated defeats in the Lords. Much later, in the final months of the parliament, ministers tried to replace the provision of detention without trial with a form of house arrest known as a control order. Then the Liberal Democrats opted for a more autonomous style of opposition of looser coordination with the Conservatives that was probably closer to Charles Kennedy's instincts. But the mature scrutiny of the counter-terrorism legislation was another illustration of the Lib Dems finding their feet as an independent opposition.

The most unexpected outcome for Charles Kennedy of the events of autumn 2001 was that he acquired a fifty-third Lib Dem MP. Within months of being re-elected as Labour MP for Shrewsbury & Atcham, Paul Marsden had been in excitable negotiations with Liberal Democrat MPs representing nearby constituencies about defecting to their party. His motivation was complex and as much personal as political. He had been in dispute with Labour Party whips after his wife was injured in a car accident. He then emerged as a vocal critic on Labour's back benches of the bombing of Afghanistan, making clumsy attempts to demand a vote on the military action.[6] Paul Marsden was summoned to see the government chief whip, Hilary Armstrong. In a highly provocative, indeed unprecedented, move he responded by passing his account of the meeting to a Sunday newspaper, portraying his chief whip as slow witted and authoritarian.[7] This was bizarre behaviour. During the passage of the government's anti-terrorism legislation, Marsden again clashed with his party's whips and protested to Tony Blair and the Commons Speaker, Michael Martin, that Labour whips had threatened and assaulted him. Again, a detailed account from Paul Marsden appeared in the Sunday press.[8] During this period of trauma Marsden was befriended by several Lib Dem MP in conversations over drinks in the Strangers' Bar of the Commons, notably Lembit Öpik, Paul Keetch and Matthew Green. He returned to Paul Keetch's flat in south London for several discussions into the night about the possibility of defecting. Mark Oaten, now chairman of the parliamentary party, was summoned more than once to answer Paul Marsden's nocturnal questions and listen to him agonising aloud, but none of these meetings bore fruit. As his estrangement from the Labour Party began to be played out in public, Hilary Armstrong wrote Paul Marsden a letter, rapidly publicised, informing him that he was the subject of an inquiry. She summoned him to a meeting on 10 December at which she would seek an undertaking that he would follow the code of conduct of the Parliamentary Labour Party.

This proved to be Paul Marsden's cue to jump ship. After further contact with Lembit Öpik he was introduced to Charles Kennedy, who invited Marsden to his flat for a preliminary discussion. The details of his defection were sealed largely in Kennedy's absence at another meeting in his flat on a Friday evening, three days before Marsden was due to see the government chief whip. Tim Razzall, Anna Werrin and Jackie Rowley, who had joined the leader's office as press secretary, conducted the talks with Paul Marsden. Kennedy himself was attending an annual Liberal Democrats dinner in

Winchester, the constituency of his friend Mark Oaten, and by the time he returned by train the terms were settled. Four years later Paul Marsden published an account of the evening, saying he and Kennedy stayed up until midnight drinking;[9] in fact, the others present desperately wanted him to go home so they could go to bed. Eventually Marsden was offered a makeshift bed on the sofa, where he spent the night.

Although Charles Kennedy's inner circle were excited at landing their first defector, the announcement the following Monday that Paul Marsden was to cross the floor of the Commons was not seen as the coup they thought it was. He had pretty much burnt his boats with the Labour Party through his erratic behaviour. Nor was this an obvious act of principle. The policy issue with which Marsden was most associated was his vocal opposition to the bombing of Afghanistan, a campaign the Liberal Democrats had supported. This risked giving the impression that the Lib Dems were simply a depository for people wishing to register a protest. Over the weekend, with the plans for his defection already sealed, Simon Hughes suggested that Marsden should sit as an independent MP. Two days after his defection, Menzies Campbell found himself on his feet in the Commons speaking in a debate on international terrorism. Pointedly, Campbell began with the wry observation: 'In the light of recent domestic political events, it would be right for me to restate once again Liberal Democrat support for government policy since 11 September.'[10] There was some discussion within the parliamentary party over the procedure for deciding to accept a defector. But, on precedents such as that of Emma Nicholson, whom Paddy Ashdown brought over from the Conservatives in 1995, MPs accepted that the decision lay with the leader. Marsden's subsequent decision to rejoin Labour on the eve of the 2005 election, having stood down from the Commons, appeared to confirm the folly of embracing a defector in such circumstances. On the same day he defected to the Lib Dems, a group of former Conservatives also joined the party. They were led by John Stevens and Brendan Donnelly, both ex-MEPs disillusioned with the increasingly Eurosceptic tone struck by successive Tory leaders, and had unsuccessfully formed the Pro-Euro Conservative Party for the 1999 European elections.

During the opening months of 2002 a far more difficult development in foreign policy began to take shape as President Bush turned his sights on Iraq. The prospect of American military action against Iraq had been discussed in Washington within days of the 11 September terrorist attacks and the decision by President Bush to focus initially on Afghanistan had been greeted by much relief. In reality, plans for an attack on Iraq had simply been put into abeyance and were revived by George Bush in his State of the Union address in January 2002, when he identified North Korea, Iran and Iraq as part of an 'axis of evil' threatening the peace of the world. Iraq, under its brutal President, Saddam Hussein, was in breach of a host of outstanding United Nations resolutions dating back to the Gulf war of 1990–1, had expelled UN weapons inspectors in 1998 and was subjected to restrictive trade sanctions. Following the overthrow of the Taliban from Afghanistan, President Bush began to articulate a new national security policy of pre-emption, of identifying and taking action against future threats to America's security even before these were fully realised. After a meeting between George Bush and Tony Blair at the President's ranch in Crawford, Texas in April, Bush stated explicitly that his aim was the removal of Saddam Hussein from power. As Bush talked simply of a policy of achieving regime change in Iraq, Blair began making a more complicated case for action against Saddam based on Iraq's potential possession of illegal weapons of mass destruction: chemical, biological or even nuclear weapons.

Large sections of British public opinion were at once appalled and bemused by the prospect of invading Iraq. Unlike Afghanistan, whose regime had harboured training camps for al-Qaeda, the terrorist network responsible for the 11 September attacks, there was no proven link between Saddam Hussein and Islamic terrorism. Under Iain Duncan Smith, who had contacts among neo-conservatives in Washington, the Tories were enthusiastic in advocating military intervention against Iraq. Despite having supported the Afghan campaign, the notion of such an invasion of Iraq presented political difficulties for the Liberal Democrats. Under Charles Kennedy the party had pursued an undeclared strategy of 'two against one', by siding with Labour on big issues against the Conservatives. To break ranks with the government over Iraq implied a new strategy which carried greater risks. Moreover, by its nature, part of Tony Blair's developing case that Britain should stand ready to support any American invasion of Iraq was based on secret intelligence material. Charles Kennedy was being invited to support a policy on the basis of evidence he could not share. Twice Kennedy was given confidential briefings by John Scarlett, then chairman of Whitehall's joint intelligence committee, on assessments of Iraq's illegal weapons. He remained sceptical. Dick Newby observed:

> I think he thought John Scarlett didn't tell him anything he hadn't read in the papers,

because, of course, it is a great way of sucking somebody in – you know, meeting with John Scarlett on Privy Council terms in the Cabinet Office, you can't bring anybody with you. He was never taken in by all that sort of flummery and status.

Charles and Sarah Kennedy were away on their honeymoon in Malaysia for much of the summer of 2002 as media speculation, particularly in the United States, hardened about the likelihood of war with Iraq. Menzies Campbell, left to determine the Lib Dems' response, was alerted by diplomatic and military contacts to the doubts within Whitehall about the course of action taken by Blair and adopted a fairly challenging tone on behalf of the Lib Dems. On his return, Kennedy had a telephone conversation with Tony Blair who seemed to be anxious to damp down the media speculation about military action. 'Charles was saying: "You can't be serious about military action,"' Dick Newby said. 'And Blair said: "Oh don't worry, there has been an awful lot of talk over the summer but George and I are going to calm it all down now."'

What Blair had done, particularly at a meeting at the President's retreat at Camp David in early September, was to persuade George Bush to go to the UN Security Council to get a new resolution requiring Iraq to comply with its outstanding obligations.[11] Ten days later Saddam announced he would allow UN weapons inspectors to return to Iraq, in an attempt to divide the international community. They did so in November. When the Liberal Democrats gathered in Brighton for their annual conference in late September, it was again destined to be eclipsed by events elsewhere. Tony Blair bowed to cross-party pressure and requested the recall of Parliament, to allow MPs to see and debate a summary of intelligence evidence on the threat posed by Iraq's weapons of mass destruction. A copy of the dossier was sent by courier to Brighton, where under police Special Branch rules it had to be handed to Charles Kennedy personally. He withdrew to his suite at the Metropole Hotel to concentrate on preparing his remarks for the Commons. Later the dossier became the focus of a prolonged political debate over allegations that intelligence chiefs were put under political pressure to 'sex up' its presentation to give it maximum impact. At the time the document still had a certain aura attached to it due to the unprecedented decision to publish a summary of secret intelligence material, although again Kennedy told advisers the dossier did not contain anything he had not seen before. The following morning Lib Dem parliamentarians crowded onto commuter trains at Brighton station to return to London for the special sitting of Parliament.

Tony Blair, in his opening statement to the Commons, was categorical. He told MPs the dossier showed that Iraq had chemical and biological weapons and its weapons of mass destruction programme was 'active, detailed and growing'.[12] But he added: 'No one wants military conflict. The whole purpose [is] a proper process of disarmament under the UN.' Iain Duncan Smith backed military action, and asked if a further UN resolution was actually needed. Again, Charles Kennedy struck a more questioning tone, emphasising the supremacy of the United Nations and saying from the outset that any military action must be preceded by a vote in the House of Commons. He criticised the doctrine of 'regime change' adopted by the Bush administration and raised a series of practical questions about what might happen in Iraq if there were to be military action. As he was about to conclude, beginning his sentence with 'finally . . .', he was met with ironical cheers from the Conservative benches, implying his contribution was overlong. Kennedy flashed back at them: 'I am only asking questions unasked by the leader of the Conservative Party.'

It was an important moment for Kennedy, demonstrating to the Commons his readiness to don the mantle of opposition on an issue where the Conservatives had aligned themselves so closely with government policy; it also boosted his self-confidence. In the full debate that followed Menzies Campbell, unwisely, took Blair at his word, saying at one point: 'If, as is eloquently demonstrated by the dossier and if, as we are entitled to assume, Saddam Hussein has chemical and biological weapons . . .'[13] But his speech was also notable for a telling exchange as Iain Duncan Smith took the unusual step of intervening during Campbell's remarks to accuse the Liberal Democrats of changing position on whether there were circumstances under which they would support military action. The substance of his allegation was of less interest than his wish to discredit the party that was tentatively adopting the guise of opposition in the space he had vacated. Once Kennedy and his MPs returned to Brighton, the Lib Dem conference passed a carefully worded motion calling on the government to participate in military action against Iraq only as a last resort and provided a list of conditions were met. These included a failure by Iraq to honour its offer to allow the return of UN weapons inspectors, clear and incontrovertible evidence that Iraq had the capacity to deliver weapons of mass destruction, and a full debate and vote in Parliament. It further required new UN resolutions giving a clear mandate or that military action was taken was in accordance with international law. On the final day of the conference, Charles Kennedy delivered probably his best such speech as leader, firmly committing himself to a new strategy of overtaking the Conservatives as the main opposition party in British politics. Kennedy told the conference: 'The prize is very great. There is no law which says when the Conservative Party is down it must come up again. And there is no law which says the Liberal Democrats need forever remain third amongst Britain's political parties.'

With Iraq now dominating political debate, Kennedy revived his small war cabinet from the Afghan campaign on his return to Westminster, calling meetings monthly from early autumn, then fortnightly and after that weekly. The membership grew slightly, with Andrew Stunell, his chief whip, attending, for example, and later Michael Moore, but the format was the same: a small expert team offering him analysis and advice, rather than taking decisions. Kennedy particularly valued the counsel of Tim Garden, who was able to give technical rather than political judgements but also had extensive military contacts. Tim Garden visited experts in weapons of mass destruction at NATO's headquarters in Brussels and was told they did not regard Iraq as a problem. He suggested to Charles Kennedy that he get a similar briefing from NATO. In following the discussions on Iraq on the international think-tank circuit, Tim Garden also found himself at conferences looking at planning for the aftermath of a military operation in Iraq, in further evidence of the commitment in Washington to removing Saddam. As the political stakes rose, and Kennedy and Menzies Campbell continued to question the case for war, they had expert opinion to reinforce their case. Tim Garden said:

> I saw my role as not being political at all, just trying to do the military analysis of the data as it came through. It was generally comforting to think there was a previously senior military officer, who had studied WMD and looked into it, saying what you are doing is right.

Menzies Campbell, an urbane Scottish advocate who had spoken on foreign affairs for the Lib Dems and Liberal Party since 1987 and doubled as defence spokesman for many years, was probably the party's most respected parliamentarian; he had proved an authoritative voice in questioning the need to change the previous policy of containment of Iraq via sanctions and no-fly zones. In early November he was diagnosed with non-Hodgkins lymphoma, a form of cancer, and returned to Scotland to begin a period of intensive treatment. He continued to contribute to the policy discussions on

Iraq, speaking frequently to Charles Kennedy by telephone, and he carried on giving broadcast interviews, thanks to an ISDN line in a small recording booth at his townhouse in Edinburgh. But he was away from the House of Commons for almost five months, placing still greater responsibility on Charles Kennedy in developing the party's response to what could be a fast-moving and challenging situation.

As Tony Blair had urged, George Bush did go to the United Nations to seek international support for action against Iraq. On 8 November, the UN Security Council passed unanimously a resolution calling on Iraq to comply with weapons inspections and setting a deadline for it to supply details of its weapons stocks. Resolution 1441, as it became known, threatened Iraq with 'serious consequences' if it failed to comply. There was room for doubt, however, as to whether its wording provided final authority for a military response if Saddam failed to comply, as the Americans had sought. Other permanent members of the security council, notably France and Russia, wanted a further vote explicitly authorising war should it come to that; the United States said merely that the Security Council should meet to discuss the weapons inspectors' reports. The government called a Commons debate on 25 November on a motion supporting Resolution 1441, and saying that if Iraq failed to comply 'the Security Council should meet in order to consider the situation'[14] – endorsing the looser American interpretation of what was agreed. Unusually, the Speaker chose not to select the opposition amendment routinely tabled by the Conservatives, who were supporting the government's position while urging still stronger ultimatums on Saddam. Instead the Speaker selected the Liberal Democrats' amendment, stating: 'Any decision that Iraq is in material breach of Resolution 1441 is for the UN Security Council as a whole to determine and no military action to enforce Resolution 1441 should be taken against Iraq without a mandate from the UN Security Council.'[15]

The amendment further called for a vote in the Commons before any British forces were committed to any such action. It was defeated over-whelmingly by the combined votes of most Labour and Tory MPs, although thirty-two Labour backbenchers rebelled against the government and voted with the Lib Dems to demand a second resolution before going to war. It was, however, another step for the Lib Dems as they established themselves as the voice of opposition to the war.

In Menzies Campbell's absence, the Lib Dem amendment was moved by Michael Moore, his deputy foreign affairs spokesman, who impressed colleagues by his self-possession as he was thrown in at the deep end. The Lib Dems were mindful of the risk of being cast as apologists for Saddam Hussein and he emphasised in his speech, as the Lib Dems did thereafter, that Saddam must indeed be disarmed, but through the United Nations: Michael Moore said:

> I always started with a strong condemnation of Saddam Hussein and the perils of him being allowed to continue to have WMD, followed through with the need for the UN to be given the time and resources to do a proper inspection. That was the consistent, and we reckoned pretty simple, message that developed through from that point.

Whereas Kennedy had asked his MPs to support military intervention in Afghanistan a year earlier, he was not now asking them to do anything other than endorse the authority of the United Nations. His parliamentary party meetings were passionate as MPs debated Iraq but not difficult. As he invariably did, he allowed everyone to have their say. His aim was to keep his party united, leave his options open, and decide – if he had to – at the last possible moment and with the maximum available evidence before him. As the government made a series of announcements between late December and early February about the mobilisation of a total of 40,000 British troops plus equipment to the Gulf, these were supported by the Liberal Democrats as necessary to enforce Saddam's compliance with weapons inspections. 'We did not oppose the military build-up, because to be credible about the need for Saddam to comply you had to have the backup if he didn't,' Michael Moore said.

Nonetheless Charles Kennedy was becoming increasingly associated with doubts being raised by a substantial proportion of the electorate over the case for war. At the first Prime Minister's Questions after the Christmas recess, he asked Tony Blair: 'If the UN weapons inspectorate does not produce concrete evidence of weapons of mass destruction, but the US nonetheless decides to go ahead with military conflict against Iraq, will Britain be involved?'[16] Blair replied that he would not speculate on circumstances that might arise. Thereafter, Charles Kennedy used every one of his opportunities at Prime Minister's Questions to press Blair about Iraq, often putting to him a variant of that same key question, until after the overthrow of Saddam in April.

These weekly exchanges became pivotal to Kennedy, as a chance to test Blair's case and to set out the Liberal Democrats' position. It remained a difficult forum for Charles Kennedy but, with many Labour MPs sharing his doubts, a subtle change occurred within the chamber itself. Each time he would rise to the barracking that greets any Liberal Democrat, but he developed a technique of beginning with 'On Iraq . . .' or 'Returning to Iraq . . .' and then pausing, which tended to quieten the House.[17] By this stage his war cabinet was meeting three times a week as his entire focus was on Iraq. Kennedy was always voracious in monitoring the news, whether by channel-hopping from one television bulletin or discussion programme to another, flicking through a full set of daily and Scottish newspapers or skim-reading local and free newspapers when out on the road. During this period he concentrated on little else. Visitors to his flat would find a television switched to Sky News in one room, a radio tuned to Radio 4 in another and Radio 5 Live playing in a third.

Still Kennedy had not committed himself to opposing the war; indeed, he was consciously avoiding doing so. Finally, he had to choose. The moment of decision was not a vote in Parliament but a demonstration against the war organised for 15 February by an alliance of far-left and radical Muslim groups, the Stop the War Coalition. The march through London and demonstration in Hyde Park presented Kennedy with a dilemma. He was not anti-war. As the motion passed by his party conference in the autumn made clear, he would support military action if approved by the UN and if there was evidence of illegal weapons programmes and intent to use them. Moreover, a question of credibility arose: should the Liberal Democrats associate with fringe elements whose agenda was very different from their own, and some of which bordered on anti-Semitism? As he always tended to, Kennedy put off a decision on whether to attend the march, but grassroots activists within his party tried to force his hand. On 21 January, meeting in a room in the Commons, the party's federal executive committee passed unanimously a motion that effectively sought to bounce their leader into attending. The motion, tabled by Susan Kramer, who was seeking renomination as the party's candidate for mayor of London, and James Graham, an activist, read:

> The executive . . . encourages Liberal Democrat members to voice their concerns about the Iraq situation, in particular by participating in the Stop the War demonstration on Saturday, 15 February; calls on the party to publicise this fact through the press, the party's e-mail and internet facilities and *Liberal Democrat News*; requests that the parliamentary party send one of their number to speak at the post-demonstration rally on behalf of the federal party.[18]

Disregarding the nuances of a complex, changing international situation, activists had tried to mobilise the party machine to the highest-profile demonstration against the war, regardless of the leader's position. The motion was not enacted, triggering a power struggle led by Donnachadh McCarthy, a radical Irishman who was deputy chairman of the federal executive committee, about who had authority to issue instructions to departments of the party. In the midst of this testing international crisis, Kennedy found himself sitting through endless subsequent meetings as McCarthy picked over details of the motion and reinterpreted minutes of previous meetings. Several Lib Dems later likened his tactics to those of the infiltration of the Labour Party by Militant Tendency in the 1980s.

During this period Charles Kennedy visited the offices of the *Guardian* for an informal lunch with its editor, Alan Rusbridger, and a group of his writers. Kennedy, three of his aides and a dozen or so *Guardian* journalists crowded into the editor's office, where sandwiches were laid out on an oval table. Rusbridger said a few words and handed over to his writers. During a wide-ranging discussion, several from the paper's left-wing 'Respect Tendency' pressed Kennedy on why he was not planning to attend the Stop the War march. Jonathan Freedland, one of the columnists, was particularly forceful, telling him he risked the worst of both worlds by not declaring his hand. Kennedy was hesitant, confessing, in what he considered a private forum, his worry at being criticised in the Commons if he did so. The day afterwards the *Guardian* published a letter from Donnachadh McCarthy, who, frustrated in his wish to mobilise the party machine in support of the Stop the War Coalition, issued a public appeal urging Lib Dems to join the march and implying they would be following Kennedy's lead in doing so.[19] The following day, a Saturday, the newspaper returned to the same subject in its leader column, rehearsing the arguments made at its private lunch with Kennedy. The march, it predicted, would be one of the largest in memory, a spontaneous movement of ordinary people. It said:

> Remarkably, no senior or significant political figure has managed to place themselves anywhere near the head of this oppositional movement . . . This ought to be Charles Kennedy's moment. He leads a party which officially supports next week's protest … Mr Kennedy ought therefore to be on the platform in Hyde Park next Saturday. But he is not going to be there and he does not appear to want to be there. This is an extraordinary mistake on Mr Kennedy's part.[20]

One reason for Kennedy's reticence was that opinion was deeply divided among his frontbench spokesmen over whether he should attend the march. Menzies Campbell, still speaking to Kennedy by telephone from Edinburgh, was strongly opposed, arguing that far-left elements involved in the demonstration were viscerally anti-American and that the Liberal Democrats risked being contaminated by association. Paul Keetch, who as defence spokesman was in constant touch with military contacts, was wary. So, too, was Michael Moore. Mark Oaten, the MP closest to Kennedy, also advised against, due to the likely presence of extremist elements. Others, including Jenny Tonge and a number of Lib Dem peers, announced they would attend regardless of the leader's decision. This was the occasion of the frankest discussions of Kennedy's war cabinet and was a political decision no amount of expert advice could help. All Kennedy's instincts were to keep his party together yet he could no longer procrastinate: this was another fork in the road. He had to choose which path to take. The day after the *Guardian*'s leader he was due to give a television interview and knew the subject would be raised. He spent Saturday making telephone calls to Tim Razzall, Dick Newby, Jackie Rowley and other advisers but ultimately the decision was his own. The next morning, interviewed on *Breakfast with Frost*, he announced he would go on the march, saying rather lamely he had not been invited and taking care to emphasise he was pro-UN, not anti-war. He said: 'As concerns the peace march itself, personally speaking I'd be very happy to participate in that. As a matter of fact I've not been formally invited, and I would want to make the Liberal Democrat case, which is the pro-United Nations case. It is not anti-war come what may.'[21]

Kennedy's decision to attend certainly heightened interest in the march, although, as the *Guardian*'s leader noted, large numbers were already anticipated. In the event more than one million people attended. Anna Werrin, who dealt with the organisers, asked that he be the only Lib Dem parliamentarian to speak from the platform, effectively bumping off Jenny Tonge, who had been due to speak, in order to avoid comparisons between their speeches. Menzies Campbell remained concerned about what Kennedy would tell the crowd and the text of the speech was faxed to Campbell in Edinburgh beforehand. On the morning of the march, a very cold February day, Kennedy wrapped himself in a thick coat and scarf and set off on foot from his flat in Victoria with his wife Sarah, her brother James Gurling, Anna Werrin, Jackie Rowley, Navnit and Ann Dholakia, and Gurpreet Dosanjh, who later joined Kennedy's staff. They walked across the River Thames to the Royal Festival Hall, where he addressed the contingent of some 3,000 Lib Dems from an overhead footbridge. Charles Kennedy declared this his proudest moment as a Liberal Democrat. From there he recrossed the Thames with the Lib Dem marchers, joining the main march along the Embankment and past the Houses of Parliament. From there Kennedy and his group peeled off to make their way directly to Hyde Park to address a vast audience, many of whom did not share the Liberal Democrats' nuanced position on invading Iraq. Kennedy's remarks were cautious and he spoke about the Lib Dems' policy, instead of making a pitch to lead the anti-war movement. He told the crowd: 'All other options must be exhausted before there is any recourse to force. I join with you today because I have yet to be persuaded as to the case for war against Iraq . . . without a second UN resolution, there is no way that the Liberal Democrats could or should support war.'

This final sentence was his most important. He was more firmly than ever committed to his course. Menzies Campbell sent Kennedy a pager message congratulating him on the speech but the reaction from opponents was fierce. Tony Blair, addressing a Scottish Labour Party conference in Glasgow, made a moral case for disarming Iraq and gave a message for the marchers that if peace meant Saddam staying in power 'there are consequences paid in blood for that decision'.[22] At the end of January, writing in the *Observer*, Kennedy had drawn a parallel with the disastrous British invasion of Suez in 1956.[23] Now he became the target of a different historical comparison. Even before Kennedy's decision to attend the march, Nicholas Soames, a Conservative MP and former minister for the armed forces, likened the Lib Dem leader's stance to Neville Chamberlain's appeasement of Hitler.[24] Iain Duncan Smith himself, during a trip to Gouda, Holland, called Kennedy an appeaser the following week, after his attendance at the march was announced. Quentin Letts, a sketch writer and commentator, introduced the phrase 'Charlie Chamberlain' and accused Kennedy of 'milking this war for his own political profit'.[25] Although, or perhaps because, the opinion polls suggested many of the public were with Charles Kennedy, his was not a comfortable position.

The extent to which Labour MPs shared his doubts was indicated, if not fully manifest, in a Commons debate on 26 February on a government motion consciously giving Saddam Hussein a 'final opportunity' to disarm. On this occasion the Liberal Democrats did not table an amendment but supported one from Labour rebels. This was put down by Chris Smith and

Frank Dobson, both former Cabinet ministers, who negotiated its wording with Michael Moore. It simply said the case for military action was 'as yet unproven'. The government's motion was passed but, in the largest revolt against a governing party for a century, 121 Labour MPs supported the amendment, with 52 Lib Dems and 13 Conservatives. Tony Blair was under very considerable pressure. Among those who saw the Prime Minister's performance in the Commons was Paddy Ashdown, by now the UN's high representative in Bosnia, from where he watched Blair's speech on television. While Ashdown thought the judgements much more finely balanced than the case for intervention in Bosnia and Kosovo, he had concluded that military action against Iraq was right. Paddy Ashdown wrote a short, handwritten letter to Blair acknowledging he must be going through a tough time but saying he was doing the right thing. He faxed his note that night from Sarajevo to the duty clerk at Downing Street, intending it as a purely private communication. Ashdown was surprised, therefore, to receive a telephone call soon afterwards from Alastair Campbell, Blair's director of communications, seeking permission to publish the letter. Paddy Ashdown recalled:

> I had Ali Campbell come back to me very sharply saying: 'Can we make this public, can we make this public?' And I said: 'Under no circumstances can you make this public. Whatever private opinion I may have, I am not going to embarrass my party and I am not prepared to second-guess what goes on.'

By whatever route, the fact of Ashdown's support for the war did seep out and put further pressure on Kennedy as diplomatic efforts to win a second resolution from the UN security council authorising war ran into the sand, blocked by Jacques Chirac, the President of France. At his spring party conference in Torquay, which coincided with an eve-of-war summit in the Azores between George Bush and Tony Blair, Kennedy devoted his entire speech to Iraq as he prepared his party for the decision ahead. The conference passed a motion on Iraq softening slightly its stance from the previous September, saying military action should be 'on the basis of evidence from the weapons inspectors' rather than requiring evidence of weapons capability and intent to use it. But the Lib Dems' insistence on a further UN resolution endorsing military action remained. Blair did concede to a Commons vote days later, on 18 March, before committing British troops to the invasion, and announced at short notice he would open the debate himself on a motion to authorise use of 'all means necessary' to disarm Iraq. The resignation from the Cabinet a day beforehand of Robin Cook, a former Foreign Secretary, gave opponents of the war a new champion but the debate was still a test for Kennedy. Until this point, he had quizzed Blair many times at Prime Minister's Questions and in reply to his Commons statements on Iraq, but not himself given a full speech in which opponents could intervene and challenge his arguments. Kennedy had also to keep his parliamentary party together and prepare his MPs to be disciplined in a hostile Commons environment. This was one of the rare periods in which Charles Kennedy showed genuine leadership to his parliamentary party. More than any other time, he tried to impress on his MPs his own style of politics: cautious, measured, thinking ahead. At a special parliamentary party meeting on the morning of the debate, he talked his MPs through the risks, warned them not to heckle or make interventions that would allow opponents to misrepresent their position, and said they must make their case in a restrained tone. Michael Moore said:

> That was almost like a group huddle; everybody said this is going to be tough in there, so we need maximum support, vocally and physically being there, and a lot of discipline. What we didn't want is to allow others to distract us from the case we were making and turn us into the story, not the issue.

Kennedy's foresight was proved almost at the outset of Tony Blair's opening speech, when the Prime Minister conceded that very difficult issues were at stake and spoke of 'the main parties divided'. Evan Harris shouted a challenge to the effect that the Lib Dems, at least, were unanimously against; Blair stopped, contemptuous. 'Ah, yes, of course. The Liberal Democrats – unified, as ever, in opportunism and error,' Blair spat out.[26]

During his own speech, Charles Kennedy was subjected to a torrent of abuse from the Conservatives. One Tory MP, Cheryl Gillian, shouted that he was a coward before being forced by the Speaker to withdraw her remark. Iain Duncan Smith was among the first to intervene to attack Kennedy's position. Twice there were points of order from the Conservative benches and the Speaker intervened several times to allow him to proceed. The chief reason for his difficulty was a decision taken in his war cabinet the previous week that, if the Commons were to vote for military action, the Liberal Democrats would concede that Parliament had spoken and support British troops in the field. There was wide support for this change in emphasis among Kennedy's advisers; Chris Rennard put it thus: 'When Saddam Hussein's Republican Guards are firing at British soldiers and British soldiers are firing back, you have got to know which side you are on.' Its effect, however, was to allow opponents to portray the Liberal Democrats as having switched sides, from opposing the war to supporting British troops. 'I don't think we ever were fully comfortable with the language that we were opposed to the political decision but we would do nothing to undermine the troops,' Michael Moore admitted, 'and that was a slightly awkward period.'

Nevertheless all fifty-three Lib Dem MPs voted for a cross-party amendment saying the case for war had not been made; Menzies Campbell, looking gaunt and having lost his hair, rejoined them in the lobbies for the first time since his treatment. They voted alongside 139 rebel Labour MPs and 15 Conservatives, but it was not enough. Tony Blair had the approval of the Commons to go to war. Once the fighting started Kennedy greatly expanded his war cabinet to include frontbench spokesmen from the Commons and Lords, plus their researchers. It met every morning in a room on the upper committee corridor of the Commons. Again a central figure was Tim Garden, who was giving military commentary on the BBC's breakfast television news between 6 a.m. and 9 a.m. and would arrive with up-to-the-minute information from reports of journalists embedded with coalition troops. But large, regular, formal meetings such as these were not Kennedy's style and he found the group too unwieldy. Nor was he comfortable giving media interviews while the invasion was underway. He would try to talk about the politics, but inevitably the questioning would revert to military strategy. Charles Kennedy was no armchair general and had no wish to be one. In the final week of the fighting, the meetings eased off to three a week with the last on 14 April, five days after the toppling of Saddam's statue in Baghdad.

The speed with which American and British troops took Iraq, and initial television pictures of Shia Muslims celebrating Saddam's fall, appeared to vindicate some of the arguments used by George Bush and Tony Blair, as did emerging evidence of past human rights abuses in Iraq. As a new American-led team began scouring Iraq for evidence of illegal weapons systems, it was a difficult period for opponents of the war. Tim Garden's advice throughout was that Saddam might have tactical battlefield weapons but nothing posing a wider strategic threat. He probably had some ageing chemical shells but certainly had no nuclear capability; he was unable to make an assessment on biological weapons. Comforting as such expert opinion was, it was obvious that Blair and supporters of the war would seize on any finds of weapons and use them to exonerate the invasion. A long time elapsed before the team returned, empty handed.

In the event, the Liberal Democrats' decision to oppose the war was a straightforward one; they said simply the case had not yet been made. The simplicity of this position was due in large part to Kennedy's skilful positioning. It is worth reflecting, however, on what might have been. Had France and a handful of smaller states holding rotating seats on the UN Security Council taken a different view, and passed the second resolution tabled by Britain, the logic of Kennedy's position was that he should support military action. It is very likely his party would then have split, exposing the division between those seeking to uphold the supremacy of the United Nations and those who were against any war with Iraq in such circumstances. There would have been arguments over whether the tests in the Torquay conference resolution of March 2003 were met, probably some attempts to revert to the motion passed at Brighton in September 2002, and an assertion of pacifist principles, which were strongly represented in the party. Charles Kennedy argued for a second resolution; it was fortunate, for him at least, that one did not materialise.

By opposing the war, Kennedy massively raised his political profile and that of his party. There was some evidence of Iraq having an electoral impact in the local elections in May 2003 but its full significance did not emerge until a by-election in the hitherto safe Labour seat of Brent East. The 2001–5 parliament was unusual in how few by-elections there were, due to a combination of pressure on sitting MPs not to stand down between elections and more generous parliamentary pensions, encouraging older MPs to retire. When Brent East fell vacant in June, with the death from cancer of its Labour MP, Paul Daisley, the Liberal Democrats decided to make a fight of it; indeed their candidate, Sarah Teather, an articulate and energetic young policy analyst for Macmillan Cancer Relief, had already been selected. The seat was an unlikely prospect. It had a Labour majority of 13,047. The Lib Dems began in a weak third place, had little representation on the local council and just sixty-three local members. Moreover, the Lib Dems had never gained a seat from Labour in a by-election. The nearest parallel was the SDP's victory at Greenwich, in February 1987. In late June, however, Chris Rennard commissioned some market research from Martin Hamblin, the party's pollster, which undertook in-depth interviews in Harborough, south Leicestershire, and Bournemouth East. Both were target seats and offered a mixture of rural and urban opinion. One of the questions asked about trust in Tony Blair. Chris Rennard said: ' Essentially there was an overwhelming sense of betrayal over the failure to find weapons of mass destruction. They were venomous about Blair on trust.'

As was his practice, Rennard visited the party's makeshift by-election headquarters in Brent, where the Lib Dems set up shop in a former W. H. Smith outlet near a busy junction, to take the temperature as groups of Lib Dem canvassers returned from their rounds. Chris Rennard said:

> I picked up a huge surge against Blair. I remained sceptical about the scale of it and about what canvassers were saying. I went out canvassing myself, close to the head-quarters in Willesden Green. People who just were natural New Labour supporters, well-off people, were passionate, saying it was disgraceful, calling Blair a liar. It was anger over Iraq, they felt let down.

Highly unusually, Rennard decided to tap into such sentiment by using photographs of Blair on Liberal Democrat by-election literature. Scowling pictures of Tony Blair standing beside George Bush appeared on hundreds of thousands of newspapers and leaflets over the summer in the first sign that Blair, for so long a powerful electoral asset, had a negative appeal among certain Labour supporters. Canvassers also found that Charles Kennedy was recognised for the first time among ethnic minority voters, particularly the large local Hindu community and smaller Muslim population, many of whom applauded his stance in opposing the invasion of Iraq. The controversy over the war refused to go away as a government scientist and former weapons inspector, David Kelly, apparently took his own life in mid-July after being linked to criticisms that secret intelligence over Iraq's weapons systems had been exaggerated. Blair set up an inquiry into his death, chaired by Lord Hutton, who took evidence in public over the summer, including from the Prime Minister himself, which became the focus of intense public discussion.

Even so, the Lib Dems would have had little chance of gaining the seat were it not for a series of errors by their opponents. Labour decided to delay the by-election, miscalculating that the obvious unease over Iraq would fade over the summer. The Lib Dems, struggling to make bricks without straw in unfamiliar territory, suddenly found they had months to build the foundations for a by-election upset. A battered visitors' book at the reception desk of their campaign headquarters was testament to the steady stream of

Lib Dem volunteers who made their way from all corners of Britain to deliver leaflets in Kilburn, Dollis Hill and Cricklewood over the long, hot summer. Then came an error from the Conservatives. The Tories chose as their candidate Uma Fernandes, a community nursing sister and local councillor originally from Mauritius. In an interview with the *Daily Telegraph* that made much of her background, hailing signs that the Conservative Party was embracing modern Britain, Uma Fernandes admitted she expected not to win. 'Let's not kid ourselves. Brent East is a strong Labour seat,' she reasoned.[27] She added that she hoped for a better seat in future. This was a cardinal error in politics and allowed the Liberal Democrats to present themselves as the only challenger to Labour. All kinds of improbable bar charts appeared on Lib Dem literature, claiming the campaign was a two-horse race with Sarah Teather starting in close second instead of distant third, which the Conservatives never successfully countered.

It proved a bizarre by-election. Having put off moving the writ, Labour made little obvious effort at campaigning in the early summer. Its candidate, Robert Evans, a London MEP, continued with his duties in the European Parliament and gave one by-election interview by telephone from Phnom Penh in Cambodia, where he was visiting as an EU election observer.[28] Labour's main by-election headquarters, run largely by professional party staff wearing suits, had the atmosphere of a building society branch; it produced glossy literature on the improvements to schools, hospitals and police numbers made possible by the Labour government. Even a leaflet attacking the Lib Dems as 'soft on yobs' had the glossy feel of information on financial services products. The Conservatives, discovering that Robert Evans lived in Weybridge, Surrey, distributed a leaflet carrying a photograph of his house. These accused him of living in a 'millionaires' row', a curious nod to the politics of envy from the Conservatives. Sarah Teather began to undertake 'casework' on behalf of local people, giving her an opportunity to attack the Labour council on topics ranging from housing to litter, graffiti and potholes in pavements. Lib Dem newsletters called her a 'local campaigner' and said artfully she 'will be an excellent local MP' or was 'the best choice for our local MP', neglecting to mention she was already a councillor in Islington, another London borough, where she lived.

Again Kennedy threw himself into the by-election, making a series of early campaign visits, sometimes at very short notice. The focus on Tony Blair in the Lib Dem campaign was not something he was entirely comfortable with. Kennedy was sensitive to charges of negative campaigning and still had a relationship with Blair; although it would never again be as close, Kennedy always took care never to criticise the Prime Minister's integrity, only his judgement. Later in the campaign he proposed using an opposition day in the Commons to debate the euro but was overruled by members of his shadow cabinet, who insisted the party must debate Iraq.[29] Rennard quietly told the by-election team that Blair and Bush should continue to feature in leaflets but all references to Iraq must mirror exactly comments made by Charles Kennedy and Menzies Campbell. Chris Rennard retreated to the south of France for a three-week summer holiday but, communicating by laptop computer and mobile telephone, he read all leaflets in advance to check they did not stray from the party's national message. Kennedy had further reason to be nervous. Following the attempt by the federal executive to mobilise the party to back the Stop the War rally, members of this committee, led again by Donnachadh McCarthy, forced through a restructuring of the party headquarters: its campaigns and organisation would all be run by a single chief executive. Both Chris Rennard and Hugh Rickard, a formal naval officer who was the existing chief executive, applied for the post in what again threatened to become a power struggle with activists on the federal executive committee. Interviews were conducted in Kennedy's office in September, with the by-election building to its climax. There was some relief among those close to Kennedy when the job was offered to Chris Rennard.

The result in Brent East, when it came, was another sensation. Sarah Teather overturned Labour's majority to win by 1,158 votes, on a turnout of just 36.4 per cent. Kennedy awaited the result in his flat with Sarah, his wife, Anna Werrin and Jackie Rowley, whom Rennard telephoned as he was being driven to the count just after 10 p.m. Pressed for his verdict, a reluctant Chris Rennard told her: 'If you really push me, I think we have got this by 500.' The three women with Charles Kennedy burst into tears; Rennard's driver, the by-election's agent Vicky Marsom whom he had not yet told, almost crashed her car in surprise. Recalling television pictures of David Owen joining the early-morning celebrations of Rosie Barnes's victory at Greenwich, Rennard urged Charles Kennedy to come over to the campaign headquarters at Willesden Green that night. After a circuitous journey through north London, Kennedy arrived to hail a spectacular result that owed much to his decision to oppose the Iraq war. Suddenly a new battle front opened up in two or three dozen seats where the Lib Dems would take on not their old enemy, the Conservatives, but Labour.

8

Demons and drink

Late one quiet Friday afternoon, Charles Kennedy's closest staff and advisers slipped away from the House of Commons to reconvene in the privacy of his mansion flat behind Victoria Street in Westminster. There, the Lib Dem leader was joined by Tim Razzall, his principal strategist, Dick Newby, his chief of staff, Anna Werrin, his assistant and closest ally, and Jackie Rowley, his press secretary. Over glasses of Diet Coke and mineral water, they reached a momentous decision: that he should make public the corrosive secret that threatened to destabilise his leadership.

It was 4 July 2003, three months after the initial phase of the Iraq war had ended. A series of newspaper stories had been published reporting concerns about Kennedy's recent performances or alluding to his drinking. His advisers feared another was imminent, possibly with undignified photographs that risked serious damage to his authority as a political figure. They agreed he should hold a press conference and set the record straight on years of rumours about his drinking. Charles Kennedy, they decided, would say this had been the subject of a great deal of speculation; much had been printed on the subject, some of it untrue, some of it exaggerated. But, he would say, he wished to stress clearly he did indeed have a drink problem and was seeking to address and resolve it. This was an oblique reference to professional help for alcoholism he had been receiving for more than a year.

The group knew he was taking a risk. He planned to make clear he would remain as leader; commentators would question his fitness to do so, and might subject him to endless questions about drinking. Henceforth he would be watched like a hawk for the slightest sign of a lapse. His inner circle calculated, however, that by making such a public admission he would stop the continual innuendo of press stories linking him to alcohol. He might even elicit public sympathy by finally being open about his condition. Having taken the decision, the group determined to act almost immediately. The press conference was scheduled for late the following morning, 5 July – a Saturday – at the Liberal Democrats' headquarters at Cowley Street, twelve days before Parliament rose for the summer recess. Calling notices would be issued to the media on the day itself to avoid advance publicity. Since it was summer, if the weather was fine Charles Kennedy would make his announcement from the steps outside Cowley Street; if it was overcast or raining he would do so inside in the boardroom. Menzies Campbell, the deputy leader, who had travelled home to Edinburgh for the weekend, would be asked to return to London and stand behind Charles Kennedy or sit at his side during the press conference in a demonstration of support. After about an hour, the meeting broke up as the team dispersed to make preparations for the biggest personal gamble of Charles Kennedy's career.

On receiving the summons Menzies Campbell cancelled his weekend engagements and, on Saturday morning, caught the early morning train from Edinburgh to King's Cross to attend the press conference. His journey was well advanced when he took a call on his mobile telephone from Anna Werrin. She told him Kennedy had changed his mind. No further stories about his drinking had appeared in the weekend newspapers. Having slept on it, Charles Kennedy decided he no longer wished to go through with such a public declaration and would deal with his condition in his own way, she said. Menzies Campbell, having braced himself for a momentous event, got off the train and caught another back to Edinburgh, saying nothing. To say Charles Kennedy's change of heart came at the eleventh hour would be an understatement. Arrangements had been made to open Cowley Street over the weekend. A handful of senior party officials were forewarned of his announcement, due to its possible impact on the Brent East by-election campaign that was getting underway. The text of his statement had been drafted by Jackie Rowley. But, crucially, calling notices announcing the press conference had not yet been dispatched. The plan was quietly cancelled and the paperwork destroyed.

It was a pivotal decision. The risks were undoubtedly high and, as an intensely private man, the thought of such a public declaration made Kennedy instinctively recoil. But at that time the Liberal Democrats were winning recognition for their controversial decision to oppose the invasion of Iraq. It was in the middle of a parliament, just before a summer recess. If ever there was a moment for such an announcement, surely it was then. It certainly would have been done in very different circumstances to the statement he was ultimately forced to make two and a half years later, as he was fighting a revolt by his MPs and simultaneously announced a leadership ballot. Instead, having cancelled the press conference, Charles Kennedy continued to battle with his alcoholism in private. MPs who raised concerns with his staff or with their chief whip, Andrew Stunell, were assured that appropriate action was being taken but told little else. Some knew or learned of his condition, many more did not. For those that did, the only support they were able to offer was patience. Increasingly this became tested by exasperation.

Charles Kennedy struggled with a severe alcohol problem throughout his period as leader. He did not drink excessively every day, colleagues said, but every so often would go on a spree of very heavy drinking. Contrary to a mythology drawn from a caricature of a Highlander, whisky was not his tipple of choice. Nor did he care for champagne, despite at times being dubbed 'Champagne Charlie'. He drank gin and tonic, or wine, although on occasions he would drink beer or whisky. When Charles Kennedy drank to excess his condition might simply manifest itself with a pungent smell of alcohol around him the following day. After more serious episodes, his hands would shake, particularly in the morning, and he would perspire, take on an unhealthy pallor and suffer from flu-like symptoms. As its most acute, his drinking would from time to time leave him obviously unfit to perform in public. His staff quickly learnt to throw a protective shield around him during such periods and, where possible, keep him completely from view. For the first three or four years of his leadership they were largely successful, although increasingly chinks in his armour began to show. As rumours of drink-related incidents started to circulate at Westminster, a private medical condition took on a political significance. In fact Charles Kennedy was progressively drinking less, not more, but its political importance grew as the secret of his alcoholism slowly seeped out.

'I don't know when heavy drinking, which a lot of people do, suddenly becomes problem drinking,' said Anna Werrin, who was his closest assistant and friend over twenty-three years. 'It is something that you see in retrospect. I cannot tell you when he started to have a drink problem.' Her own concern at his drinking stemmed back, she said, 'well before he became leader'. 'I think the difference between pre-leader drinking and leadership drinking was that he drank less,' Werrin said. 'For many years he was cutting back, cutting back. But you are suddenly more exposed, aren't you?'

There was no pattern to his bouts of alcoholic excess that colleagues could discern. Some who saw him less frequently thought them linked to periods of high pressure or their immediate aftermath, but those who worked with him most closely insisted that was not so. As Dick Newby said:

> Charles was at his worst when there wasn't much going on and when he wasn't under much pressure. He was at his absolute best when there was pressure, when he was negotiating with Blair, when he was standing up to people, when he was very, very strong. One of the reasons why I was happy to carry on working with Charles was I knew that under pressure he was really good.

Anna Werrin concurred:

> I never felt that it was due to pressure. When pressure increased upon him at times of high stress, like Iraq, I didn't ever see him unable to make a decision or his judgement impaired on a big issue because of drink. I didn't ever see him drinking more at times of pressure. I think he drank heavily as a young man and a student, and he was elected when he was very young and he was single and he was enjoying a young, very male single life, predominantly in London, and he carried on with his student-type drinking. The truth of the matter is I could not tell you necessarily what the pattern of his drinking was. He wasn't somebody who was drinking all the time in the office. He drank in private, by and large, and drank more than he ought.

Stories of drinking attached themselves to Charles Kennedy throughout his political career. It was even suggested he had 'too much to drink over lunch' before the critical meeting of the SDP's national committee in June 1987 when he switched sides to back a merger with the Liberal Party.[1] Contemporaries of that era recalled that he would, if having lunch at a restaurant, drink a gin and tonic or two beforehand and share a bottle of wine, often pushing his food around the plate and eating only a quarter of it. But drinking heavily is a far cry from alcoholism. It was not until the mid-1990s that those who worked closely with him noticed some of his brilliance as a speaker and performer had dulled.

To concentrate solely on his drinking, however, may be to miss the point. The most arresting change in Charles Kennedy as he progressed from star student debater to contender for party leader was in his self-confidence. As a young man Kennedy exuded boundless self-belief as he befriended academics, politicians and journalists twice his age. By the time he was in his late thirties, such assurance had gone. His status as a prodigy may have been his undoing. Having arrived in Parliament at his first attempt, after a few weeks' campaigning, and within five years been marked as a future leader, he had no experience of the application and self-discipline required to fulfil such expectation. Meanwhile, from the age of twenty-three, all his opinions, his relationships, his indiscretions were liable to find their way into the public gaze. Matthew Taylor experienced something similar when, at twenty-four, he won the seat of Truro for the Liberals in 1987:

> It creates a distance. It also creates a pressure. Coming in here, for the first year or two there was a fear of letting people down because inevitably you are presumed to have a self-confidence you are unlikely to have at the age of twenty-three or twenty-four, and I don't think either Charles or I did. Charles was clearly capable. Like me he had done public speaking; I was president of the student union of Oxford. We would not have got here without being capable but nevertheless there is a huge level of expectation.

The mid-1990s was also a very unsatisfying period for Kennedy in political terms, after he stood down as president of the party and no longer had a key frontline role. This was when a serious lack of self-esteem became apparent to some of those around him. Alcohol may have been a symptom rather than a cause. Becoming leader certainly heightened the pressure upon him. For one thing, as a large fish in the Liberal Democrats' small pond, he had been able to live on his wits, sail through media interviews and give plausible Commons performances with minimum advance preparation and without exerting himself hugely. While he was a frontbench spokesman for the Liberal Democrats, which was still then very much a minority party, it did not really matter. Once he was the party's leader, suddenly it did. Intellectually he was subjected to a much greater level of challenge and scrutiny, more from the media than in Parliament. At times, especially in his early years, he doubted his own capability in the role. In the only interview he gave on his drinking, to the *Sunday Times* the day before he resigned, Kennedy referred to the need in the past to 'have a drink to calm your nerves' if feeling apprehensive before such an interview.[2]

On a different dimension, Kennedy was never entirely comfortable with his persona as a public figure once he was leader. Anna Werrin said: 'He is a different person than the much larger version of himself. He doesn't like the public introspection, in a sense, that goes with the leader thing. He had to project himself the whole time. Charles the private man is not the same as Charles the public man.'

As an up-and-coming MP, Charles Kennedy never made a secret of the fact that he was a heavy drinker. Newspaper articles about him routinely referred to his liking for alcohol. With breathtaking candour, in one interview he gave before undertaking a sponsored slim for charity, he was reported to have confessed to a 'constant craving' for whisky, red wine and lager as well as for fast food.[3]

During the leadership election in 1999 the symptoms of his alcoholism were glimpsed by a number of party members and journalists who met him in the course of the campaign. At a mid-morning hustings meeting at a leisure centre in Basingstoke, one of many organised for Lib Dem members, his behaviour left a lasting impression on Sandra Gidley, later MP for Romsey but then a local activist. She was assigned the role of candidates' aide and helped to lay out a breakfast of croissants, pastries, tea, coffee, orange juice and water for the five contestants. 'Charles arrived late, literally stinking of whisky, even then. We offered him breakfast, he turned his nose up at the whole thing,' she recalled. Instead his eye alighted on a vending machine and he asked for a can of Coke. Sandra Gidley and other Lib Dem helpers hunted first for the correct coins, then for the building's caretaker as the vending machine was not working, and eventually produced a can of Diet Coke; Charles Kennedy later left it behind unopened. Sandra Gidley, thoroughly unimpressed by his demeanour and his lacklustre contribution at the hustings itself, placed him fifth of the five candidates on her ballot paper.

Many newspaper profiles of Charles Kennedy during the leadership election raised the subject of his fondness for a drink, although he skilfully used humour to parry questions about alcohol. His standard response was: 'I make no apology for being a fully paid-up member of the human race.' Another was to joke that he would only sue if someone called him a teetotaller.[4] Rumours of a drinking problem, and indeed a completely false suggestion that he was a cocaine user, did circulate around Westminster during the leadership election, which senior Lib Dems attributed to supporters of certain rival candidates. Some of this speculation Charles Kennedy rebutted personally by talking himself to journalists who tried to check such rumours. But he emerged from the campaign with the full extent of his drinking still largely unknown, assisted by allowing anyone who enquired about his intermittent aroma of alcohol to believe it was due to his choice of aftershave[5] or an alcohol-based mouthwash.

On becoming leader Charles Kennedy still regarded himself as a social, if heavy, drinker. The consensus among senior Lib Dems was simply that he drank too much. They assumed the demanding schedule required of the leader would leave little time for such a lifestyle; he had, after all, been a capable and successful president of the party until 1994. In addition, some hoped his election as leader would boost his self-esteem and give him a status and sense of purpose he lacked as he idled away the mid-1990s in peripheral posts, ultimately as Paddy Ashdown's agriculture spokesman. Within months such optimism proved misplaced. A trickle of complaints about his performances at public engagements and visits to local Lib Dem parties began to reach the office of the new leader, typically that he had arrived smelling of alcohol, often in the morning as well as later in the day. Kennedy would carry a breath freshener and mints to mask the aroma of alcohol. Within a year his closest advisers confronted him and told him his pattern of drinking could not continue. Anna Werrin said:

> It was made very clear to him, and he took on board, that you could not combine drinking on anything other than a very social basis with being leader. He knew where a complaint had been made. I would help him. He acknowledged that you can't turn up smelling of drink.

After such incidents Charles Kennedy would scale back his alcohol consumption for periods, anxious not to jeopardise his position, although neither he nor his inner circle thought at that stage he might need professional help to do so. Lib Dems attending early evening meetings in his Commons office were still routinely invited to stay afterwards and join him for a glass of wine. There was nothing unusual in that: Paddy Ashdown's diaries are peppered with references to plotting with colleagues over late-night glasses of whisky. But after phases when Charles Kennedy tried abstinence, or at least moderation, the pattern of poor performances or complaints would resurface: from shopkeepers in Hampshire, after touring a Dorset hospital during a party conference at Bournemouth, from farmers he met over breakfast in Devon during the foot-and-mouth epidemic. On occasions, journalists, particularly broadcasters who came into close contact with him, would leave suspecting he had been drinking. This is not to suggest the media colluded in concealing his alcoholism; in such circumstances, Kennedy's comments might be more meandering, and so less easy to condense into clips for television footage, but rarely worse. On days when he was in a very poor state, his office refused media bids. Instead rumours would circulate that he had been drinking. MPs in the House of Commons chamber, from his own side and among the Conservatives ranged around them, sometimes reached the same conclusion.

As the 2001 general election approached, close colleagues began to worry about what lay ahead. One journalist, Lesley White, researching a detailed biographical profile of the Lib Dem leader for publication during the election campaign, wrote a vivid description of his poor physical state as she called at his croft in Fort William at 9.30 one morning:

> He looks as if he has been up all night carousing, with a hot pink face, watery eyes, frail and shivery. Knowing he has spent the best part of recess week recuperating here with his aged parents for company, it seems odd. Has he been out on the razzle, I ask? . . . Is it flu that makes him look so wan as he greets us, cigarette in hand, which makes that hand shake so visibly when he picks a raffle ticket at an old folks gathering – or anxiety?[6]

The few Lib Dems who realised the severity of Charles Kennedy's condition shared with the leader's office a keen awareness that he would be exposed to media scrutiny as never before for the duration of the election campaign. Anna Werrin explained:

> We were all very well aware that the campaign was going to be enormously stressful, that he would be under a huge amount of pressure, that he would be in the physical gaze the whole time. He would be travelling around with a packload of journalists on the bus, spend evenings doing television and media. He knew, as did we all, that he couldn't afford to drink. It was a given that the campaign was dry for pretty much everybody. We started our day at 6.30 in the morning, kept going until midnight or one o'clock. You can't do that and drink at the same time and get through to the end of it. There was an acknowledgement before the election that he had to be in good shape for it.

At one of a series of rehearsals for election events at Local Government House, Malcolm Bruce, then chairman of the parliamentary party, was surprised to be asked to take a mock press conference. On seeking clarification of his role, he was told to assume that as chairman of the parliamentary party he was standing in for the leader. This led to speculation among some MPs of contingency planning in case things went awry for

Charles Kennedy during the election; in fact, Kennedy had been due to attend the rehearsal but sent word at the last minute that he was unable to get there. In the event, however, the election campaign passed off exceptionally well, with no drink-related episodes. The campaign was very punishing on Kennedy. Before addressing big election rallies he would be physically ill with nerves and stress before going on stage. Charles Kennedy did not forgo alcohol during the campaign but his drinking was carefully controlled by those around him and afterwards he resolved to use the post-election summer recess to get himself in better health. Anna Werrin said:

> On his part there was an acknowledgement that he felt better during the campaign, that he felt healthier when he was not drinking, and therefore the summer was the time . . . he has always got this thing, 'I need to get healthy, I need to stop drinking, I need to stop smoking, I need to eat properly.' At this time he wasn't married, he lived on a diet of Diet Coke, Mars bars, pizza, grossly unhealthy food, smoking far too much.

Senior party figures, although hugely relieved at his performance during the election campaign, told the leader's inner circle he must use the summer of 2001 to seek professional treatment for alcoholism, if necessary abroad – for example, in the United States – where he was less likely to be recognised. Some were of the view that, on his return in September, he should make a public statement to announce he had sought treatment for a drink problem. By doing so, they reasoned, he would take a major step towards accepting his condition and signal to people whom he met in social situations that they should not offer him alcohol. Yet here the dilemma faced by Liberal Democrats not in his small inner circle became apparent. Some thought he needed residential treatment to overcome his alcoholism. Yet they felt unable to ask about details of medical treatment he might have. Charles Kennedy, an intensely private man, was loath to make any public statement about his drinking and wished to deal with it privately, on his own terms. There was never any feedback from the leader's office on what exactly he would do to ensure that the destabilising symptoms of his alcoholism would not recur during the 2001–5 parliament.

He sought professional help for the first time to control his drinking early in 2002, before his marriage. Anna Werrin would not disclose details but said she was not aware it had ever involved residential treatment. Charles Kennedy talked much later of being helped to look at his life in compartments and planning how to avoid the temptation for alcohol in each, a feature of behaviour therapy counselling for alcoholics.[7] Wine was no longer offered in the leader's office after meetings; indeed, none was kept in the office at all. Anna Werrin said:

> He didn't want to drink and the last thing anybody else wants to do when somebody doesn't want to drink is to be sitting there drinking around them. We didn't have drink in the office. We had parties in the office, we'd bring wine for that and then it was cleared.

Charles Kennedy began to settle his domestic life with his engagement in January 2002 and marriage in July. Almost twenty years of living as a bachelor in the demanding role of a member of Parliament were about to come to an end, offering him for the first time a wife to return to rather than an empty flat. This was a powerful spur to redouble efforts to conquer his drinking problem. But it was also a complicating factor, meaning two people, rather than one, had to come to terms with his alcoholism.

Four days before they married Charles Kennedy was invited to be interviewed for BBC Two's *Newsnight*. It was filmed in the library of the National Liberal Club, where beforehand Charles Kennedy met Jeremy Paxman, the interviewer, for a genial chat over a cup of coffee. But once filming began, after a series of questions on Iraq and other current topics, the questioning suddenly turned personal.

> *Jeremy Paxman*: Does it trouble you that every single politician to whom we've spoken in preparing for this interview said the same thing – 'You're interviewing Charles Kennedy, I hope he's sober'?
>
> *Charles Kennedy*: No, it doesn't trouble me at all. I mean, this is the kind of thing that goes around the hothouse at Westminster.
>
> *Paxman*: But it matters, if that's the instant response of people, including MPs in your own party.
>
> *Kennedy*: It matters if people allow that kind of rumour or slur to achieve a level of prominence that it doesn't otherwise require. All our MPs, unanimously, have just re-elected me leader for the rest of this parliament. I don't think they'd do that if there were serious questions about my political judgement.
>
> *Paxman*: How much do you drink?
>
> *Kennedy*: Moderately, socially, as you well know.
>
> *Paxman*: You don't drink privately?

Kennedy: What do you mean, privately?

Paxman: By yourself, a bottle of whisky late at night?

Kennedy: No, I do not.

Another two questions followed about why he was marrying, which further upset those close to the couple. The tone of the broadcast prompted complaints in Parliament,[8] and Jeremy Paxman was forced to apologise, saying: 'Maybe there was one question too many on drink.' But members of the Lib Dem leader's own circle were careful not to protest and tried to play down the episode, anxious not to attract further publicity. It was the first time alcohol had become the subject of intensive questioning during a prominent, serious television interview. And until that point Charles Kennedy had laughed off questions about his drinking or used his essentially truthful formula of calling himself a fully paid-up member of the human race. Now he had lied about his alcohol consumption, which in bad periods was neither moderate nor sociable. He had crossed the Rubicon to enter a land of dissembling and denial about his drinking from which he never returned until it was too late. It was a dark moment.

After their wedding Charles Kennedy took much of the summer off as he and Sarah honeymooned in Malaysia and settled happily into their married life together. Although they began hunting for a family house, this took much longer than either had anticipated and they lived together at his flat for almost eighteen months before they were able to move. The period after his marriage was one of his most demanding but ultimately successful, as he was preoccupied more and more by how the Liberal Democrats should respond to the prospect of military intervention in Iraq. It was after the invasion that his demons once again became evident. The final Commons debate to approve the role of British troops in the invasion was traumatic for him. He had been called a traitor – as he had after breaking ranks with colleagues to become the first MP from the SDP to back a merger with the Liberals. The charge was no less wounding fifteen years on. Friends said in the weeks after the invasion of Iraq he went 'into his shell', exhausted and emotionally drained. His performances slumped. As attention turned back to domestic British politics, his colleagues found him introverted and lacking in ideas. Having been absorbed in the Iraq crisis, the party's domestic policy framework needed his attention but Kennedy did not involve himself in it as some colleagues wished. Although the Lib Dems did exceptionally well in the local elections in May he was less active in the campaign than in previous elections, and much less so in the Scottish parliamentary and Welsh assembly elections held on the same day.

On 9 June an important statement was made to the Commons by Gordon Brown, the Chancellor, announcing that four of his five tests for British entry into Europe's single currency had not been met. This was a hammer blow to supporters of the euro. It was clearly unlikely all five tests would be met before the next general election and therefore the question of a referendum on joining the euro would be academic for several years at least. It was the most important government announcement of the parliament, on a policy close to his heart, yet Charles Kennedy was absent from the Commons chamber. He was not due to speak, but this was nonetheless thought odd for a committed pro-European. Matthew Taylor, his Treasury spokesman, saved his leader a place on the Lib Dem front bench; Charles Kennedy's staff said later he watched the statement from his office on a television monitor. In retrospect, they said, he ought to have attended the chamber in person but it was an error of judgement and no more. Few of the senior Lib Dems who knew of his alcoholism accepted this explanation. That night a wealthy Lib Dem supporter threw a party to celebrate the twentieth anniversary of Charles Kennedy's election to Parliament. Ramesh Dewan, a publisher known for sending boxes of Indian sweets to Lib Dem MPs every Christmas and Diwali, hired a fleet of coaches to transport MPs, party officials and other guests from Cowley Street to his mansion in Harrow Weald, north London. A large marquee was erected in the garden and there was a buffet supper and live music for the 400 guests and a lively atmosphere. Some MPs present noticed Kennedy had been drinking heavily, although his host noticed nothing untoward. Ramesh Dewan said:

> It was a jolly party, it was good fun. If I had been an MP for twenty years and you gave a party, you would expect me to have a couple of drinks. As the host, I would have been offended if he did not have a couple of drinks. My recollection is that he was not drunk. The few drinks that he had he could handle. My recollection is that he was very sociable. He was amongst friends.

When Charles Kennedy came to make a speech later in the evening, however, parts of it were incoherent. Some Lib Dems could not bear to watch and walked out of the marquee in embarrassment. 'Yes, it was one of those incidents where he was drunk in public,' Anna Werrin admitted. 'But you would have a lot of twentieth anniversary celebrations for a lot of MPs and you would find very few of them sober at the end of the evening.'

Accounts of the two events became conflated. Some MPs, who tended to see very little of their leader other than at formal events or in the throng of Commons divisions lobbies, knew for certain only that he had missed an important ministerial statement and later that evening had been very drunk at a private, although large, party. The episode generated great concern among senior Lib Dems. In the following weeks they also had ample evidence that Charles Kennedy was in a poor state. Sandra Gidley said:

> I was sitting on the front bench for PMQs; he would walk past reeking of alcohol. He probably had not drunk since the night before; I would not say he was actually drunk at PMQs. Some days he did very good performances. Sometimes he was shaking so much he could hardly hold the papers. He would come to parliamentary party meetings and sit there looking totally disinterested.

Sandra Gidley grew so concerned she made an appointment to see Charles Kennedy and, alone in his office, urged him to seek professional help over the summer, if necessary handing the leadership temporarily to two or three senior colleagues until his return:

> I actually said to him: 'Look, there is a problem, you have got a problem and you have got to sort it. I actually think what you should do is take some time to go away and get a proper detox.' He said: 'Yeah, yeah, things cannot go on the way they are. I give you an assurance I will deal with it. That's not the way I am dealing with it, but I am dealing with it'.

After articles appeared in *The Times*[9] and the *Guardian*[10] reporting concerns about Charles Kennedy's leadership, serious unrest began to grow amongst his MPs for the first time. Some went to see Menzies Campbell, others approached Andrew Stunell, the chief whip, or members of the leader's inner circle; this was the context in which Charles Kennedy and his advisers were on the very brink of a public admission that he was undergoing treatment for a drink problem in July.

Concealing his alcoholism placed considerable strain on those working with Kennedy. Several times during his leadership members of his team considered or even threatened to quit unless he dealt with his drinking. Dick Newby said:

The conversations were on the lines of 'we can't go on, none of us can carry on like this. We can't carry on attempting to keep the show on the road unless there is a show to keep on the road.' A number of people made it clear we just couldn't carry on, which of course he knew intellectually.

Anna Werrin agreed:

> It was often very tense in our office. Charles and I have known each other for twenty years, it was like brother and sister. I did tell him he had to sort things out or I would not stay, not because I had lost confidence or wanted to leave. I wanted him to sort himself out and was determined to make him. I did it to scare him into sorting himself out. The reality was I would never, ever have walked out on him. He was always saying to me: 'You promise you won't leave?' I would never have left and he knows it.

Fortunately for him – and not for the first or last time – a by-election was on hand to save him. Chastened by the media criticisms and the restive mood in his parliamentary party, he threw himself instead into campaigning in Brent East as his route back to political salvation.

Another perceptive newspaper article, by the journalist Anne McElvoy, observed over the summer that he had lost some of his spark:

> Something is not quite right with Mr Kennedy. He looks terribly unhealthy and, uncommonly for him, rather shrunken and nervy. When I first met him as the new leader of the party, he possessed a Tiggerish bounce that was infectious. Now he seems tentative and too reliant on the received wisdom of others. The spontaneity is gone.[11]

The Lib Dems' by-election victory in Brent East, in the week before the autumn party conference, therefore came at a critical time for Kennedy. One opinion poll in target seats, by NOP for the *Guardian*, put the Lib Dems on 28 per cent, within touching distance of the Conservatives, on 30 per cent, and Labour on 35. A mood of optimism, suffused with a considerable degree of complacency, was palpable among Lib Dem delegates as they gathered in Brighton, giving an enormous boost to Kennedy's standing as leader. His message to the conference, in his leader's speech, was a restatement of his strategy of seeking to overtake the Conservatives, which was well received. In the weeks afterwards Kennedy executed his boldest reshuffle, appointing as his Treasury spokesman Vince Cable, formerly chief economist with Shell International, whose understated manner belied an impressive mixture of intelligence and surprising radicalism. This meant demoting Matthew Taylor, the man who chaired Kennedy's leadership campaign, who received a pager message asking him to telephone the leader's office 'to discuss your next job'. Kennedy offered Matthew Taylor the post of health spokesman, but accepted his request to become chairman of the parliamentary party and retain his role in writing the election manifesto. Kennedy also removed the home affairs portfolio from an unwilling Simon Hughes, the party's candidate for mayor of London, who wanted to keep the post for a while longer. Kennedy gave it instead to his ally Mark Oaten with a brief to toughen up the Lib Dems' law and order policies.

Iraq still cast a shadow over British politics. Much attention was now focused on the outcome of the Hutton inquiry, whose report was being drafted. During the interlude before its publication, President Bush made a state visit to Britain as a means of thanking Tony Blair for his support in the Iraq war. By convention Charles Kennedy was invited to meet Bush, a potentially awkward encounter given his opposition to the invasion. The meeting, on 19 November, took place in an elegant state room at Buckingham Palace where Kennedy, Menzies Campbell and Michael Moore were ushered in to see the President after a similar delegation of Conservatives had left. With Bush was Colin Powell, his Secretary of State, Condoleezza Rice, his national security adviser, Karl Rove, his political strategist, and William Farrish, the American ambassador to London, who said nothing throughout. The Liberal Democrats noticed it was Colin Powell who stood out as the most charismatic of the Americans; George Bush did not dominate the room but set the tone in an easy, courteous, welcoming manner and began a rather folksy discussion by observing that Kennedy and his two spokesmen were all Scots. Bush told anecdotes about visiting Scotland as a young man to stay on a farm in Perthshire with Bill Gammell, whose father was a family friend. It was only after such friendly preliminaries that Bush allowed the conversation to come around to the issue that divided them. Kennedy was polite, saying his party had taken a different view and explaining why. Bush took the discussion himself, with his team only participating at his invitation, as he talked of the task of creating stability in Iraq and building a democratic government there. Kennedy and Menzies Campbell raised with him the status of a small number of British citizens arrested in Afghanistan or elsewhere and held as terrorist suspects in Guantanamo Bay, the prison and interrogation centre set up in Cuba outside US legal jurisdiction. Bush then made a concession to them. He made a gesture with his hands to indicate an airline ticket and told them: 'There are tickets for these guys to come home if you guys want them back.' They also briefly discussed the Middle East peace process, although Kennedy and his colleagues surprised the Americans by taking their leave before the time allotted for the meeting had elapsed, explaining a vote was expected in the House of Commons on the government's plans for self-governing foundation hospitals.

During the autumn, the Liberal Democrats found themselves once again eclipsed from the news by changes in the Conservative Party. Tory MPs, taking fright at Iain Duncan Smith's faltering leadership and spurred, perhaps, by the party's irrelevance in the Brent East by-election, brutally exercised for the first time a new procedure to trigger a vote of no confidence, which Iain Duncan Smith lost by ninety votes to seventy-five. Belying fears that a bloody and divisive leadership election would follow, he was replaced without a vote by Michael Howard, an aggressive figure from the party's right and the only member of the Tory front bench with Cabinet experience. Michael Howard's style in his opening weeks as leader was decisive, his tone modernising and Conservative MPs appeared to have united behind him. His leadership heralded hopes of a Conservative revival that dominated the news agenda for several months.

With Blair's authority weakened by the controversy over Iraq and divisions in Labour's ranks, Michael Howard's instinct was to go for a knock-out blow and he latched on to the impending publication of the Hutton report as the means to deliver it. In January 2004, at Prime Minister's Questions in the Commons, he prepared the ground by trying to implicate Tony Blair in leaking the name of David Kelly, whose death was the subject of Hutton's inquiry. He told Blair, and Blair accepted, that if the Prime Minister was shown to have lied to Parliament it would merit his resignation.[12] It was a dramatic exchange and created an expectation that Tony Blair's future depended on the conclusions of the Hutton report. Charles Kennedy was put under considerable pressure in media interviews to join the attack but held back, waiting to see what the inquiry's findings actually were. In the meantime Kennedy showed a flash of steel when Jenny Tonge, now his spokesman on children's issues, enraged international opinion by telling a meeting she would consider being a suicide bomber if she were a Palestinian. In a curt telephone conversation, Kennedy dismissed her from his front bench, although he did later nominate her for a peerage.

As the publication date for the Hutton report approached, a second peril loomed for Tony Blair. His legislation to enable universities to levy top-up fees for students' tuition, which many Labour MPs felt breached their manifesto, faced a critical vote in the House of Commons. This fell the day before the Hutton report was due to be published, creating twin threats for Tony Blair that the Conservatives did all they could to exploit. The legislation on top-up fees passed with a majority of just five, as seventy-three Labour MPs joined the Tories and Liberal Democrats in opposing the measure. The following morning it was snowing and bitterly cold as, at 5.15 a.m., Charles Kennedy and Menzies Campbell were collected from their homes and driven to the Cabinet Office in Whitehall. There, by agreement, they were given six hours to read Lord Hutton's report before it was published, the same as that allowed to Michael Howard. His findings, written in the measured tone of a judge, fell far short of the indictment Michael Howard had anticipated. It cleared Tony Blair of dishonourable or underhand conduct in the chain of events that led to David Kelly taking his own life. Furthermore, it rejected as unfounded the allegation that the government exaggerated the threat from Iraq's weapons of mass destruction to make the case for war. In exchanges in the Commons later that day, Tony Blair angrily demanded that Michael Howard withdraw the charge that he had lied; Charles Kennedy concentrated instead on why Britain went to war when weapons of mass destruction had not been found.

Blair had faced political pressure since the previous year, including from the Conservatives and Liberal Democrats, to hold a much fuller inquiry into the events that led Britain into the Iraq war. Having escaped censure in Lord Hutton's tightly focused inquiry, and with George Bush conceding to an independent inquiry into intelligence failures by the United States, Blair now followed suit. Amid speculation in the media about a fresh inquiry, the Prime Minister telephoned Charles Kennedy at around 7 p.m. on the evening of 2 February with a proposition. He had, he said, asked Robin Butler, a former Cabinet Secretary, to chair an inquiry into the pre-war intelligence and he offered a place on the inquiry committee to a senior Liberal Democrat. A Downing Street official had already approached Alan Beith, a Privy Counsellor, and member of the parliamentary committee with oversight of the security services, to ask him to take part. Alan Beith was keen to participate but replied, dutifully, that he could do so only with the approval of his leader. Blair clearly expected Charles Kennedy to agree and wanted to announce the inquiry that evening. Instead, put on the spot, Kennedy demurred. He pressed Blair on the inquiry's proposed terms of reference and, never comfortable rushing to judgement, said he wished to think about it overnight. Alan Beith and Menzies Campbell were then asked to come to the leader's office. Both thought the Liberal Democrats should be represented on the inquiry, with Menzies Campbell concerned that the party would be isolated if he refused. But by then Kennedy's mind was made up. He would not endorse an inquiry that excluded the political decisions based on intelligence available in the run-up to the war. The following morning, at the weekly meeting of his shadow cabinet, he told colleagues of his decision, explained his reasons and invited comments, but made it very clear he would not be swayed. Robin Butler's appointment met with widespread scepticism, on the ground that he was an 'Establishment' figure unlikely to criticise the way intelligence was handled within Whitehall; this was unfair given his subsequent censure of Blair's informal style of decision-making and bypassing of Cabinet government. Michael Howard initially backed the Butler inquiry but a month later abruptly withdrew his support on the pretext that Robin Butler had chosen to interpret his remit in a restrictive fashion. To Howard's embarrassment the Conservatives' nominee, the Tory MP Michael Mates, refused his leader's request to leave the committee. The saga marked the end of Michael Howard's long political honeymoon as, on this issue at least, Kennedy's judgement proved the sharper.

In the months since abandoning his plan for a public announcement acknowledging his alcoholism, Kennedy did cut back his drinking but severe lapses continued. Anna Werrin said:

> Charles has acknowledged that he had a serious drink problem. There were obviously days when he had been drinking. He has acknowledged that, I am not going to pretend that these days didn't exist. He drank less when he was married and he stopped living that single man's lifestyle, he had a home that he wanted to go home to. I would say that in the years since he became leader he has drunk progressively less each year, but the ability of his body to tolerate what he drank has also got regressively less.

As his own MPs became more conscious of its symptoms, but remained unaware of how exactly he was seeking to deal with it, the danger grew that any mishap, however accidental, would be assumed to be drink related. The night before the Budget statement in March, Charles Kennedy stayed at the Commons until 8.30 p.m. working on his draft response, one of the most testing duties of an opposition party leader. He was, his staff said, on good form, sober and cheerful, and shared a taxi home with Phil Willis. The following morning, however, he failed to arrive for work and members of his staff were unable to reach him by telephone. A young assistant, Gurpreet Dosanjh, was dispatched to his town house in Kennington, south London to bring Kennedy to the Commons. He was admitted into Kennedy's house but Charles Kennedy then disappeared into the bathroom. Anna Werrin made a series of frantic telephone calls to Gurpreet Dosanjh, saying: 'Get him out, get him in here.' The pair finally arrived at the Commons after 11 a.m., with less than an hour until Prime Minister's Questions and the Budget statement immediately afterwards. It was obvious that Charles Kennedy was very ill.

'We dragged him in and we said: "Why didn't you tell us?"' Anna Werrin said. 'And he said: "I knew I had to do it. I have to do it."' She told him he was in no state to sit in the Commons chamber for more than two hours. Both of them knew, however, that his absence would set off a frenzy of speculation that he was incapacitated by drink. The discussion delayed them still further. Anna Werrin said:

> It was a combination of being physically ill and knowing what was going to come in terms of what was going to be written. That was all he had in his head: 'I have to do it, I have to do it. I have got to go and do PMQs, I have to do the Budget.'

When they at last agreed he should not, she telephoned Menzies Campbell with barely half an hour's warning and asked him to stand in at Prime Minster's Questions. She could not at first reach Vince Cable, the Treasury spokesman, to ask him to respond to the Budget statement; when she did there were less than fifteen minutes until the beginning of PMQs. Both men performed creditably, in the circumstances, but the episode was handled in a chaotic fashion due to Charles Kennedy's fear of generating fresh speculation about his alcoholism. Again, although understandably this time, most Lib Dems did not see him during the day and knew only that he had pulled out of appearing in the chamber at short notice.

By another unhappy coincidence, the Lib Dems' spring conference fell four days later at Southport, at which the leader had duties throughout, culminating in a platform speech. On its opening day, Lib Dem MPs were sent an optimistic pager message telling them: 'Charles Kennedy is back on the go and looking forward to seeing you all in Southport.' In fact he remained very ill. He lost a stone in weight in four days and was unable to eat anything but toast. MPs who saw him during the period accepted his explanation that he had a severe stomach bug. Whether it was exacerbated by a combination of stress, nerves and a constitution weakened by alcoholism is another question. He made a campaign visit to a hospital en route – not a good idea, since Sky News carried a strapline saying Charles Kennedy was at a hospital – but spent much of the conference confined to his hotel room. Around the bars in Southport's conference hotels the mood among Lib Dems was very bleak and the state of their leader's health dominated conversations. Jackie Rowley scripted a defensive conference speech for Kennedy setting out his qualities as leader and comparing them with recent judgements by Michael Howard. Charles Kennedy did venture out for a series of meetings and media interviews but it was clearly an effort to do so and those present noticed his hands shook violently.

At first his absence from the Budget statement elicited little press comment. By the weekend newspapers were full of stories about his health and comments from unnamed Lib Dem MPs saying, unhelpfully, he needed to make a good speech to restore his authority as leader. There was further speculation that stage fright or some other psychological trigger was the reason he pulled out of replying to the Budget statement. On Sunday, the day of his speech, Charles Kennedy looked gaunt and pale, and clearly far from well, as he struggled through the text. His performance in the hall itself was laboured but adequate; his voice was gruff and grew hoarser, and halfway through he began mopping his brow with a handkerchief. But it went well enough to educe a polite standing ovation of two and a half minutes from delegates. The television pictures, however, were terrible. In close-up footage it looked disastrous. Under the heat of the stage lights, his perspiration was cruelly magnified, as were his shaking hands. Clips of him mopping his forehead as he struggled through the speech were shown remorselessly on news bulletins.

The coverage in Monday's newspapers was even worse. Many Lib Dem MPs had not been in Southport and had not watched the speech in person. As they returned to Westminster after the weekend they were plunged into a panic. Some had never experienced such negative headlines about their party. Individual MPs or deputations went to see Andrew Stunell, who several felt failed to grasp the scale of their anxieties, Chris Rennard, the party's chief executive, and Menzies Campbell, who a month earlier had been elected deputy leader. Some MPs and senior party figures feared there was a possibility that Kennedy's illness was such that he might have to stand down as leader. With a general election expected in fourteen months' time, this was not a moment to spend three or four months on a leadership election.

Menzies Campbell was urged to be prepared to take over as acting leader to steady the ship and, if necessary, steer the party through for an interim period until perhaps six months after the election. Simon Hughes told Campbell that, in such circumstances, he would not oppose him as a candidate in a leadership contest. The party's MPs appeared ready, if required, to offer Menzies Campbell a 'coronation' in the same way that Conservative MPs anointed Michael Howard unopposed as their leader the previous autumn.

At the height of this turmoil Charles Kennedy gave a television interview to ITN in which he was asked directly if he had a drink problem. He replied: 'I certainly do not have a drink problem. I have always been a sociable person over the years and I have no intention of changing that. But that has no impediment or interference with my life in general or leadership in particular.' Challenged a second time, he replied: 'It is absolutely, categorically untrue and very unfair to me personally to try and make that kind of innuendo.'

Jenny Tonge, who shared serious concerns about his drinking and was herself a doctor, called for him to have a 'top-to-bottom health check', saying: 'If he is chronically ill in some way then he should decide for himself whether he wants to carry on with the job.'

The situation was now critical: his public denials had reached the stage of serious deception and MPs were clamouring for action. The following morning came the moment every leader dreads. A delegation of senior party office holders filed awkwardly into his Commons room to confront Kennedy over the issue he had avoided discussing with them for four and a half years. It comprised Menzies Campbell, Matthew Taylor, Andrew Stunell and Chris Rennard: the party's deputy leader, parliamentary party chairman, chief whip and chief executive. Charles Kennedy, seated to the side of his desk as the others perched on chairs and his green two-seat sofa, was in a very low state. Menzies Campbell, looking uncomfortable, said little, as did Andrew Stunell, and the discussion was led by Chris Rennard and Matthew Taylor. Rennard pressed his leader to talk not about the previous week's illness but the underlying problem of his drinking. At first Charles Kennedy was unwilling, but Rennard pushed him again and again, saying they needed to know what the problem was.

Finally, Rennard asked him directly: 'You are an alcoholic, aren't you?'

After a pause, Charles Kennedy answered with a single word.

'Yes,' he replied.

He did not use the word himself, but it was the first occasion he had made such an admission beyond his tight circle of staff and advisers.

Chris Rennard told him: 'What the party wants, what the party needs, is to have you as leader, but without alcohol.' Matthew Taylor was harder, telling his leader: 'You must never drink again. The next time you pick up a drink, you give up being leader.'

They told him the party could not afford a repeat of such a leadership crisis linked to his health; he must get himself well and look after himself. Critically, however, they said they would support him in doing so. They discussed the forthcoming elections and how important they were to the Lib Dems. Charles Kennedy told them about some of the steps he was taking to avoid alcohol, by altering his routine and focusing on interests as an alternative to drinking. Given the gravity of the circumstances, it was a remarkably friendly and constructive meeting. But implicit in their exchanges, and their emphasis on the next set of elections, was a coded warning. He had three months to prove himself worthy of their trust and support.

That evening, as a series of Commons votes were held on the Budget resolutions, Charles Kennedy made a point of speaking to as many of his MPs as he could in the chamber and division lobbies, telling them he felt better. By then the leadership crisis was subsiding. The following night he addressed his weekly parliamentary party meeting, emphasising his commitment to the summer's elections and outlining to them the broad themes for the general election manifesto, which were to be freedom, fairness and trust. But he addressed directly the question of his health, telling them: 'My health is a legitimate issue and I will take steps to address it.'

The immediate crisis had passed but, to survive, Kennedy had been forced to confront his demons. The onus was now on him to slay them.

9

The campaign trail

To his great good fortune, a target presented itself for Charles Kennedy to aim at. Elections for local councils, and London's mayor and assembly, had been delayed a month to coincide with polls for the European Parliament in June. It would be the biggest political test before the general election. Kennedy returned from the Easter recess refreshed, in a positive frame of mind and eager for the challenge ahead. When members of the four-strong delegation from March assembled again in his Commons office for a follow-up meeting, they were heartened to find his self-assurance and confidence seemed to have returned.

A further reason for optimism rapidly emerged. In a spectacular U-turn, Tony Blair announced he would submit the constitution being hammered out for the European Union to a referendum.[1] Although motives were complex, it was a hugely significant decision. With one bound Blair weakened the negotiating position of Jacques Chirac, the President of France and increasingly his adversary in the European arena, and blew a hole in the Conservatives' manifesto for the European elections. The Tories and Lib Dems, as on the Maastricht treaty and on the euro, had pressed for a referendum on the constitution. For Michael Howard and the Conservatives it meant a chance to kill the constitution, which opinion polls consistently suggested a majority opposed. Tony Blair's move ensured the case against the constitution would instead be channelled into the referendum campaign, when it came. For Charles Kennedy, it presented a double benefit. The Lib Dems, as well as Labour, stood to gain from spiking the Conservatives' guns in the European elections. Moreover, with the prospect of Britain joining the euro effectively dead, a referendum on the constitution offered Charles Kennedy a place on the national stage addressing an issue with which he and his party were indelibly associated: Europe.

In a sign of his bullish mood, Kennedy stamped personally on a fresh flurry of speculation about his leadership. A newspaper report[2] suggesting he consulted friends about standing down after the general election prompted a discussion on the Sunday morning television programme hosted by David Frost.[3] Half in jest, on air David Frost invited Charles Kennedy, if he was watching, to telephone the show and clarify his position. Kennedy, an inveterate follower of political programmes, was indeed tuning in at his croft in Lochaber. Shortly afterwards, the crackly but distinctive voice of the Lib Dem leader was transmitted live as, taking up the offer, he declared: 'This is just complete fiction from start to finish. Full stop.' Lib Dem MPs, some slightly bemused, soon found their pagers humming with messages telling them the matter was dealt with, and concluding: 'Any further comment would be unnecessary and unhelpful – CK.'

As Kennedy divided his time between preliminary campaign visits and Westminster, colleagues noticed their leader made himself more available to them, staying around after Commons divisions instead of returning to his room, and appeared keen to demonstrate that he felt back on top form. Tentatively, he discussed in an interview some of the medical advice he was following, confirming he had seen a doctor and saying he was trying to establish a daily routine that allowed time for three reasonable meals, one of them hot and eaten properly.[4] 'I'm medically MoT-ed fine at the moment,' he said.

Predictably, the Lib Dem campaign for the European elections made Iraq a predominant theme. At its launch in Cowley Street this was justified by Kennedy on grounds that the poll had an international dimension. Although his parallel effort for the council elections dealt ostensibly with local issues, much of the literature at grassroots level similarly highlighted the Lib Dems' opposition to the invasion of Iraq. The elections were, however, rapidly gatecrashed by the UK Independence Party, a small, fractious single-issue movement dedicated to Britain's withdrawal from the European Union. Fortified by a £2 million war chest, chiefly from Paul Sykes, a Yorkshire millionaire disillusioned with the Conservatives, UKIP suddenly let rip. It retained the services of Dick Morris, once a strategist to Bill Clinton, and Max Clifford, a publicist attuned to tabloid newspaper instincts, and produced a campaign that combined celebrity kitsch with singular clarity of message. Robert Kilroy-Silk, a controversial daytime television presenter, stepped forward as a UKIP candidate. Endorsements came from Geoff Boycott, the cricketer, Joan Collins, the actress, and from four rather obscure Tory peers. Suddenly opinion polls forecast that the UKIP was on course to win between 14 and 18 per cent of the vote, leapfrogging the Lib Dems into third place, a prophecy that became self-fulfilling.[5]

Robbed of a distinctive policy on Europe, the Conservatives watched in horror as core supporters threw themselves into UKIP's embrace, epitomised briefly by the handsome and media-savvy Robert Kilroy-Silk. The Tories managed to win the election but their share of the vote plunged by 9 per cent, and Labour's by 5.4 per cent. The Lib Dems experienced the indignity of being pushed into fourth place by a ragbag band of opponents whose outlook was the polar opposite of their own. But their vote share rose 2.3 per cent and their tally of seats went up from ten to twelve as they gained MEPs in the north-west and, for the first time, the north-east, despite a cut in the number of British MEPs. This fell one short of Chris Rennard's goal of thirteen as hopes of another in London were frustrated by a poor Lib Dem performance in the capital. Privately some Lib Dems pinned the blame on a lacklustre bid to be London's mayor by Simon Hughes, who trailed third as Ken Livingstone, having rejoined Labour, was re-elected. This was Tony Blair's sole consolation on a wretched night for Labour. In the local elections the Conservatives gained 283 councillors. Charles Kennedy was given a boost as his party came second in terms of share of votes cast, gaining 137 council seats. The Lib Dems dramatically won control in Newcastle-upon-Tyne and Pendle in Lancashire but lost power in Cheltenham, Winchester and Eastbourne. Here was a pattern that foretold the Lib Dems' prospects in the general election, of big swings from Labour in the north but a loss of ground to the Conservatives in parts of the south. Labour lost 479 seats in the local elections, coming third in the share of the vote and prompting David Blunkett, then Home Secretary, to declare himself 'mortified'.

Charles Kennedy had reason to feel well satisfied by these results and fate conspired to give him a further opportunity to demonstrate his flair for campaigning. The death of Jim Marshall, Labour MP for Leicester South, created a by-election in the very type of constituency, part inner city, ethnically mixed, where Lib Dems had picked up support from a sense of disillusionment with the government. The party lay in third place but the city's two universities offered a student population ripe for incitement over tuition and top-up fees. Unlike in Brent East in 2003, the Lib Dems had a substantial local government base in Leicester, having won minority control

of the city council the previous year, and a reasonably sized local membership. With the ingredients on hand for a classic Lib Dem by-election upset,
Chris Rennard advised Kennedy from the outset that they had a realistic
chance of winning. The Lib Dem leader told his staff to reorganise his diary
where necessary to free up big blocks of time for by-election visits. Swiftly the
Lib Dems selected as their candidate Parmjit Singh Gill, a local Sikh city
councillor, and as a campaign headquarters took a lease on a cavernous
former bank building with a warren of offices on a floor above. Thus
prepared, they began their practised arts of street level agitation over sub-post
office branch closures, council tax bills, university top-up fees, and most
heavily, the occupation of Iraq.

Labour, planning its defence of Leicester South, drew three conclusions
from the party's humiliation in Brent East. It planned a relatively quick
campaign. It chose a candidate with strong local credentials, the city council's
former leader Peter Soulsby, who opposed the Iraq war. Most importantly, it
turned its back on a campaign based on reciting achievements of the Labour
government and resolved to attack the opposition. The gloves came off. On
his visits to Leicester, Charles Kennedy found himself intercepted by small
but vociferously hostile counter-demonstrations by Labour supporters.
Parmjit Singh Gill was pilloried for his record as the city's cabinet member
responsible for social care after the council's withdrawal of £2 million of
grants to voluntary groups and a proposal, although hastily dropped, to cut
bus passes. While Parmjit Singh Gill, who was not a charismatic candidate,
was attacked politically he was not attacked personally. This was at the
insistence of Phil Woolas, who ran Labour's campaign, to avoid accusations
of racism. But Labour seized on the fact that Lib Dem literature on some
largely white council estates called him Pramjit Gill, and dropped Singh from
his name. The Lib Dems responded with ferocious attacks on the tenure of
Peter Soulsby – 'Tony Blair's man' – in eighteen years running the city,
saying, gleefully, he awarded himself 'fat cat pay rises', raised council tax bills,
closed schools and homes for the elderly, and was 'thrown out by voters last
year'. As the mud-slinging intensified, leaflets without a publisher's mark
were distributed in Asian communities carrying a photograph of Parmjit
Singh Gill shaking hands with a transsexual, and the heading: 'Is this the man
you want as your MP?'

The Conservatives tried to make this a three-cornered fight. Michael
Howard, facing his first by-election as leader, made three visits to Leicester
to signal his determination to mount a challenge and test a 'diversity'

initiative to reconnect with black and ethnic minority voters. His chief whip, David Maclean, took a close interest in the Tory effort and dispatched regular coach parties of Conservative MPs to help. The Conservatives made crime a core theme and experimented in new electoral arts they used later in the general election, but by and large concentrated on policy. Copying the Focus leaflets developed by Liberal councillors in Liverpool forty-two years earlier, the Tories produced ward-level news sheets. Borrowing from Republican congressional campaign techniques in the United States, they took full-page colour advertisements in the *Leicester Mercury*. Yet as Tory handbills began to attack the Lib Dems, not Labour, it became clear Michael Howard's efforts were failing.

With electioneering in Leicester South in full swing Terry Davis, Labour MP for Birmingham Hodge Hill, resigned his seat on being elected secretary general of the Council of Europe. It meant another by-election in similar circumstances; again Kennedy agreed his party should fight to win. Shrewdly, Labour moved the writs for both seats for the same day, 15 July, ensuring a snap campaign in Hodge Hill, and stretching the Lib Dems' resources with simultaneous by-elections. The Lib Dems had never successfully fought two by-elections on the same day. The closest parallel was in May 1986 when Liberal candidates, under the aegis of the Liberal/SDP Alliance, won Ryedale in Yorkshire but narrowly failed to replicate the upset in West Derbyshire. The Liberal Party had last pulled off a double by-election coup at Ripon and the Isle of Ely in July 1973.

With two campaigns in progress, the by-elections became a major focus for Charles Kennedy. Labour's tactics in defending Birmingham Hodge Hill, led by two of its tougher MPs, Tom Watson and Fraser Kemp, duplicated the roughhouse politics in operation 45 miles away in Leicester. Demonstrators rocked Kennedy's car during one of his five visits to the constituency. But in one regard, Labour went farther, ruthlessly targeting the Lib Dem candidate, Nicola Davies, who in her professional life worked for the Mobile Phone Operators Association as its council liaison officer. Tom Watson and Fraser Kemp portrayed her as a campaigner for installing mobile phone masts and called her 'Nokia' Davies, after the manufacturer of mobile phone handsets.[6] To their delight, Charles Kennedy repeated this moniker in one interview as he tried to protest at the treatment of his candidate, reinforcing their 'attack line'. Labour branded the Lib Dems soft on crime and against summary justice powers to curb anti-social behaviour; the Lib Dems claimed the constituency had been neglected under Labour, which had lost control of Birmingham City Council to a Tory–Lib Dem coalition, and campaigned heavily on Iraq. As in Leicester South, the Conservatives threw considerable resources into contesting Hodge Hill, delivering 300,000 leaflets over the three weeks and again flooding wards with coach parties of Tory MPs, who sipped Pimm's on the journey home.

Two weeks from polling day the spectre of Iraq returned to haunt both Tony Blair and Michael Howard. Robin Butler's inquiry into pre-war intelligence arranged to publish its report on 14 July, a day before the by-elections. Tony Blair had scheduled major government announcements on health and education spending to coincide with the campaigns, culminating in the Chancellor's three-year public spending statement; instead, as voters visited polling stations, the news would be dominated by the war. Newspapers began to talk of a difficult forty-eight hours facing the Prime Minister[7] and, before long, of a defining week in British politics.[8] The air of anticipation created just the kind of pressure-cooker feeling required for a Lib Dem by-election upset. Chris Rennard, making triangular train journeys between London, Leicester and Birmingham, faced competing internal pressures to devote more resources to help a woman candidate or to secure the party's first non-white MP; he went for broke in both, but Leicester South looked the better bet.

With days to go, Lib Dem canvassers in Leicester South found the Tory vote firmer than expected in the affluent suburbs thanks to the intensive Conservative activity. A letter in Charles Kennedy's name was delivered saying the Tories could not win and that only the Lib Dems could beat Labour, a classic squeeze of Conservative support. Final Lib Dem canvass returns suggested they were just ahead in Leicester South and that Hodge Hill would go to a recount. The party was very keen for Charles Kennedy to be associated with a victory in either. In secret Kennedy, Dick Newby, Tim Razzall and Anna Werrin drove up during in the evening and checked into Weston Hall, a country house hotel near Nuneaton, equidistant between the two, where they watched coverage from both counts on television. Had they won both, Charles Kennedy would have gone immediately to Birmingham, the longer shot. In the event, Labour held Hodge Hill by a margin of 460, on a turnout of 37.9 per cent. As she conceded defeat, Nicola Davies was subjected to a final indignity as Labour supporters pre-programmed their mobile handsets to greet her remarks with the sound of ringing mobile phones. The Lib Dems achieved a 27.7 per cent swing from Labour in three weeks and were convinced they could have won with more time, but

Labour's tactics paid off. In Leicester South the swing was smaller, at 21.5 per cent, but enough to give Parmjit Singh Gill a majority of 1,654. His victory speech, written by Chris Rennard knowing it would be televised live, gave credit to Charles Kennedy. Within a couple of hours, the Lib Dem leader arrived at a victory party in a neon-lit bar in Leicester. Despite getting lost as he was driven back to their hotel, he returned the following morning for a walkabout in the constituency. Charles Kennedy was prominent in all the media coverage of the by-election triumph. There could be no doubt whose victory this was.

The loss of a safe Labour seat was an embarrassment to Tony Blair but was contained by holding Birmingham Hodge Hill. John Reid, then health secretary, cleverly portrayed the results as 'a score draw'.[9] The Conservatives, pushed into third place in both despite fighting full-scale campaigns, were seen as the biggest losers and hopes of a Tory revival under Michael Howard began to fade.[10] Commentators began to talk of a Lib Dem bandwagon,[11] or at least of taking the Lib Dems seriously for the first time,[12] while the Sun paid the back-handed compliment of branding them 'the most dangerous party in Britain'.[13] Remarkably, given Charles Kennedy's precarious position in March, his authority was restored. A week later another opportunity, albeit an unlikely one, beckoned. The day after Parliament rose for its summer recess, Tony Blair nominated his long-time confidant Peter Mandelson as Britain's next European Commissioner, requiring him to resign his seat in Hartlepool and precipitating a third by-election. Such a move had been the subject of considerable speculation, including about the possibility of holding all three by-elections on the same day, but the Lib Dems were astonished nonetheless. So keen was Charles Kennedy to get back on the campaign trail that, with the date of the by-election unclear, he discussed several times with colleagues a plan to cancel a forthcoming trip to the Democratic national convention in the United States and rent a house over the summer in the north-east, within striking distance of Hartlepool.

In the event, with the likelihood of a quick poll in Hartlepool receding, he went to the Democratic convention in Boston – his first – with a Lib Dem party of his wife Sarah, Tim Razzall, Jane Bonham Carter, Chris Rennard, Menzies Campbell and Richard Holme. Its scale and carnival-like atmosphere made a powerful impression on Charles Kennedy. As a former student of political rhetoric he was fascinated by the speeches. He watched the acceptance speech of John Kerry, the Democrats' presidential candidate, and was captivated by Bill Clinton, who had to accelerate his remarks to fit network television schedules; effortlessly Clinton condensed his speech to exactly twenty-two minutes. Charles Kennedy took a close interest in the use by Democrats of internet fund-raising, which he discussed in detail with members of Howard Dean's campaign for the presidential nomination. While Kennedy was there an opinion poll put the Lib Dems on 28 per cent, with Labour and the Conservatives both on 30 per cent.[14] To his own surprise, and delight, the Lib Dem leader found himself recognised on the streets of Boston by followers of Prime Minister's Questions and after the four-day convention, he and Sarah stayed to spend a weekend together in the city before returning to London.

Up in Hartlepool, the by-election was shaping up to be predictably bruising. Tom Watson and, replacing him later, Fraser Kemp, the brutally effective duo responsible for Labour's victory in Birmingham Hodge Hill, were dispatched to Teesside to repeat the feat while the Lib Dems, with a whole summer to prepare the ground, set to work on overturning a Labour majority of 14,571. Unbeknown to them, Labour began with a crucial advantage for which, ironically, they could thank Arthur Scargill, the hard-left former president of the National Union of Mineworkers. In the 2001 general election, Scargill, a bitter opponent of New Labour, stood for the Socialist Labour Party against Peter Mandelson in Hartlepool. He had no chance of winning – he polled just 912 votes – yet Peter Mandelson took the threat sufficiently seriously to ensure thorough canvassing was done to get out the Labour vote. He memorably made a hoarse and rather triumphal speech at the Hartlepool count saying his re-election showed 'I am a fighter, not a quitter.' As a result, Labour began its defence in the Hartlepool by-election with much better canvass records than in most safe seats.

Charles Kennedy again threw himself into the by-election. The Lib Dems tried to turn the contest into a referendum on the future of Hartlepool's hospital, saying ministers wanted to close it. Labour responded with its familiar criticism that Lib Dems were soft on crime and yobs. But the campaign took off over an unforced error by the Lib Dem candidate, Jody Dunn, a multilingual family law barrister who practised in Hartlepool. Eager to break new ground, the Lib Dems announced their candidate would write and publish a by-election blog, or online diary, of regular updates on the campaign, the first candidate to do so in a British election. Jody Dunn turned herself to the task with alacrity and, hoping if she won to interest a publisher in reproducing them as a book, placed a premium on adopting a lively, readable style. One wet night in late August, canvassing with Simon Hughes, now the party's incoming president, they began knocking on doors. Of the householders at home, one had been in the bath and answered the door wrapped in a towel, another had been drinking, a third was accompanied by a barking dog and a fourth was a Labour Party member. It was a dispiriting experience but made humorous reading for her blog. 'We'd picked what appeared at first to be a fairly standard row of houses,' Jody Dunn wrote. 'As time went on, however, we began to realise that everyone we met was either drunk, flanked by an angry dog or undressed.'

As usual her copy was checked by a Lib Dem minder, Ed Fordham, who removed a reference to the Labour Party member she tried to canvass, but thought the rest fine to be posted online. Within a day Labour inflated her remarks as an attack on the entire 67,500-strong electorate of Hartlepool, in a leaflet headed 'Outrage at candidate's insult to town'. As the story took off, Jody Dunn was interviewed on BBC Radio 4's *Today* programme. Rather than explain she had been referring to three or four householders in one street, and that she certainly did not think them typical of Hartlepudlians, she declared she had nothing to apologise for. Labour's campaign team recorded her interview on a CD-ROM which they distributed in Hartlepool, and toured the town's streets in a bus playing clips of her defiance over a loud speaker.

Despite these shenanigans, the Lib Dems made Jody Dunn the star turn of their party conference in Bournemouth. With her parents and eldest child, she was flown down from Durham and Tees Valley airport in an eight-seat aircraft piloted by Lembit Öpik, the Lib Dem MP, and introduced with great razzmatazz to the conference. In response to her speech delegates broke into chants of 'Jody! Jody!'. After Charles Kennedy's own speech, with a sense of theatre, he joined her in the aircraft to fly to Hartlepool, in an attempt to create a buzz in the Teesside media. The *Guardian* now began to get very excited about the impending by-election, for which, unusually, the writ was moved during the summer recess for the concluding Thursday of Labour's conference in Brighton. The *Guardian* sent a reporter to Hartlepool for an entire month, who produced a very long dispatch[15] that included a flattering profile of Jody Dunn and suggested Labour's candidate, Iain Wright, had little to offer beyond his Hartlepool roots. If he won, the *Guardian* reported, he might even face moves to deselect him. On the same day the paper's respected commentator Martin Kettle wrote that the result would determine whether Tony Blair stayed to fight the general election or quit and handed over to Gordon Brown.[16] On polling day itself the *Guardian*, usually if begrudgingly supportive of Labour, published an extraordinary leading article announcing: 'If this newspaper had a vote in Hartlepool today, it would go to the Liberal Democrats.'[17] It continued: 'We still support most of the aims of this Labour Government. The Liberal Democrats, though, are the one party to have consistently opposed the war and to have consistently tried to hold the executive to account. This election is about the effectiveness of Parliament.'

Its intervention came too late to tip the balance and Labour held Hartlepool with a majority of 2,033. As Jody Dunn spoke at the count she was struck by a powder bomb of purple dye thrown by a candidate for Fathers4Justice, a direct action group targeting her over her legal work in family courts. The Lib Dems achieved another large swing, of almost 19 per cent, while the Conservatives were humiliated, pushed into fourth place behind the UK Independence Party. The by-election reinforced Charles Kennedy's party as the chief challengers to Labour in many of its traditional heartlands and boosted its media profile. Yet Labour's victory checked the Lib Dem bandwagon and, sub-consciously, set a ceiling on what the party could achieve.

As he had at Romsey in 2000, Chris Rennard used the four by-elections in the latter half of the parliament to 'road test' campaign themes for the general election. For him, no amount of market research could beat listening to a group of experienced canvassers reporting their findings on a busy Saturday with a by-election in full swing. There were, however, drawbacks to such an approach. All four by-elections were in predominantly urban seats and pitched the Lib Dems against Labour, not the Conservatives. Moreover, as the *Guardian*'s leading article on Hartlepool suggested, by-elections are an opportunity to send a message rather than choose a government. The Lib Dems developed a series of such messages that apparently resonated with the electorate, at least in Labour-held inner-city seats where these were most tested, and compounded them into a draft manifesto for the Bournemouth conference.[18] This so-called pre-manifesto, 5,000 words long and produced as a tabloid newspaper, was half the length of the equivalent document before the 2001 election and was to be the centrepiece of the pre-election conference. It still tried to convey values, through its title *Freedom, Fairness, Trust*, but it gave priority to a list of policy pledges, styled 'ten reasons to vote Liberal Democrat'. They were wearyingly familiar; by the time they were reproduced in the manifesto itself the following spring, the document had been shorn of any unifying theme and was slightly anodyne. Hence huge interest was sparked when the party's younger generation of MPs came up with a radical policy agenda of their own: *The Orange Book.*

Policy discussion should, in theory, have been channelled via working groups and into the manifesto. The policy commission set up by Charles Kennedy after the 2001 election under Chris Huhne's chairmanship succeeded in drawing some of the sting from an ideological argument within the party over the role of private companies in providing public services. His report[19] left the door open to the private sector but laid emphasis on a greater role for mutual and other not-for-profit groups to run services. It was one of the clearest statements of Kennedy's own ideals. It also proposed devolving responsibility for key public services, and taxation powers, to regional or local government. This emphasis on regional government was removed after people in north-east England voted in November 2004 by a four-to-one margin against a regional assembly in a referendum. The Huhne commission also proposed replacing national insurance contributions with a ring-fenced tax for the National Health Service. The nature of political debate over funding public services changed, however, after the Budget of 2002, in which Gordon Brown raised national insurance contributions by 1 per cent, generating £8 billion a year more for health services. In a move of profound strategic importance, Charles Kennedy subsequently dropped the Lib Dems' pledge of adding 1p to income tax to raise money for education, which had seen them through three elections to become their best-known policy, and decreed his party would no longer advocate higher taxes for basic rate taxpayers. As with previous strategic shifts, he handled this gradually, conceding the opportunity for an arresting act of political positioning in order to achieve maximum consensus within his party. Higher rate taxpayers would still have to pay more, at a new threshold of 50p on incomes over £100,000 a year, from which the revenue would fund three commitments: to abolish university tuition fees, reintroduce free personal care, and subsidise the transition between abolishing the council tax and replacing it with a local income tax. In a new approach to signal greater financial discipline, Charles Kennedy announced in spring 2003 that his frontbench spokesmen would seek cuts in existing Whitehall budgets of £5 billion a year, including privatising services, to fund any further spending commitments.[20] This exercise was led by David Laws, the party's former policy director and now an MP, in the relatively new Lib Dem post of shadow Chief Secretary to the Treasury. It produced some eye-catching results, such as a proposal by Vince Cable to abolish the Department of Trade and Industry, and some heated internal quarrels as Lib Dem spokesmen adjusted to the discipline of cutting budgets rather than advocating higher taxes to enable their inexorable expansion.

David Laws was, therefore, already a controversial figure when, in the summer of 2004, he lobbed a grenade into his party's pre-election policy mix. Originally an investment banker, he made his name in the City when as a junior member of staff he was left to run the US dollar treasury at J. P. Morgan while more senior colleagues went on a golfing trip to Ireland. In their absence Alan Greenspan, head of the US Federal Reserve and the man responsible for setting US interest rates, released a characteristically Delphic letter about the health of America's economy. David Laws made a snap decision to buy over $1 billion's worth of eurodollar interest rate futures on the Chicago market, effectively betting that American interest rates would fall. The young banker's judgement was subsequently vindicated with a quarter-point cut in US interest rates, making a profit of more than $10 million for the bank. David Laws was able to retire from the City aged twenty-eight to devote himself to politics. He and Paul Marshall, who stood as an SDP parliamentary candidate in Fulham in 1987 and later founded a successful investment fund, co-edited a book of policy essays seeking to apply liberal principles to the emerging policy challenges for the twenty-first century and reclaim the strands of economic, political, personal and social liberal thought. Of the eight MPs or candidates who contributed, several were economists and David Laws himself, Vince Cable, Chris Huhne, Ed Davey, Susan Kramer, Nick Clegg and Mark Oaten were all on the party's centre-right. Only Steve Webb, whose chapter on the family and the state was co-written with his researcher Jo Holland, wrote from a left-of-centre perspective. Several essays were challenging. Vince Cable proposed greater plurality and choice in public services. Nick Clegg argued Lib Dems must be stronger advocates of reforming the European Union. But David Laws's twin contributions were incendiary. His first, striking at a social liberal mindset predominant amongst Lib Dem activists, argued for more choice, competition and consumer power in public services to achieve social policy goals and reasserted Gladstone's commitment to free market principles, saying these were unnecessarily ceded to the Conservatives in the 1980s. His second was more specific, accusing the National Health Service of failing to meet contemporary expectations and proposing a national health insurance scheme in which health services would be provided by competing private, employer, not-for-profit or mutual insurers for an annual charge per patient met from taxation. This was directly contrary to the Lib Dem policy in the pre-manifesto, which supported the existing National Health Service while proposing decentralisation and greater use of preventative medicine.

The Orange Book stimulated considerable interest from commentators keen to look beyond the limited and carefully chosen policy offerings served up at the Bournemouth conference, which Charles Kennedy intended to use as a shop window for the rigorous approach to costing spending commitments he had ushered in. It created confusion, too, among the Lib Dems' critics. The *Sun* portrayed Charles Kennedy as a spitting cobra, calling him a danger to the nation with plans for 'a staggering forty tax hikes'.[21] On the same day, the *Daily Mirror* ran a front-page headline of 'Orange Tories' with a photograph of Charles Kennedy's face superimposed with Margaret Thatcher's, saying his party's soul was 'no longer to the left of Labour' on tax and spending. But many Lib Dems were furious with David Laws. A fringe meeting to launch *The Orange Book* was cancelled as his fellow contributors got cold feet and pulled out; they included Mark Oaten, who became involved after meeting Paul Marshall through his centre-right pressure group Liberal Future. By this stage Mark Oaten had resigned as chairman of Liberal Future as he positioned himself for a leadership bid, but his involvement left one legacy. He persuaded Charles Kennedy to pen a foreword to the book, which, although just 178 words long, gave it the leader's seal of approval. The foreword encouraged lively debate within the party, and said: 'Not all of the ideas in *The Orange Book: Reclaiming Liberalism* are party policy, but all are compatible with our Liberal heritage.'

Charles Kennedy's position was awkward. There was a case for sacking David Laws for contradicting party policy and undermining the health spokesman, Paul Burstow. David Laws had submitted a paper proposing such a health insurance system to Chris Huhne's commission on public services, which rejected it; his critics pointed out that David Laws, a member of the commission, did not even attend the session when it was discussed. The by-election in Hartlepool, where the Lib Dems were campaigning to save the National Health Service hospital, was in its penultimate week. At the first parliamentary party meeting after the Commons returned, David Laws was given a roasting by fellow MPs. Sarah Teather, who telephoned David Laws beforehand to forewarn him, opened by criticising his timing, saying he had overshadowed a launch of the party's health policy. About a dozen MPs piled in after her, led by Alistair Carmichael, calling it irresponsible to propose an alternative health policy so close to an expected general election and with an important by-election in progress. Members of the 2001 intake, who had often been exhorted not to rock the boat, asked why the principle of collective frontbench responsibility was not applied to the shadow cabinet. Some of the attacks were sharp and personal, and there was criticism, too, of the brief contribution to *The Orange Book* from Charles Kennedy. He stayed silent during the exchanges. David Laws defended himself, saying he had not known the book's publication would coincide with a by-election, but it was a very bruising encounter.

Although Charles Kennedy had to engage in firefighting to douse down tempers, his chief of staff took a more relaxed perspective. Dick Newby said:

> Certainly my view was that people like David Laws had clear views which they expressed in *The Orange Book*. People were up in arms against them but what was required from those people was equally clear views about what they wanted to do, which were not forthcoming. I think Charles's view was to encourage them to make a response, to have a debate.

Alistair Carmichael and two activists, Duncan Brack and Gareth Epps, considered publishing a left-of-centre riposte after the general election but it was overtaken by events and failed to materialise.

During the months since March, Charles Kennedy's public performances had, by and large, been good. Privately some Lib Dem MPs, including some close to Kennedy, still wondered if he enjoyed his role and thought he would stay until the election and then bow out, given the crisis that had engulfed his leadership in the spring. Charles Kennedy was drinking more infrequently, although there were sporadic lapses, and he continued to make occasional, coy references to his battle with alcoholism. In an interview with *The Times* at the Bournemouth conference he disclosed he had all but given up drinking,[22] moving away from his standard response of two years that he drank moderately and socially. Kennedy said:

> I haven't bothered with alcohol, hardly at all, just because I have been busy and physically active, which has been good. When I was not well earlier this year, when you are cooped up in one room with nothing to look at but four walls and a field for a few days, it does give you time to think. I had quite a spring cleaning with myself. I said, you are coming up to forty-five and this is a pretty gruelling job, you can't get away with things that you can get away with in terms of your own physique when you are twenty-five. You just have to accept the graceful passage of time.

Although he referred to taking walks, regular meals and sleeping better, he was clearly hinting at a determined effort to improve his health, in the same breath as renouncing alcohol. Once the interview was finished, and they were alone in a makeshift room in the conference hotel, Kennedy turned to Jackie Rowley and told her: 'That was quite deliberate. I meant to do it.'

He was not quite able to escape the shadow of the crisis caused by missing the Budget statement in the spring. During the week of the Lib Dem conference Mary Ann Sieghart, the author of occasional but well-informed commentaries on the Liberal Democrats, wrote an account in *The Times* of the events of March. She attributed Kennedy's failure to appear in the Commons not to illness but to drinking too much as he 'decided to fortify himself in advance', and said he had done the same before missing the statement on the euro in June 2003.[23] Charles Kennedy's staff was furious, believing that if left unchallenged, such allegations would resurface in the coming general election campaign, and demanded a retraction; *The Times* stood robustly by her story and refused. Two days before her piece appeared, Mary Ann Sieghart had been spotted by several conference-goers having lunch at the Highcliffe Hotel in Bournemouth with Menzies and Elspeth Campbell. In an illustration of the difficult relationship between Charles Kennedy and his deputy leader, Menzies Campbell subsequently agreed to write a private letter to *The Times* admitting he had discussed the episode with Mary Ann Sieghart and admitting he had not seen Charles Kennedy in person on the day of the Budget and could not therefore say whether he had been drinking. On that basis, the newspaper published a brief correction, saying it accepted Kennedy had not been drinking on the day of the Budget and apologising for any misunderstanding.[24]

The conference season produced one further twist. Labour politicians tended to ignore the Lib Dems and attack the Conservatives. This time they put the Liberal Democrats in their line of fire, too. Tony Blair led the way with his speech to the Labour conference at Brighton, although he did so in curious fashion by first mentioning his own regard for Charles Kennedy: 'I know people say we should take the Lib Dems seriously. But I can't. I like Charles, incidentally. But . . . the great advantage of the Lib Dems is precisely that no one knows what they stand for. If they ever find out, it'll be the end of you.'[25]

That autumn, as his general election preparations gathered apace, Charles Kennedy announced that he and Sarah were expecting their first child, due by a quirk of fate in April, when the campaign was likely to be underway. It looked as though his transition from hard-living bachelor to settled family man might soon be complete. The following spring, in Harrogate at the final Lib Dem conference before the anticipated election, Charles Kennedy again gave a rare glimpse of the inner man. Addressing the conference's closing session, he added some highly personal remarks, paying warm tribute to Roy Jenkins, who died in 2003. 'I miss him dearly, particularly when the going gets rough politically,' he said. 'That's when you need your principles.' With the air of one walking, hesitantly, in his mentor's footsteps, he compared the Lib Dem's chances in the coming general election with those of the founders of the Liberal/SDP Alliance, saying the opportunity now was greater, given the Lib Dems' broader political base. Charles Kennedy then thanked Sarah, his wife, saying: 'On a personal level Sarah and I have never been more happy. I have never felt more personally fulfilled.' He told his Lib Dem audience they owed her a debt of gratitude, as a councillor, wife and, soon, mother of their child.

For a reason known only to a handful, Charles Kennedy had another motive to view the approaching election with excitement. In December, an e-mail arrived at the Lib Dems' headquarters in Cowley Street posing some questions on details of policy. The correspondent, Michael Brown, was particularly interested in Third World debt and asked if he might meet representatives from the party over lunch. Chris Rennard took the inquiry sufficiently seriously to ask two of his senior staff, Ben Stoneham and Kate Haywood, to arrange to see Michael Brown at Cowley Street. As he was leaving one of them noticed their visitor had a chauffeur. It was only then that the Lib Dems decided they should introduce Michael Brown to the party's treasurer, Reg Clark. He was duly invited in January to a discreet lunch in Dining Room D, a small room for private functions in the House of Commons, where a dozen or so potential donors were introduced to Charles Kennedy. Michael Brown was sufficiently impressed that, on 10 February, he gave the party £100,000, a big sum for the Lib Dems but not seismic. Since he lived in Majorca and had not registered to vote in Britain, either as an expatriate or by registering at his London flat, he was not permitted to make a personal donation. Instead he paid the money via an investment company in London he had bought the previous summer, 5th Avenue Partners. That was not all. He liked Charles Kennedy. After further contacts, in which he expressed interest in coming to the spring conference, Charles Kennedy accepted an offer to travel to the conference with Michael Brown in a private aircraft, enabling him to visit a mosque in the target seat of Rochdale en route, and back afterwards to be with his wife Sarah, by now eight months pregnant. On 25 February, a week before the conference, Michael Brown gave the party a further £151,000, through the same route. In Harrogate he attended a dinner for around twenty wealthy financial supporters and, as his liking for Charles Kennedy grew, the tenor of their dialogue began to change. Senior Lib Dems told Michael Brown of the financial firepower deployed by their opponents in elections, saying in rough terms Labour and the Conservatives had spent £20 million each on election budgets in 2001, compared to the Lib Dems' £2 million.

While in Harrogate, Michael Brown produced a letter for Charles Kennedy, which he presented to Anna Werrin, containing a startling proposal. He offered to double the Lib Dems' financial firepower for the election and asked how such extra resources would be spent if he did so. He wished, he explained, to create a more level playing field in British politics. Michael Brown was invited to a meeting soon afterwards in an interview room at the House of Lords with Anna Werrin and Tim Razzall, who outlined his election campaign budget and how any extra donation could be spent. There was no time to hire more staff or invest in an enhanced telephone call centre operation, as the Conservatives had done. Instead Razzall proposed a massive blitz of advertising via posters, newspaper display advertisements and leaflets. Afterwards an e-mail was dispatched to Michael Brown taking him at his word and outlining a business plan to double campaign spending, implying a donation of between £3 and £3.5 million; he replied saying they could have another £2 million. On 22 March, his company transferred to the Lib Dems' bank account £1,536,064.80, by far the biggest donation in the party's history. Eight days later came a further £632,000. Michael Brown, after an acquaintance with the Lib Dems spanning barely four months, had given the party fractionally over £2.4 million – more than its entire budget for the 2001 general election. It gave Kennedy a huge opportunity in the forthcoming campaign; when things began to go wrong, however, the unconventional circumstances of the donation caused him great damage.

The sums cleared literally days before Tony Blair was expected to go to Buckingham Palace and ask the Queen to dissolve Parliament, the formalities required to call the general election for 5 May. Chris Rennard embarked on a round of newspaper advertising and billboard posters on a scale the party had never seen. Press advertisements were the most flexible, enabling the Lib Dems to combine appeals for support in national newspapers and websites with large display advertisements in regional and local newspapers in target seats. Reinforcing this, eleven million tabloid campaign newspapers were distributed as inserts in free local newspapers. Buying up poster sites in such constituencies at very short notice was difficult and the location of Lib Dem billboards was dependent on finding available hoardings, which tended to be in more deprived areas. But 2,200 Lib Dem election posters with large pictures of Charles Kennedy were displayed. It was still a sea change for the Lib Dems, whose advertising budget had, until Michael Brown's largesse, been limited to a handful of poster vans touring target seats. The week before the campaign proper Michael Brown again stepped in to help, providing a private aircraft to enable Charles Kennedy to fulfil a four-day dash around each of the television regions for press conferences in airport hotels, aimed at the regional media.

Charles Kennedy's schedule was intended to create a sense of momentum and seize the opportunity of greater media coverage that was so important to Lib Dems during past general election campaigns. This was stalled by the death of Pope John Paul II, as the public reacted strongly with a sense of mourning and reflection. Tony Blair postponed for twenty-four hours his visit to Buckingham Palace, planned for 4 April, and campaigning activity was suspended, as it was again on 8 April for the Pope's funeral, for which Tony Blair, Michael Howard and Charles Kennedy travelled to Rome. The wedding of Prince Charles and Camilla Parker Bowles, due the same day, was put back to 9 April, losing another day's electioneering. Lib Dems were, therefore, already frustrated at the loss of three days' activity from their election grid when the first full day of the campaign, 11 April, was interrupted by the birth of Charles and Sarah Kennedy's son.

Having declared beforehand that their baby would come first, Charles Kennedy was as good as his word. He navigated his first 7.30 a.m. election press conference at Local Government House, sparsely attended as Michael Howard launched his Conservative manifesto at 8 a.m. and Labour retaliated with a 7.20 a.m. press conference. Kennedy was driven to Godalming Sixth Form College in Surrey, where he addressed sixty politics students and felt sufficiently emboldened to risk inviting a show of hands on how they would vote – almost half said Lib Dem. Just after press notices were dispatched from Cowley Street for the planned launch of the Lib Dem manifesto the next morning, and with Charles Kennedy about to board his campaign aircraft at Farnborough airport, he took a call from Sarah, who told him after a routine check-up she was being admitted to hospital with early signs of labour.

Abandoning his schedule, he returned to London immediately, driven by his Special Branch protection team, and arrived at St Thomas' hospital in good time for the birth of Donald James, shortly after midnight, named after his grandfather, the Fort William crofter, and James Gurling. The following afternoon the Kennedys, accompanied by two community midwives, posed for a huge press pack outside as they left the hospital and returned home for a brief period of privacy. For two days Menzies Campbell stepped into the breach to carry out the leader's tour engagements, although it was the story of the Kennedy's election baby that made the news. Pictures of a proud Charles Kennedy, with his arm around his wife as she cradled their child, or even just of the sleeping infant Donald, were published widely but the Lib Dems' plans to establish and reinforce their political message early in the campaign had been thwarted.

On the second day after Donald's birth, Tim Razzall, Chris Rennard and Anna Werrin visited his leader at home in south London to ask if he felt ready to return to launch the manifesto the next morning. Chris Rennard was very keen that Kennedy himself should do it, to get the media focused on Lib Dem policy messages. Charles Kennedy, although tired, explained he had been watching the election on television, felt he had kept apace with events and, indeed, had gained a broader perspective than he otherwise might out on the road. He agreed to do it.

Even without a newborn child sleeping in a cot in his bedroom, the election schedule was a punishing one for Charles Kennedy. He was due at Cowley Street at 6.30 a.m. for the first briefing on the manifesto launch, but failed to arrive. There was another meeting for the press conference panel at Local Government House at 7 a.m., which again he missed. There had been a heated dispute over the panel's composition at Cowley Street with some officials, led by Sandy Walkington, a former communications director at BT hired for the campaign, arguing vociferously that Vince Cable should be on the platform. Sandy Walkington was overruled, despite asking that his objection be recorded, and the panel chosen to flank Charles Kennedy was Tim Razzall, as campaign chairman, Menzies Campbell, the deputy leader, Matthew Taylor, the manifesto's author, and Sarah Teather, for gender balance. At last Charles Kennedy arrived, unbriefed and ten minutes before the press conference, saying he had overslept. He went outside for a cigarette before facing the media. As he stepped onto the platform, he looked awful. His face was pasty, his eyes sunken and bloodshot. He laboured terribly in reading his opening remarks. These ran to three and a half pages of double-spaced paragraphs, longer than he was comfortable with. Once he concluded the final page, which looked an ordeal in itself, things got much worse as journalists challenged him over details of the local income tax policy. First, Adam Boulton of Sky News asked if its overall effect was tax-raising or tax neutral. Incorrectly, Charles Kennedy answered it was the latter – 'not a penny more, not a penny less' – disregarding a proposed £2 billion subsidy that made it a tax cut. Vince Cable, confined to the back of the room rather than on the platform, was overheard by journalists groaning in frustration and protested later his leader had been 'irritatingly wrong'.[26] Next Andrew Marr, from the BBC, asked the rate at which a dual-income couple paying local income tax would become worse off. For several seconds, Charles Kennedy floundered, struggling to recall past briefings, and had to be prompted by Matthew Taylor. 'You are talking in the region of twen . . . twent . . . twen . . . twen . . . yuh, I mean if you [pause] take [pause] a double-income couple, uh, 20,000 each that's what you are talking about, 40,000. Yeah, £40,000 . . . sorry. Yes, £40,000', he said at last.[27] In the unforgiving medium of television clips his stammering search for an answer made a macabre piece of political theatre. It was replayed again and again. The launch was a disaster.

During subsequent exchanges with reporters Charles Kennedy joked of how little he slept the previous night with a new baby in the house, and most accounts of his performance attributed his confusion to fatigue. Once the press conference ended he was taken by Anna Werrin to the flat she was using during the election a stone's throw away, loaned by Norman Lamb, where he slept for an hour. She gave him coffee and toast before he returned, revived, to Local Government House for a round of television interviews hastily arranged in an attempt to mitigate the damage. In these his performance was markedly better but, at close quarters, the broadcasting crews noticed something that struck several Lib Dems whom he spoke with earlier: he smelled powerfully of alcohol. There had been some premonitions that Kennedy had resumed drinking in the run-up to the election, including a fraught visit to Richmond, south London days before the campaign started. His alcoholism had reappeared at the worst moment.

Anna Werrin said later she did not know if alcoholism was the cause of his disastrous manifesto launch. 'I don't know if he'd been drinking,' she said. 'I have never said to him: "Did you get drunk the night before?" I dealt with the situation as it was at the time, with somebody who was exhausted who clearly needed to sleep.' Several Lib Dems were convinced, however, that alcohol was indeed behind his calamitous performance, not simply lack of sleep. Such people came to regard the derailment of their manifesto launch as close to unforgivable. Charles Kennedy resumed his battlebus and aircraft election schedule but his self-confidence had taken a knock, and the Lib Dems failed to get the early lift they hoped for in their poll ratings, which remained fairly static. Indeed the underlying figures were worse. Charles Kennedy's own performance rating fell markedly over several days before it stabilised and picked up, dramatically, only in the campaign's closing stages.[28] All in all, it was a terrible start.

Gamely, the Lib Dems continued with their day-by-day election plan. Each morning's press conference was devoted to a policy theme which Charles Kennedy would reinforce in visits to key seats later that day. He would generally fly from London City airport to a regional airport from where a battlebus would take him and accompanying television crews to their destination: on crime policy day he would tour a police station, and so on. Charles Kennedy was disciplined in sticking to the message, aware that public service broadcasting rules guaranteed his party airtime. He deployed his sense of humour well and he tried to strike a positive tone. Bu the local income tax policy continued to prove problematic. During a radio election phone-in programme Simon Hughes was asked if owners of second homes would pay more and admitted he did not know, despite exhaustive background material circulated by Ed Davey, although on air he found a briefing note explaining they would pay a business rate. Charles Kennedy mixed up the party's key message that the average family would be £450 a year better off, mistakenly giving a figure of £540 in television interviews. While such slip-ups were a source of mirth to the media, the local income tax policy had a strategic drawback, too. It was relentlessly presented by opponents and many journalists as a tax rise for many people, obscuring the Lib Dems' shift to a tax-neutral manifesto for basic rate taxpayers, some of whom would pay less tax. When coupled with the 50p income tax threshold, undoubtedly a tax rise but applying only to around 400,000 people with six-figure incomes, it reinforced an impression that the Lib Dems remained a high-tax party.

Towards the end of the second week Charles Kennedy's mood began to brighten. As in the run-up to the 2001 election, the Lib Dems had discussed campaign strategy beforehand with Labour. Again Tim Razzall conducted these talks for Lib Dems, with Sally Morgan representing Labour. Sally Morgan told him that, as previously, Labour would use the campaign's first week or ten days to attack the Conservatives' economic policy and urged Razzall to do likewise. He was happy to agree since, if the Lib Dems were to advance, they needed to stop the Tory vote from going up. And while Labour were attacking the Conservatives, they would not be attacking the Lib Dems. Tim Razzall and Sally Morgan agreed to speak daily during the campaign, and began by doing so for five or ten minutes each morning. Such cooperation held for the first two weeks, although it was soured when the Lib Dems refused to join Labour in attacking Michael Howard's uncompromising messages on immigration. Tony Blair had discussed the election with Charles Kennedy during one of the journeys to and from the Vatican for the Pope's funeral. They agreed neither wanted immigration to dominate the election. But Blair thought he secured an undertaking from Kennedy to join him in denouncing Michael Howard if the Conservatives made immigration a central election issue. When Tony Blair went to Dover, flying in by helicopter with its famous white cliffs as a backdrop, to deliver a speech condemning the Tories' decision to campaign on immigration, he expected Charles Kennedy to follow suit. Sally Morgan made a series of heated telephone calls to Tim Razzall urging the Lib Dems join the attack and isolate the Conservatives on the issue of immigration. Kennedy refused, saying he had never agreed to coordinate responses; while he had consistently called for tolerance, he was determined not to fight the election on immigration. Tim Razzall said: 'In our rolling polls, every time the issue of the day was immigration or asylum, the Tory polling went up. Every time it was health or education or the economy they went down.'

The Lib Dems' relations with Labour were more fraught this time for more fundamental reasons. Unlike in 2001, the Lib Dems were now targeting three or four dozen Labour-held seats and knew they would make gains from Blair. Moreover, in the latter half of the campaign grid the Lib Dems planned to switch from domestic policies to the invasion of Iraq, and take the fight to Labour. This was when Charles Kennedy's campaign sparked into life.

As Kennedy was about to introduce the Iraq war he was aided by the leak of a summary of advice to the government from the Attorney General, Peter Goldsmith, before the war. The Attorney General gave six reasons why the use of British troops might breach international law, although he concluded it would nonetheless be legal, the *Mail on Sunday* reported.[29] Michael Howard responded by branding Tony Blair a liar. Charles Kennedy consciously held back from doing so, but questioned Blair's judgement and said the public's trust in the Prime Minister was at stake. His first press conference devoted to the Iraq war was a tough encounter, as journalists asked Charles Kennedy if the world would be a better place with Saddam Hussein still in power. For the first time in the campaign, however, the Lib Dems led the news bulletins. They continued to do so the following day as, at his morning press conference, Tim Razzall played his ace. Brian Sedgemore, a retiring Labour MP from the hard left, announced he was joining the Liberal Democrats and appeared with Charles Kennedy on the platform, where he spoke from the lectern and took questions, evidently enjoying himself after years of obscurity as a Labour backbencher. Brian Sedgemore said: 'I urge everyone from the centre and left in British politics to give Blair a bloody nose at the election and to vote for the Liberal Democrats in recognition of the fact that the tawdry New Labour project is dead.'

In their excitement, the Lib Dems appeared not to have calibrated the impact on floating or soft Conservative voters as Charles Kennedy embraced an embodiment of the Labour left. But the stimulus it gave to their campaign was palpable. That evening the Lib Dem leader arrived to address a rally at the guildhall in Cambridge to find all 500 seats taken and hundreds more people queuing outside in teeming rain. Before delivering his speech Charles Kennedy insisted on going outside to speak, unscripted, to those locked out who thronged in a semi-circle six or seven deep as the rain receded. Shirley Williams and Matthew Oakeshott, who had both stood as parliamentary candidates in Cambridge for the SDP, made similar open-air speeches, as did Menzies Campbell. The atmosphere of expectation in Cambridge, which Charles Kennedy caught, was never replicated and illustrated how the Lib Dems' two strongest themes, of opposition to the Iraq war and student tuition fees, appealed most powerfully in certain constituencies – typically university towns or those with large ethnic minority communities. Nevertheless, thanks to the attention given to Iraq, the Lib Dems' support had begun to pick up when the war became the dominant story of the election. A full account of the Attorney General's advice on the legality of the invasion was broadcast by *Channel 4 News*, revealing his opinion was that the safest option would be to secure a second resolution from the United Nations Security Council. Tony Blair, who days before going to war published a short statement from the Attorney General saying the first UN resolution gave authority to use force, now released his full legal advice. This coincided with a special edition of BBC One's *Question Time*, in which the three main party leaders appeared consecutively before an assertive studio audience, and the issue of Iraq dominated the programme. Charles Kennedy, who was quizzed first, was on brilliant form. He was composed, fluent, responded openly to criticism, and on the side of the audience on Iraq. Michael Howard looked uncomfortable as he was grilled on his immigration policy, accused of negative campaigning, and declared he would have invaded Iraq in the same circumstances but would have been honest about why. By Tony Blair's turn, the studio lights were so hot he began perspiring as he was pressed on Iraq and public services and looked out of touch by admitting he was unaware patients were often unable to book a doctor's appointment more than forty-eight hours in advance. In performance terms, Charles Kennedy came out on top. It was his high point of the election.

Just as the wind began to fill his sails, Charles Kennedy was blown off course by the superior campaigning of his opponents. In spring 2005 Tony Blair was very unpopular with sections of the electorate, and spent much of the campaign side by side with Gordon Brown, his Chancellor, in an attempt to broaden the appeal of Labour's campaign. Michael Howard, advised by an Australian political strategist, Lynton Crosby, had from the outset urged voters to 'send a message' to Tony Blair rather than return a Conservative government. This was cunningly pitched, implying Michael Howard did not expect to win but conjuring in the electorate's mind a vision of a triumphant Tony Blair and inviting voters to burst his balloon. On the doorstep, Lib Dem candidates found Michael Howard's 'send a message' theme resonated strongly with wavering voters, even in Tory/Lib Dem marginals. In the final week before polling day Tony Blair produced another highly effective 'air war' message that the Lib Dems found still harder to counter. Aware of surging support for the Lib Dems in certain Labour/Tory marginals, the Prime Minister issued a series of strong warnings to Labour voters that, by switching to the Lib Dems, they would let the Conservative candidate win. Although there were only two or three dozen such seats, he conflated the message to claim this could even lead to a Conservative victory. 'There are three ways to get a Tory MP. One is to vote Tory, one is to stay home, one is to vote Liberal Democrat,' Tony Blair warned them, as he and Gordon Brown toured marginal seats in the south-east. 'Take nothing for granted. Unless people come out and vote Labour, it is a Tory government they will wake up to on 6 May.'

How the Lib Dems should react was the subject of heated discussion in Cowley Street. Tim Razzall and Chris Rennard, seated at one end of a horseshoe of tables in Cowley Street's open-plan 'war room', said the response should simply be the Conservatives could not win. Dick Newby, who sat across from them and kept in touch with Charles Kennedy, disagreed, saying Kennedy found it difficult to rebut the point without putting it in context. By now Charles Kennedy was conducting three campaign visits a day and coordination became more difficult as much of Kennedy's time was spent clambering in and out of his aircraft, battlebuses and cars. Kennedy was also worn out. He tried to summarise Tony Blair's claim and then knock it down but, each time he did so, he repeated Labour's message and inadvertently reinforced it. 'Let's give the lie to this last-minute desperation from Tony Blair that if you go out and vote Lib Dem, you get Michael Howard as Prime Minister,' Charles Kennedy said in a shopping centre in Edinburgh. 'It's not going to happen.'

Tony Blair's intervention achieved its aim and arrested the fall in Labour's vote as he returned to Downing Street with a reduced, but still comfortable Commons majority of sixty-seven. Ironically, in Tory/Lib Dem marginals, its effect was the opposite of what he had claimed. To gain seats from the Conservatives, Lib Dems needed to persuade Labour supporters to vote for them tactically. In the final days, frustrated Lib Dem canvassers in places such as Orpington encountered Labour voters determined not to switch for fear of seeing Michael Howard win the election; in fact, the sitting Tory MP in Orpington increased his majority. Lib Dem campaign strategists privately conceded their 'air war' message was not sufficiently effective in the final week. They were clearly outdone in 'ground war' tactics, too, as some Lib Dem candidates struggled to match the Conservatives' expensive armoury of marketing software for voter identification, call centres for telephone canvassing and use of direct mail for election literature. These helped Michael Howard to gain a total of thirty-three seats even though the Tories' share of the vote stayed almost static at 32.5 per cent, up by just 0.6 per cent from 2001.

The Lib Dems won almost 6 million votes, nearly 1.2 million more than in the previous general election, and 22.1 per cent of votes cast, up from 18.3 per cent last time. They took eleven seats from Labour, including the unexpected prize of Manchester Withington, overturning a majority of 11,524. They gained Ceredigion from Plaid Cymru, another surprise, and three seats from the Conservatives: Taunton, Westmoreland & Lonsdale and Solihull. The latter was targeted in absolute secrecy by Paul Rainger, the party's campaigns director, after an encouraging run of local by-elections.

But there were five losses to the Conservatives: Newbury, Devon West & Torridge, Guildford, Ludlow and Weston-super-Mare. In a further thirteen Tory-held key seats the Lib Dems lost ground, including those of four senior Conservative frontbenchers who were targeted in what became known universally as a 'decapitation strategy', which backfired disastrously. The Lib Dems emerged with sixty-two MPs, a net gain of eleven, after allowing for Scotland's boundary changes. This was four short of Chris Rennard's private prediction of sixty-six. But a sizeable number of party members expected to gain another fifteen or twenty seats, or perhaps more, and had assumed net gains from the Conservatives as well as from Labour. The Lib Dems faced the unique circumstances of a Labour government whose popularity was crumbling and a relatively weak Conservative challenge, and held a distinctive position as the only major party to oppose the Iraq war.

A sense that the Liberal Democrats had failed to capitalise on an historic opportunity created a powerful, destabilising undercurrent within the party in the traumatic months that followed.

10

Losing the leadership

Charles Kennedy returned to Westminster after the 2005 general election intending to hit the ground running; instead, he fell over. Things began to go wrong within weeks. During the course of the election, as he idled away the hours in his fleet of battlebuses, his campaign aircraft or his Special Branch car between public appearances, Kennedy had wrestled with mounting frustration at some of the dottier Lib Dem policies foisted on him by his free-spirited activists. In interview after interview, he found himself forced to defend plans to liberalise pornography law, tax plastic bags and give the vote to convicted prisoners. Such commitments provided a rich seam for the Conservatives to mine for lines of attack. The Tories orchestrated small groups of demonstrators to chant feigned disapproval at policies to end mandatory life sentences for murder and require dog owners to microchip their pets. None was in the Lib Dem manifesto, from which the party's wilder and wackier policies were carefully excluded, but all had been formally endorsed by the party's sovereign twice-yearly conference. Kennedy resolved enough was enough. Never again should he, nor any leader, be so entangled by the foliage from the more exotic trees within the far-reaching forest of Lib Dem policies.

On the first Monday back at Westminster, still on a high from election adrenalin, he gathered his sixty-one MPs at Local Government House determined to show from the outset the smack of firm leadership. In a coded criticism of Chris Rennard and Tim Razzall's election planning, Kennedy declared the party must study and learn from ground war tactics used by their opponents and examine how to communicate Lib Dem messages better at all levels. Policy development, too, needed to change. He proposed a 'clean sheet' approach to policy, forcing the Lib Dems at the start of every parliament to look afresh at all proposals to ensure they remained relevant to changing circumstances. 'We must reconsider whether it should be possible to commit the party to specific and controversial policies on the basis of a brief, desultory debate in a largely empty hall,' Kennedy told his MPs.

His comments, composed by a fatigued Dick Newby over the weekend, were well received by MPs and in the press, but raised hackles among the few hundred activists who had long exercised massive influence over policy by virtue of the party's democratic structure. Having set such hares running, Kennedy subsequently did little to chase them up. Thus he generated suspicion from defenders of the status quo and frustration among reformers, a pattern all too familiar to some MPs. Opponents, meanwhile, moved quickly to exploit his reference to a clean sheet on policy. Labour's chairman, Ian McCartney, sowed confusion by suggesting the Lib Dems had dumped their flagship proposal for a local income tax to replace the council tax.[1]

With disquiet over the debacle of Kennedy's election manifesto launch still fresh in MPs' minds, his inner circle moved swiftly to deal with the awkward formalities of his renomination as leader for the new parliament. Kennedy's office began the process immediately: Anna Werrin asked every Lib Dem MP to sign his nomination papers at their first meeting, effectively tying them to a declaration of confidence in his continuing leadership and snuffing out the prospect, however remote, of a challenge. All did so but one, John Hemming, an eccentric newcomer and deputy leader of Birmingham City Council. Even though Kennedy was re-elected, the month-long period until nominations closed concentrated minds on the leadership question and Kennedy's allies were jumpy until he was returned unopposed early in June.

Next, Kennedy set about the task he consistently found most difficult, that of reshuffling his frontbench spokesmen. On his election odyssey around Britain, another resolution he came to was to appoint a smaller, less unwieldy shadow cabinet. Tony Blair immediately executed a government reshuffle and Michael Howard, despite announcing his intention to resign, made changes to the Tory front bench. Kennedy did not complete his until ten days after the election. The hiatus unsettled some MPs, who were unsure whether they were expected to bid for a post or await his decision. The more self-assured wrote letters to Kennedy or told his staff the job they wanted; others waited on tenterhooks. Menzies Campbell, Vince Cable and Mark Oaten remained in the most senior posts as spokesmen for foreign policy, economics and home affairs. David Laws, Ed Davey and Steve Webb were promoted, Norman Lamb, Sarah Teather and Michael Moore were brought into his shadow cabinet and, just a week after entering the Commons, Nick Clegg and Chris Huhne were given prominent frontbench roles. MPs who made way for them were, however, enraged by their treatment. Phil Willis, who told Kennedy he wanted to move from the education portfolio, was telephoned by Anna Werrin and informed that a statement was about to be released saying he had 'asked to leave the shadow cabinet'. Paul Burstow, who had struggled as health spokesman, told his leader he would take anything but international development; he was duly offered just that and opted instead to return to the back benches. Others forcibly resisted his attempts to slim down the shadow cabinet, insisting that special interest groups they dealt with would feel snubbed. At the first weekly meeting of Lib Dem MPs, Kennedy told them he wanted 'stability' in the elected posts of parliamentary party chairman, held by Matthew Taylor, and chief whip, held by Andrew Stunell, for which both Phil Willis and Don Foster harboured ambitions. Lib Dem MPs muttered to themselves that neither post was the leader's to give.

Kennedy, exhausted from the election and still adapting to a baby a few weeks old at home, ploughed on with setting up his policy review *Meeting the Challenge* to channel the party's internal debate between social and economic liberalism. This further reflected his preoccupation with criticism that the Lib Dem manifesto had been too much of a shopping list of pledges and would next time need a theme, or narrative, rooted in liberal values to convey what it meant to be a Liberal Democrat. Kennedy approved a commission to look at his tax plans and a committee to reconsider the process for making policy. He tried to start developing a new four-year strategy, thinking ahead to the positions Labour and the Conservatives might take at the next general election, what policy areas might come to the fore and how he might navigate a separate, distinctive path for the Lib Dems. Characteristically, he kept such nascent thinking to himself, and colleagues involved in the initiatives he set up complained that he failed to follow them through. Instead he became increasingly bogged down in internal, housekeeping matters. Several of the party's defeated MPs and candidates were critical of Kennedy's policies and election campaign, fuelling the feeling that the Lib Dems ought to have done much better, especially against the Conservatives. Ambitious Lib Dems and commentators alike began pressing for clarity over the strategic direction in which Kennedy intended to lead the party. Many of the twenty new MPs, comprising a third of his parliamentary party and full of enthusiasm and ideas, began grumbling about delays in being allocated Commons offices and the frustrations that confront all newcomers to Parliament. Their gripes were exacerbated when, ten days after his shadow cabinet reshuffle, Kennedy completed his junior frontbench appointments by promoting six more of the 2005 intake: Susan Kramer, Lynne Featherstone, David Howarth, Danny Alexander, Julia Goldsworthy and Jo Swinson. This confounded past practice that novice MPs were given at least a year to find their feet in Parliament. It caused irritation among longer-serving MPs and the remainder of the newcomers who were overlooked. Several of those appointed had only just been allocated Commons offices and computers. A tetchy atmosphere took hold in the parliamentary party, worsened by the death from cancer of the Lib Dem MP Patsy Calton, causing a difficult by-election in her marginal seat of Cheadle, Greater Manchester. The by-election became a preoccupation for Andrew Stunell, as both chief whip and MP for its neighbouring constituency, Hazel Grove.

As frustration over the management of the parliamentary party grew Phil Willis, still sore from his treatment in the reshuffle, returned from a short break brooding at his weekend retreat determined to challenge Matthew Taylor for the post of party chairman. Willis canvassed widely among fellow MPs, pledging to recast the role as backbenchers' representative rather than one of the frontbench team. Don Foster developed similar plans to challenge the chief whip. Realising two contested elections risked seriously destabilising the leadership, Willis and Foster backed away after Charles Kennedy offered a review to re-examine the party's organisation in the Commons, the way its elected posts were filled and the management of the Lib Dems' £1.77 million of Short money and Cranborne money, public funds to subsidise an opposition party's parliamentary work in the Commons and Lords. Willis, placated by an invitation to conduct the inquiry himself, offered to nominate Matthew Taylor as parliamentary party chairman.

But one of Willis's supporters, Paul Holmes, remained dissatisfied. He was wary of Kennedy's forthcoming policy review, and decided to stand himself. Holmes, a suspicious left-winger convinced of a perpetual plot to drag his party to the right, was an unlikely candidate yet he tapped into wider unrest among fellow MPs from his 2001 intake who felt overlooked in the reshuffle. His campaign was run by Alistair Carmichael and John Barrett, MPs also on the party's left who were unhappy that the principle of collective responsibility had been breached by contributors among the shadow cabinet to *The Orange Book* the previous autumn. A general complaint about lack of communication with backbench MPs, who at times learned of policy or strategy developments via the media, further permeated the air. Even so, Paul Holmes looked to have little hope of winning until the day of the vote itself. Five minutes before the meeting, Matthew Taylor popped into the leader's office, where Charles Kennedy offered to nominate him. Taylor begged him not to, saying this would be unhelpful. When they joined the assembled MPs in Committee Room 11, Kennedy did so anyway. Matthew Taylor then made a gravely misjudged speech. Instead of offering himself as the establishment candidate, he distanced himself from Kennedy and issued an on-your-side message to restive backbenchers, reminding them of his own sacking as Treasury spokesman two years earlier. 'I accept things have not always been done well. I have been a victim of that as well,' he told unconvinced MPs. 'You rescued me from that,' he added referring to his position as party chairman, which he had, in fact, negotiated with Charles Kennedy. The reaction of his colleagues was swift. They rejected Taylor by thirty-six votes to twenty-three, removing from this powerful position an experienced media performer, policy spokesman and author of Charles Kennedy's two general election manifestos, and substituting him with Paul Holmes, a little-known figure who saw himself as an old-fashioned backbenchers' shop steward.

The episode was obviously damaging to Charles Kennedy, who was by now gloomy, tired and bruised from confrontation. As the Conservatives appeared ready to turn their own forthcoming leadership election into another period of infighting, commentators puzzled at a lack of leadership from the Lib Dems and thought Kennedy curiously inactive.[2] Senior Lib Dems saw ominous signs by mid-June that their leader had lapsed into one of his periods of introspection that were a pattern of his alcoholism. He went rapidly downhill. His manner in meetings was dull and accepting, his responses vague rather than lively or sharp. His office cancelled meetings at short notice. Several of his performances in the Commons were rambling and lacked focus or bite. A sense of drift set in.

With a vacuum at the top of the party, the usual post-election manoeuvrings by politicians, freed from the constraints of campaign discipline, had a greater impact than they otherwise might. Menzies Campbell appeared ready to relinquish his unspoken position as leader-in-waiting should Kennedy's alcoholism render him unable to carry on. Although Menzies Campbell remained deputy leader, a vacancy seemed to be opening up in the party's hierarchy. Shortly before the general election, Campbell told friends he no longer expected a chance to become leader.

Kennedy's relative success in eschewing alcohol in the months before the campaign had removed the need for a short-term caretaker in charge for the election. Menzies Campbell, about to turn sixty-four and still relieved to have survived cancer treatment, thought the new parliament might be his last and contemplated alternative roles during what might be his final term. If he could not realise his ambition of becoming Speaker, a prominent chairmanship held considerable attractions for him, such as heading the Commons Foreign Affairs or Defence Select Committees, if Labour would grant the Lib Dems such a concession. In another valedictory move he announced in mid-June an agreement with Hodder and Stoughton to write his autobiography, for publication in autumn 2006, suggesting he was at the stage of looking back upon his political career. He was, he said, 'looking forward to revisiting my past' and would talk for the first time in his memoirs about aspects of his political career.[3] He did not look to be a man pondering a tilt at the party leadership.

Simon Hughes, meanwhile, became more hyperactive than ever. During the election, in his role as party president, he visited several dozen constituencies, some of them marginal seats but others with comfortable Lib Dem majorities and large numbers of party members. Charles Kennedy and his inner circle suspected Hughes was deliberately raising his profile and might even challenge him for leadership, despite having given his leader a letter assuring him he would not do so. This explained why the renomination process was pushed through so quickly. Simon Hughes further protested about the number of media interviews given by Matthew Taylor as chairman of the parliamentary party, saying the presidency was a constitutional position and should take precedence. In the reshuffle, Hughes requested he be made shadow Attorney General, a post already held by Martin Thomas in the Lords, or shadow Leader of the Commons. Either would enable him to carry out a frontline role in Parliament without the additional demands of scrutinising legislation or policy development, allowing time for his duties as president. Kennedy refused and, unwisely copying Tony Blair's division of Cabinet roles, asked Hughes to shadow the Office of the Deputy Prime Minister, while making Sarah Teather responsible for local government and communities, which came under the same Whitehall department.

Days into his new role Hughes, in a television interview,[4] turned up the gas on the simmering debate over Kennedy's election result, declaring: 'We went up. We didn't go up as much as we hoped we might. It was good progress but it was disappointing compared with the upper limit we hoped to get.' As if that were not mischief enough, Hughes shot a hole through the policy of a local income tax: 'I supported local income tax as a change. But there was a flaw. And that was it meant different things in different parts of the country. And that's why I don't think actually, in the end, it worked well.'

His remarks, which were widely publicised, generated intense irritation among fellow Lib Dems. Charles Kennedy was forced to clarify the policy's status amid confusion over whether local income tax would stay. Sarah Teather, technically the spokesman for local government policy including town hall finance, was also in a difficult position. She and Simon Hughes had previously crossed swords when she replaced him as London spokesman in 2004 after his unsuccessful campaign to become the capital's mayor; Hughes tried to bar her from commenting on London's bid to host the 2012 Olympic Games, saying he should continue to do so. Now their relationship came under serious strain. Sarah Teather, urged on by colleagues and Kennedy's allies, who told her it was time someone stood up to Simon Hughes, tried to assert her right to take charge of local government policy. After the pair argued in public, at a meeting of Lib Dem councillors in the Local Government Association, Charles Kennedy was finally persuaded to intervene. He began a series of difficult negotiations with Simon Hughes that led to him switching portfolios the following month to become shadow Attorney General in the Commons.

Few MPs doubted that Simon Hughes's assertive behaviour was, in part, a response to the vacuum in the leadership caused by Charles Kennedy's exhausted introspection and Menzies Campbell's apparent readiness to surrender the crown of leader-in-waiting. Other potential leadership candidates, too, began to hoist their flags aloft. Vince Cable gave a presentation on National Health Service reform, well beyond his frontbench responsibilities, which he later published as a pamphlet.[5] He wrote another pamphlet on Britishness for the party conference.[6] Mark Oaten agreed to address Policy Exchange, a think tank with close links to liberal Conservatives, on his vision for liberalism in the twenty-first century. He threw a drinks party, ostensibly to celebrate his move to a new office in Norman Shaw South, but clearly aimed at schmoozing opinion formers in the party. Ed Davey gave a series of media interviews defending robustly his local income tax policy and planting reminders of his role in developing previous policies while he was the party's economics adviser, namely the penny on income tax to boost education spending and giving the Bank of England independence to set interest rates.[7]

Charles Kennedy's torpor was not entirely self-induced. During these weeks, politics was dominated by Tony Blair's policy on Europe, after France and the Netherlands rejected the European constitution, and the G8 summit at Gleneagles in Scotland, which at Blair's behest discussed aid for Africa. On both issues, the Lib Dems broadly supported the government, making it difficult for Kennedy's voice to be heard. Part of Charles Kennedy's plan for the opening weeks of the parliament was to deliver a speech charting the broad strategic direction in which he now intended to lead his party. One of the earliest initiatives by Paul Holmes as party chairman was to demand that Kennedy outline its message first to his MPs. This was to placate those on the left fearful of being bounced into further concessions of political territory in the ongoing struggle between social and economic liberals. Kennedy agreed to postpone his speech on the party's future prospects, due on 23 June. Instead he came to 'road test' his remarks at a weekly meeting of his parliamentary party that coincided with the nadir of his malaise. MPs, and a handful of peers and party staff, trooped into Committee Room 11 to hear Kennedy, seated and facing them from his place on the chairman's platform, deliver one of the worst orations any had witnessed. Head down, and reading from a dense text, he delivered it with a lacklustre quality few of the newer MPs had witnessed from their leader. Rapidly he lost the attention of the room, but ploughed on for almost half an hour, oblivious to the reaction of his aghast audience. The leader, who weeks earlier had held his own under tough interrogation from Britain's foremost media interviewers, whose disarming frankness and quick-witted humour sparkled in the latter stages of the election campaign, had become an embarrassment to his own side.

When, finally, Kennedy finished, things got worse. Questions were invited. Steve Webb, an erudite MP not in sympathy with Kennedy's leadership and a close ally of Simon Hughes, was among those who responded. He thanked his leader for sharing his thoughts with parliamentary colleagues.

'I would just like to know: what motivates you? What gets you up in the morning?' Steve Webb asked his leader. It was interpreted by those present as an open challenge to Kennedy's commitment to his role. By coincidence, the same evening a celebratory dinner had been arranged for the party's twenty new MPs as an opportunity to toast their arrival in Parliament and get to know one another. Straight after the parliamentary party meeting they made their way along Whitehall in the balmy late June sunshine to the National Liberal Club. There they dined in the Lady Violet Room, with its high ceiling, arched alcoves and dense, brown patterned wallpaper. The hosts, Julia Goldsworthy and Danny Alexander, suggested each of them should make a few remarks. They might talk about themselves, their constituency, experiences of the Palace of Westminster, whatever they wished. As they proceeded around the long, oval table lit with candles, contributions were universally negative. They voiced dissatisfaction at the sloth-like pace at which the Commons authorities enabled them to establish offices and let them get down to work. They expressed impatience and disappointment at the Lib Dems' own organisation in Parliament, that at times appeared to them illogical or plain incompetent. John Hemming launched a direct attack on Charles Kennedy but, as ever, missed the mood. They complained that more experienced Lib Dem MPs were unfriendly, the parliamentary party lacked cohesion and a sense of purpose, of a feeling of drift and lack of communication between the leader's office and MPs. Initially the mood was one of anger. Then it turned to relief that everyone was feeling the same. Nick Clegg, another of its organisers, said:

> I was genuinely struck by the depth and strength of feeling amongst twenty newcomers about how poorly organised and unprofessional our induction in both Parliament, but also the parliamentary party, was. These two things came together. There was concern at not having computers and offices. That combined with real frustration about the way in which the parliamentary party meetings were conducted.

Many of the new intake of MPs were young, half of them under the age of thirty-five. The majority had left successful careers to take up politics and shared a sense of professionalism and keen ambition that they and their party should achieve greater things. Several arrived in the Commons believing they owed their electoral success to Charles Kennedy, to his opposition to the Iraq war, his campaigning skills and his relaxed style with voters. Before and during the election they had seen their leader well briefed, focused and full of energy. They arrived at Westminster, flushed with success and brimming with anticipation, to find him awkward, slightly reclusive, inconsistent and presiding over a chaotic system of internal party management. As they traded confidences over the dowdy English fare in the high Victorian grandeur of the National Liberal Club, the new MPs were sharing a profound moment. Consciously or not, they were coming to terms with the collective shock of joining a profoundly dysfunctional parliamentary party; one that since 1997, when Paddy Ashdown more than doubled his Commons representation, had been in transition. It was moving from a small grouping of outsized local personalities loosely bound by a political philosophy to a bigger, more cohesive movement with a common identity. Stalling this gradual process was a dark, brooding secret as senior MPs, party officials and the leader's office had become complicit in containing and covering up Charles Kennedy's alcoholism as he pitched from one self-inflicted crisis to another.

After supper, as many of the group retired to the club's stone terrace facing towards the river Thames, they sat in the evening air cradling glasses of wine, and talked for the first time together about Charles Kennedy, of their bewilderment at his performances since the election, epitomised by the awful speech they had witnessed earlier that day. Some expressed irritation, too, at Simon Hughes's conduct since the election. Their leaders, they were discovering, had feet of clay after all.

Such was the fractious, faintly dangerous, atmosphere among Lib Dems at Westminster when another foaming wave of leadership speculation crashed over their heads. On 28 June, as the Commons debated the second reading of the government's revived legislation for national identity cards, the BBC's then political editor Andrew Marr telephoned Charles Kennedy's press secretary and put to her a specific story he was preparing to break as the lead item on the six o'clock news: that Kennedy had undergone treatment for an alcohol problem. Andrew Marr made further approaches to a small number of Lib Dems, including newer MPs who sought advice from colleagues and, inevitably, were referred to the chief whip. Jackie Rowley telephoned shortly before the bulletin and issued a categorical denial to the BBC, killing its story, but rumours of its content spread rapidly around Westminster. Several newspapers, including the *Daily Mirror* and the *Glasgow Herald*, were on the brink of publishing similar stories but were threatened by Jackie Rowley with legal action if they did so.

The following day Kennedy stalked into the weekly parliamentary party meeting and attempted, with uncharacteristic force for a mild-mannered man, to lay down the law. He tackled the rumours head on, declaring himself fed up with speculation over his position. This was bizarre, since some MPs were unaware that rumours were in circulation. Now they knew. Kennedy went further, effectively accusing two of them of plotting against him, and threatening to sack any front bench spokesman who spread such stories. 'These rumours are being fed by someone,' Kennedy told them. 'I trust fifty-eight members of this parliamentary party,' he added, in a peculiarly precise aside. Following Patsy Calton's death, and excluding himself, sixty Lib Dem MPs remained, two of whom he was charging with disloyalty. Most assumed

Simon Hughes to be one. Much intellectual energy was expended by Lib Dems in seeking to identify the second.

Charles Kennedy's position, which had been shaky since the disastrous manifesto launch two months earlier, was now precarious. The emerging group of talented, economically liberal spokesmen pressed in vain for clarity of strategic direction. Those on the sullen left suspected a right-wing plot. New MPs simply craved professionalism. Most significantly, a gradually widening circle of senior party figures suspected an ominous, prolonged lapse in his battle with alcoholism. Fortunately for Kennedy, in a by now familiar pattern, an election campaign offered him a lifeline. He grasped it as a drowning man would clutch a serpent.

By this stage the by-election in Cheadle, set for mid-July, was giving cause for concern in Cowley Street. It was no time for MPs to take action against their leader and Kennedy threw himself into the fight with gusto. The Lib Dems had never in the party's seventeen-year history successfully defended a seat in a by-election. The closest parallel was the Truro by-election, where Matthew Taylor held the constituency for the Liberals in 1987 after the death of David Penhaligon, a year before the merger. Cheadle was, furthermore, highly marginal. Patsy Calton gained it from the Tories in 2001 by just thirty-three votes. Although she pushed her majority up in May to 4,020, early exploratory visits to the constituency by Chris Rennard left him concerned that the personal vote built up by Patsy Calton might not transfer to the Lib Dem candidate. The Conservatives reactivated their national campaigning centre at Coleshill in the West Midlands to fight a high-octane campaign with tactics copied directly from past Lib Dem by-elections, from bar charts showing a close two-horse race to blue Focus leaflets. Tory literature denounced Mark Hunter, the Lib Dem candidate, who lived eight miles from the constituency boundary, as an 'unpopular outsider', a line of attack used by the Lib Dems themselves against Tory and Labour opponents in the Romsey and Brent East by-elections. Conservative campaign newspapers savaged his record as leader of Stockport Council in direct emulation of literature used by Lib Dems against Labour's candidate in the Leicester South by-election a year earlier.[8] The Conservatives' output lacked vim and sophistication – Mark Hunter could not simultaneously have been 'responsible for leading the desperately unpopular local council' and 'an outsider . . . who most people have never heard of'[9] – but it was bruising stuff. Nor was the Labour Party content to be a bystander in this bare-knuckle fight. One Labour leaflet branded Mark Hunter 'unfit to be our MP', a 'grave wrecker', a 'criminals' friend' and 'financially incompetent' and carried a petition headed 'say no to . . . Lib Dem plans to give votes to child killers, murderers and rapists'.[10]

Chris Rennard, well aware of Kennedy's perilous position, issued a series of curt all-points bulletins summoning any available party officials, MPs and peers' staff and volunteers to Cheadle. Kennedy himself made five visits. Chris Rennard, no stranger to roughhouse politics of his own when it suited him, saw a chance to deflect the aggressive onslaught back on his opponents. Lib Dem by-election material went for the moral high ground, criticising the Conservatives for 'negative American-style campaign tactics'[11] and was peppered with references to the memory of Patsy Calton and her record as Cheadle's MP. An A5-size typed letter on headed paper from her widower, Clive Calton, endorsing the Lib Dem candidate was distributed with only a tiny printer's mark at the bottom of the back page revealing it to be by-election literature.

One the eve of polling day, some of the tensions now simmering within the Liberal Democrat party spilled into the open. Showing the sort of self-indulgence for which Liberal Party activists were once notorious, Donnachadh McCarthy chose a moment forty-eight hours before the by-election to resign his membership and call on Charles Kennedy to quit.[12] His lengthy charge sheet ran from timidity in opposing the Iraq war to Kennedy's attempt to loosen the grip on policy-making of the unrepresentative activists whom he epitomised. But he made telling criticisms, too, of Kennedy's failure to lead or take clear positions. Tony Greaves, unbelievably for a peer in a small party with a keen sense of common purpose, weighed in the day before polling with similar protests over Kennedy's attempt to change policy-making.[13] He went further, attacking Mark Oaten and David Laws as economic liberals out of touch with the Lib Dem membership and com-plaining about the party's general election performance. Such indiscipline notwithstanding, Chris Rennard's team saved the day as the Lib Dems held Cheadle with a majority of 3,657, actually achieving a swing from the Tories given the lower turnout. Had the Conservatives captured the seat, there is little doubt Kennedy would have faced moves to force his resignation. Vince Cable said: 'If we had lost the Cheadle by-election he would have been out. There was clearly an increasing negative mood that was reflected in many semi-public and private discussions, although I personally believed at that time, and continued to believe, that he was a net asset to the party.'

Freed from initial fears of losing the by-election, and with the summer recess of Parliament beckoning, Charles Kennedy at last gave his long-awaited speech on his future strategic direction.[14] A sizeable number of his MPs joined journalists and party staff in the Wilson Room, a modern meeting room in Portcullis House, to listen although it did not quite match expectations. He gave a lengthy run round the course of current challenges to face and reviews in place but little sense of which way he would jump, other than an oblique hint at dropping the 50p tax rate pledge. On this, he said: 'We do not need and we should not seek a punitive taxation system. High taxes are not a moral good in themselves.' The remainder was diagnostic but without prescriptions, and clearly intended to placate – his policy review, he emphasised, was 'not about lurching to the left or right'. The question mark over strategic direction remained. For a more substantial message, Lib Dems would have to wait until his speech to the party conference in September. Before his parliamentary party dispersed for the summer Charles Kennedy pulled one further rabbit from the hat, reshuffling his junior frontbenchers to find jobs for the remainder of the new intake of MPs. Several longer-serving colleagues, who had been forced to wait for preferment, quietly seethed.

During the summer Charles Kennedy recharged his batteries, spending time with his family in Lochaber and going on holiday to the south of France, but broke off to intervene in a growing debate over counter-terrorism powers. Since 7 July, when four young British Muslim men blew themselves up on London Underground trains and a double-decker bus, killing fifty-two people, public attention had focused on steps to root out religious extremism. While treading with care, Kennedy pointed out that Britain's role in the occupation of Iraq was being used by extremists to spread violent fundamentalism.[15] But he held to a cross-party consensus under which ministers would consult opposition parties while considering how to react. Early in August, with such talks well advanced, Tony Blair intervened. The Prime Minister unveiled a list of new proposals[16] including powers to deport extremists and radical imams, close mosques, ban two Islamist organisations and strip British citizenship from certain people engaged in extremism. He proposed a new offence of glorifying terrorism. If necessary the Human Rights Act, one of the keystone achievements of Labour–Lib Dem co-operation from the 1990s, would be amended. 'Let no one be in any doubt. The rules of the game are changing,' Tony Blair famously declared. He won broad backing from the Conservatives[17] but, taking a political risk, Charles Kennedy demurred. Protesting at the absence of prior consultation, he gave warning that the cross-party consensus was 'under serious strain'.[18] Lib Dems would examine the measures but Mr Blair should not count on their support, he said. Charles Kennedy was roundly attacked in the tabloid press[19] but again demonstrated his judgement in going against the crowd.

In advance of the Lib Dem conference, held in unfamiliar territory in illiberal Blackpool, Tim Razzall gave two unnecessary hostages to fortune. He penned a six-page memorandum to Charles Kennedy on strategy for the forthcoming parliament, which, with surprising candour, addressed weaknesses in his leadership and proposed a four-year plan to 'build you up as a future Prime Minister'. It advised: 'We need to boost the leadership questions – which I suspect must be done by a combination of big speeches, well trailed in the media, and the development of an international expertise commensurate with a potential Prime Minister.'[20]

A summary of the Razzall memo was published in *The Times*,[21] causing embarrassment that Charles Kennedy's closest adviser was conceding that there were questions over his leadership. In a briefing for journalists a week ahead of the conference Tim Razzall, ever the optimist, painted the brightest gloss possible on the Lib Dems' election results, saying: 'Inevitably, there will be an element of celebration about the conference.'[22] A substantial number of Lib Dems thought otherwise and were impatient for an honest debate about what went wrong as well as what went right in the party's general election planning. Only the most diehard were granted a chance even to raise the issue as Tim Razzall and Chris Rennard offered a consultative session in the Baronial Hall within the Winter Gardens entitled 'general election debrief' at 9 a.m. on the opening Sunday, when most Lib Dems were still setting out for Blackpool.

From the beginning, the conference was a disaster. The Kennedy camp had been focusing on Iraq; they feared a 'troops out' motion from the conference floor at a time when party spokesmen believed their demands for the withdrawal of British forces by the year end should be extended for pragmatic reasons. Too little thought was given to other bear traps. The opening debate was on the European Union, on a motion advocating a cap of 1 per cent on the EU's budget until radical financial reforms were achieved. The party's twelve MEPs claimed not to have been consulted. Due to a proportional voting system of closed regional lists in European Parliament elections – a legacy of Paddy Ashdown's 'project' – MEPs did not face the electorate directly and thought that the move was populist. Furious MEPs, led by Chris Davies, queued up to denounce the motion and defend EU spending in their constituencies. Their ire combined with further suspicion among left-wing activists that the *Orange Book* economic liberals, epitomised by Vince Cable, who concluded the debate, were trying to inch the party in a Eurosceptic direction. Despite passionate pleas from Vince Cable and Nick Clegg, who moved the motion, it was ignominiously thrown out.

Next Charles Kennedy threw himself to the conference wolves. He arrived on the stage in the Winter Gardens' Empress Ballroom, peeled off his jacket and settled in an easy chair for a question-and-answer session chaired by Simon Kelner, editor-in-chief of the *Independent*. Lib Dems, who take a stubborn pride their refusal to stage-manage such events, allowed Kelner to choose from among the pre-submitted questions. With a journalist's instinct for a story, Kelner selected among his crop a question on leadership. Nasser Butt, fresh from standing as a parliamentary candidate in the safe Conservative seat of Mole Valley in Surrey, told Kennedy: 'I spent a lot of time defending, successfully, my party leader, on the doorstep and to my members. But should the candidate be spending so much time defending the party leader rather than converting the voters?'

It was a minor, if rather undignified, incident but a more significant blow was to follow. Economic liberals from the *Orange Book* tendency had, in the absence of a strategic lead from Charles Kennedy, invested great hopes in a new policy to privatise the Royal Mail. This had been mooted first by Vince Cable, attempted by Malcolm Bruce and now refashioned by Norman Lamb, who proposed a third of the shares be held in a trust for employees. Eager for the policy to be in place to demonstrate bold Lib Dem thinking, he bypassed the conventional route of a representative working group to consider the policy. After a battle with left-wing MPs, Norman Lamb won support to table it directly as a motion to the conference. Charles Kennedy backed the plan when asked in a pre-conference interview,[23] and did so again when doorstepped by reporters on the morning of the debate, but there was little effort by the leadership to mobilise supporters to attend the vote. Again the tenor of the discussion was coloured by suspicion that it presaged a new, economic liberal agenda. Speeches opposing it during the debate were often cloaked in procedural protests about the unconventional route by which it reached the conference agenda, and the policy was blocked and referred back to be reworked. Afterwards, a visibly upset Norman Lamb was asked for his reaction by journalists at the side of the stage. He was interrupted with extraordinary discourtesy by two of his triumphant social liberal opponents, Tony Greaves and Gareth Epps, a member of the federal policy committee.

Hijacking the exchanges, Tony Greaves declared: 'The economic liberal people have got to realise they are going to lose the debate.'[24]

Clearly the tensions between social and economic liberals risked getting out of hand. Leadership was needed. Richard Grayson, who had left the leader's office to return to academia, gave an interview in which he urged a change in approach from Charles Kennedy, using the memorable phrase 'his style is more chairman than leader'.[25] This comment caught the mood and it was put to Charles Kennedy himself during a radio interview.[26] Not grasping its significance, nor wishing to contradict his one-time friend, Kennedy replied: 'I quite accept these things. It is a reflection of what I am feeling myself.' Kennedy was presented as having acknowledged a failure of leadership. Simon Hughes duly revealed he had felt the need in Blackpool to promise Charles Kennedy he would not challenge him for the leadership, repeating a commitment he made after the general election.[27]

While apparently trying to be helpful, Simon Hughes added to the impression that his leader was in trouble. Charles Kennedy had no alternative but to tear up his prepared text and insert an extended passage to his conference speech in defence of his qualities as leader: getting the big decisions right, taking the party along with him and knowing when to listen rather than act.[28] Four months after a successful general election seemed a good time to take stock and listen, he said. There was no contradiction between economic and social liberalism, he continued, or financial discipline and social justice. But he added: 'What people don't want, don't deserve and don't demand is yet another conservative party in British politics . . . and I can assure all of you – I did not enter public life with the ambition of leading yet another conservative party in British politics.' This was applauded loudly but smacked of playing to the gallery and belittling the aims of economic liberals. The speech, his last as leader, was well received, delivered with confidence and some passion, but left longer-term strategic questions unresolved.

As the Lib Dems left Blackpool, bruised by unnecessary accidents, one final misfortune befell them. *The Times* published an investigation into the background of Michael Brown, the party's expatriate £2.4 million election benefactor, revealing details of past bounced cheques in the United States for which he had been arrested.[29] More importantly, it reported ongoing inquiries by the Electoral Commission into the permissibility of his donation via a nascent company in London. The newspaper carried criticisms from Michael Brown himself of his treatment by the party. This was very bad news for the Lib Dems' high command. Michael Brown had intended to give further, very substantial sums to the party, heralding an historic opportunity to fight Labour and the Conservatives on something approaching a more even footing. His public falling out with his Lib Dem handlers, exacerbated over the ensuing months, closed the door on that prospect, at least via his largesse. The story was followed by other newspaper investigations probing the financing of some of Charles Kennedy's pre-election aircraft flights[30] and his private office,[31] and how these were declared. Cumulatively, these created a sense of siege within the party's upper reaches during the autumn. Six months later Michael Brown was arrested in Spain and extradited to London to face fraud charges involving millions of pounds. In July 2006 he pleaded guilty at Southwark Crown Court to perjury and making an untrue statement to obtain a passport. HSBC, his bank, brought separate proceedings against him.

Regardless, Charles Kennedy pressed ahead with executing the plan to boost his leadership credentials set out in Tim Razzall's summer memorandum. He embarked on a series of speeches, of which the ill-fated excursion to the LSE was only the second. He laid plans for fact-finding visits to China, Israel and the Palestinian Authority and, the following year, Africa and India. After some diplomatic overtures and juggling of dates, a six-day trip to Beijing was arranged in early November but, to some frustration, cancelled to due to a clash with the report stage of the Terrorism Bill. Anxious not to repeat the embarrassment of missing a vote on counter-terrorism powers in March, this ensured Charles Kennedy was in the division lobbies as a proposed power to extend the maximum period of detention without charge to ninety days was lost by one vote, Tony Blair's first Commons defeat. Kennedy did at least see China's President, Hu Jintao, who was making a state visit to Britain, and used his audience with President Hu at Buckingham Palace to register concern at China's record on human rights and industrial pollution.[32] This was an important personal milestone for Charles Kennedy, who greatly regretted not having criticised the suppression by the Metropolitan Police of protests during a visit to London by China's previous President, Jiang Zemin, soon after he became Lib Dem leader in 1999.[33]

The gravity of Charles Kennedy's position became apparent to his inner circle only about three weeks after his final, calamitous, drinking episode, when he arrived still unwell to chair a morning meeting of his shadow cabinet, struggled through his lunchtime speech at the LSE and abandoned a train trip to Newcastle. Through loyal MPs, and a handful with feet in both camps, his staff first heard suggestions of moves to mobilise a delegation of senior MPs to tell the leader they had lost confidence, then of a plan for a letter with a larger number of signatories conveying the same message. Kennedy himself focused on his duties but Anna Werrin began questioning MPs and went to see Menzies Campbell to extract from him an assurance that he would do nothing to bring a premature end to Charles Kennedy's leadership. She also encouraged Mark Oaten to let it be known that, if a vacancy were to arise, he would stand as leader, thus disrupting moves to position Menzies Campbell as the only candidate able to beat Simon Hughes.

Even when his shadow cabinet revolted against him on 13 December, demanding the chief whip take soundings to see if Kennedy held their confidence, it never occurred to Charles Kennedy to resign. He returned to his Commons office for a pre-arranged sandwich lunch with a group of backbenchers, Paul Holmes, John Pugh, Adrian Sanders, Richard Younger-Ross and Susan Kramer, and used the occasion to seek their views. All were supportive but Susan Kramer. That evening Kennedy made an awkward tour of Christmas parties around Westminster, accompanied by Simon Hughes, who was now making an obvious statement of loyalty. One of their calls was to Dining Room C in the Commons, where the 2001 intake of Lib Dem MPs were having a fraught Christmas dinner. In an attempt at jollity Kennedy presented Paul Holmes with an award for chairing the longest parliamentary meeting. But once Charles Kennedy and Simon Hughes left the dozen MPs remaining embarked on an extended discussion on whether Kennedy should quit, initiated by Chris Rennard, who joined them. It was clear that the discontent extended beyond the shadow cabinet, although the MPs were split. The evening was soured when Paul Holmes accused Sarah Teather of briefing the press against Kennedy; she left the room in tears.

By now Kennedy knew he would lose his shadow cabinet's support in a vote of confidence. This was obvious from his one-to-one meetings and telephone calls with senior frontbenchers and MPs, and from the report he was receiving from Andrew Stunell regarding those who saw the chief whip. This view was reinforced by Chris Rennard, who had kept in touch with discontented MPs and wrote a devastating aide-memoire to the chief whip saying Charles Kennedy's position would become untenable if he tried to dismiss his critics in his shadow cabinet or if any resigned. He wrote:

> Current discussion and debate in the parliamentary party is now between those who say that 'Charles has had his last chance' and those who say that 'this is his last chance'.

A very substantial proportion of the shadow cabinet, quite possibly more than half, are probably in the 'had last chance' category.[34]

Chris Rennard gave warning that Kennedy's strongest support was from the diminishing number of MPs still unaware of his alcoholism and said others offering their backing were being duplicitous. In a coded reference to Menzies Campbell's readiness to stand as leader, Rennard advised: 'Perhaps in desperation, but in any event, new alternatives have emerged.'

Kennedy thought, however, that he would command a majority in his wider parliamentary party. He extended his one-to-one meetings and telephone calls to backbenchers to shore up support among them. His staff asked the whip's office about the procedure for calling a confidence motion themselves in that evening's parliamentary party meeting, only to be told it would be out of order since this required a week's notice. Instead they bought time as contributions at the meeting were dominated by loyalists while Kennedy's critics remained silent.

Thereafter Charles Kennedy, Dick Newby and Anna Werrin sought to prevent key members of the shadow cabinet from resigning, and to peel off any wavering rebels, hoping that by doing so he could survive until the local elections in May. They hoped that strong results then – that in the event failed to materialise – might rescue him. He also wanted to lower the temperature and let things calm down. This was misinterpreted by many, who could not understand why Kennedy himself did not spend the first few days of the Christmas recess exhaustively telephoning Lib Dem MPs, peers, council leaders and regional party officers to bolster his position. Dick Newby said: 'His plan was to go off, and give everybody the period between Christmas and New Year without disturbing them, but come back immediately after the New Year and spend the week on the phone then.'

Time was not, however, on his side. As the crisis spiralled out of control his advisers were split on whether he should make a public declaration that he was an alcoholic but had sought professional help, as he so nearly had in the summer of 2003. Tim Razzall and Anna Werrin were in favour, Dick Newby and Jackie Rowley against. Kennedy himself changed his mind several times. His team was dispersed when the fatal call came from an ITN executive with a warning that its bulletin would reveal the story of the delegation that confronted Kennedy over his alcoholism in March 2004. Tim Razzall was at the hospital bedside of a critically ill friend; Dick Newby was halfway up a mountain in a national park in north-east Hungary;

Matthew Oakeshott, another peer close to Kennedy, was in Kenya. In a hasty series of telephone calls they decided that Charles Kennedy must make a statement himself, in a dignified way and in his own words, rather than be forced to react to a media story. Andrew Stunell and Paul Holmes were forewarned, plus key allies such as Phil Willis, and Jim Wallace in Scotland.

At this moment of crisis Kennedy withdrew alone to the study of his south London townhouse to work on his statement. He was joined during the afternoon by Anna Werrin, Jackie Rowley, James Gurling, who came later, and Ben Stoneham, the most senior Cowley Street official in the absence of Chris Rennard, who had been away in Liverpool. During a discussion in the slightly cluttered, low-ceilinged family kitchen in the basement, Ben Stoneham was told of their plan simultaneously to call a leadership ballot; by now Kennedy's circle assumed he would do badly and might even lose the support of the Parliamentary Party should MPs table a no-confidence vote on their return to Westminster the following week. The ballot was a means of going over their heads to appeal for the support of members. Ben Stoneham was taken aback and advised against such a move, saying a leadership election in such circumstances would be a disaster, but his objections were waved aside. Stoneham persuaded them that he should telephone Chris Rennard, who as chief executive would be returning officer for the ballot, to at least give him warning, and was left alone in the kitchen while he did so. Rennard, who was driving back to London, strongly opposed the plan for a leadership ballot and said that Kennedy should confine his statement to an appeal for support from the party. Chris Rennard tried to evoke the memory of Roy Jenkins in a last attempt to make Kennedy change his mind. After their conversation Ben Stoneham sought out Charles Kennedy, who had returned to his study, and passed on a message from Rennard. It was a reminder of a phrase used by Roy Jenkins in praise of Paddy Ashdown during a turbulent period in his leadership, saying he had shown 'grace under pressure'. Kennedy, still demonstrating the remarkable calm he had throughout the crisis, smiled. 'Ah yes, typical of Chris to quote Roy Jenkins at me,' he said.

But Kennedy and his team would not be moved. They held a further discussion in his first-floor sitting room about the logistics for the press conference. Their chief concern was that Kennedy should be able to leave the room immediately after reading his statement, and not be boxed in by a crowd and subjected to questions. With little more than two hours' notice they proposed reconfiguring the room so that the podium was next to the door. Ben Stoneham told them there was too little time and instead organised a team of people ready to usher Kennedy into the room and out straight afterwards.

Early the following morning it was clear the plan had failed. As Lib Dem parliamentarians took to the media airwaves to demand Kennedy's resignation, Jo Swinson telephoned the leader's office to report moves to coordinate a mass resignation from the front bench unless he quit that day. She later joined the rebels, although several similar calls followed from MPs still supportive. Later Andrew Stunell called to confirm that at least twenty MPs had threatened to quit. When, in mid-afternoon, Charles Kennedy telephoned Ed Davey, the rebels' coordinator, he asked for forty-eight hours to reflect on his position. In fact, his mind was made up. He knew he must resign but not immediately, as the twenty-five signatories demanded. Typically, he wanted to sleep on it. He also wanted time to construct a thoughtful resignation statement. Dick Newby, who by then was at a castle in Visegrad and talking to Kennedy by mobile telephone, said:

> By Friday lunchtime he knew the game was up but he decided he was just going to sleep on it. The advantage of not rushing to judgement was that he was thinking about what he was going to say. If he had made a statement on Friday it would not have been as good as the statement he made on the Saturday.

On Saturday morning Kennedy returned to the computer in his study, on a mezzanine level at a turn in the stairs and overlooking the courtyard garden, this time to craft his swansong. Ever the performer, he ensured his last statement as leader was among his best. As he addressed his final press conference from the podium in the boardroom at Cowley Street, he read it with extraordinary composure.

'I have been in politics for far too long to be overly sentimental about this sort of moment,' he said immediately after announcing his resignation. He thanked just two people by name: Sarah, his wife, and Anna Werrin, saying he could not have wished for a finer friend and colleague. On leaving Cowley Street for the last time as leader, he and Sarah were driven back to the house, where they were joined by Tim Razzall, Anna Werrin, Jackie Rowley, Mark Oaten, Lembit Öpik and Kennedy's junior office staff, who had been told of his announcement earlier in the day. There were no more speeches but Kennedy thanked them individually for their support.

Such plaudits as he received at the end, however, could not hide the fact that his resignation had been an unbelievably messy, drawn-out affair. Part of the explanation was that, far from being ruthless, his critics wanted to allow Charles Kennedy to depart with dignity, a fact even his supporters recognised. 'One of the reasons that the whole thing became so messy was that they were such unwilling assassins. They didn't want to do it, really, because they did have a lot of affection for him,' Dick Newby acknowledged.

There were two further factors. The betrayal of the conspirators' plans, notably by Mark Oaten, frustrated their attempts to confront Kennedy in conditions of absolute secrecy with evidence of a loss of confidence among his frontbench colleagues. Furthermore, until the end Charles Kennedy himself stubbornly failed to accept that his position was irrecoverable. No leader can survive if they forfeit the support of their most senior colleagues, no matter what the fine print of a party constitution might say. From the moment six of his shadow cabinet told him he should go, and the same number raised grave doubts or offered only qualified support, his leadership was over.

Things rapidly grew worse for the Liberal Democrats after his resignation. Menzies Campbell declared that he would be a candidate on the day Kennedy quit, after being advised by Archy Kirkwood that he had damaged himself by prevaricating in the party's previous leadership election in 1999. Campbell's move, however, looked hasty and calculating and fuelled an atmosphere of recrimination among Lib Dems. This was stoked up by Simon Hughes, ostensibly fulfilling his role as party president by speaking on behalf of members but also furthering his own candidacy, as he attacked as 'unacceptable and inexcusable' Mark Oaten's behaviour in having a leadership campaign already in place. Tim Razzall and other Kennedy supporters protested angrily that criticism of Charles Kennedy on the day before he resigned had been unnecessarily brutal. Mark Oaten declared himself a candidate but withdrew after finding insufficient support with just one MP, Lembit Öpik, ready to vote for him. Days later Mark Oaten resigned as home affairs spokesman after newspaper revelations of past visits to a male prostitute. Simon Hughes, who also stood as a leadership candidate, was forced to admit to homosexual relationships, having denied that he was gay in newspaper interviews to publicise his candidacy.

The assumption had been that these three candidates would stand. This was confounded by Chris Huhne. On returning from a skiing holiday in Davos, Switzerland, Huhne went to see Menzies Campbell and asked to be released from his commitment given the previous month to support him in a leadership election; he wished to stand as a candidate himself. Huhne said he would honour his word if Campbell held him to it. Menzies Campbell released him from the commitment, saying he was free to stand – 'Of course, dear boy,' he said – but after a long discussion on policy appeared to have talked him out of doing so. Huhne left, saying he was 'minded' to support Campbell after all. After discussions with his wife, however, Huhne returned the following day to say he would be a candidate himself. Chris Huhne's candidacy drew bitter criticism from other potential candidates who had held back to support Menzies Campbell.

These were terrible circumstances for a leadership ballot. Mark Oaten was disgraced. Simon Hughes was damaged, although he battled gamely on. Chris Huhne attracted brickbats from seething colleagues for breaking his word but plaudits from the media and many activists for his courage. Menzies Campbell, cursed with the handicap of being the frontrunner, struggled due to a combination of his age at sixty-four, caution from not wishing to offer hostages to fortune, and over-organisation owing to a large campaign structure. Permeating the contest were the emotions stirred up by the bewildering and bloody events that forced Charles Kennedy's resignation. Such sentiments remained among the active membership but were at least soothed among MPs themselves thanks to their culture of collegiate discussion. At their first parliamentary party meeting after the Christmas recess, with Charles Kennedy absent, they held an extraordinary session. It began with backbenchers such as Bob Russell, Paul Rowan and Mike Hancock venting anger at what had happened. But the tenor changed when a series of protagonists gave candid accounts of why they acted as they did. Vince Cable explained the genesis of his infamous letter to Kennedy. Ed Davey, David Laws and others said they were motivated not by plotting against Kennedy but by what they thought was in the party's interests. Matthew Taylor described being forced to deny Kennedy's alcoholism to the press. As accounts of Kennedy's difficulties at the manifesto launch and at events the previous November were given, it became clear that some Lib Dem MPs were still unaware of the nature of the problem. Andrew George explained why he had called for the resignation of the leader he admired and had served as parliamentary private secretary. John Thurso spoke movingly of how difficult he found it to sign a letter of no confidence in Charles Kennedy, who was MP for his neighbouring Highlands constituency. Several were angry that shadow cabinet members had not spoken up at their last confrontational parliamentary party meeting in mid-December, but accepted it was unrealistic to expect them to do so with Charles Kennedy present and reporters camped outside. Andrew Stunell explained the role he had played as chief whip. There were frank accounts from MPs about cases of alcoholism within their families. At least half of those present spoke. The meeting, which was emotional and subdued, was twice interrupted by Commons votes and ran for four and a half hours. It did not draw all the bitterness from the saga but flushed out the worst of it and dispelled many misunderstandings. There was, too, a powerful view that all should now support Charles Kennedy. The atmosphere was of a tentative reunion after a fierce family quarrel.

Kennedy himself took a holiday, spending a fortnight with Sarah and Donald in the Bahamas at Tim Razzall's villa, where he had enjoyed his first summer holiday after being elected leader. On their return, faced with the difficulties of adapting to life as a former leader and post-devolution backbench Scottish MP, Kennedy took a remarkable decision. The day before Kennedy resigned a Labour MP, Rachel Squire, died after a long illness. Her death meant a by-election in Dunfermline & West Fife, where the Lib Dems were a long way behind but in second place, narrowly ahead of the Scottish National Party. Several times by-elections had rescued Kennedy's leadership; this one arose just too late. As the leadership election to choose Kennedy's successor lurched from one setback to another, few people beyond Scotland took much notice of the by-election in Dunfermline. It was assumed the Lib Dems should aim simply to avoid being pushed into third place by the Scottish nationalists. The one point of interest was that the constituency was next door to Kirkcaldy & Cowdenbeath, the seat of Gordon Brown, the Chancellor, who was universally assumed to be Labour's next leader. The Lib Dems, however, were fighting to win. They knew the SNP could not match their local organisation and activists and, in Willie Rennie, a former Scottish party official, the Lib Dems had an experienced candidate. Somehow, they managed to blame Gordon Brown for plans for steep toll rises to cross the Forth Road Bridge, even though these were determined by the Scottish Executive in which they were junior coalition partners. The Lib Dems were making a fight of it.

As he had many times before, Chris Rennard called upon Charles Kennedy's campaigning skills to boost the by-election campaign. Kennedy accepted immediately and, thus, his first public appearance since his resignation was in the thick of a by-election campaign on 2 February surrounded by a scrum of reporters and photographers. 'I know there were people who were not very keen on the idea,' said Jim Wallace, who had just stepped down as leader of the Scottish Lib Dems and who accompanied him. 'The Scottish party were doubtful, they thought it might be awkward, for him and the party, people might ask questions.'

By coincidence, each of the main parties contesting the by-election sent their big guns to Dunfermline on the same day. Gordon Brown arrived to have a lunch of carrot and coriander soup in the upstairs room of a local café. David Cameron, in his first by-election campaign as Conservative leader, opted for a walkabout in the high street. Alex Salmond, leader of the SNP, arrived to discuss plans for improving Dunfermline's town centre. The media entourage, a fickle but telling bellwether, showed polite interest in Gordon Brown but swamped David Cameron. Poor Alex Salmond found himself treated as a sideshow. When, several hours later, Charles Kennedy arrived he was, if anything, the subject of still more interest than David Cameron, making his walk along Dunfermline's main shopping street a chaotic one. Reporters thronged around him and shouted questions about whether he had stopped drinking, who he blamed for his downfall and the damage wreaked on his party by recent events. Kennedy dealt with them calmly, with good humour and relentlessly talked up the Lib Dems' chances in the seat. It was a brave performance in what could have been difficult circumstances.

One week later, shortly before midnight, astonishing news began to break from Dunfermline. The Liberal Democrats won the by-election, overturning a Labour majority of 11,562 to win by a margin of 1,800 in the constituency bordering that of Gordon Brown. It was an incredible result, ranking with the great Lib Dem by-election upsets in political history. For five weeks the party had been treated as a joke as it endured regicide, alcoholism, sex scandals, infighting and public scorn. Victory in Dunfermline & West Fife confounded the Lib Dems' critics. The campaign was won when the party was without a permanent leader. All three remaining candidates had visited and could claim a share of the credit, but only a share. So, too, could Charles Kennedy. Nobody could quite quantify the impact of his visit during the by-election but it was clearly significant and one of the talking points of the campaign. The result demonstrated that, despite the foibles of a handful of its senior figures, the Liberal Democrats' potency as a campaigning force remained intact. It was, too, a poignant reminder of the electoral appeal of Charles Kennedy, the brilliant prodigy turned politician whose star burned too brightly, too early, and whose promise was blighted by a tragic flaw.

11

In search of a role

At 46, Kennedy still had much of his working life before him when he resigned as leader. The Lib Dems were a relatively small party with few politicians recognised and liked by the public; he remained one of their greatest assets. He could, of course, have contemplated a second career outside frontline politics, such as in broadcasting, leaving the Commons straightaway or at the next general election and accepting a peerage. Neither crossed his mind. Kennedy remained to his fingertips a politician, the only job he had ever known. Some months after his resignation as leader, he told an interviewer: "I've never been tempted during this year since stepping down to do anything else."[1]

Remaining in the Commons did mean finding a new role appropriate to his talents and status as an ex-party leader, that suited his temperament yet did not get in the way of his successor. The circumstances were not easy. The media had, by and large, been baffled and enthralled in equal measure by the savagery of the blood-letting that forced Kennedy's departure. The Lib Dems, thrown into a leadership election to replace him, were widely portrayed as a remote tribe engaged in some obscure internecine war. While Kennedy was not naturally one to nurse a grudge he felt Menzies Campbell, who won the ballot to be his successor, could have stopped the revolt against him. There remained coolness on Kennedy's part, and outright hostility among some of his close allies and departing staff, towards the Lib Dems' new leader. Before confirmation of the result Campbell's campaign chairman Archy Kirkwood had lunch with Kennedy's former chief of staff Dick Newby and discussed his future role. Kirkwood told him that, should Campbell win, he would issue an invitation to Kennedy to take a senior role in his shadow cabinet. Kennedy declined this overture and made clear he did not wish to return as a front bench spokesman for the duration of the parliament, although would rule nothing out beyond that.[2] In the months that followed he tried to keep a low profile and stayed away from the Lib Dems' spring conference at Harrogate, where Campbell made his first speech as leader. He was keen, however, to show willingness to campaign on his party's behalf and braved the inevitable media attention by making by-elections in Bromley & Chislehurst, where the Lib Dems narrowly failed to overturn a large Conservative majority, and Blaenau Gwent in the south Wales valleys, which Labour lost to an independent.

Kennedy's most prominent public appearance after his resignation came in the autumn, after he accepted an invitation to address the Lib Dem conference at Brighton. This may have been intended as a valedictory address, a chance to bid a dignified farewell to party activists; instead Kennedy and his friends saw it as a moment to signal his return although what exactly he intended to return to was never quite clear. Certainly his closest advisers, Anna Werrin and Dick Newby, wanted him back as leader once he could show he had conquered his alcoholism. In his first television appearance since re-joining the backbenches, on *Question Time*, Kennedy himself refused to rule out regaining the Lib Dem leadership at some stage in the future. 'Who knows? The one thing we can all be sure about in politics is you are as well to expect the unexpected,' he replied when asked.[3] Asked by a member of the audience whether he was now teetotal, Kennedy did not answer directly, saying simply: 'My health is good and it's up to me to keep it that way.'[4]

With Menzies Campbell struggling to make an impact in his first months as leader and Lib Dem poll ratings sliding, the prospect of Kennedy's speech was given a sharper edge. While their friendship went back many years, the pair had a strained relationship since the events of December and January, despite overtures from Campbell; a plan to meet with their wives at the Edinburgh Festival was cancelled; Campbell arranged to go to Kennedy's new office on the third floor of Portcullis House, Westminster to discuss arrangements for the speech, but they did so in a telephone call instead. Kennedy said he wanted no fuss, no one on stage other than the conference chairman and aide, no party grandees to welcome him, no welcoming handshake on stage from Menzies Campbell, who instead sat on the conference floor in the front row. In the event the pressure eased of its own accord. When he took the stage in Brighton, looking remarkably trim having lost a great deal of weight, Kennedy received a rapturous reception and spoke fluently without notes. He was studiously loyal and talked with optimism of the future for the Liberal Democrats. But, as he ruminated on the Iraq invasion, social justice, reforming the House of Lords and global warming, his skill in reading an audience appeared to let him down; very subtly, there was a sense that his speech was overlong and lacking in clarity of message. He ended to warm applause, but it felt a moment had passed. Most reaction was kind. But Paddy Ashdown, loyal to Campbell and unwilling to indulge Kennedy, was merciless in his assessment in a radio interview the following morning. 'The perfect ex-leader's speech does two things: it says goodbye to the party and it does not take the spotlight away from the party's present leader,' Ashdown said, archly. 'I think Charles succeeded in both those things very well.'[5]

The episode diminished Kennedy's potency as a king over the water for restless Lib Dems, despite the Jacobite appeal of such a notion, but he ploughed on with a political rehabilitation in his own image. Initially, and somewhat awkwardly, he was allocated the Commons office previously used by Menzies Campbell in Portcullis House. Kennedy arrived to take possession and noticed his name plaque beside the door said simply 'Charles Kennedy' without the prefix 'Rt Hon' that was his due as a privy councillor. He was never pompous yet he was a traditionalist and liked things to be done in a proper way. He insisted that the Commons authorities replace the plaque with his full title. Several months later he was able to relocate to another office overlooking the Portcullis House atrium, with a balcony on which he could smoke. He chose to make his first Commons speech from the backbenches a month later, during an Opposition day debate seeking a Privy Councillors' inquiry into the Iraq invasion. Kennedy noted he had spent more time on this than on any other issue as Lib Dem leader, and challenged the criticism that a full inquiry would undermine British troops still serving there. He described attending a memorial service for British personnel killed in Iraq, saying he spoke to every bereaved family to ask if it was right for him to question the invasion. Whatever their views on the war, he said, all had acknowledged his right to do so. 'On the political tombstone of this Prime Minister will be the word 'Iraq',' he told the Commons presciently. 'For hundreds and thousands of innocent civilians in that country there will never be a tombstone, and we will never know their names.'[6]

Thereafter he resumed speaking in the Commons from time to time on issues close to his heart, such as Europe and his opposition to university tuition fees, and on constituency matters like the impact on island com-munities of a postal workers' strike, although his attendance at Westminster was sporadic. On occasions he would attend the weekly parliamentary party meeting of Lib Dem MPs, sitting on a side bench, sometimes making a contribution. He took up a visiting parliamentary fellowship to St Anthony's College, Oxford, a graduate college specialising in politics and international relations, giving seminars on the roles of religious and ethnic minorities in democracies;

academic life interested him and he spent considerable time preparing these. He became vice-president of Liberal International, the international federation of Liberal parties, worked with the Westminster Foundation for Democracy, taking a particular interest in human rights issues in Russia and visiting opposition politicians there. Within a year Kennedy was elected president of the European Movement in the UK, the cause at the core of his political creed that he learned from his mentor Roy Jenkins.

He picked up other threads from his former life, too, making several television documentaries that allowed him to explore recent political interests. In a *30 Minutes* programme for Channel 4 he looked at the then still relatively recent phenomenon of declining trust in politics, which he linked to political parties and leaders playing down or neutralising divisive issues of concern to many voters, such as the Trident nuclear missile system, civil nuclear power or Britain's place in Europe, and electioneering tactics of ruthlessly targeting swing voters in target seats. In another documentary for the BBC, *A Chip on Each Shoulder*, he marked the 300th anniversary of the Act of Union, charting Scotland's history within the United Kingdom and exploring its national identity. Not all his broadcasting was as cerebral, as the faint tug of celebrity found him filming shows on his favourite garden and the thirty greatest political comedies. He wrote occasional newspaper articles, taking meticulous care with these and returned, too, to the after-dinner speaking circuit where he remained in demand as the star turn at awards evenings, conferences and corporate events, earning substantial amounts for each. They carried risks, and a handful of times he would turn up at these or other speaking engagements the worse for drink, illustrating that his battle with alcohol was not conquered as he claimed.[7]

While Kennedy was, to some extent, recreating a political comfort zone in which he felt at ease, Menzies Campbell found life as leader ever tougher. When Gordon Brown flirted with a snap election in October 2007 before losing his nerve and calling it off, Campbell stood down precipitating the second Lib Dem leadership election in nineteen months. Had Kennedy really harboured hopes of a comeback this was his moment; the caravan had, however, moved on. Chris Huhne, assertive and aggressively populist, moved quickly to stand a second time while Nick Clegg, the protégé of party king-makers, stood as a centrist moderniser. Kennedy swiftly made clear he would not be a candidate. 'I didn't think there would be a vacancy in the Lib Dems in this parliament, and certainly not to contest one; I'm quite happy with the role I've got," he declared.[8] This time Anna Werrin and Dick Newby ran the Huhne campaign. Several more of Kennedy's allies also backed Huhne and there were concerted attempts to persuade Kennedy himself to declare. 'We desperately wanted him to come out and endorse Chris because if he had Chris would have won,' said Matthew Oakeshott, a Lib Dem peer. Kennedy did agree to a request that Huhne's campaign literature could feature prominently a photograph of the two men together at the Stop The War demonstration against the Iraq war but refused to take sides publicly. Clegg, the front-runner, fought a lacklustre campaign and won by the narrowest of margins.

By this time, however, a new opportunity had presented itself which would fill the void left in Kennedy's life since he was forced out as leader. Early in 2007 he attended an event at the University of Glasgow, his alma mater, and while there was approached by students about a forthcoming vacancy as rector. This post, unique to Scotland's ancient universities, is elected by students to represent their interests to the university court or council. Kennedy had turned down previous invitations to stand as rector before he became Lib Dem leader. This time he thought the moment right and signalled his interest. One of the student leaders Jamie McHale graduated that summer and got a job in the constituency office of Jo Swinson, Lib Dem MP for East Dunbartonshire, and put Kennedy in touch with a current student willing to run his campaign.

One complication was that Glasgow university has two students unions, with a keen rivalry between them. Kennedy remained a life member of the Glasgow University Union, in its handsome stone building with grand oak panelled rooms, previously the men's union.

It was at the Queen Margaret Union, formerly the women's union, that Kennedy's nascent rectorial campaign met for the first time in functional 1960s premises, in November. McHale and Niall Rowantree, former president of the GUU, explained a wish among students for a working rector. The incumbent was the Israeli nuclear technician Mordechai Vanunu who had revealed secrets of his country's nuclear programme; at his installation the rector's gown was draped over an empty chair since he was detained in Israel. With growing debate at Westminster over raising university tuition fees, and pressure on higher education budgets in Scotland, undergraduates wanted a more visible champion to represent them. Kennedy, accompanied by an aide, explained he was willing to be an active rector but wished to stand on an apolitical, broad-based platform able to reach out to all shades of student opinion. The university's students had a long tradition of electing political rectors, eminent but largely absent figures who included eleven former prime ministers. Kennedy would be both a political figurehead and a presence on campus. Their objective, they agreed, must be to set aside student factionalism and get the backing of both campus unions, plus the non-political Glasgow University Sports Association – the campaign was on.

While Kennedy started with the advantage of name-recognition, the contest was keenly fought. It was soon clear that Aamer Anwar, a left-wing human rights lawyer, would be a candidate and that a Green Party politician in the Scottish parliament, Patrick Harvie, would stand. SNP students also wanted a nationalist candidate and settled on Hardeep Singh Kohli, a comic broadcaster and writer. Kennedy took the contest seriously; he submitted himself for interview by the QM board of management, a large body of students, to convince them he was serious about reaching out beyond his old stamping ground of the rival union and its legendary debating chamber. Throughout the autumn he made regular visits to the campus, stopping en route to his constituency, to meet his student campaign team, review strategy and be updated on progress. They used the slogan 'working rector' and he promised in his manifesto to be 'a constituency MP for the campus'. Anxious to avoid imagery associated with political parties, they settled on sky blue T-shirts designed by art and graphic design students: probably the only time Kennedy stood for election in blue campaign colours.

Given that it was a campaign run by undergraduates, not everything went according to plan. Niall Rowantree, who became campaign manager, spent considerable time setting up and publicising a surgery-style drop-in session for international students at Glasgow, setting aside three hours on a Friday afternoon. Kennedy arrived as scheduled to find only four overseas students had turned up. 'It was really embarrassing but he couldn't have been more understanding,' a mortified Rowantree recalled. 'He said that was four people higher than the lowest turnout for a meeting he'd had.' Other events were, however, a triumph. Kennedy, whose interest in sport was close to zero, was honorary guest speaker at the university sports association's annual black tie ball at the Thistle Hotel. It was a raucous atmosphere of more than 1,000 hard-drinking rugby, football and hockey players, cheer leaders, trampoliners and athletes. 'He had that crowd eating out of his hand,' Rowantree said. Another key moment was the end of term 'daft Friday' ball at the Glasgow University Union, an all-night party with a Hollywood theme at which exuberant students queued up to have their photographs taken with Kennedy before going up the hill to the QM building on the other side of the campus to do the same.

By January 2008 Kennedy was visiting the campus weekly and made six visits in February and stayed in the city for the final week when the vote took place by electronic ballot, a first for a rectorial election. He had by this time around fifty student volunteers in sky blue T-shirts, handing out campaign fliers and urging fellow undergraduates to attend hustings. 'He would sit down with you all in the QM canteen and it was just like he was one of the team, but was then able to stand up in front of whatever crowd – four international students or 1,000 sports students – and be able to pitch a message that was just right,' Rowantree said. When the result was declared, Kennedy won comfortably: he was just short of the required threshold after the first round of counting, but after the second emerged with 2,605 votes to 1,414 for Aamer Anwar, his nearest challenger. Kennedy arrived an hour late for the declaration in the university's Bute Hall and gave an emotional acceptance speech in which he spoke of the death from cancer the previous summer of Murdo Macdonald, his best friend and university contemporary. 'I wish he was here tonight,' a tearful Kennedy said, pausing to compose himself. 'He would be very proud.'[9]

Having offered himself as a working rector, Kennedy was as good as his word. He treated the three-year post with the utmost seriousness, devoting considerable time and energy to the task, yet fulfilling it with a lightness of touch that endeared him to students and staff alike. At his installation ceremony two months later, resplendent in the rector's black and gilt tasselled gown, he recalled an episode from his undergraduate days when a professor summoned him to suggest, gently, that he was spending too much time on debating and campus politics and too little on his studies. The academic asked the young man what he actually wanted to do with his life. Perhaps teaching, or journalism, Kennedy had replied tentatively. Both careers would need a degree, the professor pointed out, before adding: 'In your case, Charles, I suppose if all else fails you could always go into politics.' A couple of years after graduating, Kennedy told his audience, he received a letter at the House of Commons from the same professor. It read: 'Dear Charles, Congratulations upon your most unexpected election to the House of Commons. From which I can only conclude that all else has failed.'[10]

During his term as rector it was his annual freshers' address that became a highlight. Wide-eyed freshers, in their first week at university, would troop meekly into the Gothic splendour of the Bute Hall to be greeted by a wall of noise as chanting groups from the rival student unions cheered on their respective presidents as they waited to speak. These so-called freshers' helpers, in garish matching T-shirts and sometimes fancy dress, would pack the side aisles and balconies and chant, whoop and cat-call as a procession of student leaders made its way to the platform with the vice-chancellor, chaplain and rector. It must have been a bewildering, slightly intimidating, atmosphere for many of the new foreign students. But Kennedy, ever the internationalist, would always make a point of asking for a show of hands from overseas students. As, hesitantly, hands would creep up across the hall, the rector would bid them stand up and invite fellow undergraduates to give them 'a warm Glasgow welcome' with a round of applause. 'And I have to say that because you pay a bloody fortune to be here,' he added on one occasion, with a mischievous twinkle. Another theme was his urging of students to make the most of campus life. 'It's often said of Gilmorehill [the Glasgow campus] that if you're lucky then eventually the university awards you a degree,' he would tell them, 'but it's the university unions that give you the real education in life.'

This theme of the importance of extra-curricular activities was one of those Kennedy championed on behalf of students as he embraced his new duties. He raised with the university authorities students' concerns that lectures and seminars were beginning to encroach into Wednesday afternoons, which traditionally were kept clear for sporting fixtures and student-led events. The rector began holding monthly constituency-style surgeries on campus, using a room in the Students' Representative Council offices and arranging for staff from the student council and university's court to act as case-workers. He made a point of visiting its small vocationally-focused campus two hours' drive away in Dumfries. A new item headed 'report from the rector' began to appear on the agenda of the university court, which met five times a year, as Kennedy updated the university hierarchy on his whirl of activity. In one such item, the rector even reported he had made time to attend 'the end of year graduation at the university nursery', perhaps taking his new duties a little too far.[11]

It would be easy to misrepresent this newfound passion as Kennedy retreating to and reliving the familiar echoes of his own extended period as a student but the role was not merely as a students' champion. As rector he chaired the university court, which held detailed discussions on the performance and strategic development of its academic departments and estate; the internal politics of a world class research university fascinated him. It gave him a new perspective, too, on the interface between higher education and national politics, both at Westminster and Holyrood. Kennedy was active in breathing life into a Scottish rectors' group with his four counterparts at Edinburgh, St Andrews, Aberdeen and Dundee, was rapidly elected co-chairman of the House of Commons all-party parliamentary universities group, and took a close interest in emerging debates on university funding and immigration rules for international students. While rector, Kennedy tabled nineteen separate questions in the Commons on higher education issues.

The enthusiasm with which he embraced his role as rector reflected a profound change that was under way in his life: his centre of gravity was tilting away from London and back towards Scotland. He loved Glasgow, where he spent five years as a student and where his mother grew up. Increasingly, urban life for him revolved more around Glasgow and less around London, and he spent more time, too, at his constituency home in Fort William. It also reflected changes in his personal relationships. The death of his best friend Murdo Macdonald was a great blow. Although many people counted Kennedy as a friend, very few were actually close to him; they knew Charles the public persona, not the slightly withdrawn, somewhat anxious private man within. He also missed terribly the support of Anna Werrin, who had worked for him since his earliest days in the Commons, organised much of his life, pushed him when he was idle and was his protective shield when coping with his alcoholism. She and Murdo Macdonald were the two friends who had supported Kennedy with his drink problem since it developed in the early 1990s. She left his staff when he quit as leader and initially worked as an executive at the BBC, where she was on hand to keep him in touch with London friends. Werrin later moved with her family to Cornwall, from where she continued to support him although it was less easy from afar, but died from a stroke in 2010. For many years his constituency office had been run by Shanae Fraser, daughter of his great friend John Farquhar Munro. She dealt with casework and correspondence from an office off the high street in Dingwall and was also central to his support network: on occasions he would stay in her home in Inverness when he wanted a bolthole away from the world. She, too, left a year or so after he stopped being leader to spend more time with her young family. Kennedy could be very difficult: disorganised, lazy, disappearing for days on end, refusing to answer his telephone. These two women knew how to manage him. Gradually, he lost touch with or distanced himself from some of his political friends in London. Kennedy had always been assiduous in dropping short notes hand-written in fountain pen to political contacts, and sometimes opponents. Gradually these dried up. In their place came chatty, carefully phrased though sporadic text messages, always signed off 'CK'. It meant he kept in touch yet friends could never quite be sure where he was.

Kennedy did make strenuous and genuine efforts to conquer his alcoholism. These began in earnest in his final years as leader. It was a subject he never liked to speak of other than to a handful of closest confidants. Over the tears his staff and advisers tried to encourage him to seek treatment at a specialist clinic, or even spend a summer at a rehabilitation centre in Arizona, but he refused and believed he could manage it himself. Finally, in the summer of 2005, he relented and checked into a residential clinic for several days to 'dry out' and arrange on-going specialist counselling. It worked up to a point: he learned to discipline himself so that he would not drink at all for weeks on end but then would lapse. It was a pattern he never broke out of. When he made his statement in 2006, acknowledging a drink problem days before resigning, he received hundreds of letters of support, many from people giving testimonies of a relative who was an alcoholic. Kennedy's staff replied politely to them all but did not show him many of the most heart-rending; these were too close to the bone. Similarly, he received many requests from the media organisations and charities asking him to talk about his struggle with alcoholism. He never did.

His drinking was coupled with periods of depression, sometimes linked with stresses or anxieties in his personal life. He grew nervous before confrontational or judgmental situations and, as he felt tense, drank more as a way of dealing with this. The unravelling of this critically important support network of friends and aides made it harder for him to keep on top of his drink problem and, in consequence, he tipped into an acute downward spiral. His drinking became so heavy and his mental health so poor that in 2008 he had to be checked into an alcohol rehabilitation clinic in Glasgow for a period. He found the initial treatment, which usually includes medically assisted detoxification, helpful and thereafter resolved to continue with the clinic's recovery programme himself. He wanted to avoid further residential treatment, for fear that the news that he was an in-patient would leak to the press, but he was assigned a substance abuse counsellor who he continued to see regularly over several years. Initially they usually met weekly, although appointments would be interrupted by his diary commitments as an MP. Counselling sessions helped him to identify trigger points or situations linked to his patterns of drinking and to develop strategies to avoid or manage these.

As part of his treatment, his counsellor also recommended group therapy and suggested he attend an Alcoholics Anonymous group in Glasgow. This was another giant step for a man who was both a public figure and yet inherently private, who recoiled from discussing his drink problem. Again, however, the first meeting was a success. He began to block out time in his diary to allow him to return to the AA group on a weekly basis, although this wasn't always possible. Two things appealed to him about the AA's approach. One was its founding principle of anonymity. The group kept no record of who attended or how often, didn't require him to join and he could attend or quit whenever he chose. The second was its notion of fellowship. He was surprised and interested by the characters he encountered at his AA meetings as they discussed the impact alcohol had on their lives and how they coped with their addictions. They included professional people – one was a police officer, another a teacher – but were a wide social mix, as one might expect in Glasgow, and completely unconnected to his life in politics. They never broke the circle of fellowship or its core principle of anonymity. Other members of the group knew, of course, who he was when he first arrived yet the fact of his attendance never leaked, which he valued and made it a safe place for him. He was offered a separate introduction to an AA group in London, where he knew some of the people who attended, but declined and decided he was happier with his circle in Glasgow. He continued with his treatment programme, regular counselling sessions and AA meetings for around three years, and on occasion had short stays in the clinic after lapses in his drinking. By 2011 he felt he was better and had regained control over his life and stopped the meetings, although he kept in touch with his counsellor. He was, however, unable to commit to a core element of the AA's approach. Its programme of recovery, like all such treatments, emphasises that an alcoholic should give up alcohol and stay away from the first drink. He could not.

Charles Kennedy went through periods when he would stop drinking and others when he might drink in moderation: a glass or two of red wine with a meal, a tumbler of whisky afterwards, a pint of beer. There were other times, although infrequent, when he would lose control and go on a drinking spree. One evening before his resignation he left the Lib Dem leader's office in the Commons with several of his staff but told them he had forgotten something and went back inside, asking them to wait. After a quarter of an hour or so he returned, drunk. They discovered that he had opened a presentation bottle of whisky left for him to sign for a charity auction, and drunk well over half of it. Other occasions were less spectacular. With close friends he might have several glasses of wine over supper, followed by glasses of Scotch: steady heavy drinking. Latterly he drank less but its effects would be more evident and the damaging impact on his body was compounded by a thoroughly unhealthy lifestyle. He smoked heavily, had a poor diet and took almost no exercise, and would drive his car rather than walk on even the shortest errands. The most striking thing, however, was that during his latter years in Parliament few people actually saw him drinking even if they noticed its effects. He drank in private, both in London and especially on returning home to Fort William and the tight-knit community in which he grew up. His crofter's cottage was where he liked to disappear, to ignore telephone calls, to play music and collect his thoughts in a place that to him was both quiet and safe. One long-standing family friend said: 'I can remember him saying to me one time he liked being back in Lochaber because, if he was in London, if he went into a shop to get a bottle of whisky or a bottle of gin or a bottle of wine it would be in the papers within seconds. He could go and get a bottle in Lochaber and no one was going to say anything. He kind of liked that protection that he enjoyed within the area.'

He did have support at home in dealing with his alcoholism, too. His elderly parents discussed his drinking with him many times and encouraged his treatment: his father, ironically, was teetotal. John Farquhar Munro, his long-time political ally in the constituency, who had himself overcome a drink problem and attended Alcoholics Anonymous meetings, spoke with Kennedy about his drinking many times as did his wife Celia, who regarded him almost as a member of their family. These candid conversations were important as Kennedy refused point blank to acknowledge to many of his political friends based mainly in London, that his drinking was still a problem. When some did try to raise the subject with him, he would tell them disarmingly: 'I'm fine' and offer a winning smile but little else. One of the few he did confide in was Alastair Campbell, Tony Blair's former director of communications, whom Kennedy first met as a political journalist in the 1980s. Despite their different party allegiances they developed a strong friendship, which deepened once Kennedy became rector at Glasgow, where Donald, Campbell's brother, was the university principal's official piper. Alastair and his family would rent a house near Fort William every Christmas or Easter and invite the Kennedys to visit, sometimes staying the night. There they would have long talks about his drinking since Campbell, too, was a former alcoholic and knew the torment of battling with an overpowering urge to open a bottle. He knew that Kennedy had sought help but pressed him to be open about his problem, although the two obstacles of family privacy and fear of a political and constituency backlash always held him back.

On one occasion, during a family supper, Kennedy asked his host to join him for a walk in the garden even though it was raining. 'We went out there and we didn't walk very far and he said, 'look it has been getting worse and I know I have got to do something'. He said, 'just tell me again, how did you stop, how did you do it'?' Campbell said. 'I just let him talk. He talked a bit and said when he has one drink he was finding it hard to stop.' Kennedy was not in a good state: his hands were shaking so heavily when he placed a cigarette in his mouth he was unable to light it; he had to clamp the cigarette butt with his thumb and forefinger to keep it to his lips. Campbell took the lighter from his friend's unsteady hand and lit it. 'So I said, "look Charles you have taken a massive step if you really, really, really mean what you say. If you really meant it when you say you have got to do something, you have got to confront it and it has got to be for good",' Campbell said. 'And he said, "there is no doubt about it, I have to".' Campbell recommended an in-patient addiction clinic, Castle Craig Hospital in Peeblesshire, and told his friend it might require a residential stay lasting months. They discussed the cost, which would be considerable. Kennedy assured him he was ready to do whatever was necessary. 'He gave the sense that a big burden had lifted,' Campbell said. 'We went back in and he was just quite chirpy.' The next morning Campbell called Castle Craig, told them he was close to persuading a friend who was a well-known public figure to come to them. The clinic was heavily booked but offered to take him in a fortnight's time. 'I phoned him that night and said, 'are you up for this because they can get you in in two weeks?' Campbell said. 'And he said "leave it with me, I'll see what is in the diary that has to go out". I thought straight away he is not going to do it.' He didn't.

Colleagues at Westminster, too, tried to help. Reports would circulate occasionally of an event at which Kennedy turned up to speak in a poor state or, more commonly, did not turn up at all. Similarly in his constituency he would sometimes not appear for surgeries or meetings. It was not always clear whether such absences were drink-related or due to disorganisation. In the spring of 2013, during a period when he was distraught over his mother's failing health, Kennedy arrived at a 'sale of work' fund-raising event in Dingwall in his constituency. He was drunk but, worse, looked in a shocking physical state. His skin was red and blotchy, with blistery sores on his face, and his body gave off a pungent chemical-like alcohol smell. One friend who was present emailed a senior Lib Dem peer close to Kennedy afterwards to say he felt deeply worried for his health. Within weeks a dinner took place in the National Hotel in Dingwall to mark the 30th anniversary of his election to the Commons, with guests including Willie Rennie, Jim Wallace, Bob Maclennan and Danny Alexander. Kennedy, in a suit and tartan tie, arrived almost incoherently drunk, refused to eat and at one point had to be taken outside. The principal guests persuaded him not to make a speech himself although he spoke a few words of welcome and thanks. Both episodes were conveyed to the party whips in London, who consulted Kennedy's closest friends about his past treatment at addiction clinics and sought fresh medical advice about whether he might even be referred for rehabilitation against his will. In the event two Lib Dem peers who knew him best were asked to speak to him separately about his drinking but when they did he looked much better and brightly assured them he was fine and his drinking was under control. 'Did the whips send you?' he asked one of them, watchfully.

Charles Kennedy's unsuccessful battle with alcoholism put great strain upon his marriage. He was a gentle and loving husband but unreliable and often absent. He and his wife Sarah shared a conviction that they must deal with his drink problem themselves, and privately, which at times made it more difficult for close allies to press him to seek more sustained professional help. As his drinking lapses continued and they spent more time apart the marriage broke down and they announced their divorce in August 2010, although they continued to be on cordial terms. Kennedy moved out of the family home in Kennington, south London into a rented flat across the road so he could be on hand when he was in the capital to share in the upbringing of their son Donald, who inherited his father's red hair and twinkling eyes. He would have Donald on Tuesdays, collecting him from primary school – sometimes arriving in a rush by taxi – and walking him back to the flat when they would spend the evening together. He enjoyed taking his son to Common's events, such as the Christmas party for MPs' children and, best of all, advanced screenings of the Christmas episode of Dr Who, and at half terms and holidays would fly with Donald to stay at his crofter's cottage in Fort William and see his grandparents. To Kennedy's delight, although his son was growing up in London he embraced his Highland heritage, loved to listen to bagpipes and wore a kilt on formal occasions such as the Trooping the Colour ceremony in Horse Guards. Fatherhood didn't always come easy. Like many small boys Donald developed a passionate interest in football and adopted Liverpool as his favourite team. His father found most sport incomprehensible but dutifully began to log on to sports websites and ask his staff and friends for news of Liverpool matches and player transfers to pass on to his eager son.

He found deep comfort, too, from another quarter. Charles Kennedy was raised within a devout and close Catholic family and throughout his life kept Catholic points of reference. He never, for example, when making a speech described himself as proud of something, pride being a sin. He used the word 'pleased' instead. As a young man, enjoying success in politics and a bachelor's lifestyle, his faith faded but he returned to it as he grew older and became a deeply committed Christian. 'He was brought up with his faith, with Catholicism, and then like most people he quietly wandered away from it,' said Father Roddy Johnston, who for many years was the priest at St John's in Caol where the Kennedys worshipped. 'Many years ago, I had met Charles, we had chatted away, we were fine, and he was saying he had to get back in touch with his Catholic roots.' He returned to attending mass every Sunday, or on Saturday evening if he had engagements the following day, always sitting unassumingly at the back of the church. He would also go to confession. He attended services in London, too, including at St George's Cathedral in Southwark and Westminster Cathedral, and at the Commons would join Catholic MPs for their weekly mass on Wednesday evenings at St Mary Undercroft in the crypt, again sitting quietly at the back of the chapel. As he grew older, Kennedy took his worship so seriously that he would attend weekly mass even when on holiday abroad, taking care to look up local Catholic churches and times of services before travelling. 'There was almost a feeling he had been the boy from Lochaber who had gone down to London and had tried very, very hard to fit in and to be a part of the Westminster crowd and the whole bit down there, and this was him saying he had found there was something very good and wholesome about who he was and what he was in himself,' said Father Roddy. 'I spoke to him a lot and he was a man of extraordinary faith and yet, that's the paradox of it, it is an extraordinary sophistication of faith and yet it's the most simple faith that you can't articulate.'

When he married Sarah, an Anglican, they signed a declaration that their children would be brought up to practice the Catholic faith and he took seriously his duty to do so. He insisted that Donald was baptised a Catholic. When Donald was staying with him in Fort William he would accompany his father to mass and, when they went forward for communion, would fold his arms to accept a blessing from the priest. Father Roddy McAuley, who took over the parish in 2011, found Kennedy a most humble parishioner, never questioning his preaching, always encouraging and kind. 'People treated him here as one of their own – he was born and bred here, he came to church. Nobody bothered him really, he was Charles, Charles Kennedy,' he said. 'They were very, very comfortable with him and he was very comfortable with them.' Interestingly, Kennedy kept his faith private among most of his London friends, many of whom were unaware he even went to church.

Despite his somewhat detached status from Westminster, Kennedy enjoyed the House of Commons when an issue caught his interest. In the autumn of 2008 he was ambling through Parliament when a colleague told him the annual ballot for the right to bring in a Private Member's Bill was about to take place and suggested he enter. Without any piece of legislation in mind, Kennedy did so and found himself drawn at seventeenth in the ballot: each of the top twenty has the opportunity to introduce a Bill. Kennedy consulted carefully, as he did before any decision, and chose to take up a measure on behalf of an environmental group seeking to clean up power stations by setting a mandatory performance standard for carbon emissions. His Industrial Carbon Emissions

(Targets) Bill attracted wide cross-party support and considerable interest from conservation and international aid charities. Private Members' Bills are one of the key ways that backbench MPs can advance a cause or get themselves noticed but, in twenty six years in the House, Kennedy had never introduced one as a primary sponsor. By this time he needed reading glasses, usually perched on the far end of his nose. At first he bought prescription glasses, which were expensive, but kept losing them on aeroplanes or buses. Over time he switched to buying batches of women's reading glasses with red frames from Poundstretcher, at £1.99 each, and would keep several spare pairs in his pockets. As he moved the Bill for its second reading in July 2009 he spoke fluently on the technicalities of carbon capture and storage but made one or two minor slips that betrayed his lack of familiarity with the formalities of backbench legislation. Rather pompously a Labour MP, Andrew Dismore, intervened to correct him on a small point, noting as he did so that Kennedy was not a regular attender on Fridays, when such Bills are generally debated. 'There are advantages to having a constituency that is an awfully long way away - it provides a very useful excuse at times,' Kennedy replied, with disarming candour.[12] He withdrew the Bill, which would not have progressed without government support, but it was seen as a success in raising the profile of the issue.

Unlike his relations with Menzies Campbell, where a shadow remained between them, Kennedy got on well with his successor Nick Clegg although they were not close. Clegg had arrived in the Commons in 2005, when Kennedy was in the embattled latter stages of his leadership, and the two had had little chance to get acquainted. Once Clegg became leader, however, the pair made a point of meeting every six months or so, usually for lunch at the National Liberal Club where Kennedy felt comfortable and liked the plain food. Clegg had very different political instincts, particularly in being more hostile to Labour, but valued these discussions: Kennedy never gilded the lily and told him straight how he saw things. Both knew, too, the loneliness of leadership. Clegg could seek his advice in a way he could from few others and knew it would be given dispassionately and with absolute discretion.

Freedom from the duties of being party leader allowed Kennedy to spend more time in Fort William. For the first time since he entered the Commons boundary changes meant that, from 2005, his home district of Lochaber was part of his constituency. It was a source of deep satisfaction to him to represent the Highland community where he and generations of his family had lived and the feeling appeared to be reciprocated. Fort William, and in particular Caol, the working class suburb next to which he lived, had been a predominantly

Labour-voting town but local allegiances transferred to a personal vote for Kennedy, one of their own. The difficult circumstances in which he resigned the party leadership were not an issue within his constituency at that stage. 'He was very much here the local hero, the local boy done good,' said Duncan Mackay, his constituency party chairman. 'Even if they weren't of that particular political persuasion, people were genuinely proud for him and proud of him. There was this recognition that this was a national figure. Everybody knew the reason why he stood down because that was made public, but that was never held against him.'

He was in demand to speak at business dinners and Burns suppers, sometimes arriving with television cameras in tow, to the excitement of those present, as he resumed the role of a more active constituency MP. One thing that had changed since his days before becoming leader was that his areas of responsibility had reduced since the creation of the Scottish Parliament: constituents with a complaint about a hospital, housing or school places, for example, would go to the constituency's MSP. This reduced Kennedy's profile slightly on campaigning issues although he and the incumbent John Farquhar Munro were personal friends as well as political allies and worked closely from a shared constituency office in Dingwall. The seat fell into three geographical areas far apart, Fort William and Lochaber in the south, Skye to the west and Ross-shire and Black Isle two hours' drive to the north, each with their own local newspapers, so appearing active in all three was hard work. Within a year local campaigning switched to the Scottish parliamentary elections in spring 2007 and Kennedy pitched in to secure Munro's re-election, with a fractionally reduced majority although the SNP enjoyed a swing of 12 per cent in Ross, Skye and Inverness West, finishing a strong second by squeezing the Labour and Tory vote. Nationally the Lib Dems returned with sixteen seats, down one, while Labour suffered a net loss of four – enough for the Lib-Lab coalition to lose its majority at Holyrood. The SNP, after spectacular gains, returned with 47 MSPs making it fractionally the largest party. Alex Salmond, the SNP leader, offered coalition talks with the Lib Dems, who refused to meet his price of an independence referendum, and instead formed a remarkably successful minority administration. The nationalists were on the march although it was not clear then if the Highlands, historically apart from Scotland's political trends, would remain immune to the SNP's advances.

When the 2010 general election approached Kennedy, free from the burdens of leadership, told his local party he wanted to fight an old fashioned campaign based around public meetings across the constituency's disparate villages. He never knocked on doors, to which he held a strong aversion, but when visiting a community would make a point of popping into a local shop, usually to buy a can of Diet Coke. In this way he could engage people in conversation and, as he walked along tiny high streets, shoppers would cross the road to come and shake his hand and say hello. This highly personalised style of campaigning was beneficial for fund-raising, too, as well-wishers would often thrust a £10 or £20 note in his hand 'for the campaign', which an aide would collect on walks-about and public meetings. Kennedy would enjoy swapping jokes and banter with farmers at auction marts and stood outside the gates of Ross County football ground in Dingwall to chat with supporters, although he refused all entreaties to buy a ticket and mingle with fans watching the match. He insisted that, as he didn't watch football throughout the rest of the season, it wouldn't be right to give an impression of sudden interest during an election campaign.

Although the schedule of public meetings was Kennedy's own idea, he found even these tiny events nerve-wracking. He didn't like driving himself the often long distances involved and was always allocated a driver. When the task fell to his local chairman Duncan Mackay, the ex-party leader who had addressed one million people at a Stop The War rally in Hyde Park would confess his apprehension. 'I genuinely believe he did not have a lot of confidence in himself,' his chairman said. 'I would sometimes drive him round to meetings: he had spoken to party conferences but this meant going to a wee village hall. But it never failed to hit me that he really was incredibly nervous about anything like that.' Afterwards, even after a flawless perfor-mance, he might ask anxiously: 'Was that okay?' Nerves aside, it was an otherwise enjoyable campaign. Opponents fought their corners but there was no sense of any real attempt to unseat the ex-Lib Dem leader with his large majority. On the night of the election he polled 18,335 votes, or 52.6 per cent, with his majority down somewhat but still huge at 13,070. Labour remained far behind in second place but only two votes ahead of the SNP, whose vote had increased. The SNP candidate requested a recount in the hope of overtaking Labour to establish the nationalists as challengers in the seat. The returning officer refused but this was a straw in the wind: the SNP was making in-roads in the Highlands.

12

Highland man

The 2010 general election result was a relief to Kennedy in his constituency but the outcome across the country as a whole heralded his worst fears. Gordon Brown lost badly yet David Cameron had not won; Conservative gains of ninety six seats left them with 305 MPs, some 21 seats short of a majority. After a roller-coaster campaign, in which Nick Clegg triumphed in the inaugural television debates and his party's poll ratings soared above 30 per cent before dropping, the Lib Dems confounded commentators as they ended up with MPs, a net loss of five from the peak achieved under Kennedy. Still, however, they were kingmakers. The scale of Brown's defeat meant a Lib-Lab coalition would still be a dozen seats short of a majority, although a 'rainbow' alliance with minority parties was mathematically possible. Clegg sent negotiators to talk to both Labour and the Conservatives but it was Cameron's 'big open and comprehensive offer' of a deal with the Lib Dems that gained momentum.

It was a sign of Kennedy's detached status that, as Labour power-brokers lobbied senior Lib Dems to salvage Lib-Lab talks, he played little part in the frenetic five days that followed the election. When an outline coalition agreement between the Tories and Lib Dems emerged, Kennedy called Nick Clegg to say he could not support it. His objection was not with the terms of the agreement, which he thought excellent, but the strategic risk: every time previously it was the Conservatives who gained in the long term when Liberals went into coalition with them.[1] The mood among Lib Dems, however, was strongly in favour. The party's MPs, peers and federal executive committee gathered that evening at Local Government House for their verdict, with individuals unhappy or uneasy but the predominant mood one of determination mingled with some excitement. Clegg, on arriving, was met with cheers, applause and a standing ovation.[2] Notwithstanding the shared sense of resolve Kennedy, sitting hunched two thirds back, made a brief contribution setting out his objections. When separate shows of hands were called for MPs, peers and federal executive members, he had intended to vote no but consulted a handful of friends who persuaded him to abstain. 'He wanted to vote against,' his former adviser Tim Razzall said. 'He was advised not to do that on the grounds that if he voted against that would become the story. If he abstained he would always be able to say he was not in favour of it, which he wasn't.' The votes were overwhelmingly in favour with just one member of the federal executive, ex-MP David Rendel, voting against. Kennedy waited until the weekend to make public his opposition to the Con-Lib coalition. It drove 'a strategic coach and horses through the long-nurtured realignment of the centre-left to which leaders in the Liberal tradition, this one included, have all subscribed since the Jo Grimond era,' he wrote in *The Observer*. 'It is hardly surprising that, for some of us at least, our political compass currently feels confused.'[3] He would have preferred to explore a 'progressive' Labour-led coalition, he said, or remain in opposition and offer a minority Tory administration a 'confidence and supply' agreement to get its key business through the Commons.

Neither did Kennedy, who held a prominent role as rector of Glasgow university, play much part in the tortured discussions within the Lib Dem parliamentary party on university tuition fees, as the coalition trebled these to £9,000 a year. Quietly, however, he let it be known that under no circumstances would he change his position and he would vote against this. His intransigence bolstered resistance among other Lib Dem MPs as did that of Menzies Campbell, who was also unhappy at a coalition with the Conservatives. He was also by this time, Chancellor of the University of St Andrews. When the key votes in the Commons came in December, therefore, the right to abstain had been overtaken by events. With so many Lib Dem MPs in the 'no' lobby, the government would have faced defeat. The parliamentary party split three ways, twenty seven voting for, eight absent or abstaining, and twenty one including Kennedy against.

Kennedy did not like disloyalty and, bar these instances, took care not to be cast as a serial critic. Instead he picked his battles. On issues he disagreed with most strongly he signalled his opposition or voted against: he did so on the 'bedroom tax' which reduced housing benefit for claimants with a spare room, and he fought boundary changes that would have merged his constituency with that held by Danny Alexander to create a single seat of Inverness and Nairn. In the early days of the coalition Lib Dem MPs faced heightened expectations to show discipline and support the coalition in Commons votes, with endless three line whip divisions. Even senior MPs were told they must fill out an absence request slip if they wanted to miss a vote, and permission might be refused; Kennedy slipped the yoke with a genial shrug. Alistair Carmichael, the Lib Dem chief whip, invited him for a cup of coffee on the Commons terrace to explain the obligations of government. 'So,' Kennedy asked him, with polite amusement, 'you want me to sign a slip of paper?' He never did. As Lib Dem colleagues settled in to ministerial posts across Whitehall, he took the opportunity to upgrade his Commons office to one in Portcullis House with a river view, which he specifically wanted, but then spent spent less time at Westminster. Rapidly the party's whips stopped including him when totting up the numbers to ensure they did their bit to keep the government's majority intact: if he turned up, it was a bonus. If he was around he would attend the weekly parliamentary party meeting, again sitting on one of two benches at the back, and ask questions on strategy or speak on campaigning rather than policy. Kennedy was appointed to the Speaker's advisory committee on works of art, which is responsible for the extensive House of Commons art collection, but rarely attended. He took much greater interest in his appointment to Britain's delegation to the parliamentary assembly of the Council of Europe, meeting four times a year in Strasbourg. This suited his keen interest in international affairs, especially on supporting democracy and human rights through its legal affairs committee, which met in Paris, but impacted further on his attendance and voting record at Westminster. It also added further geographical complexity to his public life, split as it was between London, Glasgow university and his Highlands constituency.

His rectorship at Glasgow continued to give him particular satisfaction. As his three year term neared its conclusion Kennedy was invited to speak at a Dialectic Society dinner in the intimate splendour of the university union Bridie Library, and found himself seated next to Chris Sibbald, a student who was planning to run as the union's next president. 'I asked him how he had enjoyed his first term and I then said to him, 'would you be interested in standing for a second term?'' Sibbald said. 'He was very modest, he said, "well if the students would ask me to do it again I would certainly be very interested". And I said: the students *are* asking.' They arranged to meet several times over the summer of 2010 and Kennedy subsequently asked Sibbald to run his campaign, which they announced at a 'daft Friday' end-of-term dinner in December. Such was his profile and popularity on the campus that it was a relatively straightforward affair: again they agreed on an apolitical platform, sought and secured the endorsement of both student unions and the sports association. They used the simple slogan 'Charles Kennedy: re-elect your rector' and printed campaign T-shirts in green. He hosted a student pub quiz in the Queen Margaret union to raise money for the campaign, some short videos in which he talked about his student surgeries and stance on tuition fees, and made repeated visits to canvass students during lunchtimes on campus. They even enlisted the university *a cappella* group to sing during campaigning on the hill. This time around he faced only one rival candidate, the Scottish writer and comedian A.L. Kennedy who stood on an anti-cuts platform and cheerfully admitted she held 'no illusions of winning'.[4] Typically, her namesake told his own team he admired her writing and thought her a formidable opponent; the result told its own story. He was returned with 2,601 votes to her 565, 82 per cent of the vote, and in doing so became Glasgow's first rector to serve consecutive terms since Benjamin Disraeli in 1874-77. Kennedy asked the *a cappella* group to sing at his second installation ceremony, to the chagrin of the university's choir.

Student anger at the trebling of tuition fees added an edge to his second term as rector. Undergraduates had previously occupied a computer science building on the Glasgow campus in solidarity with Palestinians in Gaza. In February 2011, just before his re-election, a more serious occupation began as students seized a vacant university research building, Hetherington House, in protest at higher education cuts. Glasgow university, relying on the Scottish government for much of its funding, was implementing a programme of £20 million in cuts, causing concern among students which Kennedy relayed to the university authorities and raised at court. To an angry minority this was not enough. A hard core embarked upon a long occupation, and caused controversy by 'kettling' the president of the National Union of Students, Aaron Porter, during a visit to the campus. After clashes with elected student representatives, who criticised the occupation, the university made the mistake of calling in Strathclyde police to evict the occupiers by force, generating considerable adverse publicity. The university announced an independent inquiry, chaired by Kennedy as rector, which drew the sting by concluding that the occupation went beyond legitimate protest but said the university should have obtained a court order to authorise the eviction.[5] The rector intervened on another issue of greater concern to the mainstream student body as the university drew up plans to knock down a nightclub, The Hive, and two bars in an extension building beside the Glasgow University

Union and replace them with a gym. These premises, popular with students, generated three quarters of the union's £1.3 million annual turnover and threatened it with financial catastrophe, although the university offered £250,000 a year in recompense.[6] Kennedy, who needed little prompting to go into battle for his beloved union, helped to broker a compromise for the university and union to share a redeveloped building.

The breakdown of his marriage meant that Kennedy once again had to fend for himself when staying at his London flat and, to a degree, at home in Fort William. He was a very poor cook. He could serve guests a bacon butty and make himself baked beans on toast: he amused staff by arriving at his constituency office one morning full of indignation having driven to his local Co-op supermarket the evening before to find it had no tins of baked beans. 'It's important for people who can't cook,' he told them emphatically. 'It's a basic foodstuff and they should stock it.' Other simple culinary tasks were beyond him. He arrived one day in his constituency office in Dingwall after the long drive from Fort William and asked if he could make himself a cup of coffee. His party chairman Duncan Mackay, who was going out, showed him where they kept the jar of ground coffee, the percolator and mugs and spoons. On his return he found Kennedy mistook it for instant coffee and was puzzled when it would not dissolve in his cup. He liked only plain food, such as fish fingers, scampi or pies, and when back in his constituency home would be spoiled by his mother, who cooked and cleaned for him. When he was travelling home he would even telephone ahead and ask her to turn on the electric blanket on his bed.

Unexpectedly and gradually, Kennedy found happiness again in his personal life as he developed a relationship with Carole Macdonald, a teacher and widow of his best friend Murdo. They were long-standing friends, having been students together at Glasgow, and their families were close – Murdo had been godfather to his son Donald. Kennedy stayed frequently at their family home in Renfrewshire near Glasgow when performing his duties as the university's rector and often left his car there when he flew to London. He supported Carole in her bereavement, and she helped him in his struggles with alcohol, as she and Murdo had done over many years. As their relationship developed, Kennedy was accepted by her four adult children as part of their family but he was much more cautious about their relationship in his constituency, wanting to protect her from the public eye. When she came to stay with him in Fort William he would always introduce her as 'my friend Carole' although many more people understood her significance to him than he realised. They noticed that he seemed more relaxed when she was around, drew strength from her companionship and enjoyed her company. He was happy again.

Coalition with the Conservatives at Westminster made campaigning much tougher for Lib Dems in Scotland, where the Tories remained viscerally unpopular, while Alex Salmond's cunning in leading a minority government made the SNP an incumbent party of government. In Kennedy's constituency there was a further complication as his friend John Farquhar Munro was retiring as its MSP. Some Lib Dems urged Munro to step down a year early to force a by-election on the day of the 2010 general election, giving his successor almost a year in post before the Scottish parliamentary elections in spring 2011, but he refused. Worse, during the campaign itself the SNP released a statement in which Munro, always a maverick, offered 'a message of support' to Alex Salmond, saying the SNP leader had done an excellent job as First Minister and he was 'quite happy to support him for a second term'.[7] Munro appeared to be saying he preferred Salmond for the role over Iain Grey, lacklustre leader of the Scottish Labour Party, but his remarks were presented by the nationalists as a personal endorsement of the SNP leader.

Members of Kennedy's local party knew they faced strong political headwinds in the Holyrood election, compounded by boundary changes as the seat became Skye, Lochaber and Badenoch, making it more marginal. They selected as their candidate Alan MacRea, who grew up in Uig on Skye and ran a restaurant business in Edinburgh but had little political experience; at the adoption meeting in Dingwall, Kennedy made a point of giving the speech to propose him as their Lib Dem candidate and put in appearances during the election but had commitments elsewhere and left his local party to run the campaign. Despite their best efforts, it was a disaster: the SNP, rampant across Scotland, took the seat with a swing of 13 per cent from the Lib Dems, delivering a majority of 4,995. To the north Caithness, Sutherland & Ross also fell with a still larger swing to the nationalists, who gained another MSP on the regional Highlands and Islands list. Overall the SNP triumphed with 69 seats, enough to give Salmond a majority government, with the Lib Dems the biggest losers, down by twelve to just five MSPs. 'It was dreadful,' the party chairman Duncan Mackay said, 'and if I analyse what it brought home to us it was that the Highlands was no longer different in terms of politics in Scotland.'

Alex Salmond pledged during the campaign to hold a referendum on Scottish independence within three years if he won. Such a decision was not in the First Minister's gift but was a 'reserved' power held by the United Kingdom government. With polls suggesting a clear majority of Scots wanted to remain in the UK, David Cameron moved to seize the initiative and agreed to a referendum on his terms with a single question on the ballot paper rather than a second option of greater fiscal autonomy. Details were agreed later the following year, although Salmond secured his preferred date of autumn 2014, the 700th anniversary of the Battle of Bannockburn. The question was to be: Should Scotland be an independent country?

As opposing sides prepared for the referendum, there was a widespread expectation Kennedy should play a prominent national role in the 'No' campaign. 'Better Together', the cross-party organisation, commissioned polling to identity key 'message carriers' who would command most credibility among undecided Scots voters and two figures stood head and shoulders above the rest: Gordon Brown was top and Charles Kennedy second, well clear of the others. It was agreed Kennedy would be a patron of Better Together with Annabel Goldie, former leader of the Scottish Conservatives, and it would be led by Alistair Darling, the former Labour Chancellor: these three would be the 'main faces' of a cross-party pro-union campaign.[8] From the outset, however, Kennedy's involvement was sporadic. For the formal launch of Better Together, at Edinburgh Napier University in June 2012, he, Darling and Goldie were scheduled as speakers but he pulled out at 24 hours' notice. Craig Harrow, a public relations professional who was a Lib Dem director of the campaign, received a text message from Kennedy at 5pm the previous day, a Sunday, saying his parents were both unwell and he could not attend. For a cross-party campaign, this presented a severe problem. Harrow and Darling agreed to ask Willie Rennie, leader of the Scottish Lib Dems, to step into the breach but kept this secret; neither Johann Lamont nor Ruth Davidson, respectively leaders of the Labour and Conservative parties in Scotland, would be on the platform making the protocol awkward. It passed off with only minor references to Kennedy's non-appearance but the episode, followed by other examples of cancelled meetings, added to his reputation as unreliable and made the No camp wary of using his name for events in case he failed to turn up. When he was used for Better Together events, a contingency plan was always in place should a substitute be required, due both to Kennedy's family commitments and risks linked to his drinking.

Nonetheless Alistair Darling remained very keen to use Kennedy and in the two years leading up to the referendum the Better Together organisers frequently pressed him to do more. He did some events, media appearances and press articles but over time detached himself somewhat from the formal cross-party campaign and focused more on local events in the Highlands. Later Alex Salmond generated considerable controversy by suggesting 'I don't think his heart was in the Better Together campaign'.[9] Kennedy was certainly a passionate and committed unionist but did grow exasperated with poor organisation on the No side and its negative message. His approach to politics was always to accentuate the positive and show respect for opponents, even when he disagreed with their position. At a training event for Better Together supporters in Inverness in February 2014 he told those present the tone of the campaign thus far reflected that of a battle between Labour and the SNP in the Central Belt of Scotland and would not work in the Highlands, whose geography and political history required a more constructive, positive approach. 'Voters here do not want shrill exaggeration, they want sensible engagement,' he argued.[10] A month later he went further, voicing frustration that the rhetoric from Labour's Scottish party conference presented the debate as 'Salmond versus Scotland', saying this would only bolster the nationalists' appeal. At the Scottish Lib Dem conference in Aberdeen, Kennedy broke a taboo by becoming among the first to predict a close result. Presciently, he appealed to No supporters to think ahead to the legacy the referendum would leave. 'Mrs Thatcher won most of her big political battles but she did so with terrible wreckage in the wake,' Kennedy said. 'We've got to win and take with us the ones who did not vote our way.'[11]

His discomfort with the Better Together campaign reflected, too, a much broader sense of the role he had developed since returning to the back-benches. He wanted to be his own man, to do things his own way. Other Lib Dems shared his frustration with the Better Together operation and he attended more No campaign events with his own party. But his relationship there had changed too. He was careful not to appear disloyal in public yet gave a sense of being one step removed as a Lib Dem. This was sensed by Alastair Campbell, with whom he kept in frequent contact. 'After being leader Charles found a greater sense of fulfilment in the freedom that he had and was always reluctant to get too sucked in to formal structures,' Campbell said. 'He had developed a sense of his own persona, which had been totally subsumed when he was the leader, for obvious reasons. When you are the leader of a party you become the face of the campaign but that doesn't mean you are in total control of it. He felt much more comfortable when he was both able to be a voice that people understood about the party but not totally of the party. He liked that slight separation.'

He liked to do things at his own pace, too, which generally did not match the energy of others, and he was continually pressed to do more for the No side. Brian Wilson, a former Labour minister who was founding editor of the *West Highland Free Press*, a left-wing weekly newspaper based on Skye, urged Kennedy to campaign harder when the pair met in the lounge at Glasgow airport awaiting the same flight for London. 'I thought he should be doing a lot more. In particular I said he had to do something in his own patch because by then the danger signs were showing,' Wilson said. 'I got the real impression by then of a real lack of confidence.' Once they had landed in London, Kennedy sought him out on the Heathrow Express and asked if they could speak at some meetings together. Wilson did set up meetings at Portree on Skye and in Fort William at which they both spoke, although the latter was thinly attended. Kennedy was happy to share platforms with people he felt comfortable with. He liked Wilson, with whom he had campaigned on many issues such as against Skye bridge tolls and to save the Fort William and Inverness sleeper trains but he resisted requests to speak at meetings with the left-wing firebrand George Galloway. A further issue was that Kennedy did not like to stay overnight away from home after campaign events, and wanted to get back to visit his ailing family.

His mother Mary, to whom he was very close, had been very ill around the time of the 1997 election when she developed a heart condition due to a clotting of one of her main arteries. She made a remarkable recovery and for many years returned to an active life, even enjoying again a cigarette and a glass of whisky. By 2012, however, her health was declining. She was no longer able to play the keyboard at the Saturday evening vigil at church in Caol, where her name was added to the list of sick parishioners for whom prayers were said at mass. The priest would call at their home once a month to bring her communion, and she had interludes in Belford Hospital in Fort William. Mary Kennedy died in April 2013, aged eighty seven. At her funeral at St John's church, attended by hundreds of mourners, her grief-stricken son was unsure whether he would be able to keep his composure to read a short eulogy in her memory. He insisted on remaining in a pew amongst the congregation, rather than speak from the lectern at the front of the church. He nodded to the priest moments beforehand to signal he felt able to speak without breaking down, and a lectern was brought to him down the nave of the church. His father Ian, too, became increasingly frail and developed a form of Alzheimer's disease. He was taken on occasions to Raigmore Hospital sixty five miles north in Inverness. There was a shortage of places at care homes in Lochaber and, once a place became available, his father moved to a care home, Moss Park, four minutes' drive away from the family home and next to the church.

When he was in Fort William, Kennedy would visit his father, sometimes taking him to a lunchtime mass at a Gothic-style church at Glenfinnian, a picturesque spot twenty minutes' drive away overlooking Loch Shiel. In spring 2014 his family responsibilities increased hugely after his older brother Ian slipped in his kitchen at home nearby in Caol and suffered a terrible spinal injury. He underwent a series of operations at a spinal unit in Glasgow that saved his life but left him quadriplegic, barely able to move. After some months Ian was transferred to Belford Hospital in Fort William; the family decided not to tell their father about his son's accident, which meant he couldn't be moved to a care home in case the two met. Charles Kennedy would often help by giving his brother's partner Caroline a lift to the hospital if she didn't take the bus. They agreed that Ian should move into the parental home once the cottage was adapted with ramps and widened doors. After Kennedy returned from a day's campaigning across his vast constituency, he would do a round of family visits to check on his brother and father; he would also sometimes look in on a frail aunt and uncle in Claggan on the other side of Fort William.

Kennedy was juggling these caring responsibilities as he spent more time campaigning in the Highlands for a No vote, sticking to a reasoned tone, reaching out and acknowledging why some people were drawn to the Yes side, and talking up the positive benefits of the union. The previous summer a blogger from his local Yes group in Lochaber posted a description of Kennedy visiting the Mallaig and Morar Highland Games as that year's chieftain of the games. In that role it fell to Kennedy to lead a parade around the field where, among the stalls at the far end, a handful of Yes supporters had pitched a gazebo and were handing out leaflets between a lady and her daughters selling cupcakes and the Royal British Legion Scotland tent. The blogger reported, with light mirth, that the chieftain appeared to avert his eyes as he led the procession past the Yes supporters, wearing blue tabards and holding placards. Faithfully, however, the blogger added: 'Later in the day Mr Kennedy did a reverse circuit around the field and did stop at our tent to have a chat with two of my colleagues.'[12]

Affability notwithstanding, the Yes side was building a formidable grass-roots organisation and as the poll approached it was clear that support for independence was strong in parts of Kennedy's constituency. In contrast the local No movement, and Kennedy's own party organisation, were in poor shape. His constituency party had just over 100 members, mostly concentrated around Dingwall, and many of advancing years. Such a small membership had not represented a problem in previous campaigns as, often, apolitical volunteers would pitch up to help. It also suited Kennedy's old-school approach of addressing public meetings or impromptu walks-about rather than door-knocking, running street stalls or social media messaging. This meant, however, that his team had little data on his supporters from canvas returns and telephone canvassing was difficult in the Highlands as fewer people gave permission to accept calls. This was further compounded by staffing changes in his constituency office. Once his long-serving office manager Shanae Fraser left, subsequent employees had to adapt to Kennedy's hands-off style and inconsistent record in keeping appointments. Initially, institutional knowledge among other staff kept the office running but for a period there appeared to be a break down and one member of staff went on long term sick leave. Kennedy was not good at confronting such issues; his reaction to a staffing problem was to back away, just as if someone upset him or let him down he might blank them to avoid a quarrel. Finally in spring 2014 he asked a friend Peter Ellis, a businessman and Lib Dem supporter, to reorganise his constituency operation. The upshot, not without tension along the way, was a second office was opened that summer in Fort William so members of his campaign team could be near to Kennedy's home and keep in more regular contact with him. Previously he had quietly resisted having staff based so close to his home, where sometimes he liked to ignore telephone calls and disappear. He was forced to accept that there had to be changes.

In Fort William, where Kennedy would regularly make the three minute drive to shop at the Co-op or attend mass in Caol, tightly packed lines of yellowing bungalows and slate grey pebble-dashed houses began to be bedecked with Yes stickers and even flags. These were classic one-time Labour voters embracing independence from a sense of alienation despite previously having voted for Kennedy, their local man. Skye, too, with its Liberal tradition in tension with a truculent island mentality, showed signs of becoming a Yes stronghold, which seemed to appeal to the romanticism of coach parties of American tourists. Kennedy knew he had a fight on his hands yet was determined to keep his approach positive. With the campaign in full swing, he addressed a Better Together meeting at the National Hotel in Dingwall with two MSPs, one Labour and one Conservative, who both approached and embraced him on arrival. He exuded geniality. 'What struck me, as always, was his ability to communicate a message to people in a way that made it easily understood and this superb command of English, but without notes and without hurting anybody. And at the end people were coming up to speak to him and see how he was,' said Duncan Mackay, his party chairman. 'I remember thinking "you really are one of the most skilled politicians in our country". It had never left him – that great ability.'

With eleven days before the vote, an opinion poll for the *Sunday Times* showed the Yes campaign ahead for the first time, by 51 per cent to 49, sending shockwaves across Britain.[13] David Cameron, Ed Miliband and Nick Clegg agreed to cancel that week's Prime Minister's Questions and travel north to try and save the union. By coincidence, that Wednesday the Scottish Lib Dems had scheduled an event in Kennedy's constituency where their leader Willie Rennie and Alistair Carmichael, the Scottish Secretary, were due to join him for a cable car ride up a mountain side at Aonach Mor, north east of Ben Nevis. It was a spectacular setting and would have yielded striking images: Lib Dems suggested Clegg join them, but Kennedy vetoed the idea. 'It would have made absolute sense once Clegg said he was coming to Scotland for Clegg to come there and join what was going on,' Conn O'Neill, Kennedy's campaign manager said. 'But Charles said, "no way, I'm not having that", and told Willie no.' His objection was not personal but political: he judged Clegg's unpopularity would do damage, not help.

In the final stages of the campaign Gordon Brown rang Kennedy to discuss plans for them to make joint appearances at rallies in Perth, Inverness or Stirling; at this critical juncture Kennedy was the only Lib Dem he was prepared to share a platform with. Brown then had a change of heart and decided he would appear at events alone. While sentiment across Scotland veered back towards the No side, in Kennedy's constituency it felt different. 'On the day of the referendum we went around five or six polling stations in Lochaber and then I drove Charles home and he just said "this isn't going well",' O'Neill said. 'Charles and I both thought this is a definite Yes - this has gone.' Exhausted from the long campaign, Kennedy remained at home while his team assembled at the Highland count in Dingwall. By the early hours it was clear the No side had won with a bigger margin than expected: the final result was 44.7 per cent for Yes and 55.3 per cent for No. With ballot boxes driven in from remote communities to be counted, the Highland region result was the last to declare at 8.15am, with the margin of victory only fractionally lower. Results by constituency were not published but Lib Dems at the count watched votes being sorted from each ballot box as it was opened. Their own tally confirmed their fears - in both Lochaber and Skye, a majority voted Yes.

Over a period of years, Kennedy had spent progressively less time in the Commons. In the final session of Parliament, from June 2014 to March 2015, he spoke on just twelve occasions, usually to ask a brief question, and tabled two written questions to ministers. During the coalition's five years in office he took part in 30.4 per cent of the divisions called, among the lowest of any MP. Some explanation is important here. Both his parents and then his brother had been seriously ill and Kennedy had made clear his opposition to the coalition. In the latter half of the Parliament, as relations between the two governing parties became more strained, MPs also had very little to do. Little legislation of note was passed and much parliamentary time was given to Opposition day debates and other non-binding motions. Kennedy was first elected in an era when MPs tended not to have research staff to put down parliamentary questions on their behalf: he would table questions or motions himself, with advice from parliamentary officials. But the figures did not lie: he had been progressively less active at Westminster. His expenses claims were also among the highest of any MP. There was nothing improper here: when the *Daily Telegraph* published a vast batch of expenses claims from every MP, the worst it found among Kennedy's claims were three boxes of chocolate mints and two toffee bears.[14] Indeed like many MPs Kennedy hated the bureaucracy of parliamentary expenses but his claims were inflated by his attachment to the Highland sleeper train services to Fort William and Inverness, which were more expensive than flying when travelling to and from his constituency.

He was therefore vulnerable to attack on his record. After the Scottish referendum campaign, as his focus switched to the general election due in May 2015, Kennedy was one of the few to realise that defeat for the Yes side would not spell the end of the nationalist fervour that had swept Scotland. When David Cameron responded to the result by making greater powers for Holyrood conditional on limiting the voting rights of Scottish MPs at Westminster, it triggered accusations of betrayal that quickly transferred to a renewed surge in support for the SNP. Early election literature produced by the Lib Dems for Kennedy's constituency highlighting the coalition's achievements at Westminster looked irrelevant, even counter-productive. In the autumn his team adopted a new strategy with a personalised message about Kennedy himself: the popular local figure with 30 years of service for the Highlands. Rapidly, the nationalists sought to turn this on its head. The SNP candidate for the constituency Ian Blackford, who was selected in

January, immediately launched a personal campaign targeting Kennedy over his voting record. This was, of course, a legitimate line of attack although the SNP's message often appeared to carry a subtle innuendo about Kennedy's alcoholism. Within days of his selection Blackford's attack on his opponent was reported by the *Sunday Times* in an article whose opening line said Kennedy had been 'branded unfit to remain an MP' and quoted the SNP candidate saying: 'I'm saddened to see such a poor voting record.'[15] He reinforced his attack with social media messages using the hashtag 'Where is Charlie?' Later in the campaign SNP leaflets were left on cars parked at a hustings at Portree on Skye with a photograph of Kennedy and Willie Rennie, leader of the Scottish Lib Dems, with the phrase 'the party's over'.

In readiness for the campaign, Kennedy's team relocated their Fort William office from an industrial estate to a former florist's shop on the high street. He resumed speaking at public meetings and made visits to local secondary schools when, in late March, he was hit by twin calamities. Kennedy took a call from the care home to say that his father Ian had fallen and damaged his hip, and was being taken to hospital in Inverness. That same evening Kennedy was due to appear on BBC One's *Question Time*. Throughout the day his staff were unable to get hold of him and he didn't go to his Commons office. The Lib Dem press office was making arrangements for a substitute to appear on the programme in his place, as they had on several past occasions, when he arrived by train in Leeds where it was being filmed. Kennedy's appearance was a disaster. He was clearly the worse for drink, slurring his words in some answers and losing his train of thought several times. His staff later said he had been upset by news of his father's fall but, by coincidence, at 8.30am that morning a friend catching a bus in south London had sat in a seat next to Kennedy, who was asleep, red-faced, with a blotchy complexion and reeking of alcohol.

His appearance was widely commented on over subsequent days, with the *Daily Mail* reporting in detail on the 'recovering alcoholic's rambling performance'[16], and caused grave damage by appearing to reinforce the SNP's portrayal of him as no longer able to represent his constituency effectively. *The National*, a pro-independence daily newspaper launched after the referendum, carried a damaging cartoon of leading Lib Dems that portrayed Kennedy clutching a pint of lager and sweating profusely. Worse, the episode unleashed a torrent of online abuse and vilification of Kennedy by 'cybernats', the fanatical nationalists whose internet trolling of opponents had been a feature of the referendum campaign.

His father was subsequently discharged from hospital and returned to the care home in Caol where, a week before the election campaign began, he died. Kennedy withdrew from the campaign for several days, again speaking at the funeral from amongst the congregation rather than the front of the church, and returned the following Monday for his first hustings. Although it took place at a community centre near his home in Caol, where he grew up and was widely known, the area had been a Yes stronghold during the referendum and the atmosphere was poisonous. A woman in the audience asked the panel whether public servants should be prevented by the Official Secrets Act from giving evidence on historic child sex abuse and then rounded on Kennedy, saying he had failed to support an amendment moved by a Labour MP, John Mann, to prevent this. The Conservatives' young candidate, Lindsay McCallum, sitting next to Kennedy on the panel, was shocked by the venomous mood. 'It was like everything was planned, quite contrived, the questions - it was definitely full of nationalists,' she said. 'It was just hostile and vicious, very much out to get Charles over his voting record. They didn't seem to hold back.' She was struck, however, by his calm demeanour while under attack and his kindness towards her, too: he leaned across, *sotto voce*, to congratulate her on her introductory remarks, knowing she was a first-time candidate. 'Charles was just so kind to me. He had such a generous spirit,' McCallum said. 'He always rose above whatever he came across. He never lowered himself to their level, he never got annoyed. They were so personal - he must have been hurt, he must have been exasperated sometimes.'

The exchanges at Caol set the tone for others that followed. The woman who challenged him on historic child sex abuse turned up at subsequent events and asked similar questions until, at a public meeting in Bellachulish, Kennedy asked her to leave. Other opponents also regularly attended meetings to bait Kennedy, either in person or online afterwards. One of them Brian Smith, a former police officer who was convenor of the SNP's branch for Skye and Lochalsh, would sit in the audience wearing a hat, scribbling furiously in a note pad. He or his friends would ask questions, listen politely to Kennedy's replies and, later, he would go home and post abusive commentaries online. In one post, replying to an SNP MP, he said: 'We have a different target here though with the Quisling-in-Chief Lib Dem St Charles of Kennedy.' Later he referred to Kennedy online as 'a drunken slob'. Smith later resigned from his SNP post but he was by no means alone.

Kennedy was an experienced politician and accepted that his was a rough trade yet he took care to treat opponents with respect. He instinctively shared too, the Highland tradition in which politics was conducted robustly but with a degree of courtesy. He felt perplexed at the ferocity and personalised nature of the SNP's campaign against him, and a little hurt too. Two weeks before polling day, in the constituency office in Dingwall, he approached his party chairman Duncan Mackay and asked for 'a word in your ear'. They went outside and Kennedy, his face grave, assured him he had not behaved improperly over the Commons vote on historic child sex abuse or with his expenses. Astonished, his chairman told him there was no need for an explanation. 'It would be wrong to say that it didn't affect him. He was hurt by it, he really was hurt,' Mackay said. 'What was happening on social media was something we had never, ever experienced before, from a number of people that would appear to be supporters of the Scottish Nationalists. It was horrific.' The campaign was further soured when the SNP candidate stormed in to the Lib Dems' office in Fort William and began shouting and stabbing his finger at Conn O'Neill, Kennedy's young agent, complaining at literature that called him 'a well-funded banker from Edinburgh'. (Blackford had been managing director of Deutsche Bank and ran its Dutch equity business.) 'The thing that really upset Charles was when he had a go at his staff,' said Candy Piercy, who came to help in the final weeks. 'Ian Blackford was wagging his finger in Conn's face saying, "You have dragged this campaign into the gutter I am going to have to retaliate".'

Despite the death of his father and the ferocity of the nationalists' attacks, Kennedy fought a good campaign. There were no further drink-related episodes and he threw himself into the demands of long-car journeys criss-crossing the constituency, walks-about in tiny Highland streets and villages, gruelling hustings and occasional media commitments elsewhere. Sometimes he would be accompanied by Carole, who would help him to compose himself before meetings, but more often by his young agent Conn O'Neill who also acted as his driver. Most mornings, as they left Fort William, Kennedy would ask him to stop at a BP service station 'to get the *Press and Journal*', the regional daily newspaper for the Highlands. He would return with his paper and two packets of Silk Cut Blue cigarettes; for longer journeys, he would appear with a carrier bag containing two large bars of chocolate, usually a Yorkie Bar or Cadburys Dairy Milk, and a can of Diet Coke. As the campaign wore on, this would be supplemented with a can of Red Bull caffeine drink and he would 'cat-nap' to catch up on sleep during the drive; he was exhausted. His constituency party chairman Duncan Mackay noticed this fatigue in the month before the election started, at the opening of the town centre campaign headquarters in Fort William. 'That day I thought CK didn't look himself,' Mackay said. 'When I said, "how are you today" I will never forget what he said. There's a word people don't use so much but he said, "I am weary today; I am really weary".'

Tired as he was, he was on good form in the final days of the election, as friends who came to help testified: energetic, focused, cracking jokes, enjoying electioneering. 'He was brilliant,' said Jim Wallace, who accompanied him to Dingwall auction mart and a couple of visits nearby. 'People were crossing the road to shake his hand.' Candy Piercy said: 'By the end of the campaign he really was firing on all cylinders again. It was like working with Charles of ten years before, and he loved it. He loved that contact with the public and he loved the response he got.' But there were moments of levity, too. In the final week a hustings was hosted by Lochaber High School, within walking distance of Kennedy's home, where Kennedy had been a pupil and star debater. The event was for S1 pupils, aged 11 and 12; unaccountably, Kennedy decided not to take it seriously. First he suggested to other candidates that they swap speeches, saying they each knew what the others would say; his opponents objected. Then, when it came to his turn, he abandoned politics and decided to harangue the unfortunate children about litter. 'Who's been dropping litter outside my house in the mornings?' he harrumphed. 'I won't have it and I'm fed up with it.' At the end the pupils voted and got their revenge on their grumpy neighbour: he got just two votes, one more than the Green Party candidate.

For all the effort that went in to constituency campaigning, there was a far more significant dynamic to the election. Across Scotland a mood had taken root that was akin to a revolutionary spirit, fuelled by anger at a feeling of betrayal that promises made during the independence referendum had not been honoured. Many, many Scots wanted to smash the system. For months opinion polls suggested an incredible surge was underway for the SNP, with projections that the nationalists would win at least 50 of Scotland's 59 seats at Westminster. Constituency polls commissioned by the Conservative peer Michael Ashcroft put the SNP five points ahead of Kennedy in February and 15 points ahead in April. A swing to the nationalists of seismic proportions was under way. Cunningly, David

Cameron reacted by warning English voters that a minority Labour government would be reliant on the votes of Scottish nationalist MPs and urged them to vote Conservative; in Scotland, this stoked the fear of a majority Tory government and drove the defiant electorate deeper into the embrace of the SNP. Charles Kennedy, an experienced politician, had a fairly realistic idea of what was coming, despite hopes that local campaigning might stem the tide. On the night of the election he watched the exit poll at home in Fort William, which correctly forecast a Conservative majority and an SNP rout in Scotland. 'Exit poll spells defeat. Do keep me posted re early boxes / impressions,' he texted to his agent. When Conn O'Neill texted back saying such a poll could not pick up nuances in his own seat, Kennedy replied 'Dream on. CK.' He and Carole drove up to Dingwall for the count for Ross, Skye & Lochaber and checked in at the National Hotel, the setting for so much of his constituency life. From there, they continued to watch the unfolding results, which for his party were a disaster far beyond that which anyone had foreseen. Carole dropped him off at 5am at the count at Ross County football stadium where he was met by Candy Piercy. She found him disappointed but remarkably composed. He even predicted what his SNP opponent would say in his acceptance speech, having noticed a pattern of words from elected nationalist MPs while watching declarations across Scotland on television. His own result was brutal. The SNP polled 20,119 votes to Kennedy's 14,995, a swing of almost 25 per cent. Kennedy, wearing his favourite tie, a green tartan designed by children at Mulbuie primary school in Ross-shire, made a short gracious speech. 'I am very fond of political history,' he said. 'If nothing else, we can all reflect on and perhaps tell our grandchildren that we were there on the night of long sgian dubhs.' This was a reference to the knife worn with a kilt as part of traditional Highland dress (pronounced *skean dhus*). With that, his staff ushered him out and he was collected outside by Carole and, as the sun rose, they drove back to the croft. He just wanted to be with her.

Many friends tried to get hold of Kennedy over the following three weeks to ask how he was and wish him well. He didn't answer most telephone calls, although this was not unusual. He was worn out and wanted to rest. He also wanted time to reflect on his changed circumstances. Until now, he had never lost an election in his life as a candidate, from student union ballots to seven previous general elections. Defeat hurt but Kennedy was unsentimental about politics and new options lay before him. For one thing,

Carole had retired from teaching at Christmas and they could spend more time together.

The weekend after the election he travelled down to London to start packing up and vacating his Commons office and to see Donald. A fortnight later his ten-year-old son came up to stay with him over half term: he flew up to Glasgow, his father picked him up from the airport and drove him back to Fort William. It proved to be a very difficult week for Kennedy, who took Donald to visit the grave where the boy's grandfather was buried two months earlier in the same plot as his grandmother. Kennedy suffered a severe relapse in his drinking during the week and was very unwell: so poorly he booked a doctor's appointment and expected to be admitted to Belford hospital in Fort William the following Monday. Donald returned home to London on the Saturday. Over that weekend Kennedy sounded sober in telephone conversations, but remained very unwell. On the Monday morning, June 1st, Carole Macdonald drove up from Glasgow expecting to take him to hospital but arrived at the croft and found him dead after suffering a major haemorrhage in his stomach. A post mortem later concluded that his death was a consequence of sustained damage to his body caused by his alcoholism.

After the funeral at St John's, the modern white church where he worshipped, his coffin was driven the twelve miles northwards on narrow country roads to the extraordinary spot that Kennedy had always known would be his final resting place. The hearse drove on the single track lane through the Achnacarry estate, seat of the Camerons of Lochiel, until it stopped by a metal gate. Mourners proceeded on foot across a field where sheep grazed, beside a fast-flowing stream, and up a track into a pine forest. At the crest of a hill, topped by old pines and oaks, they reached the family's ancestral graveyard, which dates back more than 200 years when the Kennedys were followers of clan Cameron and tenants of land at Clunes. He was buried beside the graves of his parents, near that of his beloved grandfather, next to Kennedys before them. It is a beautiful place, a small clearing with a grassy knoll, dotted with moss-covered boulders, bracken and the roots of ancient trees, with the smell of fresh-cut pine from the working forest beside it. A short distance up the hill is a second burial plot, enclosed by a low stone wall green with moss, a graveyard of Camerons who were involved in the Jacobite uprising. Through the trees are views of Loch Lochy, part of the Great Glen that cuts through Kennedy's former constituency from Fort William to Inverness. There he lies, in a unique and tranquil place resonant with centuries of Highland history, a son of Lochaber who transcended his roots yet never forgot them; a Highlander to the last.

13

A place in history

News of Charles Kennedy's death prompted a remarkable public reaction. It dominated news bulletins and headlines for two days and many, many people appeared to be personally touched, and spoke of his death as though they had known him. There were tributes in the House of Commons during which several MP from other parties, as well as former Liberal Democrat colleagues, talked of him with deep affection and respect: Liam Fox, the Conservative backbencher and Glasgow contemporary of Kennedy, paused and blinked back tears during his short speech[1]. The *Daily Record*, a Labour-supporting tabloid, caught the mood in its leader column, noting: 'His death has prompted a wave of sadness because we feel he was neither elite nor remote as a politician. He was one of us.'[2] The *New Statesman* similarly observed: 'That the passing of the former Liberal Democrat leader... has been greeted with such sadness is a reflection of his qualities: decency, principle, kindness and wit.'[3] Newspaper cartoonists paid tribute: Steve Bell in *The Guardian* drew the Lib Dems' yellow bird of liberty with an outline of Kennedy's face, flying above the Highlands; Peter Brookes in *The Times* showed Kennedy as a giant, dwarfing Tony Blair and Michael Howard with his opposition to the Iraq war. Several television programmes on which Kennedy had been a frequent guest, including *Question Time* and *Have I Got News For You* recorded compilations of archive clips of his past contributions that were widely shared on social media sites.

His funeral was attended by hundreds of people including Gordon Brown and many senior Liberal Democrats, with several dozen mourners sitting outside on chairs in the sunshine. Neighbours, friends and well-wishers lined the street afterwards and applauded as the hearse left the church. The following week the University of Glasgow held a memorial service in its Bute

Hall to remember Kennedy as 'one of its beloved sons'. Alastair Campbell and his brother Donald played the bagpipes to lead in the academic procession with *The Skye Boat Song*. Nicola Sturgeon, the SNP leader and First Minister of Scotland, read a lesson as did David Mundell, the Conservative MP and Secretary of State for Scotland. Hymns included *I Vow To Thee My Country*, one of Kennedy's favourites that was sung at his wedding. Glasgow university launched a memorial fund and announced that it would name a large lecture theatre after its former undergraduate, student leader and rector.

In the many tributes Charles Kennedy was widely described as the most successful third party leader for more than eighty years. In terms of the total number of seats in the House of Commons, this was true. The tally of sixty two MPs achieved under his leadership was the largest for a third party since 1923, when the coalitionist Liberals of David Lloyd George and independent Liberals of Herbert Asquith reunited to win a total of 158 seats. Such an assessment of Kennedy's place in history is factually accurate but over-simplistic, and ignores the achievements of some of his predecessors in much more difficult circumstances. The Liberal Party had faced extinction before Jo Grimond became its leader in 1956; from a precarious base he spearheaded a revival which re-established the Liberals as a permanent fixture in Britain's political firmament. When David Steel, his next-but-one successor, took the helm in 1976 the Liberal Party was tarnished by Jeremy Thorpe's resignation and later trial for conspiracy and incitement to murder, in which he was acquitted. It took formidable skill for Steel to have foreseen the threat of being steamrollered by the launch of the SDP and instead form an alliance that polled more than a quarter of the votes cast in the 1983 general election. Again, when Paddy Ashdown was elected to lead the newly formed Liberal Democrats in 1988 the party faced the very real threat of extinction. Ashdown's strategy of moving the Liberal Democrats so close to Tony Blair and Labour was controversial within his own party but, in electoral terms, extraordinarily successful. Under Paddy Ashdown the Lib Dems' number of MPs more than doubled, from twenty to forty six. The party's representation broadened significantly, too, in the European Parliament, Scottish Parliament and National Assembly for Wales during Ashdown's tenure. In proportional terms, Paddy Ashdown was the most successful third party leader since the Edwardian Liberals, not Charles Kennedy.

The place in history earned by Charles Kennedy is real, nonetheless. He deserves to be remembered for his decision to oppose the deployment of British troops to invade Iraq. He was the first main opposition party leader to oppose military action involving British forces since Hugh Gaitskell attacked the disastrous attempt by Britain and France to seize back control of the Suez Canal from Egypt in 1956. The stance taken by Kennedy helped to establish the Liberal Democrats as a more credible and mainstream political force as, in voting against the Iraq war, the Lib Dems articulated the views of many voters whose political sympathies had traditionally lain elsewhere or had simply not taken them seriously. Kennedy's predecessors readily acknowledged the importance of the stance he took on Iraq. David Steel said:

'His big achievement was simply taking the major decision to oppose the Iraq war. It was not popular and it was to his credit. And the fact that he capitalised on that in the election and returned the largest number of MPs that we had had in 80 years is undeniably to his credit. It was risky and could have been highly unpopular with Government and Opposition both supporting, but it turned out to be very popular.'

David Owen similarly singled out Kennedy's position on Iraq among his achievements. 'Although I supported the war, I think it was constitutionally necessary that a political party opposed it,' Owen said. 'It was a tough call and he took that call, and I think that was to his great credit.' While most Liberal Democrat members appeared comfortable with Charles Kennedy's decision to oppose the war, it was not inevitable that the party's leadership would do so. Menzies Campbell, Kennedy's successor, opposed the invasion itself but would not have addressed the Stop the War Coalition rally in Hyde Park attended by more than one million people. That, more than any other event, defined the Liberal Democrats' position as against the Iraq war. Paddy Ashdown freely admitted that, had he still been leader, he would have backed the invasion when the House of Commons voted, and so split the party.

'If I had been leader I am very confident that the party would not have followed me and I would have ceased to be leader that day, or sometime over that period, when it became evident that the recommendation I was making to the party would not have been followed. 'I could never have suppressed that view since I believed it to be the right one. I also am very well aware that I could never have carried the party and that would have been the end. That is why Charles was the right person for the time.'

Still, Charles Kennedy faced criticism for not being more robust and assertive in his opposition to the Iraq war. Such criticism underestimates his achievement in guiding the Liberal Democrats through this period united, and indeed strengthened. It also underestimates the gravity of the political decision to oppose military action when British forces would risk their lives, which Kennedy tried clumsily to alleviate with his pledge to 'support the troops'. But the question goes to the heart of Charles Kennedy's style of leadership. His tone, and indeed his popular appeal, was not as a belligerent, aggressive politician but as a man who put his case in a reasoned manner. More importantly, in the months before the invasion of Iraq he was trying hard to keep his options open and not commit himself to one position or course of action but give himself flexibility as events developed. Most obviously, a second resolution by the United Nations Security Council authorising military force against Iraq would have required the Liberal Democrats to change their position. This was typical of Charles Kennedy. He disliked making snap judgements, avoided closing off options, and would reach decisions gradually, seeking minimum confrontation and maximum consensus, but with an acute sense of political positioning. In this, as in so many ways, he was the exact opposite of Paddy Ashdown, as Ashdown himself acknowledged.

> 'There are it seems to me two broad types of politician,' Paddy Ashdown said. 'One is what I would call the position taker, and the other is the positioner. David Steel was a superbly gifted positioner, he positioned the party exactly where it needed to be to take advantage of the huge forces that were around him with Labour and the Conservatives so the party could advance. Margaret Thatcher was a position taker, David Owen was a position taker, I am a position taker. I take positions and I enjoy taking positions. Charles' unique skill was to have a sense of what was right for the moment and to position the party in the right place. In that sense he was far more like David Steel than like me and the party benefited hugely from that.'

David Steel, too, acknowledged a similarity between his own style of leadership and Charles Kennedy's, with both of them having an eye on the big picture rather than details, and neither being much interested in policy. 'People talked about my laid back nature,' David Steel said. 'I certainly didn't take the detailed interest in policy that Paddy, for example, did. Paddy's approach was very successful, I am not decrying that, but it was very different from both me and Charles. Charles got into the public's empathy just by the stance and demeanour of his approach as leader.'

Charles Kennedy's skill at positioning was best illustrated by the way he extricated himself and the party from the failure of Paddy Ashdown's strategy of constructive opposition to Labour. Its goal of a new voting system for the House of Commons was clearly out of reach but the legacy of Ashdown's relationship with Tony Blair remained, symbolised by the Joint Consultative Committee of Cabinet Ministers and senior Liberal Democrats. Even Ashdown admitted this was no longer in the Lib Dems' interests; widening its remit in November 1998 was a final, unsuccessful attempt at getting his strategy to bear fruit. But, typically, Ashdown would have brought matters to a head sooner and more directly than Charles Kennedy did. Ashdown said:

> 'I didn't agree with everything he did. 'I would have actually broken the relationship with Blair earlier because I think the party had ceased to get anything out of it, but I think Charles thought it was right to let it wither on the vine. It was clear we weren't going to get anything more out of that and it was clear it wasn't serving any purpose. It was diminishing our capacity for clarity.'

But Kennedy's skill lay precisely in the gradual way that he executed his profound change in strategy. Its supporters were given every chance to make it work. Its critics could see it was unlikely to have a future. Kennedy himself never discussed the JCC or relations with Labour if he could avoid doing so. By withdrawing, politely but determinedly, from Labour's embrace only after the 2001 general election, he ensured that the Lib Dems continued to benefit from tactical voting by Labour supporters.

Skilful positioning, however, has its limits. Both temperamentally and politically, Charles Kennedy was generally reluctant to commit himself to irrevocable decisions but it is noticeable that some of his best judgements were made when he was forced to do so. He came out and backed a merger between the SDP and Liberal Party when he could no longer take refuge in having friends in both camps and when the scope for compromise ran out. He opposed the Iraq war when Parliament was asked to vote either for or against a motion authorising force to disarm Saddam Hussein; abstention was not a credible course. The decisive moment in taking a stance against the invasion probably came a month earlier when he was forced to decide whether or not to address a mass anti-war demonstration. He had to take sides, and did so. Similarly, when Kennedy was telephoned without warning by Tony Blair in February 2004 and asked whether or not he would support the Butler inquiry into intelligence failures before the Iraq war, there was little scope for equivocation: he could either answer yes or no. Kennedy said no, although even then he asked if he could sleep on it. Charles Kennedy was sometimes best when pushed into taking a decision. Without such pressure, his instinct tended to be to avoid confrontation or to compromise. The result in the later stages of his leadership was a lack of clarity, particularly on policy, as he tried to appease radical and conservative forces within his party, social and economic liberals and disillusioned Labour and Conservative supporters. Kennedy was consistent and principled in his support for the European Union but his lack of interest in ideas or involvement with policy development allowed opponents to portray the Liberal Democrats as a party of protest motivated by opportunism. The Lib Dems did not lack policies; twice-yearly conferences churned these out in bewildering detail. What they did lack under Kennedy was a clear set of principal policy ideas that conveyed the party's vision and sense of purpose.

Another of Charles Kennedy's achievements was at once ephemeral and profound. People liked him. His style was different and unconventional for a politician. He was approachable, proportionate in his language, softly-spoken, very witty but modest and self-deprecating, too. He admitted to his political short-comings, agreed with opponents when their views chimed with his own and, sometimes, gave the impression he knew very well that voters did not like politicians to take themselves too seriously. David Owen thought this Kennedy's greatest feat.:

> 'The most important thing he achieved was he gave the impression as party leader that he was part of the human race, which is quite an achievement. People began to like him and therefore when they liked him they liked the Liberal Democrat party. That is not necessarily to say they took them seriously but they began to like them, and I think that was a very attractive aspect.'

Although he managed to convey a sense of an easy-going man able to chuckle at the absurdities of politics and life, Charles Kennedy found aspects of being a public figure very, very difficult. He used his sense of humour and air of stoicism as a shield to mask just how shy and private he was. During the leadership election in 1999, for instance, he endured endless questions about his relationship with Sarah Gurling and whether they would marry; very personal territory for both of them. He was subjected to more of the same during the general election campaign of 2001. Similarly, the birth of their first

child during the 2005 election campaign put his family life under the glare of
media attention once again. It was very hard for such a private man to do so.
That he did it largely with grace and good humour is a tribute to him.

An obvious question arises of how and why a politician with a reputation
for honesty and for being straight with the electorate could for years conceal
an alcoholic condition so serious that it led to his enforced resignation as
party leader and, ultimately, was the cause of his death. He certainly lied to
hide his drinking problem, as did those around him. There is little point in
being unduly censorious about this. Of course, he should not have lied; but
denial is part of the condition of alcoholism. Indeed, before that Kennedy
was remarkably open about the fact that he enjoyed drinking and did so
frequently. He continued to be so for his first three years as leader. It was only
once he was challenged about secret drinking and drunkenness during an
interview with Jeremy Paxman for *Newsnight* in July 2002 that a pattern of
deception set in. Within a year of that, Charles Kennedy was on the brink of
making a public admission that he had a drink problem and only abandoned
the plan hours beforehand. He was not a man who set out to deceive or who
was comfortable doing so. Voters sensed this and this was part of the reason
he was held in such public affection: people caught his vulnerability and this
made him appear more rounded as a person and a politician.

Nevertheless some of his actions while leader pushed uncomfortably at the
boundaries of legitimate journalistic questioning of a politician's private life.
Every time a senior politician lies about a matter clearly linked to his fitness
for office he invites more persistent, even intrusive inquiries by the media in
future cases. Concealing his alcoholism also placed intolerable strains on
those in senior positions in his party. They faced the dilemma of becoming
complicit in a continuing deceit or precipitating a crisis that could ruin
Kennedy and severely damage their party.

The more pertinent question is whether the Liberal Democrats could have
advanced further in this period had it not been for their leader's alcoholism. This
is very hard to quantify, since when Kennedy had been drinking to excess his staff
took care to conceal him from public view. But there were certainly opportunities
missed, decisions delayed and plans postponed or not followed through as, at
times, they resorted to crisis management during and after drinking episodes.
The most graphic illustration was Charles Kennedy's disastrous launch of the
Liberal Democrat's manifesto in the 2005 general election campaign, after which
the party's opinion poll ratings remained static for more than a week before
starting to tick upwards. The weeks after the same election, when Kennedy

exasperated party colleagues by failing to follow through the launch of a policy review and other initiatives, provided similar examples.

The general election in 2005 is thus a double-edged sword in terms of Kennedy's achievements. Yes, the Liberal Democrats emerged with sixty-two MPs, the highest number for a third party in three generations. But doubts remain over whether the Lib Dems should have done better still, especially in Conservative-held seats. This highlights a paradox in Kennedy's strategy. The hallmark of his approach tended to be caution, often to the frustration of other Lib Dems. And yet, his strategy for the latter half of his leadership was essentially very bold, carrying massive political risk. Previous post-war Liberal and Liberal Democrat leaders tended to position themselves closer to the Labour Party, both as a means of winning electoral support and as a short-cut to power as potential junior partners in a coalition. Jo Grimond talked of a realignment of the left, either with a new, progressive political party for Liberals, Labour supporters opposed to state socialism and liberal Conservatives, or a merger between the Liberals and most of the Labour Party. In his pamphlet *The New Liberal Democracy*, written in 1958, two years after becoming leader of the Liberal Party, Grimond ruled out joining a coalition in the event of a hung Parliament and proposed moderating the policies of the majority party. But with just six Liberal MPs in the Commons, the question did not seriously arise at that stage[4]. When Jeremy Thorpe, with unseemly haste and little consultation, accepted an invitation to see Edward Heath in Downing Street after the inconclusive general election of February 1974, the hostile reaction from Liberal activists confirmed that the party's centre of gravity lay to the left. David Steel was always committed to working with Labour politicians or a Labour Government without a Commons majority, as he did to questionable effect in the Lib-Lab pact from 1976-78. Steel's preference to work with Labour to offer an alternative to the Conservatives was a major stumbling block in the electoral strategy of the Liberal-SDP Alliance before the 1987 election. While David Owen's readiness to work in coalition with the Conservatives afterwards broke this pattern, the very purpose of forming the SDP was to seek a realignment of the left by breaking up the Labour Party. The goal of a progressive alliance drove Paddy Ashdown's 'project' to seek a coalition with Labour after the 1997 general election, even in the event that Tony Blair won a working majority. For this reason, Liberal and Liberal Democrat support tended to be tied inversely to the strength of the Labour vote, doing better when Labour was relatively weak but being squeezed in periods when Labour was in Government.

Charles Kennedy's approach from the period after the 2001 general election was to break with the Grimond/Steel/Ashdown strategy of a realignment of the left and to chart an independent course for the Liberal Democrats. Instead of seeking to be a junior coalition partner in Government his intention, first set out in his conference speech at Brighton in the autumn of 2002, was to establish the Lib Dems as a stronger opposition party. His stated aim was to overtake the Conservatives and to make the Liberal Democrats the main party of opposition, and therefore the chief challengers to Labour. In the event that no party emerged with a majority in the House of Commons after the 2005 election, as proved to be the case, Kennedy was determined not to enter into a coalition with either Labour or the Conservatives but to act as a moderating, reasonable, independent force and hope for a breakthrough in the following general election. Such a strategy required a consolidation of Lib Dem support, going beyond a reliance on the fickle backing of tactical voters to build a body of electoral opinion that was consciously Liberal Democrat. The figures suggest some success in doing so. From the 2001 general election, Lib Dem poll ratings bucked previous trends of falling support between elections. They rarely dipped below 17 per cent and for most of the following four years stood at around 20 per cent or higher, rising to 22.1 per cent in the 2005 election. It was clear, however, that Charles Kennedy failed to define adequately what actually it meant to be a Liberal Democrat, both in philosophical terms and particularly in his policy programme. It was this weakness that his post-election policy review, *Meeting the Challenge*, was set up to address.

That challenge passed first to his successor, Menzies Campbell, who from the outset tried consciously to set a different tone as leader. Allies said he intended to bring a sense of professionalism to the role, clearly implying a criticism of Kennedy's informal style. More importantly he tried to show boldness and clarity on policy, breaking with the Liberal Democrats' commitment to higher taxation to advocate tax plans that were fiscally neutral but distributed between rich and poor by cutting taxes on income and increasing taxes on wealth and environmental pollution. But he struggled to project the party more widely, facing frequent comments about his age and scornful reviews for his early performances at Prime Minister's Questions in the Commons.

But Menzies Campbell faced a difficulty that his predecessor had not in the form of lingering ill-feeling within sections of the party over the events that led to Charles Kennedy's resignation. This was heightened by the fact that several of those involved in confronting Kennedy were prominent supporters of Campbell and were given key roles in his team: Archy Kirkwood became his political counsellor, Norman Lamb his chief of staff, Ed Davey the chairman of the party's campaigns and communications committee, which is responsible for elections. The suspicion, held by some, that Menzies Campbell plotted the overthrow of Charles Kennedy was simply wrong. Kennedy's enforced resignation was as drawn out and messy as it was due to the absence of an orchestrated plan to remove him and a lack of ruthlessness on the part of most of his critics, who wished him to leave with dignity; there was no plot. The process was as destructive as it was because of a failure of those around Charles Kennedy, notably Andrew Stunell, his chief whip, to recognise and act upon the scale and seriousness of the loss of confidence in Kennedy's leadership arising from his failure to deal with his alcoholism. Where Menzies Campbell was at fault was in allowing a conflict of interest to arise between his duty as deputy leader and his position as a potential candidate when the final crisis in Kennedy's leadership arose; Simon Hughes, the party's president, was similarly compromised. With the chief whip, deputy leader and president unwilling or unable to take a lead, it was left to more junior members of the Liberal Democrats' shadow cabinet to take matters into their own hands. Several paid a high political and emotional price for doing so. They faced hostility from other Lib Dems in some quarters, were cast as plotters by the media and a handful were then accused of lacking the courage to stand as candidates in the ensuing leadership election. But to blame others for the events that toppled Kennedy is to miss the point. Ultimately, and tragically, Charles Kennedy himself was the architect of his own downfall having been unable to act on repeated pleas and warnings from colleagues that he must stop drinking.

That Menzies Campbell proved to be an interim leader was unfortunate for him but in the interests of his party, and he deserved credit for standing down after Gordon Brown's loss of nerve in calling off a snap general election in autumn 2007. It is the legacy of the party's next leader, Nick Clegg, that is likely to be the most fiercely debated. In the wake of the unmitigated disaster of the 2015 election result there were widespread signs that many were ready to rush to judgement while the bitter taste of election defeat was still fresh; history was in danger of being written too quickly.

There ought to be no doubt about the severity of the Lib Dems' defeat. The party plummeted from fifty seven MPs to just eight, from 6.8 million votes to 2.4 million, from 23 per cent of votes cast to just 7.9 per cent. It terms of popularity the Lib Dems came well behind the United Kingdom

Independent Party (UKIP), which won 3.8 million votes or 12.6 per cent of those cast; in terms of seats they were eclipsed by the Scottish National Party, with fifty six MPs, and suffered the humiliation of being on a par with the Democratic Unionist Party in Northern Ireland: well and truly minority party status at Westminster. Nor was a route to recovery obvious. In very many seats, Lib Dem candidates came fourth or worse, including in constituencies where the party been the chief challengers in second place after many years of development.

It should be acknowledged, however, that the coalition government was successful, that Nick Clegg and many of his colleagues proved to be effective ministers and, in Parliament and beyond, the Liberal Democrats showed discipline and resolve. The question is why becoming a party of government, the long-held strategic aim of many Lib Dems, proved so catastrophically damaging in electoral terms.

Some electoral damage was inevitable. Charles Kennedy in particular bequeathed his party an inherent tension that could be fudged or managed in opposition but meant a day of reckoning the moment the Liberal Democrats tasted power at a national level. He positioned the party as an opposition movement; his stated aim from the 2005 election onwards was to offer 'effective opposition'. He attracted support from a wide and fundamentally incompatible array of people who wanted to protest, many of whom were unprepared and unwilling to face the clarity of definition and compromises that come with wielding power. The revival of the Conservative Party in the 2010 general election, even though David Cameron fell short then of a Commons majority, ended any notion that the Liberal Democrats might replace the Tories as the main opposition and challenger to Labour. The instinct of Kennedy was to fall back on the Grimond/Steel/Ashdown strategy and seek a power-sharing deal with Labour or stand apart. Being prepared to negotiate only with Labour was not a strong or even realistic position from which to enter negotiations and expect anything but the slightest of concessions. The alternative of remaining resolutely in opposition, with a 'confidence and supply' agreement to keep a minority government in office - his preference - cannot be the permanent aspiration of a serious political party.

Nick Clegg and his colleagues were right to enter into a coalition with the Conservatives and in doing so knew they would forfeit the support lent to them over successive elections by voters from the disaffected left. So it proved. Within weeks the Lib Dems' poll ratings dropped by 10 points to 13 per cent, around which figure they stabilised for about another year.

Governing parties often reap unpopularity mid-way through their term. In the Lib Dems' case they never recovered. There was never any sign of picking up new support among voters ready to take the party seriously due to being in government. When the Lib Dems' ratings moved again the direction was downwards until, in early 2013, they were overtaken by UKIP and for the final year of the Parliament settled at a rock bottom of eight per cent.

The decision of Lib Dem ministers to support the trebling of university tuition fees was not, therefore, the cause of the party's demise but did become a symbol of it and inhibited all efforts to reach out to new supporters. The seeds of this debacle were sown long beforehand. Clegg inherited from Kennedy a policy of abolishing tuition fees altogether, a stance that remained popular with many activists. Several of the Orange Book modernisers, including Clegg himself, wanted to drop this commitment and believed better funded nursery places were a more effective means of challenging inequality. Clegg and Vince Cable tried before the election to abandon the policy but were defeated in a bad-tempered meeting of the party's federal policy committee. Instead they settled for an uneasy compromise, pledging to phase out tuition fees over six years. Lib Dem MPs and candidates then all signed a pre-election pledge circulated by the National Union of students to 'vote against any increase in fees in the next parliament'.

The appointment of Vince Cable as business secretary was a further complication, since his responsibilities included university funding. Conservative ministers assumed the Liberal Democrats would exercise their right, carefully written into the coalition agreement, to abstain if they could not support the government's response to a review of higher education funding chaired by John Browne, the former BP group chief executive. Indeed their Tory partners were astonished that Cable involved himself in the policy, rather than wash his hands of it, as he embarked on exhaustive but fruitless examinations of variants of a graduate tax. The Lib Dem leadership thought Clegg's careful consultation on the terms of the coalition agreement, culminating in a series of votes, superseded previous pledges: that MPs in particular had endorsed their right to abstain in votes on tuition fees.

The outcome, raising the cap of tuition fees to £9,000 albeit with a much more generous student loan repayment system, was undoubtedly a breach of faith with the electorate. The argument that the Lib Dems didn't win the 2010 election and therefore could not implement their manifesto was a nonsense. No reasonable person would expect a party to say one thing before an election and, in government, do the direct opposite on such a talismanic issue: the student vote was a core element to the Lib Dem's support. Breaking a pledge is a serious matter and the Liberal Democrats therefore deserved a degree of electoral punishment in consequence. Yet the voters' retribution proved unremitting and far out of proportion to the offence, grave as it was. From the elections in May 2011 onwards, when Liberal Democrats were routed in English town halls and in Scotland and Wales, the electorate vented its anger. The accusation of betrayal created a powerful undercurrent of mistrust in the referendum on the alternative vote, held on the same day. The result, rejecting voting reform for the House of Commons by a margin or more than two to one, ended any Lib Dem hopes of breaking the mould of the two-party system. Voters went on and on punishing the Lib Dems at each opportunity, steadily destroying the party's local government base that for twenty years had been basis for its grassroots strength and, in 2014, its representation in the European Parliament.

So why this disproportionate revenge? The reason lies in the brief yet phenomenal surge in support for the Lib Dems during the 2010 election campaign after Nick Clegg's success in the first television debate. The party gained around 10 points in the polls, reaching 30 per cent, and edging further upwards to a peak of 34 per cent before dropping sharply in the campaign's final days. While the Con-Lib Dem coalition was attacked from the outset by many on the left, in its early days it generated considerable interest and goodwill among the electorate at large. Clegg in particular became a symbol of hope for a new type of politics, one that put the national interest before party advantage. The inaugural press conference given by Cameron and Clegg in the rose garden at Downing Street captured this mood of optimism, confounding a widely held assumption that a coalition would mean endless wrangling and weak government. It was this spirit that Clegg punctured with his breach of trust on tuition fees, magnifying its impact.

Could he have played things differently? Certainly the position on tuition fees was punctuated by mistakes throughout although, ironically, the policy itself achieved its objectives in avoiding large cuts to university funding, allowing a significant expansion in undergraduate numbers and increasing numbers of poor students. Clegg's strategic response to the defeat of voting reform in the AV referendum was certainly an error. He spent the coalition's first year accepting shared ownership of the government's whole programme, extolling enthusiastically the benefits of working with the Conservatives. Thereafter he tacked to the opposite, beginning an approach of 'differentiation' by making public his disagreements with the Conservatives on a series of real, and some imagined, policy disputes. This may have been helpful from a party management perspective. Many Lib Dem activists wanted to see and hear more about what their small band of ministers were doing and liked this. To the public at large it was much less appealing. Most people are not impressed by politicians bickering and, much more importantly, it gave the overall impression that the Liberal Democrats were uncomfortable and slightly unreliable partners in government. Differential between the two governing parties would have occurred naturally, driven not least by dissatisfaction and indiscipline amongst restive Conservative backbenchers. Perhaps he could have held out for Liberal Democrat ministers in different Whitehall departments, or even run one himself, but this could not have altered the fundamental issue.

History ought, nevertheless, to be kinder to Nick Clegg and give full credit to the maturity and judgement shown for the most part by the Liberal Democrats in government. It will be tempting for his successor Tim Farron to distance himself and the party from its role in the coalition, especially given that Farron himself did not serve as a minister; he should resist this lure and claim credit when he can for the party's achievements in office. The Conservatives' unlikely outright victory in the 2015 brought a narrow majority of sixteen, lower than that achieved by John Major in 1992 and which he lost over the following five years. The period of coalition government may come to look stable in comparison. Farron now faces a monumental task, with the perennial challenge of being noticed made much harder by broadcasting rules limiting the airtime given to Liberal Democrats due to their much weaker showing in the general election. Despite his own shortcomings as leader, these stark realities make Charles Kennedy's achievements appear all the greater.

Appendix A

Order paper, Glasgow University Union debate, January 1980

Glasgow University Union.
Union – Dialectic Debate
in
the Debating Chamber
on Friday, 18th January, 1980 at 1.15 p.m. and 7.30 p.m.

<u>Time Schedule.</u>

1.00–2.30 p.m.	Opening Period
2.30–3.00 p.m.	Open Period
3.00–3.30 p.m.	Committee Stage
3.30–4.15 p.m.	Mid Afternoon Round
4.15–4.45 p.m.	Open Period
4.45–5.30 p.m.	Closing Afternoon Round
7.30–8.30 p.m.	Opening Evening Round
10.00–10.30 p.m.	Question Time
10.30 p.m–	

Speakers in the Open Period will be allowed 4 minutes for the completion of their speeches.

Distinguished Strangers in the gallery must observe strict silence.

Members of the House are asked to remain on the Floor of the House and to refrain from entering or leaving during speeches.

On entering or leaving the House the customary tribute must be paid to the Mace.

SOCIAL DEMOCRATIC GOVERNMENT IN POWER.

Members of the House and Distinguished Guests (including Ladies) may obtain refreshments in the Coffee Room.

Resolution.

'THAT THIS HOUSE HAS NO CONFIDENCE IN HER MAJESTY'S GOVERNMENT IN WESTMINSTER'

The Cabinet.

Rt. Hon. CHARLES P. KENNEDY (Lochaber)	Prime Minister and First Lord of the Treasury
FIONA KENNY (Jam Tart)	Lord President of the Council and Deputy Prime Minister
LIAM FLYNN (Immaculate Conception)	Secretary of State for Foreign and Commonwealth Affairs
JOHN J. WALLACE (My Little Chickadee)	Lord Privy Seal and Minister Without Portfolio
PETER YOUNGER (Tartan Special)	Chancellor of the Exchequer
IAN CAMERON-MOWAT (Samarkand Central)	Minister of Defence
MAUREEN LINDSAY (Token Broad)	Secretary of State for Home Affairs
RON GRAY (Cunning Linguist)	Secretary of State for Scotland
GRAHAM WATSON (Stuffed Whale)	Secretary of State for Education
DAVID JOHNSTONE (Head of Programmes)	Secretary of State for Industry
GERARD FRIELL (Inspiration)	Minister for Sport and Recreation
COLIN G. McGEACHIE (Quiet Man)	Postmaster General
JOHN T. MACDONALD, LL.B. (Cock o' the North)	Attorney General

KEITH MOLLISON (Hundred Acre Wood)   Minister of Agriculture and Fisheries

COLIN STEPHENSON (Turncoat)   Minister of Transport

Privy Council.

Rt. Hon. GERARD REILLY, M.A.	Expletive Deleted
Rt. Hon. BRIAN J. McBRIDE, M.A.	Paradise West
Rt. Hon. ROBERT V. SERAFIN	Vaulting Ambition
Rt. Hon. MICHAEL A. FOSTER, LL.B.	Dr. Gloucester
BRIAN WILSON	(Inverness-shire)
Rt. Hon. DONALD C. DEWAR, M.P.	(Garscadden)

Appendix B

Minutes from Charles Kennedy's leadership campaign team, 19 May 1999

Follow-up points from meeting of 13 April
Mechanics of nomination procedure being clarified – need definite answers on whether forms can be faxed, actual verification deadline for completed forms etc **JG/AW/SNC**
Freepost address needs one week to organise – confirm Atul's office as receiving address? **CaP**
Remaining membership lists to be obtained from Euro candidates; Scotland, Wales, Northern, North West and West Midlands remaining. **JB**
Presentation Bill may not now be on food labelling – topic/date to be decided **RG/DN/LD**

New points
Euro campaign in Highlands potentially tricky because of coalition talks; **CaP** suggested addressing question of tuition fees etc via use of advertorial in local press. Stressed the importance of 'bucking the trend' in Scotland and campaigning effectively. **CK/CaP** to speak re: funding/tactics.

Danger than handling of the coalition issue could effect [*sic*] CK campaign across UK; **CK** should have line on talks (**JBC** to check this) and square Scots colleagues accordingly.

RMC to draft article/letter re: CK line for LD News/Guardian, and run it past Jim Wallace

Saturday Telegraph magazine article due out on 29th May. Sunday Times postponed for several weeks. Decided to limit number of stories placed/

interviews given over first weekend of campaign. **JBC/NS/RG/CK/AW** to meet and discuss press strategy.

Identified need for full-time press office for campaign; **JBC** to speak to **AW** re possible names.

List of volunteers to be compiled for telephone canvassing help etc **SNC**

Daniel Farthing to be brought down from Inverness office for full-time help in CK office, from beginning of June

William Sieghart providing publishing/printing and designing 'the look'. 'Life story' document done, comments etc to **RG**. **RG** to speak to **DN** re: press pack. **CaP** to be involved in design of leaflets etc.

CK campaign is behind in its active supporters database and needs a big key contact list to ensure a large majority.

The gaps in the supporters list therefore needs filling in – especially for the top 150 membership constituencies. MP supporters to be asked to help and **JB** to start 'cold calling' constituency chairs etc, in an effort to build up the number of supporters around the country.

Offices need to be decided. 'Logistics' to remain at Millbank, but need to set up 'war room' for telephone canvassing etc in Atul's office **JB/AW/SNC**

Direct mailshots are possible – needs to be decided how many/what quality of people are mailed, for eg Council Leaders only? **JB/CIP**

Need to target phone calls/mailing very heavily. **CaP** to speak to Garry White for help.

Formal by-election-style practical strategy needed ASAP **CaP/JG/GE/CIP** Launch to be over three days nationally, but locally launched in Inverness on Friday 11th June.

Hustings should aim to conserve CK and provide maximum media opportunities. Suggestion that local MP should accompany CK, plus 2 people from team.

Appendix C

Charles Kennedy's feedback on 2001 election organisation, submitted to an internal Liberal Democrat review of the election

Some reflections from the leader

Two advance disclaimers by way of introduction.

First, my own impressions of the tour are likely to be exactly that – impressionistic. When you are at the eye of the storm, and increasingly tired as time goes on, you may not be the most reliable of sources.

Second, I had several ideas of my own for the components and dynamics of the tour – some of which found their way through to the final version, some of which did not. I do not complain about that fact.

However, there is one essential characteristic which the tour team got correct throughout. That is, given the intense focus upon the Leader individually as the campaign progresses, it is vital that the tour accommodates the personality and whims of the person in that role; equally, that the personnel in most immediate and politically sensitive contact with the Leader are those with whom he or she is most comfortable.

All the logistics and creativity in the world will not succeed if the above two tests are not met.

There is little doubt, as one political journo described it on air, that had the election result been awarded on the basis of the general ambience of the morning press conferences then the Liberal Democrats would have won.

The same chair each day is essential and that person has to be top drawer. A regular but not incessant presence of the Leader is necessary. We succeeded in both, but too often had too many people on the top table. The insufficient presence of elected women was a problem, which spilled into the Q&As and conference coverage generally. These two facts should be addressed for a future occasion.

Further general points

I was conscious of quite a lot of dead time between the conclusion of the press conference and setting off on the daily tour. On some occasions this was taken up by media, on other occasions it enabled informal touring of Cowley Street to chat informally with staff and volunteers. The latter is useful for morale, but not that many of the team are around first thing in the morning. Consideration must be given to filling the space with private rest time (particularly as the campaign rolls on). Perhaps I should have gone to the gym . . .

Where the bus/plane tour is concerned there is a cumulative tiredness which mounts steadily as time progresses. On our tour we were subjecting ourselves physically – leave aside every other aspect of tiredness – to a standard 10 hours of human vibration, almost every day. This takes its toll, but was unavoidable.

However, I do wonder if the bus concept will be appropriate for a future campaign. Having said that, I was scarcely making the case for the maximum use of helicopters. And they have been known to vibrate as well. Neither bus was exactly comfortable nor suitable for working (is any bus?). Most days they were overcrowded. The small plane was a joy compared with the larger one. Those servicing both travel modes could not have been better – next time we need a better, larger plane (I began to gaze with increasing envy at the Hague plane, the more airports we found ourselves adjacent to it).

On tour, the inability to 'connect' with the broadcast media was both frustrating and potentially damaging. We didn't suffer serious damage, but there were occasions when, upon arrival at your constituency stop, you would be advised as to the questions the in-house media corps wanted to put. They were more up to speed than we were – a pitfall if the going had got tricky.

If the next general election does, at last, involve broadcast leaders' debate then the entire structure of the Leader's Tour would have to be re-thought. I would recommend a pre-debate day of little more than a press conference and photo-opp, followed by a flexible post-debate day, depending on how the commentators and polls have reckoned the Leader performed.

Rest and refreshment time – private and comfortable – must be given a higher priority before evening media big interviews and rallies. The rallies worked better than I thought, although I still prefer building in a Q&A session instead of too many political speakers.

The overnight team's initial brief was very good and arrived at a good time

(11pm-ish). Having an hour or two privately after the public day also allowed for television viewing, essential in my view to get a better idea of that day's events (the Prescott punch being the most obvious example).

Media-wise we are too indulgent collectively of the insatiable media demands, particularly where the Leader is concerned. As the campaign wears on, it becomes increasingly important for the travel time in between stops to be dead time; additional off the record briefings can be extremely tiring and that's where the gaffes can most easily occur.

Generally, we all pushed ourselves to the physical limits and perhaps beyond on the tour. We only had to pull one visit, due to travel problems, a small miracle all things considered. But we could have ended up with significantly poorer major media interviews if we'd run, say an hour late on one or two occasions. Next time we may well devise a different strategy anyway – but whatever it proves to be should take account of that reality.

The above points are deliberately self-centred, at least to a point, but that strikes me as my most pertinent contribution. This election proved – in several respects – an easier ride than we might well have hoped for. Next time some of the above could lead to significant political impacts.

All those who put up with my truculence, periods of silence and increasing irritation with the bug that just would not go away deserve medals.

My final – wholly – self-serving thought is that the Leader will always turn in a better performance when allowed to reside at home.

Appendix D

Extracts of a memo from Tim Razzall to Charles Kennedy after the 2005 general election

Overall

Despite the fact that this was the best result the party has achieved since the 1920s, we have allowed certain sections of the media – encouraged by over optimism from some of our colleagues – to turn this into failure.

There is no factual evidence that this election was a missed opportunity for us. In the six months prior to the start of the election campaign our position in the opinion polls ranged from 18% to 25% with an average performance of roundabout 20%. With the current 'first past the post' election system, unless we were to break out of the 18% to 25% range, our range of seats would be from 55 to 70 depending on ground war targeting. In the event we increased our share of the vote in the course of the campaign by about 4% to just under 24%[1] and 62 seats was bang in the middle of the 55 to 70 range.

Why people did not vote for us

There were three key reasons:

1. Despite the prevailing wisdom in certain quarters inside and outside the Party, policy reasons were not the major motivation for people not voting for us. Our post election private polling shows that of those people who considered voting for us, but did not vote for us in the end, less than 25% of them could cite policy reasons as factors in not voting for us.

   Indeed five of our key policies:
   • Council Tax/Local Income Tax
   • Student fees
   • Iraq

> • Long Term Care for the Elderly
> • 50% Tax Rate

All proved extremely popular.

2. A much more significant reason why people did not vote for us was a perception of the party as not yet strong enough in all parts of the country to be regarded as challengers nationally on a par with the other two main parties.
3. The Blair campaign undoubtedly made a difference. As you will remember the Prime Minister spent the last week almost entirely on the topic that a vote for the Liberal Democrats could put Michael Howard into Downing Street. The statistics show why this was important for Labour. 50% of the seats gained by the Tories from Labour resulted in no increase in the Tory share of the vote, but an increase in our share of the vote at Labour's expense. Although this did little to minimise our gains from Labour in seats the Tories could not win, the result of the Blair campaign was to increase the Tory vote in seats where we were the challenger – particularly in the South, presumably on the basis that is was worthwhile re-electing Tory MPs if Michael Howard could win. The Labour campaign also had the effect of restricting the squeeze on the Labour vote in seats we targeted from the Tories – despite the fact Labour were in third place.

Strengths
1. Our biggest achievement was undoubtedly to persuade the media that this was a three party election. This is the first time this has happened since the Alliance Election of 1983 and the benefit clearly came through in the increase in our share of the vote.
2. Published polling confirms that we were regarded by the public as having fought the best campaign of the three parties and that you ran by and away [sic] the best Leader campaign.
3. We made a significant breakthrough this time with popular policy positions being associated with us. Our policies on abolition of Council Tax, abolition of Student tuition fees, opposition to the war in Iraq, provision of Long Term Care for the elderly and increase in tax to 50% to pay for specific items were popular and clearly associated in the minds of the public with the Liberal Democrats. This is a massive achievement.
4. We were able – probably for the first time – to fight a well funded and vigorous campaign throughout the country, whatever the type of seat. I

found the comment in the Independent editorial that we can no longer appeal to different people in different constituencies bemusing.

5. We made a significant breakthrough with voters under 30 – good news for the future.

Weaknesses

1. Our major weakness was, of course, a lack of resources. We had too few resources to fight the other parties on equal terms and the significant increase in resources came too late for it to be spent on anything other than advertisements, hoardings and newspapers and last minute leaflets. In this election, we were subject to a massive influx of resources from the Tories which clearly had an impact.

2. There can be no doubt that we scored relatively badly with the over 65's – despite the fact that we had extremely beneficial policy positions on abolition of Council Tax, Pensions and Long Term Care for the elderly. I suspect the major factor with this group is that many of them will have started voting when the Liberal Party was not a serious player and they have not managed to break their old voting habits.

3. We were clearly hurt by the short nature of the campaign. It always takes us some time to start to move opinion in the course of the campaign and this time the birth of Donald, the Royal Wedding and the Pope's funeral lost us about 25% of your available campaigning time. This could not be helped, but it undoubtedly had an effect.

4. The so called decapitation strategy was only a limited success – unseating only Tim Collins out of the five targets. Having said that, I am not sure what we could have done once the press spotted that our top seats on a swing to win included Teresa May, David Davis, and Oliver Letwin. Inevitably there would be a significant media focus, which clearly pulled up Tory turnout in those seats.

Challenges

1. We must agree a narrative (to use a word coined by Peter Mandelson) and we must remember that a narrative is not the same as a theme or a slogan. A narrative is a 'Set Britain Free' message from the Tories in 1951 or 1979 and a 'get rid of sleazy Tory' message of Labour in 1997.

   We had a narrative in 2001 which started as 'we are the effective opposition' and then morphed into 'we are the real opposition to this Government'.

I believe we should now think big in our narrative along the lines that the Liberal Democrats are now the only alternative to the Labour Party and the Tories can't win.

2. We need to re-visit our themes which are not the same as the narrative and not the same as a slogan.

    I will take a lot of persuading that the concepts around freedom, fairness and trust which have served us well for the last two elections should be abandoned. The balance between freedom and fairness at any one time is the quintessential Liberal dilemma.

3. We need to develop a new slogan and must not make the mistake of confusing the slogan with the theme or the narrative.

4. We must be conscious of our 'look'. We must always be fresh, optimistic, go-getting, young, caring.

5. We clearly need, on this occasion, to start collecting financial resources much earlier. We need to work with the new Treasurer to ensure that we have commitment in principle for some significant funding by Christmas.

6. We need to spend the next 4 years building you up as a future Prime Minister. You get extremely good ratings on honesty, trust, in touch with needs of ordinary people. We need to boost the leadership questions – which I suspect must be done by a combination of big speeches, well-trailed with the media and the development of an international expertise commensurate with a potential prime minister.

7. We need to maintain with the media the position that we are in a three-way political world.

8. We need to put in place structures under which we have the best possible candidates to fight seats we can win next time – as the media focus will be on our candidates even more strongly. Fortunately the Parliamentary Party already contains talent good enough to form a government.

9. Most importantly, we must not get drawn into the sterile debate as to whether the party is moving to the right or is to the left of Labour. Any polling on this topic indicates that we are positioned marginally to the left of centre in people's minds, which is more or less where the majority of people sit, if asked, although it is clear that few modern voters define their position in left/right terms. Our objective must be not to get deflected in the futile left/right debate, but to maximise the small 'l' liberal vote which comes from both sides and is enough to give us a majority.

Appendix E

Private memo from Chris Rennard, Liberal Democrat chief executive, to Andrew Stunell, chief whip, December 2005

Current discussion and debate in the parliamentary party is now between those who say that 'Charles has had his last chance' and those who say that 'this is his last chance'.

A very substantial proportion of the shadow cabinet, quite possibly more than half, are probably in the 'had last chance' category.

Harold Macmillan sacked 7 of his cabinet in the 'night of the long knives', but he did so for issues to do entirely with politics and the performance of those people. Any sackings or resignations (which would be almost as bad) would inevitably lead to very widespread public discussion of the problems and make the Leader's position untenable.

Most of the MPs who know most about the nature of the problem are probably now in the 'had last chance' category. But many MPs remain unaware of what the real issues are and feel perplexed and angry about discussions they do not understand and about negative briefings to the media.

Support for the Leader carrying on is clearly strongest from the group of MPs who are probably least aware of the nature of the problem. The difficulty for the Leader is that more of them are becoming aware of the problem and support for carrying on is likely to continue to fall.

Amongst critics, there is some appreciation of attempts to deal with the problem and some knowledge of steps that have been taken.

Private acceptance of the nature of the problem with some senior colleagues in Spring 2004 was seen as a significant step forward. Categorical assurances were given then about the absolutely necessary course of action needed. This calmed the situation until the General Election.

Concern became more widespread as the problem resumed in the run up to and during the General Election. The manifesto episode was seen as particularly damaging to the party and it is known to some that it was not unconnected to the problem – but critics remained discreet about this.

Hope still remained that the problem would be addressed after the General Election. But it became clear that it had not been addressed. Fear of the likely only alternative was all that prevented more significant dissent on the issue.

The growing belief in the parliamentary party (MPs and peers) that we have passed 'last chance' was driven by the events of 4 weeks ago (Shadow Cabinet, LSE youth speech, failure to attend FPC and Newcastle train journey).

Many people know that truth is not being told in a number of key respects. People who have been prepared to 'cover' in the past or turn a blind eye seem less willing to do so.

Many private assurances have been given over long periods of time including word to some that the Leader's leading supporters were threatening decisive action themselves if the problem was not ended. But the problem has continued.

There is a genuine fear amongst many MPs that we face much greater exposure of the problem and they think that it will do great damage. Our opponents in the media and other parties are much more aware of the problem and will embarrass us much more in future.

Perhaps in desperation, but in any event, new alternatives have emerged.

This means that many MPs no longer subscribe to the 'no acceptable alternative yet' theory.

Confidence that the problem will be addressed, amongst those who are aware of it, now appears to be almost non-existent. Although some MPs who are well aware of the problem are duplicitous in what they say.

Some of those who are most generous towards the Leader say that the Christmas period is the time to reflect on the Leadership. They say that if there is the tiniest exposure to a drop of the problem over the recess, then resignation is the only honourable course of action.

But others say that it is already too late for that. After all previous assurances that it is possible to be Leader and address the problem, they say that it is no longer possible to accept those assurances.

Appendix F

Pager messages from Andrew Stunell, chief whip, to MPs,
December 2005–January 2006

30 December
HAPPY AND SUCCESSFUL 2006 AND COMPLETE DISCRETION
BY ALL, PLS. CHIEF WHIP

4 January
FROM ANDREW TO ALL COLLEGUES [*sic*] WE HAVE ENOUGH
FREE PUBLICITY THANKS. PLS REFER ALL MEDIA BIDS TO
MARK LITTLEWOOD [number] BEFORE YOU SAY YES

Two minutes later
TO ALL FROM CHIEF WHIP. PLS SHARE YOUR VIEWS WITH ME
[number] BEFORE AIRING THEM IN THE MEDIA

Ten minutes later
TO PPM FROM ANDREW. PUTTING IT ANOTHER WAY. USE
YOUR COMMON SENSE AND SHUT UP

6 January, 10.40 a.m.
TO ALL COLLEAGUES. RACHEL SQUIRE, DUNFERMLINE WEST
HAS DIED, BY-ELECTION, LD IN SECOND. ONE REASON TO
LISTEN TO CHIEF WHIP

8.30 p.m.
SCORE TODAY 10 OUT OF 10 FOR DAVID CAMERON. SO CAN
WE ALL THINK AND LISTEN AND NOT TALK FOR 2 DAYS?
ANDREW

Appendix G

Charles Kennedy's personal statement on alcohol, 5 January 2006

I've called this press briefing to address an issue – directly – one that has been a source of concern for myself and to others for some time.

Over the past eighteen months I have been coming to terms with and seeking to cope with a drink problem.

And I've come to learn through that process than any drink problem is a serious problem indeed – for yourself and for those around you.

I've sought professional help and I believe today that this issue is essentially resolved. People close to me know that this has been a struggle and for extended periods I have consumed no alcohol at all. As a matter of fact I haven't had a drink for the past two months – and I don't intend to in the future.

I've learnt the hard way of the need to face up to this medical problem – one that is dealt with successfully by many others on a daily basis. I have chosen not to acknowledge it publicly in this way before because, if at all possible, I wanted to overcome it privately.

In a sense, this admission today comes as something of a personal relief. I should have been willing to talk about it more openly before. I wish I had.

This issue has – understandably – been of concern to several of my parliamentary colleagues. They have been both understanding and supportive. I am extremely grateful to them for that.

It also lies beneath much of the current leadership speculation within the parliamentary party. Therefore, let me be clear. I consider myself capable and in good health – and I remain politically determined as leader of the party.

This party's members have shown me tremendous support of the years and overwhelmingly in recent weeks and days. It is a privilege to serve as their leader. I want to continue doing so, not least because the prospects in front of us in this parliament are so great.

Given my statement today I believe it is only fair now to give our party members their say over the continuing leadership. It is open to any colleague who believes that they can better represent the longer-term interests of the party to stand against me in such a leadership election. I am requesting that the party puts in place the necessary steps to enable this election to take place immediately.

Given the extremely personal nature of this statement I trust that you will understand that I do not propose to make further comments.

Appendix H

Resignation threat from 25 MPs, 6 January 2006

Liberal Democrat Education spokesman, Ed Davey, this evening said:

> Today I have had discussions with many MPs about Charles' statement. I and my colleagues believe we need to make our personal positions clear at this time.
>
> Everyone wishes to give Charles the weekend to reflect, and have [*sic*] expressed their sympathy and support for him in his battle with his serious medical condition. However, we felt we had to indicate what our personal intentions would be next week, given his statement yesterday [see Appendix G]. We have indicated to Charles Kennedy that we would no longer be prepared to serve under his leadership after this weekend and wish to give him the next couple of days to reflect on his position. Following conversations over the last few days it is absolutely clear that a growing number of MPs agree with us.

Sarah Teather, Liberal Democrat local government spokesperson said:

> I have reached the same conclusion as Ed Davey and I can say with absolute confidence that a further twenty-three of my parliamentary colleagues also concur. The following MPs have indicated to us that they would not be able to serve under Charles Kennedy's ongoing leadership. They are Norman Baker, Tom Brake, Andrew George, Sandra Gidley, Norman Lamb, David Laws, Jeremy Browne, Alistair Carmichael, Nick Clegg, Tim Farron, Lynne Featherstone, Julia Goldsworthy, Chris Huhne, Evan Harris, John Pugh, Jo Swinson, Stephen Williams, Nick Harvey, Martin Horwood, Dan Rogerson, Adrian Saunders, Matthew Taylor and Jenny Willott.

Appendix I

Charles Kennedy's resignation statement, 7 January 2006

I wished to make a statement this afternoon having, as I said yesterday evening, reflected over the leadership of the Liberal Democrats.

When I made my personal statement on Thursday afternoon I said then that I thought it was only fair to give our party members their say over my continuing leadership. Accordingly, I requested the opening of a leadership election – which the party's Federal Executive will put in train at their meeting on Monday evening.

Since then it has been open to any other Liberal Democrat MP to announce their candidacy and to stand against me. None have decided to do so.

In the recent weeks and days I have been inundated by messages of support from Party members and activists throughout the country. It means a great deal to me – which I have appreciated enormously. Many, many of them have made the point to me that we fought for and founded this party on the fundamental principle of one member, one vote. I urge them to stick with us and to exercise that right in the leadership election which now follows. However, it is clear now that such support is not reflected strongly enough across the parliamentary party in the House of Commons itself.

In all of this the interests of the party have to come first. That is where my personal, political and constitutional duty lies. Accordingly, I am announcing today that when nominations open for the leadership of the party I shall not now be putting my name forward. And I am standing down as leader with immediate effect.

I have been in politics for far too long to be overly sentimental about this sort of moment. However, I would like to pay a heartfelt tribute to the many colleagues and friends who have helped sustain me through my years as party leader in Parliament and outside. And with whom I look forward to continue working in politics for very many years to come – at constituency level and at national level. They are far too numerous to mention individually, save one – and that person is Anna Werrin. A finer friend and colleague you could not wish for – throughout my first 23 years in politics!

Personally and politically the support of my wife, Sarah, and our respective families remains beyond adequate tribute – but they know the sincerity of what I am saying today.

Now, there are very important elections in front of this party and it is essential in my view that a new, democratically elected leader is in place as soon as possible to take the party forward. And that new leader can be assured of my loyal support as a backbench Liberal Democrat MP.

That new leader – and the party – also has some serious internal political issues to address further and to resolve. And I want to say a few words about that process today.

As I have acknowledged before, there is a genuine debate going on within this party – somewhat crudely caricatured at times as being in rather redundant terms as between left and right; in rather simplistic terms as between social liberals and economic liberals; in rather misleading terms as between traditionalists and modernisers.

I have never accepted that these are irreconcilable instincts – indeed, quite the opposite. And I believe that unity remains fundamental to our further advance and success. It should be a debate driven by ourselves. It must not be allowed to become dictated by others who do not share our long-term hopes and goals. We must stand and argue – politically independent and intellectually self-confident. And it must be based on time-honoured, sound philosophic liberal principles – principles which have stood the test of generations and remain not just as relevant to, but even more essential, in British politics today.

The leadership personalities change from time to time in politics, but principles should not. Civil liberties; justice and rule of international law; Britain again seen as a force for good in the world, through our unique amalgam of roles within Europe, the United Nations and the Common-wealth; a far greater regard for our environmental challenges today and what we bequeath to future generations; and a far fairer social deal for the have-nots in our society. I look forward to continuing to contribute to that ongoing debate in due course.

My sincere parting advice as leader to the party is to keep that debate within the parameter of these principles – and not to get unduly distracted by the machinations in other parties or what the vagaries of the British voting system may offer up at a future general election. That route will blur our identity and turn away the very voters who are still looking to us – rightly so – as their best hope for the future.

It is to that future which I will continue to work with enthusiasm. First, for the people of the Ross, Skye & Lochaber constituency – whom I am privileged to serve. And also for the continuing progress and success of our Liberal Democrat values – values which, when best expressed, give voice to the many who might otherwise be insufficiently heard.

A new leader inherits a party with the largest House of Commons representation in the liberal tradition in over 80 years. We secured a million more votes in our support at the last General Election compared with the one before. We are established as serious players in the changing reality which is three-party politics across Britain.

I believe that to be a good inheritance and a great opportunity. One in which I look forward to continuing to play my part.

Thank you.

Notes

Chapter 1

1. 'Young People and Politics – Real Power, Real Responsibility', 15 November 2005.
2. *PA News*, 17 November 17 2005.
3. See chapter 9.
4. *Guardian*, 9 December 2005.
5. Mark Oaten, 'My Week', *House Magazine*, 19 December 2005.
6. *This Week*, BBC One, 9 December 2005.
7. *Daily Mail*, 10 December 2005.
8. *Daily Mail*, 13 December 2005.
9. *The Times*, 14 December 2005.
10. For example, *Guardian, Independent, Scotsman*, 15 December 2005.
11. Liberal Democrat press release, 15 December 2005.
12. Home affairs team update, 13 December 2005.
13. *Daily Telegraph*, 17 December 2005.
14. Paul Marshall and David Laws (eds), *The Orange Book: Reclaiming Liberalism* (Profile, 2004).
15. *Mail on Sunday*, 18 December 2005.
16. *Jonathan Dimbleby*, ITV1, 18 December 2005
17. New Year's message 2006 from Charles Kennedy, 29 December 2005.
18. *Observer*, 1 January 2006.
19. *The Times*, 3 January 2006.
20. *Today*, BBC Radio 4, 4 January 2006.
21. *Newsnight*, BBC Two, 4 January 2006.
22. Appendix H.
23. *Today*, BBC Radio 4, 6 January 2006.
24. *Independent*, 7 January 2006.
25. *The World at One*, BBC Radio 4, 6 January 2006.
26. Appendix G.
27. *Newsnight*, BBC Two, 6 January 2006.
28. Appendix I.

Chapter 2

1.   *Herald*, 12 April 2005.
2.   Charles Kennedy, *The Future of Politics* (HarperCollins, 2000), p. 122.
3.   Ibid., p. 209.
4.   Ibid., p. 102.
5.   Lesley White, *Sunday Times Magazine*, 2001.
6.   Ibid., p. 145.
7.   Gerald Warner, *Conquering by Degrees: A Centenary History* (Glasgow University Union, 1985).
8.   Parliamentary debate report, 1 December 1978.
9.   Appendix A.
10.   Scottish Students Debating Committee minutes, *Aberdeen University Debater*, 23 February 1980.
11.   Parliamentary debate, 16 October 1981.
12.   *Daily Telegraph Magazine*, 27 May 1999.
13.   Warner, *Conquering by Degrees*, pp. 202–5.
14.   Ibid., p. 205.
15.   *Daily Telegraph Magazine*, 27 May 1999.
16.   Lords Diary, *House Magazine*, 16 January 2006.
17.   Interview, *Sunday Times*, 8 January 2006.

Chapter 3

1.   Hansard, 15 July 1983, col. 1114.
2.   Hansard, 17 February 1987, col. 877.
3.   David Owen, *Time to Declare* (Michael Joseph, 1991).
4.   Ibid., p. 714.
5.   Ivor Crewe and Anthony King, *SDP: The Birth, Life and Death of the Social Democratic Party* (Oxford University Press, 1991).
6.   Ibid., pp. 723–4.
7.   *The Times*, 7 July 1987.
8.   *The Times*, 9 July 1987.
9.   Crewe and King, *SDP*, p. 409.
10.   Ibid., pp. 408–9.
11.   *The Times*, 11 August 1987.
12.   See, for example, *The Times*, 1 September 1987.
13.   David Steel, *Against Goliath: David Steel's Story* (Weidenfeld & Nicolson, 1989).
14.   Crewe and King, *SDP*, p. 421.
15.   Steel, *Against Goliath*, p. 288.
16.   Crewe and King, *SDP*, p. 429.
17.   Ibid., p. 430.
18.   Steel, *Against Goliath*, p. 290.
19.   Crewe and King, *SDP*, p. 432.
20.   Ibid., pp. 424–5.
21.   Owen, *Time to Declare*, p. 738.
22.   Ibid., p. 736.

Chapter 4

1.   Paddy Ashdown, *The Ashdown Diaries, vol. 1: 1998–1997* (Allen Lane, 2000), p. 7.
2.   Ibid., p. 52.
3.   For example, *Daily Mail,* 18 September 1990.
4.   Ashdown, *Ashdown Diaries, vol. 1,* pp. 66–7.
5.   Ibid., pp. 58–62.
6.   Charles Kennedy, *The Future of Politics* (HarperCollins, 2000), p. 52.
7.   Hansard, 7 November 1989, col. 831.
8.   Hansard, 18 January 1990, cols 405–6.
9.   Ashdown, *Ashdown Diaries, vol. 1,* p. 6.
10.   *The Times,* 1 November 1989.
11.   Ashdown, *Ashdown Diaries, vol. 1,* pp. 198–9.
12.   Kennedy, *Future of Politics,* pp. 10–11.
13.   Ibid., p. 92.
14.   Ibid., p. 93.
15.   *Independent,* 16 October 1990.
16.   *The Times,* 6 April 1992.
17.   Hansard, 10 February 1998, col. 251–3.
18.   *Sun,* 16 June 1994.
19.   Ashdown, *Ashdown Diaries, vol. 1,* p. 452; Paddy Ashdown, *Ashdown Diaries, vol. 2: 1997–1999* (Allen Lane, 2001), p. 10.
20.   Ashdown, *Ashdown Diaries, vol. 2,* pp. 71–2.
21.   *Daily Telegraph,* 22 September 1997.
22.   BBC News Online, 25 April 1998.
23.   Ashdown, *Ashdown Diaries, vol. 2,* p. 246.
24.   Ibid., pp. 194–6.
25.   Ibid., p. 392.
26.   Appendix B.

Chapter 5

1.   For example, *Independent,* 11 August 1999.
2.   Interview, *Observer,* 15 August 1999.
3.   BBC Online, 21 September 1999.
4.   *A Report on Political Attitudes in Britain: 8 Focus Groups* (Martin Hamblin, December 1999).
5.   Hansard, 9 February 2000, cols 244–6.
6.   *The Times,* 12 April 2000.
7.   *Jonathan Dimbleby,* ITV, 30 April 2000.
8.   Hansard, 3 May 2000, col. 141.
9.   *The Times,* 1 May 2000.
10.   Charles Kennedy, *The Future of Politics* (HarperCollins, 2000), p. xii.
11.   ICM/*Guardian* poll, 19 September 2000.
12.   *The Times,* 22 September 2000.
13.   *Today,* BBC Radio 4, 17 March 2000.
14.   *The Times,* 16 March 2001.

Chapter 6

1. *Financial Times*, 24 September 1999.
2. *Jonathan Dimbleby*, ITV, 2 April 2000.
3. Paddy Ashdown, *Ashdown Diaries, vol. 2: 1997–1999* (Allen Lane, 2001), p. 384.
4. Andrew Rawnsley, *Servants of the People* (Hamish Hamilton, 2000), p. 195.
5. Charles Kennedy, *The Future of Politics* (HarperCollins, 2000), pp. 5–6.
6. *Talk* magazine, April 2000.
7. Peter Riddell, *The Unfulfilled Prime Minister: Tony Blair's Quest for a Legacy* (Politico's, 2005), pp. 159–160.
8. L. T. Hobhouse, *Liberalism* (Oxford University Press, 1911).
9. *The Times*, 16 May 2001.
10. Appendix C.
11. Downing Street press statement, 20 September 2001.
12. *Guardian*, 18 January 2002.
13. For example, Hansard, 17 December 2003.

Chapter 7

1. Liberal Democrat press release, 12 September 2001.
2. Hansard, 14 September 2001, col. 606.
3. Ibid., col. 610.
4. Ibid., col. 625.
5. Peter Riddell, *Hug Them Close: Blair, Clinton, Bush and the 'Special Relationship'* (Politico's, 2003), p. 155.
6. Hansard, 8 October 2001.
7. *Mail on Sunday*, 21 October 2001.
8. Ibid.
9. *Mail on Sunday*, 18 December 2005.
10. Hansard, 12 December 2001, col. 859.
11. Riddell, *Hug Them Close*, p. 210.
12. Hansard, 24 September 2002, col. 3.
13. Ibid., col. 44.
14. Hansard, 25 November 2002, col. 47.
15. Ibid., col. 73.
16. Hansard, 8 January 2003, col. 164.
17. For example, Hansard, 29 January 2003, col. 872.
18. Radical Bulletin, *Liberator*, issue 286, March 2003.
19. Letter, *Guardian*, 7 February 2003.
20. Leading article, *Guardian*, 8 February 2003.
21. *Breakfast with Frost*, BBC One, 9 February 2003.
22. *Sunday Times*, 16 February 2003.
23. *Observer*, 26 January 2003.
24. BBC Online, 7 February 2003.
25. Quentin Letts, *Evening Standard*, 11 February 2003.
26. Hansard, 18 March 2003, col. 761.

27.   Interview, *Daily Telegraph*, 14 July 2003.
28.   To *The Times*.
29.   Hansard, 10 September 2003.

Chapter 8

1.   Ivor Crewe and Anthony King, *SDP: The Birth, Life and Death of the Social Democratic Party* (Oxford University Press, 1991), p. 446.
2.   *Sunday Times*, 8 January 2006.
3.   *The Times*, 3 September 1996.
4.   *The Times Magazine*, 10 July 1999.
5.   Ibid.
6.   *Sunday Times Magazine*, 20 May 2001.
7.   *Sunday Times*, 8 January 2006.
8.   Hansard, 18 July 2002, col. 430.
1.   *The Times*, 30 June 2003.
10.   *Guardian*, 30 June 2003.
11.   *Evening Standard*, 17 September 2003.
12.   Hansard, 7 January 2004, col. 250.

Chapter 9

1.   Hansard, 20 April 2004, col. 155.
2.   *News of the World*, 25 April 2004.
3.   *Breakfast with Frost*, BBC One, 25 April 2004.
4.   *The Times*, 10 May 2004.
5.   *Daily Telegraph*/YouGov survey, 24 May 2004.
6.   'Scandal hits phone mast Lib Dem', Labour leaflet.
7.   *Daily Telegraph*, 1 July 2004.
8.   *Evening Standard*, 12 July 2004.
9.   PA News, 16 July 2004.
10.   *Guardian*, 17 July 2004.
11.   John Curtice, *Independent*, 17 July 2004.
12.   Matthew Parris, *The Times*, 17 July 2004.
13.   *Sun*, 17 July 2004.
14.   *News of the World*/Populus, 25 July 2004.
15.   'Today Hartlepool, tomorrow . . .', *Guardian*, 28 September 2004.
16.   'Hartlepool, not Brighton, will decide Blair's future', *Guardian*, 28 September 2004.
17.   'Sending the message', *Guardian*, 30 September 2004.
18.   *Freedom, Fairness, Trust*, Lib Dem policy document, September 2004.
19.   *Quality, Innovation, Choice*, Lib Dem policy paper, August 2002.
20.   'Tough Choices: Delivering Public Service Priorities', speech, 4 March 2003.
21.   *Sun*, 21 September 2004.
22.   Interview, *The Times*, 20 September 2004.

23.   Times 2, *The Times*, 23 September 2004.
24.   *The Times*, 20 October 2004.
25.   Tony Blair, speech to Labour conference, 28 September 2004.
26.   *Daily Mail*, 15 April 2005.
27.   *Independent*, 15 April 2005.
28.   Leader campaign performance index 2005, British Election Study, Essex University.
29.   *Mail on Sunday*, 24 April 2005.

Chapter 10

1.   Labour Party press release, 9 May 2005.
2.   Mary Ann Sieghart, *The Times*, 10 June 2005.
3.   Hodder & Stoughton press release, 14 June 2005.
4.   *The Politics Show*, BBC One, 22 May 2005.
5.   Vincent Cable, *Public Services: Reform with a Purpose* (CentreForum, 2005).
6.   Vincent Cable, *Multiple Identities: Living with the New Politics of Identity* (Demos, 2005).
7.   Guardian Unlimited, 17 June 2005.
8.   One front page read 'Shame on you Mr Hunter' over a picture of a school due to shut. A Lib Dem tabloid in Leicester South led with 'Shame on you, Sir Peter' and a photograph of a closed school.
9.   Community Focus leaflet issued by the Conservative campaign.
10.   Hunter Special leaflet circulated by Labour.
11.   News Extra campaign newspaper published by Lib Dems.
12.   *Independent*, 12 July 2005.
13.   *The World at One*, BBC Radio 4, 13 July 2005.
14.   *Conscience and Reform: The Liberal Democrat agenda for Britain*, 18 July 2005.
15.   'We Must Address the Root Causes of Terrorism', speech, 12 July 2005.
16.   Downing Street press conference, 5 August 2005.
17.   Conservative Party press release, 5 August 2005.
18.   Liberal Democrat press release, 5 August 2005.
19.   Leading article, *Sun*, 6 August 2005.
20.   Appendix D.
21.   *The Times*, 29 August 2005.
22.   *PA News*, 12 September 2005.
23.   Interview, *Guardian*, 9 September 2005.
24.   *The Times*, 21 September 2005.
25.   *Today*, BBC Radio 4, 19 September 2005.
26.   *The World at One*, BBC Radio 4, 20 September 2005.
27.   Guardian Unlimited, 21 September 2005.
28.   'Vision of a Liberal Britain', 22 September 2005.
29.   *The Times*, 23 September 2005.
30.   *The Times*, 24 November 2005.
31.   *Sunday Times*, 4 December 2005.
32.   Lib Dem press release, 8 November 2005.
33.   Charles Kennedy, *The Future of Politics* (HarperCollins, 2000).
34.   Appendix E.

Chapter 11

1.   *The Observer*, 27 August 2006.
2.   The Times, 4 March, 2006.
3.   *Question Time*, BBC One, 22 June 2006.
4.   Ibid.
5.   Today Programme, BBC Radio 4, 19 September 2006.
6.   Hansard, 31 October 2006, col 207.
7.   For example, Daily Mirror, 18 October 2006.
8.   The Daily Politics, BBC Two, 17 October 2007.
9.   The Herald, 28 February, 2008.
10. Rectorial address, University of Glasgow, April 2008.
11. Minutes, University of Glasgow court, 24 June, 2009.
12. Hansard, 3 July 2009, col 624

Chapter 12

1.   Chris Bowers, Nick Clegg The Biography, Biteback 2011, p 238-9.
2.   David Laws, 22 Days in May, Biteback 2005, p 193-4
3.   The Observer, 16 May 2010.
4.   Glasgow Guardian hustings report, March 8, 2011.
5.   Hetherington Inquiry Report, September 9, 2011.
6.   Glasgow Guardian, September 8, 2011.
7.   SNP statement, 4 April, 2011.
8.   The Guardian, January 11, 2012
9.   BBC interview, June 2, 2015.
10. The Herald, February 10, 2014.
11. Sunday Post, March 30, 2014.
12. Yes Lochaber blog, August 4, 2013.
13. YouGov / Sunday Times poll, September 7, 2014.
14. Sunday Telegraph, May 31, 2009.
15. Sunday Times, January 25, 2015.
16. Mail Online, March 14, 2015.

Chapter 13

1.   Hansard, June 3, 2015, col 598
2.   *Daily Record*, June 2, 2015
3.   www.NewStatesman.com, June 3, 2015
4.   Michael McManus, Jo Grimond: Towards the sound of gunfire, Birlinn 2001, Appendix 2

Appendix D

1.   In fact the Lib Dem share of the vote was 22.1%.

Index